POLITICALLY INCORRECT

POLITICALLY INCORRECT

THE EMERGING FAITH FACTOR
IN AMERICAN POLITICS

RALPH REED

WITH A FOREWORD BY WILLIAM BENNETT

WORD PUBLISHING
Dallas·London·Vancouver·Melbourne

PUBLISHED BY WORD PUBLISHING
DALLAS, TEXAS.

Scripture quotations are from The New
American Standard Bible (NASB), © The Lockman Foundation
1960, 1962, 1963, 1968, 1971, 1972, 1973, 1975, 1977.

Book design by Mark McGarry
Set in Garamond

LIBRARY OF CONGRESS CATALOGING-IN-PUBLICATION DATA

Ralph Reed, 1961–
Politically incorrect: the emerging faith factor in American politics/ Ralph E. Reed
p. cm.
Includes bibliographical references.
ISBN 0–8499–1172–9
1. Conservatism—Religious aspects—Christianity.
2. Sociology, Christian—United States. 3. Christianity and politics—History—20th
century. 4. Evangelicalism—United States—History—20th century. I. Title.
BR115.C66R44 1994
320.5'5'0973 — DC20
94–28095 CIP

PRINTED IN THE UNITED STATES OF AMERICA

4 5 6 7 8 9 0 1   LB   9 8 7 6 5 4 3 2 1

To Jo Anne
The light of my life

CONTENTS

FOREWORD

xi

ACKNOWLEDGMENTS

xv

CHAPTER ONE

The Winning Coalition:
People of Faith Uniting Together

I

CHAPTER TWO

What the World Would Look Like:
A Religious Conservative Vision for America

23

CHAPTER THREE

To the Back of the Bus:
The Marginalization of Religion

41

CHAPTER FOUR

The New Amos and Andy:
How the Media Portrays People of Faith

53

CHAPTER FIVE

Faith Versus Fanaticism:
How Religion Has Become Marginalized

67

CHAPTER SIX
The Fire This Time:
Family Breakup and Social Chaos
81

CHAPTER SEVEN
Adventures in Porkland:
The End of Politics as Usual
93

CHAPTER EIGHT
A Jurassic Jungle:
The Dinosaurs of Business, Labor, and the Media
115

CHAPTER NINE
Separation of Church and State:
"Christian Nation" and Other Heresies
131

CHAPTER TEN
We Stand at Armageddon:
Religion and the Reformist Impulse
141

CHAPTER ELEVEN
The Electronic Godzilla:
Television, Talk Radio, and Politics
157

CHAPTER TWELVE
The Smoking Volcano:
Ross Perot and the Populist Revolt
171

CONTENTS

CHAPTER THIRTEEN
Miracle at the Grassroots:
Christian Coalition and the Pro-family Movement
189

CHAPTER FOURTEEN
Clinton Agonistes:
Woodstock Goes to the White House
203

CHAPTER FIFTEEN
To Cast a Wider Net:
Why We Need a Broader Issues Agenda
221

CHAPTER SIXTEEN
The Curse of Ham:
Religion and Racism in America
235

CHAPTER SEVENTEEN
What is Right about America:
How You Can Make a Difference
249

NOTES
269

INDEX
293

ix

FOREWORD

IN READING *Politically Incorrect*, I am reminded of a November, 1956 sermon delivered by Rev. Martin Luther King, Jr., in Montgomery, Alabama. During that sermon King said, "Always be sure that you struggle with Christian methods and Christian weapons. Never succumb to the temptation of becoming bitter. As you press on for justice, be sure to move with dignity and discipline, using only the weapon of love."

Ralph Reed, in *Politically Incorrect*, does many things. He advocates. He critiques. He calls us to action. But he does all of these things with dignity and discipline. He does not succumb to the temptation of complaining about the media and the political hostility directed at religious conservatives. Rather, Reed takes a higher road than many of his critics. He offers a thoughtful and intellectually rigorous assessment of the world of politics and the world of faith. It is a very impressive work.

Politically Incorrect represents the coming of age of a movement.

Ralph Reed, the Christian Coalition, and the movement they represent defy stereotyped descriptions and caricatures. Together, they are a politically forceful movement, growing in influence, stature, and effectiveness. Their beliefs and their policies are not oppressing; they are liberating. They are not the values of an intolerant past; they are the values of a vibrant American future.

Critics of conservative Christians time and again misrepresent the aims of their political movement. In response, Reed makes a compelling argument: "[People of faith] are not, after all, asking people to subscribe to their theology; they are asking them to subscribe to their public policy views, and to respect their right to participate without their religion being impugned. This is not too much to ask in a democracy."

Reed clearly and cogently refutes the stereotype of white male religious conservatives gathering to burn copies of *The Wizard of Oz* and oppressing minorities. In an America that over the last three decades has experienced enormous increases in violent crime, out-of-wedlock births, abortion, divorce, suicide, child abuse, and the number of welfare recipients, we are deluding ourselves if we think that serious people of faith are the ones we need to fear. For those who wonder what groups like the Christian Coalition advocate, Reed spells it out: safe streets, good schools, strong families, nonintrusive government, and communities where people care for one another. Good things all. And not, one would think, particularly controversial or "divisive."

Christians should be involved in debating the great issues of our time. They should fight with heart and passion, with intelligence and integrity and a sense of high purpose, for the things in which they believe. Like others, Christians should stand up and say, without apology, what they stand for—and they should say, without apology, what they will not stand for.

Ralph Reed says some tough things. Throughout the book, he is not afraid to address some of the faults and excesses within the movement. In his call to "cast a wider net," Reed calls the church and conservatives to task for past and present racism. "We must frankly acknowledge the errors of the past, recognize the debt we owe to those who exposed the hypocrisy of the Church, and forsake racism as both an ideology and a political style. And we must do more. We must build a genuinely inclusive movement that embraces the full racial diversity of America. . . . If we flow out of our lily-white churches into lily-white organizations and support only lily-white candidates for elective office, we cannot expect the larger society to take us or our agenda seriously." Reed understands that the message of religious conservatives has a broad appeal. It is the opposite of sectarian, because it fits human nature as God created it and speaks to universal aspirations for decent communities and strong families.

According to Reed, the policies he advocates "will improve the lives of Americans who find themselves trapped in poor schools, unsafe neighborhoods, and financial poverty. But it is important to acknowledge that they will not solve what ails America's soul. They will not begin to ameliorate the spiritual poverty from which so many in our society suffer." That is the work of faith. It is not, it cannot be, the work of politics.

Back to November 1956, and Reverend King, who closed his sermon that day by saying, "I still believe that standing up for the truth of God is the greatest thing in the world. This is the end of life. The end of life is not to be happy. The end of life is not to achieve pleasure and avoid pain. The end of life is to do the will of God, come what may."

And so it is. A caution, then, is perhaps in order—one which I believe Ralph Reed shares. When Christians enter the world of politics, they should keep the "eyes of their heart" on the things that are above. One of the cornerstones of the faith is the conviction that we are pilgrims and strangers and sojourners in this world.

When the news was brought to him in Carthage that Rome had been sacked, St. Augustine—a Roman citizen and a Roman patriot—knew that the empire that had ruled most of the civilized world for centuries was dying. But he was able to remind his flock of something which we too easily lose sight of. "All earthly cities are vulnerable," Augustine said. "Men build them and men destroy them. At the same time there is the City of God which men did not build and cannot destroy and which is everlasting." St. Augustine went on to write his masterpiece, *De civitate Dei—The City of God.*

Recognizing that we are spiritual and moral beings in a human drama is at the center of the faith; it should also be at the center of our lives—even, and maybe especially, our political lives. This, too, is something which Ralph Reed believes.

On a number of occasions, I have said that the Christian Coalition is fortunate to have Ralph Reed as its executive director. With *Politically Incorrect*, I am pleased to say that the entire conservative Christian community is fortunate to have him as a leader.

WILLIAM J. BENNETT

ACKNOWLEDGMENTS

A BOOK is a little like a Broadway play. There are many people working behind the scenes who make those on stage look better than they truly are. To those who contributed to this effort, I take this opportunity to convey my gratitude. The flaws that remain are mine.

This project began with a paper delivered at the invitation of the Ethics and Public Policy Center in Washington, D.C., in December, 1993. I am grateful to Michael Cromartie and George Weigel of the Center for their encouragement and generosity of spirit. For those of us engaged in the "doing," they provide an atmosphere of thought and reflection. Adam Meyerson, the editor of *Policy Review*, encouraged me to write some of the first thoughts that later became this book. Thomas Holt, a former Heritage Foundation staffer and an editorial writer with the Richmond *Times Dispatch*, was my very able and diligent research assistant. He put in countless hours helping to run down source material and check facts under a difficult deadline. Mike Russell was indefatigable not only in his research but in his dedication to the book's purpose. Heidi Scanlon supplied wonderful ideas, as well as books from her husband's law library, which were enormously helpful.

Marshall Wittmann endured marathon telephone conversations and was a terrific sounding board on just about everything. Everyone should be fortunate enough to have a colleague like him. Ben Hart offered a first-time author sage advice that proved invaluable. Patsy Greene, my dedicated secretary, was always there through the long hours and many rewrites. I am deeply grateful to Pat Robertson and the board of directors of the Christian Coalition for allowing me to write in addition to my day-to-day responsibilities and for encouraging me throughout the project.

Stephen L. Carter sparked a lively debate on religion in American politics and culture with the publication of *The Culture of Disbelief* in 1993, and I am indebted to him for beginning a vital conversation on such a civil note. Though we come from different political perspectives, his scholarship was an inspiration. Bill Bennett was gracious and encouraging. Much of what is good and honorable in American civic discourse today is due to his forcing us back to issues of virtue, character, and moral literacy.

Kip Jordon and the fine team at Word were some of my earliest and most enthusiastic cheerleaders. That we made it under deadline is due in no small measure to their dedication. Jan Johnson was a delightful editor. She gave clarity and structure to my ideas and added a touch of grace and depth in so many places.

The staff and local leadership of the Christian Coalition have enriched my life and the life of this nation. They are the real heroes in the story related in these pages. I am honored to be on the same team with them.

Finally, my lovely wife Jo Anne held down the fort (we moved twice while this book was being written) while I hopscotched between airports and hotels. She deserves to have this book dedicated to her, not only because she so gracefully weathered the labor of it all, but also because she has contributed so much to helping to make the movement described herein a reality. She is my most indispensable asset, and the joy of my life. For that, I am grateful most of all.

RALPH REED, JR.
CHESAPEAKE, VIRGINIA
JULY, 1994

CHAPTER ONE

The Winning Coalition:
People of Faith Uniting Together

IN JANUARY of 1989 I traveled to Washington to attend the inaugural of George Bush. At a dinner one evening I was coincidentally seated next to Pat Robertson, who had recently returned to the Christian Broadcasting Network following his 1988 presidential bid. We struck up an animated conversation about the Bush presidency, the recent campaign, and the future of the pro-family movement. We discussed the successes and the mistakes of his presidential campaign. I asked about his future plans. He said that he was considering setting up a grassroots political organization to carry on the work he began while running for president.

After dinner, Pat motioned me to follow him out of the ballroom. As we walked to the elevator, he said, "I am going to start this new organization, and I think it will change politics in America. The evangelicals and Roman Catholics have more grassroots supporters than anyone, but they need leadership and direction. I would like for you to come on staff and help make this vision a reality."

"Pat, I'm very honored," I replied (surprised was more like it). "But I am still writing my dissertation, and I have to finish my doctorate."

"I understand," he responded. "But why don't you write me a memo about what the group might look like."

By then Pat and his wife Dede were on the elevator and the doors were closing. He was gone.

As I headed back to my hotel room, I was sure that it had been a chance meeting and nothing more. Although I planned to send the promised memo, I had no intention of taking a staff position with any

I

such organization. I was completing a doctorate in history at Emory University and preparing for an academic career. I was through with politics.

Over the next few days, in between teaching a class and feverishly working on my dissertation, I drafted a memo sketching out the broad outlines of a grassroots political organization. The theme was simple: Ronald Reagan was gone, and when he had departed from the national stage in early 1989, the booster rocket of the religious conservative movement flamed out with him. The proposition was that any new group must break the mold of its predecessors by building a grassroots infrastructure by region, state, county, precinct, all the way down to block captains. It must assiduously avoid a direct mail strategy that sought to gain political influence by merely assembling a huge mailing list. The memo, dated February 2, 1989, continued:

> There exists in American politics today a tremendous vacuum that must be filled. Estimates on the number of evangelicals range from a low of 10 million to a high of 40 million. Whatever the actual number, there is no constituency in the American electorate with greater explosive potential as a political force. Nor is there any constituency of comparable size and energy so pitifully unorganized and uneducated.

My memo recommended the formation of a "national political organization dedicated to mobilizing, educating, and activating evangelicals" and their Roman Catholic allies. The leadership would steer clear of "figures that might serve as lightning rods," assemble a "blue-ribbon board of directors," and require "no spiritual litmus test for membership." State and county chapters would be established by a network of roving regional field recruiters based in Los Angeles, Chicago, Atlanta, Denver, Philadelphia, and Dallas. By 1992, the memo suggested, it would be possible to construct an organization with "membership of 3 million, chapters operating in at least 350 of the nation's 435 congressional districts, a field staff of fifteen full-time recruiters, at least 5,000 graduates from training schools, and an annual budget of $10 million."

The goal of this field structure was the enfranchisement of one of the largest and most under-represented constituencies in the United States. The memo concluded:

> The half-century of retreat of evangelicals from social and political action that followed the Scopes Trial of 1925 has had many profound consequences for American society. Yet surely none is more important than this: we have now had two full generations of Bible-believing Christians ... with virtually no hands-on experience in the political decision-making process.

After completing this broad outline for a new group, I sent the memorandum to Pat—and heard nothing. Then, in late September 1989, my phone rang. To my surprise, it was Pat. He related that he was concerned that many of the local activists who had become involved during the Robertson campaign in 1988 were drifting away, their energy and enthusiasm dissipating.

Pat was persuaded that it was time to act. He had spent most of the past year rebuilding the battered finances of CBN, which had lost nearly $100 million in revenues during his absence. But time was of the essence. He invited me to attend a meeting at a downtown hotel in Atlanta on September 25, 1989, with key leaders from around the country.

The gathering was attended by former state leaders of the Robertson campaign from Michigan, Georgia, Nevada, Texas, Louisiana, and several other states. It was preceded by a strategy meeting of major religious leaders: Robertson, Charles Stanley, D. James Kennedy, and Beverly LaHaye of Concerned Women for America. These leaders collectively expressed ambivalence about the early performance of the Bush administration, disappointment that evangelicals had been largely excluded from presidential appointments, and anxiety about the future. At the conclusion of the meeting of grassroots leaders, which featured much debate but little consensus about what to do, Pat introduced me as the first staff member of a group that as yet had no name, a development that surprised me as much as everyone else.

As the meeting broke up and everyone headed for the airport, Pat walked over and shook my hand. "Congratulations," he laughed. "You have no office, no money, and no staff. Welcome aboard!" That was how the Christian Coalition began.

Many people assume that the Christian Coalition began with millions of dollars of seed capital provided by major contributors. In fact, its origins were remarkably humble. I flew home to Atlanta and met with several donors who were personal friends, and they contributed $3,000 to help defray start-up costs. Pat was never discouraged; he did not despise small beginnings. He had started CBN—which now brings in $100 million a year in revenues—with $70. "I have bootstrapped some projects before," he joked once as we sat musing in the office, "but no one is ever going to believe this." Here was a former presidential candidate who had raised $24 million during his campaign, launching a national political group with several thousand dollars, some borrowed furniture, and a small office in a ramshackle warehouse.

The Christian Coalition checking account was opened with a $100 personal check, the phones turned on with a credit card, while Pat loaned the funds to get the first fundraising letter in the mail, which went to 134,325 former supporters of his campaign. One day he drove by the office and wrote a personal check as the first contribution, which I never forgot because we had almost no funds at the time.

The task of getting out the first fundraising solicitation fell to Dick Weinhold, formerly finance director of the 1988 campaign, who now operated his own consulting firm in Ft. Worth, Texas. It was quite a gamble. Rather than testing a small segment of the campaign donor file, we decided to roll the dice on the entire list. Dick came up with an excellent letter, and over the next two months the donations gradually trickled in. By the end of November 1989 we had raised $82,000 and brought on 2,000 members of the organization, many of whom pledged to give ten dollars a month. We were off and running.

A Spiritual Ferment

The Christian Coalition is part of a broader spiritual ferment in the land. "Americans will always do the right thing, after they have exhausted all other possibilities," said Winston Churchill. In the past three decades, we Americans have experimented with just about everything. After the sexual revolution of the sixties, the narcissism of the seventies, and the acquisitiveness of the eighties, Americans are turning inward and upward to fill what Pascal called the God-shaped vacuum in every person's soul.

The signs of rising religious interest are evident everywhere. *Newsweek* recently put Jesus on its cover. One of the best-selling books in recent years was Bill Bennett's *Book of Virtues*, a McGuffey-style anthology of moral stories for children. Nesting baby boomers are flocking to the churches and synagogues of their youth, returning to their spiritual roots, and seeking values for their children. Cable television has become an electronic bazaar buzzing with the competing gospels of Christian broadcasters and New Age psychics. "Religion seems to be working its way more often into the public discourse," notes the *Wall Street Journal.*[1]

Sometimes the search for spirituality turns sour. Religious cults are sprouting in record numbers, poisonous weeds in a harvest of souls. But these are mere eddies in a widening religious floodtide. Witness the explosive growth of evangelical churches. While the share of church members claimed by so-called "mainline" denominations (such as Methodists and Presbyterians) has declined by 48 percent since 1940, membership in conservative and evangelical churches is skyrocketing. The share of church members belonging to the Assemblies of God has increased fourfold in the past half-century. The Southern Baptists, with 15.2 million members, are the largest Protestant denomination in the world.[2]

Every age can be summed up in a sentence. The sixteenth century was the "age of discovery," a time when the sails of European explorers dotted the oceans in pursuit of the New World, where they discovered gold, silver, and wealth beyond the wildest imaginations. The eighteenth century was the age of revolution, as political turmoil convulsed Europe, and a bloody war in America tore the colonies from Great Britain. The nineteenth century is best remembered as the age of empire, when Pax Britannica projected British power to the corners of the globe, and the United States, fired by the spirit of Manifest Destiny, carved out the Western hemisphere as its own.

How will our times be viewed by history? I believe these days will be remembered as a time of remarkable spiritual awakening. The greatest revival of religion in modern times is breaking out across the globe. There are an estimated 200,000 people coming to Christ around the world every single day. That is more souls won in a single day than John Wesley converted during his entire ministry. The impact of religion on our lives, our families, and our politics is likely to increase in the years ahead, not diminish.

It behooves us, therefore, to understand religion and those motivated by it. Rather than marginalize faith, we must appreciate it and welcome its influence. Rather than dismiss its adherents, we should understand them, if only because they are going to play a major role in our future. Most people of faith are average citizens with mainstream beliefs, convinced that our system of government works better when more citizens are involved.

The Culture of Disbelief

Ironically, even as millions are yearning for faith, American culture has never been more hostile to the public expression of religious ideas. Stephen Carter trenchantly observed in *The Culture of Disbelief* that American culture no longer believes that religion can make a legitimate and rational contribution to civic discourse. "More and more," observes Carter, "our culture seems to take the position that believing deeply in the tenets of one's faith represents a kind of mystical irrationality, something that thoughtful, public-spirited American citizens would do better to avoid." The consequence of this cultural bias is a false dichotomy between faith and public life. "One result is that we often ask our citizens to split their public and private selves," Carter continues, "telling them in effect that it is fine to be religious in private, but there is something askew when those private beliefs become the basis for public action."[3]

Religion has become equated with fanaticism, orthodox faith with fascism, and politically involved people of faith are painted as zealots. As a society, we have become biased against bigotry itself except when that bias is directed at religion. People of faith want to exercise their rights of citizenship and serve their fellow Americans just like anyone else in public life. But their religion makes them suspect, and a deep and abiding faith often disqualifies them.[4]

Some in our society view religion as subversive because it claims to possess the absolute truth. But what of the fact that religion is the best antidote for fascism because it denies government the honor that religion reserves only for God? Or that religion has given us some of the most cherished "absolute" truths in history, which we gladly legislate. Such as: blacks and whites are equal because God created them in His image, taxation derives from the consent of the governed, slavery is evil, and human life is sacred. These positive attributes receive short shrift from the culture.

Revolt in the Big Apple

However, sometimes people working together—democracy in action—can put these basic truths into action. Consider the story of Mary Cummins, a diminutive Irish grandmother from Queens. Encountering her wrath is like stepping into a category 5 hurricane. Just ask Joseph Fernandez, the former chancellor of the New York City schools who lost his job in 1993 after mandating the Rainbow Curriculum, a multicultural course that included instruction on the gay lifestyle to students as young as six years old. Cummins, a devout Roman Catholic and a member of the Queens school board, raised her voice in protest and sparked a controversy that rumbled across the city like a political thunderclap. She not only toppled Fernandez, she became a symbol of an emerging coalition of Catholics, Protestants, and Jews that promises to change the direction of American politics.

School board elections in New York historically have been sedate affairs. But the 1993 campaign read like a subplot from Tom Wolfe's *Bonfire of the Vanities*, complete with the histrionics, bombast, and larger-than-life politics unique to the Big Apple. The dispute began when Fernandez imposed the controversial Rainbow Curriculum. Cummins and others on the Queens school board refused to implement the curriculum; Fernandez responded by summarily firing them. This action ignited a firestorm of protest among parents that dominated city politics for six months, ultimately leading to the dismissal of Fernandez for his mishandling of the mushrooming controversy. The battle spilled over into the campaign for 288 school board seats in the city's thirty-two school districts and five boroughs.

One day in March 1993 the phone rang in my office in Chesapeake, Virginia. Jeff Baran, the state chairman of the New York Christian Coalition, was on the line.

"Have you seen the fax I sent down this morning?" he asked.

I had not yet. My secretary brought it in. What I saw was the front page of the *New York Daily News*. The cover sported a grainy photograph taken at an impossible angle of a small group meeting in the basement of a Baptist church in Brooklyn. They had gathered to organize a local chapter of the Christian Coalition.

"IN GOD'S NAME!" screamed the headline, "Christian Right's Battle Plan to Seize Control of City." Inside, the story described a "secret" plan by the coalition to take control of the New York City school boards.[5]

"What are you doing in the school board races?" I asked.

"Honestly? Absolutely nothing," came the reply. Baran explained that the meeting was informational only, and that school board elections were never even discussed.

"Well, you are doing something now," I laughed. The press had thrown down the gauntlet, I argued, and we had to jump in with both feet. Baran and Terry Twerrell, our very able New York city coordinator, established contact with Mary Cummins and other parental rights advocates. We agreed to finance an ambitious campaign to turn out people of faith to the polls.

Ironically, our effort began as a result of an inaccurate story in the press. Over the next two months, the Christian Coalition distributed 550,000 nonpartisan voter guides in 1,300 churches that informed voters where 540 school board candidates stood on a broad range of issues, including school choice, voluntary prayer, merit pay for teachers, and parental rights. The voter guides were strictly nonpartisan and endorsed no candidates.

The ACLU hysterically called the campaign "the greatest civil liberties crisis" in the history of New York City. The *New York Times* solemnly editorialized that if "right-wing Christians" gained "disproportionate influence, the results could be destructive." The Reverend Al Sharpton denounced the parents' efforts as "racist."[6]

The result was that voter turnout reached the highest level in twenty years. As 450,000 voters went to the polls, approximately 60 percent of 130 pro-family candidates were victorious, and ten school boards in the city had solid pro-family majorities. Many of the victors were political novices. Linda Garcia, a Hispanic mother, won election in Manhattan's Lower East Side to a board previously dominated by gay activists and former anti-Vietnam war protesters.

A Mainstream Agenda

Garcia and others are shattering the stereotype of religious conservatives. Some view people of faith as latter-day Babbits who troop to churches in polyester suits, handle snakes, and pray in tongues for the return of Jim Crow and patriarchy. The *Washington Post* even labeled them "poor, uneducated, and easy to command."

In fact, our faith is expansive, positive, and tolerant. Religious conservatives are overwhelmingly women—62 percent female, compared to only 38 percent male. Some, like Starr Parker of California, are African-American women who have risen up from welfare to start businesses and meet payrolls. Maraide Prior, an actress in Connecticut, lobbies the legislature and organizes like-minded citizens. Others are businessmen seeking to improve their communities. Pat Gartland, a Chamber of Commerce executive from Atlanta, Georgia, is a former University of Alabama football player and a lay leader in one of the largest churches in Georgia.

These and other persons of faith support a mainstream agenda for the country. What would the world look like if they were permitted to serve? It would not be, as some have suggested, a Victorian, patriarchal, proto-Nazi, crypto-Klansman, theocratic police state. Jews, women, racial minorities, and those of differing faith traditions would be free from discrimination and bias. Some charge that if religious conservatives held office they would destroy public education, outlaw contraception, ban the teaching of evolution, destroy the First Amendment, censor books, and force women out of the workplace and back into the kitchen. These accusations are grounded not in fact but in fear and bigotry. This book addresses how that stereotype has been broadcast by our secular culture and, tragically, reinforced by some of us with deep faith.

We live in a country in which one out of every three children is born out of wedlock, one out of every two marriages ends in divorce, one out of every three pregnancies ends in abortion, and one out of every four high school students drops out of school without graduating. We have 90 million functional illiterates in our society. Murder is the leading cause of death for African-American males aged eighteen to thirty-four, and a minority adolescent male living in our nation's capital has a higher likelihood of being killed than an American soldier did in Vietnam. And yet there are still some who believe that the most frightening thing that could happen in America is for people of devout faith to become involved in public life.

It is time to set the record straight. If religious conservatives took their proper, proportionate place as leaders in the political and cultural life of the country, we would work to create the kind of society in which presumably all of us would like to live: safe neighborhoods, strong families, schools that work, a smaller government, lower taxes. Civil rights protection would be afforded to all Americans without regard to gender, race, religious beliefs, ethnicity, age, or physical handicap. Parents would send their children to the school of their choice, and children would be able to read, write, find Mexico on a map, and perform basic math and science skills on a level exceeding that of their counterparts in other advanced Western industrial democracies.

Government would be small because citizens and private institutions would voluntarily perform many of its functions. We would not need a large, bloated welfare state to take care of us, for we would take care of each other. We would not need the law to threaten or cajole us, for a higher law would live in our hearts. Through private initiatives and sound public policy, those who were hungry would be fed, those who were thirsty would drink, those who were homeless would be housed, and those who were hurting would be comforted.

Families would function again; marriages would work; children would be considered a blessing rather than a burden; neighbors would be neighbors again; government would be the servant instead of the master of a free and educated citizenry; revitalized communities would radiate from compassionate churches and synagogues; and some of the most respected leaders in society would be pastors, priests, and rabbis.

In short, we desire a good society based on the shared values of work, family, neighborhood, and faith.

People of faith would not be denied a place at the table or an effective voice in the democratic process. "The religious person is entitled, if not to prevail, at least to be heard," argues Terry Eastland, a former top official in the Justice Department under Ronald Reagan. "He can expect that his religion will not disqualify him from speaking on political matters, and that if he offers a religious or ethical justification for his position on a public issue, it will not *ipso facto* be considered out of bounds of public discourse."[7] Most of the public policy positions advocated by religious conservatives are supported by the vast majority of the American people: 70 percent favor a Balanced Budget Amendment, 85 percent favor voluntary school prayer, 75 percent favor term limits, and 70 percent oppose abortion on demand paid for with tax dollars.

Given the public support for their views, people of faith have a right to be heard, and their religion should not disqualify them from serving in office or participating in the political party of their choice. They are not, after all, asking people to subscribe to their theology; they are asking them to subscribe to their public policy views and to respect their right to participate without their religion being impugned. This is not too much to ask in a democracy.

This is not a vision exclusively for those who are evangelical or Roman Catholic or Greek Orthodox or Jewish. This vision makes room for people of all faiths—and those with no faith at all. It is not an American vision, but a vision for people of every race in every nation in the world. The agenda of religious conservatives is informed by faith, tempered by tolerance, and guided by an abiding respect for the dignity of other human beings. Even those who do not share the theology of religious conservatives are likely to share their public policy goals. And even those who do not share their policy views should sympathize with their bringing faith into what Richard John Neuhaus calls the "naked public square." They are part of one of the most cherished and glorious of American democratic traditions: the reformist impulse that derives from religious faith. Rather than building a "wall of separation" to keep them out, we should encourage more people of faith to participate in public life. Religious people are not part of America's problem but part of its solution.

Breaking the Race Barrier

This emerging coalition of Christians and their allies is snapping the color line. Survey data reveals that African-Americans and other minorities are more religiously devout and conservative than whites. In a survey commissioned by the liberal People for the American Way, Democratic pollster Peter Hart found that 87 percent of young blacks ranked the family as their most important concern in life. Their second-most important value was "fair treatment for all," followed by faith in God (86 percent), and "emphasis on self-reliance and taking responsibility for yourself," which 84 percent ranked as very important. The same poll found blacks more likely to subscribe to these traditional values than whites.[8]

Other minority surveys reveal similar findings. A poll for the Christian Coalition conducted in 1993 found that minorities tend to be more religious than whites, with 63 percent of African-Americans and 43 percent of Hispanics identifying themselves as "born again," compared to only 40 percent of whites. More African-Americans (81 percent) and Hispanics (65 percent) than whites (59 percent) say they pray daily.

Minorities also read the Bible more frequently, attend church more regularly, and engage in other forms of devout religious behavior more than do whites. In this respect, minorities are a more natural constituency for the pro-family movement than whites because of the importance of the church to the civic advancement of their community. Blacks and Hispanics generally have a more positive view of church-based civic involvement because of the centrality of the church in their daily lives and the legacy of the civil rights movement.[9]

Is this just a pipe dream? Hardly. Indeed, growing evidence points to its becoming a reality. During the New York City school board races, some of the greatest activism came from Hispanics and African-Americans.

Or consider the Los Angeles mayor's race in 1993. The contest pitted Richard Riordan, a conservative Republican, against Michael Woo, a liberal Democrat, both fighting to succeed Tom Bradley. Woo broadcast television commercials attacking Riordan for his support by evangelical

Christians—a tactic that badly misfired in the heavily-evangelical minority community. The Christian Coalition distributed 350,000 pieces of literature in 2,100 churches, including 700 Asian, Hispanic, or black churches. For the first time ever, multilingual voter guides were printed in three languages: Spanish, Korean, and English. The result: Michael Woo, an ethnic liberal Democrat, lost the Hispanic vote and barely won the Asian vote. His campaign of religious bigotry failed, in large part due to minority voters.

Bret Schundler, a committed Christian and pro-life Republican, won the election in 1993 as mayor of Jersey City, New Jersey, by campaigning on the issues of crime and school choice. At first, pundits gave the Republican candidate no chance to win in this overwhelmingly Democratic city where minorities comprise 65 percent of the population. But minorities are the first affected by violence and poor schools, and Schundler's message of empowerment resonated among African-American voters. He pledged to crack down on crime and push an experimental voucher program through the state legislature that would allow parents to send their children to the school of their choice. Jesse Jackson came to Jersey City to stump for Schundler's black Democratic opponent, warning that his defeat would spell disaster for the cause of civil rights. But blacks voted their values, not their fears. Schundler won 40 percent of the minority vote on the way to a landslide victory.[10]

A New Ecumenism

Perhaps most encouraging is a new spirit of ecumenism that permeates the pro-family community. During the New York City school board races, John Cardinal O'Connor and the Roman Catholic Archdiocese distributed an estimated 100,000 nonpartisan voter guides in 220 churches. The pro-family movement's embrace of the Roman Catholic community in New York City was one of the most significant developments since its emergence in the late 1970s. The union of Roman Catholics and conservative Protestants could have a greater impact on American politics than any coalition since African-Americans and Jews came together during the civil rights movement.

From the rumblings of the Reformation to the nativist rantings of the Know-Nothings, Protestants and Catholics have eyed one another suspiciously across a chasm of painful history. Differences on some theological issues remain. But the darkness of the culture has become so pervasive that those of like mind and common faith feel compelled to join together in unity. They agree in their respect for the sanctity of innocent human life, their opposition to pornography, and their support of school choice and religious liberty.

A major turning point in this new coalition occurred in March 1994 when a group of Catholic and Protestant leaders signed a historic declaration entitled "Evangelicals and Catholics Together." Led by Chuck Colson of Prison Fellowship and Father Richard John Neuhaus, a Catholic theologian, thirty-nine religious leaders pledged to work together to redress hostility towards religion in the broader culture. Among the signators: John Cardinal O'Connor, Pat Robertson, Bill Bright with Campus Crusade for Christ, and Richard Land of the Southern Baptist Convention.

The statement expressed consensus on the core beliefs of the Christian faith. Areas of agreement included the lordship of Christ, the supremacy of faith, the infallibility of Scripture, and the importance of evangelism.

The statement also has important political overtones. There are approximately 58 million Catholics and 24 million evangelicals in the United States—the largest single voting bloc in the electorate. The manifesto noted a "growing convergence" among the two groups on social issues. It called on Catholics and evangelicals to "contend together for a common cause" against militant secularism, abortion, euthanasia, and pornography. The statement also called for "convergence and cooperation" in advocating school choice, religious freedom, the teaching of Judeo-Christian values in schools, racial justice, and a free market economy.

"We have differences," acknowledged Chuck Colson. "Nonetheless, on the ancient creeds and the core beliefs of Christianity we stand together. Christianity is besieged on all sides—by a militant nation of Islam, by pantheists who have invaded many areas of life, including the church through the New Age movement, and by the aggressive secularism of Western life." He added, "If we can't stand together, we have very little chance to make a common defense of our truth and our world view."[11]

Centuries of distrust are melting away and denominational barriers are crumbling. "I really do think it is a historic moment," rejoiced John White, past head of the National Association of Evangelicals. Avery Dulles, a Jesuit priest and professor at Fordham University, agreed. "A new relationship between Evangelicals and Catholics is demanded by the present situation of religion in our country," he said. "The American experiment in ordered freedom, including religious freedom, is in peril. By collaboration, we can together defend religious freedom against the encroachments of government agencies that operate in ways hostile to the free exercise of religion."[12]

I recently attended an event in New York that demonstrated the persistence of these issues and the ecumenical coalition that they have brought together. The "Proudly Pro-life Awards" dinner, sponsored by the National Right to Life Committee, was attended by over 1,100 people, filling the Grand Ballroom of the Waldorf-Astoria Hotel. The two honorees were Mrs. Nancy DeMoss, an evangelical Protestant, and John Cardinal O'Connor. Among the attendees were Representative Henry Hyde, Republican of Illinois; Governor Joan Finney, Democrat of Kansas; Governor Robert Casey, Democrat of Pennsylvania; and businessman Peter Grace. Throughout the audience, the clerical collars of Catholic priests interspersed with colorful dresses worn by women. There were also many prominent Greek Orthodox priests and lay persons in attendance.

Governor Bob Casey introduced the award recipients by asserting that the pro-life movement was on the march and that the tide was turning towards ultimate victory. He pointed to the defeat of the Freedom of Choice Act, the victory of the Hyde Amendment banning taxpayer funding of abortion, and the political trouble facing the Clinton health care plan, which included coverage for abortion.

"Casey in 1996!" someone shouted from the predominantly Republican crowd.

"It could be a good year," Casey responded to thunderous applause. How remarkable that this Roman Catholic Democrat, who campaigned for George McGovern in 1972, could conceivably run for president with the support of evangelicals. A candidacy by Casey or another Roman Catholic offers an intriguing opportunity for Democrats disaffected by Bill Clinton—or even for evangelicals if the Republicans made the mistake of dropping their pro-life stance. It could also serve as a symbol of the growing importance of the evangelical-Catholic connection.

"Falling into the sphere of pro-life activists was one of the greatest things that ever happened to me in my life," said Cardinal O'Connor upon receiving his award. "There are Protestants who have held prayer groups solely for the protection of innocent life."

Nancy DeMoss, honored for her pro-life television commercials, spoke eloquently of the ecumenical cooperation that the evening represented. "We owe you, Cardinal O'Connor, a tremendous debt of gratitude," she said. "You spoke out when others have remained silent."

As I walked through the ballroom shaking hands with evangelical friends and hugging Catholic priests with whom I had labored in previous battles, I realized that the pro-family movement was overcoming its parochialism and gaining a new ecumenical flavor. I ran into Monsignor John Woolsey, an aide to Cardinal O'Connor, with whom I had struck up a friendship during the New York school board races. "This is what will make the difference," he said, pointing to the crowd.

The future of American politics lies in the growing strength of evangelicals and their Roman Catholic allies. If these two core constituencies—evangelicals comprising the swing vote in the South, Catholics holding sway in the North—can cooperate on issues and support like-minded candidates, they can determine the outcome of almost any election in the nation. Nasty nativism and dark distrust about Popery and foreign influence have been swept away into the ash heap of history. John F. Kennedy's election in 1960 buried the Catholic bogeyman forever. No longer burdened by the past, Roman Catholics, evangelicals, Greek Orthodox, and many religious conservatives from the mainline denominations are forging a new alliance that promises to be among the most powerful and important in the modern political era.

The watershed event that propelled Catholics into the political arena was the Supreme Court's *Roe* v. *Wade* decision in 1973. In a single wrenching moment, abortion replaced race as the most divisive social issue of the post-World War II period. *Roe* politicized a religious community conditioned for generations to eschew social action (due in part to well-developed fears of inciting anti-Catholicism). It also brought Catholics and evangelicals into common cause for the first time. In a 1984 study of California pro-life activists, sociologist Kristen Luker discovered more people "joined the pro-life movement in 1973 than in any other year, before or since," and these activists "reported that they became mobilized to the cause the very day the decision was handed down." Most Catholics who flocked to the pro-life banner had never before been politically involved in any way, not even in a political party or community groups such as the PTA.[13]

In the months following *Roe*, the Catholic church formally sought a human life amendment to the Constitution. This campaign culminated in the extraordinary joint appearance in March 1974 of John Cardinal Krol of Philadelphia, president of the U.S. Catholic Bishops Conference, and three other cardinals before a Senate panel. They called *Roe* "the worst mistake in the Court's history," and argued that their intent was not "to advocate sectarian doctrine but to defend human rights." The proposed human life amendment failed to reach the Senate floor, but the Roman Catholic Church had taken a historic step: public action in defense of unborn life now bore the imprimatur of church leaders.[14]

The Catholic Church was joined in these efforts by the National Right to Life Committee and evangelical Christians who began to reenter politics at the same time. A shared vision of social justice muted theological differences. This was no small matter: the Roman Catholic Profession of Faith reads, in part, "We believe in one holy catholic and apostolic church." Cardinal James Gibbons of Baltimore, the most important Catholic churchman of the nineteenth century, had been roundly criticized for his support of the labor movement. Now the American Catholic Church jumped with both feet into the most controversial issue of the day—and allied itself with Protestants.[15]

Evangelicals poured into the political arena for similar reasons. One of the sparks inciting them was an attempt by the Internal Revenue Service in 1978 to issue regulations that posed a threat to the burgeoning Christian school movement. Paul Weyrich, one of the architects of the pro-family movement, recently pointed this out in a symposium sponsored by the Washington-based Ethics and Public Policy Center. "It is a defensive movement," Weyrich observed. "The people who are involved in it didn't want to get involved; they got involved very reluctantly." What caused the movement to flower in the 1970s, he adds, was not school prayer or abortion (though they were important issues), but "the federal government's moves against Christian schools. This absolutely shattered the Christian community's notions that Christians could isolate themselves inside their own institutions and teach what they pleased."[16]

Also important to the Catholic-evangelical alliance is the rise of sex education in undermining parental rights. From New York to California, battles over curriculum decisions are uniting evangelicals and Catholics against education bureaucrats.[17] One controversial seventh-grade curriculum in Connecticut highlights sexual activity while giving little emphasis to celibacy.[18] This issue led to evangelical-Catholic convergence in the New York City school board races of 1993. The media and most observers mistook the campaign as a religious crusade designed to take over school boards. In fact, as Richard Vigilante observes, the explanation for the revolt was "really very simple: Parents are trying to take back their schools."[19]

The movement is best understood as an essentially defensive struggle by people seeking to sustain their faith and their values. They want good schools, safe neighborhoods, faith-knit communities, and lower government debt to protect the financial future of their children. They are far less interested in legislating against the sins of others, and far more interested in protecting their own right to practice their religion and raise their children in a manner consistent with their values. As Congressman Richard Armey of Texas has recently observed, "Millions of evangelicals and orthodox Roman Catholics in the 1970s felt their way of life to be under subtle but determined attack by federal policies." They sought to reenter public life, "not to impose their beliefs on others, but because the federal government was imposing its values on them."[20]

"Thus the 'new ecumenism' has arisen almost by accident," George Weigel observes. "It is not the product of theological seminars," but the result of "a shared perception that the systematic effort to strip American public policy discourse of any relationship to the religiously-based values of the American people portends disaster for the American experiment."

In this sense, abortion is the ultimate cultural Rorschach test. Do religious values have a place in the debate over this contentious issue? Evangelicals and Catholics respond in the affirmative, and that answer has set them apart—and drawn them together.[21]

They both believe in the idea expressed by Anthony Bevilacqua, the archbishop of Philadelphia, who contended in a homily delivered in 1990 that America's moral crisis requires that we include religious values in our civic discourse. "Especially in the last three decades," he notes disapprovingly, "it is the perception of many that Church and State, religion and law, are adversaries instead of companions, enemies instead of friends, antagonists instead of partners." Bevilacqua asks, "Has the time not come for Church and State, the two travelers along the path of our republic, to stop shouting at each other and start conversing in a language both can understand?"[22]

The new ecumenism is not only political. The charismatic renewal of the 1960s brought evangelicals like Pat Robertson in contact with Catholics who believed in the work of the Holy Spirit. The charismatic movement within the Roman Catholic Church began in 1967 at a weekend retreat for students and faculty, and soon spread around the nation. Catholic charismatics are a small but influential core within the church that have led the way in encouraging fellowship with evangelicals. The marriage enrichment movement has also furthered ecumenical cooperation on restoring marriage from a Christian perspective. Marriage Encounter, which began as a Catholic organization, sponsors "encounter weekends" for couples seeking help and has become the leading organization for marriage renewal in the world. It coordinates its activities and publications with the Protestant-led Association of Couples for Marriage Enrichment.[23]

The new ecumenical coalition is also extending to the Jewish community. Jews generally remain one of the most secular and liberal constituencies of the American electorate. "With the exception of blacks, there is no group in America—including even union members and welfare recipients—more loyal to the Democratic party," notes former Bush White House official Jay Lefkowitz.[24]

This pattern may be changing. *Boston Herald* columnist Don Feder notes that overall Jewish population is shrinking because of low birth rates. Between 1970 and 1990, while the overall population grew by 22 percent, Jewish population increased by an insignificant 1.8 percent. Even this demographic growth is undermined by intermarriage and assimilation. The exception to this rule is the orthodox Jewish community, which is growing in proportion to the overall population. "American Jewry of the twenty-first century," suggests Feder, "will be strikingly different from today's community: smaller as a percentage of the population, more cohesive, more religious and once again aware of its mission in the world—to attest to the presence of a universal God and His law."[25]

There are new and emerging Jewish leaders calling for greater cooperation with evangelicals. Rabbi Daniel Lapin recently formed Toward Tradition to foster Jewish-Christian agreement on shared social concerns. He has appeared at numerous Christian forums, and was one of the most popular speakers at the Christian Coalition Road to Victory conference in 1993, receiving several standing ovations. I recently appeared with Lapin at grassroots conferences in South Carolina, California, and Washington state, where he and I both urged people of faith to get involved in local and state government.

Rabbi Joshua Haberman of Washington, D.C., has also spoken eloquently of the need for dialogue between Christians and Jews on shared concerns from religious liberty to the nation of Israel. "Christian morality, as far as I'm concerned, is very acceptable to me," says Haberman. "A secular America would be a much more dangerous place in which to live than a country that is still nourished by religious tradition, Christian as well as Jewish."[26]

Another Jewish leader blazing trails in the Christian community is Rabbi Shea Hecht of the Committee for Jewish Education, who worked with evangelicals and Catholics during the New York City school board races. Dennis Prager, editor of *Ultimate Issues*, has been a vocal leader opposing religious bigotry against both Jews and Christians. When Pat Robertson came under fire during the Los Angeles mayor's race, Prager appeared at a news conference to condemn religious intolerance. Film critic Michael Medved has also been an eloquent voice calling Hollywood to task for its negative stereotypes of religion and people of faith.

Dialogue between Christians and Jews continues to center around a shared interest in the state of Israel. Evangelicals remain some of the strongest supporters of Israel. I saw this first-hand during a trip to the Holy Land in early 1993 as the Israeli government and the PLO completed negotiations on a peace treaty. I met with former prime minister Yitzak Shamir and expressed my concerns about the peace process and the need to protect Israeli citizens from terrorist attacks. "You are not the problem," replied Shamir. "You are among our strongest supporters. Whatever problems we have now are caused by Israelis, not Americans." Agreement on foreign policy and opposition to religious intolerance could provide the basis for an expanded dialogue and greater cooperation between Christians and Jews in the United States.

The evangelical-Catholic connection is a permanent fixture on the American political landscape. A significant constituency of Jews is joining them on a range of issues. As Archbishop Roach said more than a decade ago: "The right of religious organizations of varying views to speak must be defended by all who understand the meaning of religious liberty and the role of religion." He added that religious groups "must be subjected to the same standards—rational, vigorous presentation of their views—as any other participants in the public debate." Evangelicals and Roman Catholics must not only demand a voice, they must exercise that voice responsibly. If they do so, they will have a far greater impact together than they could ever have separately.

The time is ripe for change. Spiritual ferment and hunger for faith is at an all-time high. Scarcely a person in this country would disagree with the notion that something serious ails our nation and that something must be done about it. But what kind of change do religious conservatives have in mind? How do they intend to bring that change to bear? Their vision for the future is next, and it may surprise you.

CHAPTER TWO

What the World Would Look Like: A Religious Conservative Vision for America

NOT LONG AGO I appeared on a national television news program to discuss the agenda of religious conservatives. I fielded questions on the usual subjects: abortion, pornography, church and state, education, and crime. My basic message was simple: people of faith represent one of the largest segments of the electorate (24 percent according to 1992 exit polls), and they want a role in society commensurate with their numbers. During a commercial break, one of the journalists quizzing me leaned over and asked in a hushed whisper, "What is it you people *really* want?"

The question presupposed an agenda very different from the mainstream ideas I had outlined. I answered, "I would like to see a day when an evangelical Christian could stand next to the president of the United States and oversee his transition into office—in the same way that Vernon Jordan as an African-American led Bill Clinton's transition—and never have his religion become an issue." A look of disappointment crossed the journalist's face; it was not the answer he had in mind.

This incident reminds me of a story about Richard Nixon. Nixon dropped by the office of one of his speechwriters one day, and in the midst of a breezy conversation, inquired, "What do you think Ronald Reagan is up to these days?" (Nixon, then grooming John Connally for the Republican presidential nomination in 1976, worried often about the threat of a Reagan candidacy.) The speechwriter replied that Reagan was giving speeches around the country, broadcasting a daily radio commentary, and building a direct mail list of financial supporters. He was obviously running for president. "Yes, I know that," Nixon reportedly responded. "But what is he *really* up to?"

What do religious conservatives really want? They want a place at the table in the conversation we call democracy. Their commitment to pluralism includes a place for faith among the many other competing interests in society. For too long, we have left politics to the special interests. It is time for the values of middle America to have their place at the table. For decades religious people have been on the sidelines watching everyone else play the game. They want to be on the field, if not always to win, then at least to participate. If they should win, they do not want to have victory denied them because of their religious beliefs.

Opponents of conservative Christians use shrill charges to portray them as extremists. The National Abortion Rights Action League has charged that the movement has the "potential for [the] destruction of our political, religious, and legal institutions." One wonders which aspect of the religious conservative agenda they have in mind. Their tendency to label the entire agenda of politically active Christians as dangerous is disingenuous. "Such dismissive cultural assumptions, ill-founded and blithely propagated," argues John Meacham of the *Washington Monthly*, "are keeping liberals, moderates, and even conservatives from realizing what the millions-strong movement is actually right about." Meacham concludes that religious people advocate "a fairly sensible cultural vision and a not unreasonable policy agenda that's as neoliberal as it is fundamentalist."[1] Or as Ted Koppel of ABC's *Nightline* recently suggested, "Some may not like it, but the religious right is not always wrong."

Some raise concerns about people of faith based on their theology, not their political views. E. J. Dionne of the *Washington Post* recently proffered that "a liberal, democratic society presents a certain challenge to religious people, because religious people believe, fundamentally, that they have the truth with a capital T." He suggests that politics presents a dilemma for those whose primary purpose is the fulfillment of an essentially religious vision. They may erroneously believe that politics is a Manichean clash between good and evil, a conflict in which compromise is tantamount to capitulation. Dionne is right in the abstract, but very few Christians view their political involvement as an extension of their eschatology. Their objective is citizenship, not theism. Few if any believe that the Republican party platform belongs in the canon of Scripture—or vice versa.[2]

Theodore White once remarked that Barry Goldwater found ideas fascinating because they were so new to him. The same has been true of the fascination with politics among some people of faith. They have expressed a zeal for political activism because they were so new to the process. This was especially true in the early days of the so-called religious right, when messianic language and a storming-the-barricades rhetoric prevailed. The longer people of faith have remained in the political arena, the more sensitive they have become to the limits of politics. Time has softened their rhetoric and rounded out their sharp edges. Forays into the electoral arena (such as Pat Robertson's 1988 presidential bid and Mike Farris's 1993 campaign for lieutenant governor in Virginia) have made evangelicals more subdued, seasoned, and savvy.

Political involvement is a dynamic process. Since the emergence of the pro-family movement, religion has changed our politics, but politics has also changed religious folk. It has taught them not to expect a heaven on earth, to take defeat (and victory) with a grain of salt, and to respect the right of their political foes to play on the same field. For evangelicals, who have spent most of the last half-century with their noses pressed against the glass of the culture, reentering the mainstream of American life has been a little like learning to ride a bicycle all over again. At first the pedals turn tentatively and the wheels wobble, but with practice the rider grows in strength and confidence.

Most Christians experience a religious conversion and subsequently dive into politics because of their newfound faith. My testimony is quite different. By the time I became a committed Christian in September 1983, I had already worked on Capitol Hill and on numerous statewide and congressional campaigns. Though barely out of college, I was a seasoned political veteran. My goal was to be the next Lee Atwater—a bare-knuckled, brass tacks practitioner of hard-ball politics. But my experience in Washington was disillusioning. The lofty ideals that I brought to the nation's capital were shaken by the reality of life in Congress, where votes were sold to the highest bidder and politicians shook down special interests for campaign contributions in what journalist Brooks Jackson has called "honest graft." I saw powerful people up close, became acquainted with their foibles, and witnessed the seamy underside of politics. I learned quickly that the pursuit of power is an empty and unsatisfying exercise without a moral compass to guide one's journey.

Many of my friends in college had shared their faith with me, but I was too busy riding in the fast lane of politics to listen at the time. In the fall of 1983, after leaving the University of Georgia and taking a job with the College Republicans in Washington, I realized that something was missing. Raised in a devout Methodist home where my father was active in church affairs and my mother led the youth group, I knew I had gradually lost touch with my spiritual roots. One Saturday, after an evening of socializing with friends, I felt a gentle tugging in my conscience that I should start attending a local church. New to the area and not knowing where to go, I walked to a phone booth at a restaurant on Capitol Hill and flipped through the yellow pages. My finger fell by a listing for an evangelical church in the suburbs just outside Washington. The next day, following the morning services, the pastor led an altar call for those desiring to have a closer relationship with Christ. I raised my hand in affirmation and began a new life of faith.

After making my faith commitment, I was surprised to discover that some of my fellow Christians suffered from a case of "Potomac fever." Seduced by the allure of politics, they were sometimes naive about its vanity and false pretense. Like first-time investors who sink everything they own into a high-risk venture, they poured all their aspirations for the reformation of society into politics. Some met with bitter disappointment, particularly when their high hopes for the Reagan administration gave way to many victories but a number of defeats as well. While the Supreme Court became more conservative, it did not reverse liberal decisions on abortion and school prayer as many had hoped. Political action can change laws, but it does not change hearts, a lesson that liberals as well as conservatives have painfully learned.

Religious folk are now becoming more wise to the possibilities as well as the limits of politics. While they believe they possess the truth about matters of eternity, they are less self-assured about temporal matters, which tend to be more ambiguous. There are some political issues that the Bible addresses in principle. But most matters must await the hereafter before they reach a final resolution. As the apostle Paul said in his letter to the Corinthians, "Now I know in part, but then I shall know fully just as I also have been fully known" (1 Corinthians 13:12). This fact, a vital component of the Christian faith, enforces a humility that guards against self-righteousness in the political arena.

Most of the vision that people of faith have for a caring society cannot be achieved through political action. Political victory, no matter how fervently pursued, will not lead to the promised land. Just ask the Communists in the former Soviet Union. They took power in 1917 during the Bolshevik Revolution and promised citizens a heaven on earth. Today, Lenin's status lies in rubble in village squares throughout that troubled land.

This lesson of history should give pause to the conservative religious folk in America as they pour into the political process. They are met with unbridled (and undue) fear by their opponents. Christians have every right—and indeed a duty—to vote, participate in the political party of their choice, lobby elected officials, and even seek public office. But we must also allay the fears we may elicit in so doing by acknowledging that most of what we desire for society can only be achieved through private philanthropy and personal acts of goodness—not through political means. Loving wives, faithful husbands, obedient children, honest public servants, and communities enlivened by faith must ultimately await the world to come. We must be faithful in seeking to establish goodness today while remembering that only God's Kingdom contains true peace and harmony, and His Kingdom is not of this world.

Richard John Neuhaus has argued that people of faith in the political arena should act with modesty and humility that are "not the result of weak-kneed accommodationism but are required by fidelity to the claims of the gospel." And as Tom Atwood has pointed out in a recent article on this ambiguity, "Believers are required to be reverent and cautious about speaking for the Lord, especially in the volatile, darkly glassed world of politics." This makes evangelicals and others of faith the best possible candidates to lead and serve, for they appreciate the veil that separates the eternal from the temporal. There may be only one way to get to heaven according to one's theology, but there is probably more than one way to balance the budget or reform health care.[3]

We are also growing in our understanding of government service as an extension of our obligation to witness the love of Christ. Evangelicals and their allies are concerned about better schools, public safety, strengthening the family, and protecting the unborn. But if people of faith are elected to city council or state legislature, they must strive to meet all the needs of the community. When Christ performed His first miracle at the wedding at Cana by turning the water into wine, He was not only performing a sign but meeting the need of the wedding host (John 2:7). This aspect of Christ's ministry—works of excellence that met tangible needs—should distinguish our approach to everything, including politics. Reforming education, filling potholes, saving taxpayer funds, and securing justice for the innocent will all witness to His mercy and goodness in a lost and hurting world.

Crime and Safety

In a world in which religious conservatives served, violent crime would decline and neighborhoods would return to safety. Fewer people would live in fear in their own homes. Parents would be able to send their eight-year-old son or daughter around the corner to a neighborhood playground without having to worry about whether they will come home in a pine box. Polly Klaas, the twelve-year-old girl abducted in 1993 from her home in California and brutally murdered, would be more likely to be alive today. Her murderer, Richard Allen Davis, would not have been released from prison if religious conservatives had drafted the laws on early release for convicted violent felons. Davis was a three-time loser with a rap sheet nine pages long. Despite multiple convictions on kidnapping, sexual assault, and burglary charges, he was released from prison after serving only five years of a fifteen-year sentence. If religious conservatives served in government, parole would be abolished for violent felons and repeat violent offenders would spend the rest of their lives in jail.

Building more prisons will not solve the crime problem by itself. But it is part of a broader solution to the violence plaguing America. An important reform is alternative sentencing: half-way houses for juveniles, boot camps for first-time offenders. Many of the military bases being closed in the current downsizing of the armed services should be requisitioned and used in the domestic war on crime. We must also allocate resources more effectively at the state and local level to provide for more police. While criminals stalk our streets and law-abiding citizens live in fear, corrections services in 1990 accounted for only 2.5 percent of all state and local government expenditures. Indeed, government spends more on welfare ($305 billion) than it spends for the courts, law enforcement, and prisons combined. Religious conservatives hope to reverse this equation. Drugs would not only be illegal but rare. Convicted drug dealers who peddled on school grounds or to minors would go to prison—without parole. No citizenry can prosper that is not safe, and ours is assuredly not safe.[4]

As I will point out in a later chapter, there can be no genuine solution to the crime problem without more functioning marriages in which fathers and mothers watch over their children. Part of the answer involves government action—welfare reform, ending subsidies for illegitimacy, and reforming no-fault divorce laws. But much of this agenda exceeds the scope of government. We need a spiritual and moral renewal in America that causes wives and husbands to stay together, children to honor their parents, and neighbors to help one another again.

Stronger Families

Civility would return to our public discourse as well as private affairs, and the coarseness that afflicts our culture would soften. Children would respect their parents, young people would honor authority, and more citizens would obey the law. Parents could turn on the television set without ushering their children out of the room or wincing at graphic violence, profane language, or sexually explicit scenes. Women would no longer be exploited by hard-core pornography, which would be socially stigmatized and confined to dirty old men. There would be fewer divorces, fewer children born out of wedlock, more intact families, and more live births than abortions in even our largest cities.

Part of this vision can be achieved through private action, such as boycotts by consumers against corporate sponsors of violence and sex on television. These consumer efforts have succeeded in reducing the financial bonanza for those who assault our moral sensibilities for profit. Dr. Richard Neill of Fort Worth, Texas, recently succeeded in alerting advertisers to some of the offensive programs on Phil Donahue's show on subjects ranging from transvestite nuns to children who have had sex with their step-parents. These programs were broadcast after school in a late afternoon time slot, exposing hundreds of thousands of young children to inappropriate adult sexual material. Dozens of advertisers dropped their commercials from *Donahue* after learning what they had sponsored. Neill's efforts are one small trickle in a growing flood of protests from parents who want a children-friendly culture.

Government can also play a role in reducing the trash quotient of our culture. For example, an initiative on the ballot in Oregon in 1994 would outlaw hard-core pornography that includes themes of sado-masochism, rape, and child molestation. The initiative was prompted by the murder of six-year-old Lee Iseli, who was abducted and molested in 1989 by a killer who reenacted scenes from pornographic magazines. Similar legislation around the nation in the coming years will restore civility to our society, protect children, and increase respect for women, while maintaining the First Amendment freedom of the press.

Women would be free to choose a career inside or outside the home. If they chose the workplace, it would be because they wanted to, not because they were forced by financial pressure. Women in the work force would receive equal pay for equal work. Employers would hire and promote based on ability, not the color of one's skin or gender. Women who worked at home would receive tax credits for child care that are equal to those for women who work outside in order to affirm the value of the tasks they perform every day to support their families and nurture their children.

More young people would get married and stay married. Birth rates would climb as the love of married couples spilled over into their most precious resource, their children. Fathers would honor their wives, love their children, and find their self-esteem at home rather than merely in how many hours they work at the office. Fewer men would sire children out of wedlock and abandon the responsibility for financially supporting them to the government. Deadbeat dads would be socially frowned upon and pursued by the long arm of the law, their wages garnished and their social irresponsibility discouraged.

Reducing welfare subsidies and requiring the determination of paternity will greatly reduce the bias of the current system towards illegitimacy. The Promise Keepers organization began in 1991 under the leadership of University of Colorado football coach Bill McCartney as a meeting of several hundred men and has mushroomed to over 100,000 men nationwide who are dedicating themselves to their God and their families. Each man makes a pledge to be a better husband and father—thus the term "promise keeper." More fatherhood movements are likely to spring up in the years ahead as society acknowledges that the love of fathers and mothers is more important than government programs in creating a truly caring culture.

Abortion would no longer be the most common surgical procedure performed in America. It would no longer be paid for or promoted with tax dollars. The mother's womb would no longer be the most dangerous place in America for a child. A thirteen-year-old girl, prohibited from even getting her ears pierced without the permission of her parents, would not be able to have an abortion without the approval of her parents or guardians. States would be free to restrict abortions except in cases of the endangerment of the life of the mother, rape, or incest. A majority of Americans strongly support protecting innocent human life. A March 1994 survey by the Roper organization for Focus on the Family found that a majority of Americans support restrictions on abortion except in the hard cases. Only 13 percent support abortion for any reason at all through the ninth month of pregnancy. This is consistent with polling data over the past decade.

Adoption would be accessible for couples struggling to have children. Regulatory red tape would be lifted on adoption services and surrogate mothers would be unnecessary. The decline in the number of abortions would make more children available for adoption, and the long waiting lists for those desiring them would vanish.

Unwanted pregnancies would be less common among young people as fewer teens turned to sex before marriage. Achieving this goal will require a mixture of legislation and social change. The government can do more to discourage teen pregnancy, sexually transmitted disease, and abortion. The Clinton administration recently sought to eliminate all federal funding of abstinence-based curricula in the public schools, despite the fact that these courses have been demonstrated to reduce teen pregnancy. Since 1960 the federal government has spent over three billion dollars on "safe sex" programs that have utterly failed to measurably reduce skyrocketing teen pregnancy. Teenage girls bring 500,000 babies into the world each year, and those children are four times as likely to live in poverty as children in other families. To stem this tide, religious conservatives would transfer much of the funds we currently spend on "safe sex" programs to abstinence-based education that works.

Chastity movements are filling the void where government fails, sweeping the nation like wildfire as teenagers resist the sexually explicit refrain of rap music, television, and movies. The decision by these young people to delay sexual activity until marriage is sometimes based on religious faith, and often based on concerns about contracting AIDS or other sexually transmitted diseases. California's $5 million abstinence program, now in its second year, is exposing young people to a simple message: "Don't be fooled—the only safe sex is abstinence before marriage and fidelity in marriage." Virgin clubs are popping up on high school campuses across the nation. Some students in Washington, D.C., come to school sporting T-shirts that read, "I'm a virgin and I'm proud." Over 2,500 teenagers recently packed into a high school auditorium in Tampa, Florida, for a "True Love Waits" rally to celebrate abstinence. Many signed pledge cards promising to remain chaste until their wedding night. A local beauty queen was on hand to tell the cheering audience: "Gentleman, carry this card in your wallet instead of the condom they pass out at school." Like the grassroots campaign to "just say no" to drugs in the 1980s, these efforts can make a real contribution to protecting young people from the trauma of unwanted pregnancies as well as the emotional pain of broken relationships.[5]

Successful Schools

Children would go to school without worrying about encountering other students who brandish guns or knives in the halls. Delinquent and violent youth would be expelled from school or taught in a separate learning environment. The vision that religious conservatives have for primary and secondary schools is roughly equivalent to our current system of higher education: a free market of private and public schools all offering competing opportunities to young people. America's system of higher education is the magnet and envy of the world, due in no small measure to the freedom to choose the best college for one's child. Pell grants and the G.I. bill benefits are not denied to students who attend Notre Dame, Brigham Young, Southern Methodist University, or Yeshiva University. We need a similar system of scholarships, especially in the inner city, to allow elementary and secondary students to escape the ghetto and receive a quality education.

"The nation that desires a citizenry that is both ignorant and free, desires what never has been and never will be," said Thomas Jefferson. So committed was Jefferson to education that he founded the University of Virginia and forwarded one of the first proposals for common schools in our nation's history, a radical proposal in his day. Religious conservatives share Jefferson's zeal for quality public education. Even with school choice, the vast majority of students (70–80 percent) would continue to attend public schools. People of faith support educational alternatives such as home schooling, but they believe that public schools are too important to be abandoned.

Our agenda for public education is three-fold. First, create a safe, drug-free learning environment free from crime, guns, and violence. Second, institute a back-to-basics approach to curriculum that emphasizes basic skills in math, science, history, geography, and reading. Third, provide greater parental input into school board decisions on matters affecting their children, including curriculum. Although schools perform an important function, children ultimately belong to their parents, not the government.

I recently spoke to a group of college students at Furman University in South Carolina and discussed what ails American education. One of them related the story of his mother, who was quitting her job as a public school teacher after twenty years. The woman had a student in her second grade class who came from a dysfunctional home in which both parents were alcoholics and took little interest in their children. This seven-year-old boy woke up every morning, dressed himself and his younger sister, prepared their breakfast, dropped her off at a day care center, and then caught the bus to school. In the afternoons, he picked up his sister and took her home, where they often went to bed hungry and neglected. Here was a seven-year-old boy literally raising himself and his sister—and performing poorly at school. This lad is waging a valiant struggle against enormous odds, and he may succeed. But the sad fact is that for him and millions more like him, the school cannot take the place of loving parents and a stable home.

This is why advocates of public education should welcome religious conservatives to the arena rather than falsely label them "religious zealots" and "stealth candidates." In most cases, these activists are parents with children in public schools who simply want the basic values instilled at home reinforced, rather than undermined, at school. No one has a greater appreciation of the importance of strong families to quality education. We need more citizens working to improve our schools, not less. Christians and their allies are encouraging parents and taxpayers to get involved and make a difference in giving our children the education they need and richly deserve.

A Smaller Government

In a world in which religious conservatives participated proportionate to their numbers, the government would be forced to balance its checkbook in the same way that hard-working families do. Far less of the wages of hard-working mothers and fathers would be gobbled up by the confiscatory taxes that currently consume so much of the family budget. A balanced budget amendment to the Constitution would require fiscal responsibility by elected officials, and a line-item veto would give the President the same ability to delete wasteful, pork-barrel spending currently wielded by forty-three governors.

This goal may be within our grasp. In March 1994 the Balanced Budget Amendment failed by only a handful of votes in the U.S. Senate. If the 1994 elections yield even modest gains for the Republicans, it is entirely conceivable that a constitutional amendment could be passed and referred to the state legislatures as early as 1995. A tax credit for children is also gaining momentum on both sides of the aisle. The Republicans touted a $500 tax cut per child in their 1994 budget alternative—and President Clinton is expected to unveil a similar proposal prior to the 1996 election. This is one more example of an idea first advocated by religious conservatives that is now in the mainstream and supported by many Democrats as well as Republicans.

Hard work, diligence, and frugality would be generally acknowledged as virtues that should be reinforced by government policy. Public dependency would be greatly reduced as faith communities restored respect for honest labor and support for the poor shifted from the government to private and faith-based charities. Ben Franklin once remarked, "I am for doing good to the poor, but I differ in opinion of the means. I think the best way of doing good to the poor, is not making them easy *in* poverty, but leading or driving them *out* of it."[6] Public assistance would be limited, conditional, and would address "behavioral poverty," the reality that providing subsidies without changing behavior hurts the needy more than it helps them. Welfare caseloads would shrink as fewer fathers abandoned their wives and children—and as society stigmatized the irresponsible behavior of deadbeat dads.

Lower taxes would unleash the charitable capacity of the American people. Contributions to private organizations and ministries would rise as Americans, animated by faith, took it upon themselves to feed the hungry, clothe the naked, and build housing for the homeless. Congregate care centers would reach out to abandoned children and give them love and self-esteem, freeing them from the current nightmare of the bureaucratic foster care system. Homes for unwed mothers would offer a compassionate environment for abused, frightened women who desire to give their children a fighting chance in life.

Tolerance for different faiths and ethnic backgrounds would prevail. Civil rights laws would be strictly enforced and violators zealously prosecuted. Intolerance based on race, gender, or religion would be discouraged as a matter of both public policy and civic discourse. People motivated by their faith who sought to serve in government would no longer be caricatured and ridiculed by religious bigotry. Young people who organized a Bible club at their local high school would not be hauled into the principal's office. Voluntary, student-initiated prayer in public schools would be treated as protected speech under the First Amendment. Menorahs and nativity scenes on courthouse lawns would not be ripped up by court order. The public square would be clothed with faith, and expressions of religious belief would not be expunged from public life.

Government would no longer engage in what columnist George Will has called "the bullying of religion." One recent example took place in Massachusetts, where two Roman Catholic brothers declined to rent an apartment to a woman who expressed her intent to share it with her live-in boyfriend. The renters subscribed to the teaching of their church that sex prior to marriage is wrong, and they consequently objected to being a party to the cohabiting couple's behavior. Their faith, however, ran into a brick wall in the form of a state law forbidding discrimination based on, among other things, "marital status." This happened despite the fact that fornication is still against the law in Massachusetts, punishable by a fine and three months in prison — though obviously the law goes unenforced.[7]

The state of Massachusetts seems to be saying that any kind of sex can be practiced anywhere, but religion must be kept in the closet. What these two Catholic citizens sought was not to enter the bedroom of the unmarried couple, but to prevent them from bringing their behavior into their apartment building. Their posture was defensive, not offensive; their instinct was to protect their own faith, not to express hostility to others who followed a particular practice in the privacy of their own bedroom.

There would be fewer lawsuits and less litigation as Americans solved more disputes through private arbitration or faith-based reconciliation. Those who clogged the courts with frivolous lawsuits against innocent people would be forced to pay the defendant's legal fees and all court costs. Judges would interpret the law rather than legislate from the bench. The marriage covenant would no longer be the most unstable form of contract in society.

America would look much as it did for most of the first two centuries of its existence, before the social dislocation caused by Vietnam, the sexual revolution, Watergate, and the explosion of the welfare state. Our nation would once again be ascendent, self-confident, proud, and morally strong. Government would be small, the citizenry virtuous, and mediating institutions such as churches and volunteer organizations would carry out many of the functions currently relegated to the bureaucracy. Instead of turning to Washington to solve problems, Americans would turn to each other.

Democracy in America

"Democracy is the worst form of government in the world—except for all the rest," remarked Winston Churchill. There are problems with our democratic system of government—voter apathy, corruption, influence-peddling, the prevalence of special interests. But the answer to democracy's ills is more democracy, not less. Religious conservatives have launched massive voter registration drives across the nation similar to those undertaken by the civil rights movement in the South in the 1960s. The purpose of these voter education efforts is to empower a constituency that has been disenfranchised not by literacy tests or poll taxes, but by their own failure to participate in a level commensurate with their numbers in the electorate.

We do not advocate electing officials by depressing voter turnout or taking advantage of historically low citizen participation. Some have inaccurately charged that religious conservatives hide their religious affiliation, conducting "stealth" campaigns in which they eschew public forums and campaign exclusively in churches. The *opposite* is true. The Christian Coalition, for example, distributes millions of nonpartisan voter guides every year that inform voters on where all the candidates stand. This voter educational information is distributed in shopping malls, churches, union halls, and polling locations—wherever voters gather in the days before the election. We want a more open airing of who the candidates are and what they believe.

Pro-family candidates win at the ballot box because of their views, not in spite of them. They are elected precisely because of who they are and what they stand for. Despite the efforts of some to marginalize religion in the public square, faith is still an asset to most candidates and is considered an admirable character trait to the average voter.

The religious conservative movement begins with the proposition that the government that governs best governs with the consent of the greatest number of citizens. Since 1960 the number of Americans going to the polls and participating in the political system has gradually declined until barely half vote in presidential elections and little more than a third go to the polls in congressional elections. We want to raise the number of people voting to around 70 to 80 percent, a figure roughly equal to that prevailing in other Western democracies. Initiatives and referenda will give voters a larger voice in government, term limits will restore the ethic of a citizen legislature, and the distribution of millions of legislative scorecards will inform people how elected officials are really voting. Society will be more open and participatory.

A Mainstream Proposal

The conventional wisdom that religious conservatives seek to legislate a radical agenda is not borne out by the facts. In fact, the agenda of religious conservatives seems quite minimalist and mainstream, particularly when compared with the radical ambitions of other great social movements in history. As Eric Foner has observed, the antislavery movement sought to usher in industrial capitalism and destroy the feudal economic system of the South by abolishing the enslaved labor system that was its linchpin.[8] The Populists of the 1890s forwarded a radical agenda of economic and social change, often expressed in darkly apocalyptic and paranoid rhetorical terms, that included vicious attacks on Jewish bankers and Northern industrialists. The Progressives pursued an equally far-reaching agenda that included the progressive income tax, direct election of the U.S. Senate, government control of the monetary system, child labor laws, and an internationalist foreign policy.

Against this historical background, the agenda of religious conservatives seems quite unremarkable. In terms of economic policy, the most expansive reforms advocated by people of faith involve tax relief for families and requiring a balanced federal budget—hardly frightening prospects. School choice is an idea that many liberal Democrats such as Wisconsin state representative Polly Williams advocate. One need not hold to a theologically conservative religion to believe that parents, not bureaucrats, should choose where their children attend school. Even the constitutional amendments advocated in recent years by religious conservatives are measures of last resort, defensively pursued in reaction to sweeping and liberal judicial decisions, such as *Roe* v. *Wade*.

This is not to suggest that the agenda of religious conservatives is unambitious. People of faith frankly and forthrightly seek to restore the centrality of the two-parent, intact family as the foundation of our democratic society. This alone is a remarkable undertaking given the trauma suffered by the institution of the family in recent decades. They seek to replace the bureaucratic welfare state with a culture of caring characterized by acts of private compassion and faith-based charity. They wish, in short, to repair the damage and bridge the breach in our social fabric that has been caused by the breakdown of the family and a decline in civility.

Religious conservatives want to move forward, not backward. They do not want to turn the clock back. They believe that many of the social advances of the past thirty years can and must be acknowledged and preserved. For example, the movement of women to a position of equality in the workplace where they can advance as far as their talents can carry them is clearly progress. The civil rights movement has brought minorities closer to full equality than at any time since the Civil War. Those who suggest that people of faith look nostalgically back to the 1950s and Ozzie and Harriet are mistaken.

Yet there is much work to be done. The civil rights movement secured the right to vote for minorities, but has not solved the problems of intergenerational poverty or black-on-black violence. The women's movement won the right to pursue careers for those women who wanted them—but it has not adequately addressed the victimization of women through divorce and pornography. Policy failures and cultural excesses since the 1960s must be redressed if we are to move forward. The seeds of cultural and moral decay have now flowered to full bloom, with social consequences that can no longer be ignored: illegitimacy, divorce, drug use, abortion, violent crime, pornography, and illiteracy.

People of faith hold many of the answers to these problems. For that reason alone, they must not be treated as second-class citizens whose faith may be practiced on Sunday but never in the public square. The religious conservative movement must provide a voice for that marginalized constituency, the only group in America whose role in government is almost inversely proportional to their numbers. Even those who disagree with their politics should wish them well, for if faith wins its place at the table, we will all be richer for its contribution. Society is the loser when their unique contribution to building a better America is lost. Before their voice can be heard, we must make attacks on religion as unacceptable as slurs against race or gender. None of the preceding vision can become a reality as long as the law, politics, and the culture treat faith like a toxic substance instead of the healing force that it is.

CHAPTER THREE

To the Back of the Bus:
The Marginalization of Religion

W E LIVE in peculiar times, to say the least. In a country founded on the principle of basic freedoms guaranteed to all its citizens, people of faith find themselves marginalized and ridiculed. In a nation where our coins carry the motto, "In God we trust," children are denied the right to pray in public schools. In a society hungering for character and moral fiber in its elected officials, religious people who seek public office are maligned because of their faith.

It is not so much that their views are antithetical to the values of most of the American people. Indeed, surveys show that they are almost identical. Presumably all of us want the freedom to practice our religion, to enjoy the rights to free speech guaranteed by the First Amendment, and to fully participate in our duties of citizenship. Yet intolerance towards religion has reached disturbing levels, threatening civility and undermining a basic sense of fairness.

The term "back of the bus" has come into wide use in our language. It refers not only to the system of segregation in the South that attempted to relegate African-Americans to second-class citizenship, but to all efforts to deny citizens basic rights guaranteed under the U.S. Constitution. It means denying people the right to speak, to worship, to vote, to seek public office, to live where they choose, or to influence public policy in a manner consistent with the law. Sometimes this denial of rights is accomplished through the edict of a judge, other times by legislation, still others by social stigma. No one is denying people of faith the right to vote or to live where they choose. But their rights to freedom of speech and religion are under constant attack whenever they enter the public arena. Like the "separate sphere" once assigned to women, religious people are now relegated to their churches and homes, where their faith poses no threat to the social order.

When an elementary school teacher in Colorado displayed a Bible on the desk of his classroom, school officials ordered it removed. This despite the fact that he read from it silently, that the book was part of his personal library, and that other books on display included those relating to Greek mythology and Indian cosmology. The principal of the school, apparently attempting to protect students from any book about Judaism or Christianity, also removed the Bible from the school library. The teacher—though forbidden to read the Bible—was permitted to teach students about Navajo Indian religion and read from a book about Buddha. The point is not that Eastern or Native American religion should not be discussed, but that Judeo-Christian tradition should not be excluded either.[1]

A staff psychiatrist in Kentucky had his hospital privileges revoked because of "inappropriate behavior." His error? Praying with his patients. The board that suspended him ruled that his religious beliefs were "detrimental to patient safety and hospital operations" despite the fact that several patients testified that his spiritual counseling had helped them enormously.[2]

The city of Hillsboro, Illinois, has displayed a sign on its courthouse for over 50 years that reads, "The World Needs God." The sign has enormous historical significance to the community, erected at a time when bootleggers, gambling-houses, and tippling joints dotted the county. But the ACLU has filed suit to have the sign torn down. (At this writing the suit is unresolved).[3]

Government officials tilt the playing field away from public expressions of religious faith. Sharing one's faith on the job have led to a federal lawsuit, thanks to regulations drafted in 1993 by the Equal Employment Opportunity Commission. The rules barred any discussion of one's faith that might be deemed harassment. One major airline, reacting to the guidelines, instructed employees not to "possess or display, in any manner . . . material which may be construed by anyone to have racial, religious, or sexual overtones, whether positive or negative." The regulations were overturned by Congress after pro-family groups lobbied against them. Some legal experts predicted that the rules might have prohibited the sharing of gospel literature, the reading of the Bible, or the display of a menorah on an employee's desk. In a related incident, the Department of Housing and Urban Development issued regulations against religious discrimination so strict that some nursing homes removed Christian symbols from yellow page advertisements. The symbols were reinstated after an uproar of protest forced the department to guarantee the nursing homes protection from prosecution under fair housing laws.[4]

"While government protects all in their religious rights, true religion affords to government its surest support," wrote George Washington in 1789. This conviction of our founders is reflected in the wording of the Constitution. The First Amendment protects the free exercise of religion even before it mentions the rights of speech and the press. This order was no coincidence. It codified the beliefs of the founders that religion was to liberty what gasoline is to fire, a spark that ignited a love for freedom and respect for others. They also viewed the liberty to worship as essential to good government. Yet today the First Amendment has been twisted into a weapon that billy-clubs people of faith into submission and silence. The Bible, once acknowledged as the repository of the greatest intellectual and moral traditions of Western civilization, is now treated as contraband. Our legal and political culture has created a bias in the law that borders on censorship against reading, displaying, or quoting the Bible.[5]

For example, when a group of students in Mobile, Alabama, decided in 1993 to include verses from the book of Ephesians in daily inspirational messages over the school intercom, attorneys for the school board muzzled them. The students explained that the Bible verses were no different than other readings they had included from Voltaire, Plato, and Thoreau—a source of inspiration and introspection. School board attorneys were not persuaded. "I think it would be interpreted as prayer," complained an attorney for Alabama's largest school system. The rights of the students to freedom of expression to read any passage went unquestioned until they included the Bible. At a time when the Department of Justice reports that 100,000 young people bring guns to school every day, and 160,000 students stay home every day for fear of being shot or knifed to death, one would think that school officials would want more Bible reading, not less.[6]

Public schools in the United States are now safer from religion than illegal drugs. A combination of liberal advocacy attorneys and frightened school officials seems intent on turning public schools into "religion free zones." The Philadelphia school system recently forbade teachers from wearing cross pendants because it might be considered "religious garb."[7]

In 1991 a Jewish rabbi delivered a nonsectarian prayer as part of a graduation ceremony at a Rhode Island junior high school. The text of the rabbi's prayer read in part:

> God of the Free, Hope of the Brave. For the legacy of America where diversity is celebrated and the rights of minorities are protected, we thank You. May these young men and women grow up to enrich it. For the liberty of America, we thank you. May these new graduates grow up to guard it. . . . May our aspirations for our country and for these young people, who are our hope for the future, be richly fulfilled. Amen.[8]

The Supreme Court found this innocuous prayer, which was not composed or read by school officials, unconstitutional. In so doing, it rejected America's centuries-old tradition of civil religion, expressed in respectfully nonsectarian language at a voluntary public ceremony. As Justice Antonin Scalia noted in a stinging dissent, the Court's ruling so ludicrously limits public affirmations of faith that it appears (if followed to its logical end) to prohibit the reading of the Pledge of Allegiance because of the words, "one nation under God."[9]

In 1990 two high school students in Atlanta, Georgia, who attempted to distribute flyers advertising a meeting of the Fellowship of Christian Athletes were hustled to the principal's office. One student was suspended, the other expelled. Their crime? According to the student disciplinary report, they were guilty of "possession of Christian literature." In the fall of 1991 a voluntary, student-led prayer held before classes at a high school in Illinois was declared an "unlawful assembly" and broken up by police. Two 15-year old girls were manhandled by police, forced into the back of a patrol car, and threatened with mace. Police released them only after they promised "never to do anything like this again."[10]

In late 1993 a seven-year-old girl in Buffalo, New York, was filled with joy when her teacher told her she could bring her favorite book and read it to her class. The next day, when she brought her book to school, the teacher informed her that there was a problem. The book mentioned the word "God" four times. The teacher forbade the girl to read from the offending book. After her father contacted the school board, the book was reinstated, but the girl was humiliated in front of an entire class. That a little girl's story that mentioned God would be banned—even temporarily—from a public school reveals how serious our phobia of religion has become.

Sometimes the culture's phobia of religion borders on the absurd. A recent memorandum from a public school official to teachers in New Jersey recommended that spring parties steer clear of any reference to Easter. Religious holidays, the official warned, raised the ugly specter of lawsuits, recrimination, and controversy. Just to be safe, he suggested that teachers avoid using jelly beans, wicker baskets, and the colors purple and yellow.[11]

Some of these incidents take place in the buckle of the Bible belt. In November 1993 Mr. Bishop Knox, the principal of Wingfield High School in Jackson, Mississippi, allowed students to vote on whether to permit student-led prayer to be broadcast over the intercom. The young people voted 490–96 to have the fifteen-word nonsectarian prayer included with the morning announcements. The prayer was modeled after one used to open sessions of Congress. The students found it in a government textbook. It read simply, "Almighty God, we ask that you bless our parents, teachers, and country throughout the day."

Mr. Knox allowed the prayer, basing his decision on a 1992 ruling by a federal appeals court that prayer that is student-initiated, nonproselytizing and nonsectarian is constitutional. But the Jackson school superintendent promptly fired him for permitting prayer. He was later reinstated after pro-family legal organizations threatened to sue. A protest rally at the Mississippi state capitol held four days after his dismissal attracted a throng of 4,000 people, and 280 students staged a walk out in protest over the firing. The ACLU argued that the utterance of a simple prayer over a public address system "involves the state in sponsoring religion." Warned Lynn Buzzard, the Mississippi ACLU director: "That may seem petty but the consequences of this type of action are very dangerous." What "dangerous consequences" might flow from voluntary prayer? Buzzard was not specific.[12]

"Religion is the basis of civil society, and the source of all good and of all comfort," said Edmund Burke. One would hardly recognize this sublime view of faith in federal court opinions since World War II. Rather than viewing religion as the response of the individual to the dictates of conscience, our legal culture treats religious obligations as just another lifestyle choice. The Supreme Court ruled in 1986 that the armed forces may prohibit Jewish soldiers from wearing yarmulkes while on duty. In *Lee* v. *Weisman*, the Court suggested that voluntary prayer at high school graduations could lead to psychological harm for young people who felt pressured to participate. The bias of American jurisprudence now lies firmly against expressions of faith. In this formulation, prayer is psychologically harmful, religious worship offensive, and quoting the Bible may violate another's rights.[13]

In November 1991 the Pennsylvania Supreme Court reversed the sentence of a convicted murderer named Karl Chambers. The voiding of his sentence turned on a technicality: the prosecutor had tainted the sentencing hearing, not by tampering with the jury or destroying evidence, but by excessive oratorical flair. His error? He quoted from the Bible. A close review of the court transcript revealed that the district attorney, in final arguments, said to the jury, "Karl Chambers has taken a life. As the Bible says, 'the murderer shall be put to death.'" This quotation of Scripture—which the Court called "a dangerous practice which we strongly discourage"—might have prejudiced the jury, and the Court reversed Karl Chambers's death sentence. Then the Court went a step further, threatening future district attorneys who quoted the Bible with punishment, and warning that "reliance in any manner upon the Bible or any other religious writing . . . is [a] reversible error per se and may subject violators to disciplinary action." It admonished that citing Scripture would be viewed as "a deliberate attempt to destroy the objectivy and impartiality of the jury which cannot be cured and which we will not countenance."[14]

Karl Chambers was a drifter who spent a good deal of his time drinking, smoking marijuana, and loitering outside bars. On February 1, 1986, Chambers was short of cash when seventy-year-old Anna May Morris walked into a convenience store to purchase groceries with the proceeds from her Social Security check. He followed her out of the store, robbed her, and beat her to death with an ax handle, leaving her nude body abandoned under a railroad bridge. Chambers was arrested and charged with murder in the kind of open-and-shut case that prosecutors dream about. Based on the testimony of witnesses, a jury convicted him of first-degree murder and sentenced him to die. But the sentence was voided because the prosecutor quoted from the Ten Commandments. (The murder conviction stood; the sentence was later upheld by another judge.)[15]

This bizarre decision issued forth from the highest court in a commonwealth whose legal system dates back to William Penn, who in 1682 drafted the "Frame of Government for Pennsylvania." In that charter, Penn asserted that government was "a part of religion itself, a thing sacred in its institution and end." Despite Quakerism's tradition of pacifism, it also provided for the death penalty. The government of colonial Pennsylvania rested on laws that reflected the Quaker reading of the Bible. "Let men be good, and the government cannot be bad; if it be ill, they will cure it," asserted Penn. "But, if men be bad, let the government be never so good, they will endeavor to warp and spoil it to their turn." Today quoting the Bible is prohibited under some circumstances in Pennsylvania's courtrooms.[16]

Other courts have issued similar rulings banning expressions of religious faith. California courts have ruled against prosecutors quoting Scripture no less than three times. In Nassau County, New York, in early 1993 a judge ordered a Roman Catholic prosecutor to remove the ashes from his forehead while arguing a case on Ash Wednesday. The judge feared the attorney's faith might adversely influence the jurors.[17]

William Constangy, a state court judge in Charlotte, North Carolina, once began each session with a brief prayer that asked for divine assistance to "protect the innocent, give justice to those who have been harmed, and give mercy to us all." The ACLU sued Contangy, whose prayer was later thrown out by a federal appeals court. Yet state court judges in North Carolina are required to swear witnesses in with an oath that ends, "so help me God," and deliver death sentences with the words, "may God have mercy on your soul." The U.S. House and Senate begin each day with prayer (led by government-sanctioned chaplains) and the Supreme Court opens each session by invoking God's name. What was the difference? The court's feeble reply: Constangy's prayer did not constitute a "long-standing tradition."[18]

Courts of law are not alone in their fear of faith. In 1993 a Minnesota man sued a local school board to force the removal of the Bible from the school library. This individual, who did not even have a child enrolled in school, alleged that the Bible was "obscene" and "offensive" because it contained descriptions of violence, incest, rape, murder, and child abuse.[19]

Several years earlier, the state of Indiana temporarily removed Bibles (placed there by the Gideons at no cost to taxpayers) from inns at state parks. The Indiana Civil Liberties Union and gay organizations later requested that the parks department place a pamphlet provocatively titled *Let's Have Sex* beside the Bibles in guest rooms. Another organization received permission (later withdrawn) to place a brochure next to the Bibles that admonished: "Warning! Literal belief in this book may endanger your health and life." A similar episode of Bible-banning unfolded in Florida. Officials at the University of Florida pulled Bibles from guest rooms at the campus conference center, placing them behind the front desk where they were available only upon request—not unlike pornographic magazines behind the counter of a convenience store.[20]

Whether religious people are wounded by such barbs is not the vital question; their faith is more powerful and transcendent than public persecution. Indeed, faith often thrives in the heat of opposition. Certainly those who enter the public square must be willing to take the heat or, in Harry Truman's words, "get out of the kitchen." People of faith must not adopt the status of "victims" who seek special protection from the rough-and-tumble of civic life. Christians who step into the ring can expect to get punched. But some blows are cheap shots, and attacks on religion are the rhetorical equivalent of kidney punches that should be against the rules. Our ability to listen to all sides in our spirited civic debate—including the religious view—is irreparably undermined by ongoing assaults on public expressions of faith.

It is unconstitutional today to post the Ten Commandments in a public school. In 1980 the Supreme Court struck down a Kentucky law providing for the posting of the commandments on the dubious grounds that it might "induce the schoolchildren to read, meditate upon, perhaps to venerate or obey, the Commandments." The Court cavalierly dismissed the fact that the Kentucky legislature, in drafting the law, had cited not the religious meaning of the Ten Commandments, but its "secular application" as "the fundamental legal code of Western Civilization and the Common Law of the United States."[21]

In June of 1994 the Supreme Court ruled that a courthouse in Cobb county, Georgia, must tear down a plaque from its walls bearing the Ten Commandments. The Court failed to see the irony of this decision coming from its building, which has the Ten Commandments chiseled in granite on its walls.

It is unconstitutional to erect a nativity scene on a courthouse lawn at Christmas unless one displays Frosty the Snowman or Santa Claus next to it to prevent a religious message from being conveyed.[22]

An appeals court in Colorado has recently ruled that a stone monument located on state property depicting the Ten Commandments and the Star of David violated the separation of church and state, even though the monument was erected with private funds. Similarly, a federal judge ruled in 1991 that a war memorial shaped as a cross in San Diego, California, must be torn down because it violates the Constitution.[23]

It is also unconstitutional for a school board to use the word "God" in an official document. It is a violation of the Constitution for kindergartners to recite, "We thank you for the flowers so sweet, we thank you for the good food we eat, we thank you for the birds that sing, we thank you for everything." The Supreme Court ruled in *DeSpain* v. *DeKalb County* that a child reciting this rhyme might meditate upon God, even though a deity is never mentioned.[24]

All this is part of a culture that treats faith as a form of pathology. The zealous disdain for religion in American jurisprudence amounts to intolerance. The full weight of American culture, law, and politics leans heavily against those who seek to bring their faith to bear in the larger society. Keith Fournier of the American Center for Law and Justice concludes that "the ones not being tolerated are religious people who dare make any kind of religious reference or take any kind of religious posture outside the private arena."[25]

Even the freedom of the press is jeopardized when religion raises its ugly head. In December 1993 the principal of a high school in northern Virginia ordered the student newspaper to keep its coverage of the holiday season "as secular as possible." The principal ordered the young journalists to avoid religious terms such as "Christmas." He warned that one "needs to be careful that they don't associate the upcoming holiday with any particular religion."[26]

Schools are laboratories of democracy, where students learn not only how to read and write, but how to be responsible citizens as they prepare for adulthood. When students are arrested or suspended for speech with a religious content, when Bibles are banned, when student newspapers and intercom announcements are censored, what are we teaching the next generation of citizens? They are being trained in the art of censorship and intolerance.

Students are not to read the Bible, jurors are not to hear it, prosecutors cannot quote from it, and teachers are not to display it. "If I were a dictator, the first thing I'd burn would be the Bible," said journalist Quentin Reynolds. "I'd burn it because I'd realize the whole concept of democracy came first from the Bible." Today we ban the Bible in the name of preserving democracy—a sad irony given the heavy reliance of our founders on its precepts in building the American republic. "A Bible and a newspaper in every house," said Benjamin Franklin, "a good school in every district—all studied and appreciated as they merit—are the principal support of virtue, morality, and civil liberty." Franklin was not talking about good literature or poetry only, but about the moral absolutes contained in the Bible that are the foundation of our social order. They are equally if not more relevant in an age of moral relativism.[27]

Contrast this view of faith with today's culture, which conveys the not-so-subtle suggestion that religion is at the least socially discomforting, and at worst, irrational and subversive. Freedom of religion has been replaced by freedom from religion. That which is objectionable to anyone is now inappropriate for everyone, namely the public expression of religious ideas in a political context. This creates a chilling effect for freedom of speech by people of faith that has vast consequences for us all including those with no faith. For if those with faith can be silenced today, anyone can be silenced tomorrow.

Our culture's tolerance wears thin when religion intrudes on the public discourse. When Cardinal John O'Connor criticized New York Governor Mario Cuomo's views on abortion, Arthur Schlesinger issued a stiff rebuke on the opinion page of the *New York Times*. O'Connor, warned Schlesinger, had confirmed "the fears long cherished by the No-Nothings [sic] in the 1850s, the Ku Klux Klan in the 1920s, and a succession of anti-Catholic demagogues that the Roman Catholic Church would try to overrule the American democratic process." Translation: keep quiet and stay in the back of the bus or someone might just hurt you. This is like blaming the social dissenter for the bigotry his protests elicit. Nor is Schlesinger alone. When a Catholic priest was named in 1989 to head the New York Public Library, Gay Talese and other authors questioned his ability to preside over an institution dedicated to freedom of inquiry.[28]

Our schools, courtrooms, and libraries set the tone for the entire society. The message they currently communicate is harsh and unambiguous: religion is offensive and should be kept out of public view. If government and the courts are so quick to marginalize faith, is it any wonder that American society has become what Stephen Carter has called a "culture of disbelief"? Despite the culture's ambivalence towards religion, the future does not belong to those who seek to exclude it from the public square. The energy, activism, and enthusiasm in America today lies with evangelicals, Roman Catholics, Jews, and others seeking to create a politics of virtue. They are tireless organizers, indefatigable workers, and are widely respected as more committed than their foes. Those who display intolerance towards their faith and vision of society may call them names. But their insults and abuse have not prevented those fired by faith and hungering for a good society from making remarkable progress in recent years. The final frontier for what *Newsweek* magazine calls the "Virtuecrats" to influence is the media, Hollywood, and popular culture. The next chapter examines how they have helped to create a stereotype of religious faith that provides the basis for the marginalization of their remarkably mainstream views.

CHAPTER FOUR

The New Amos and Andy:
How the Media Portrays People of Faith

How evangelical and fundamentalist Christians came to be viewed as less than full citizens is a complex story. But the central drama in their marginalization unfolded in Dayton, Tennessee during the Scopes Trial of 1925, in which a public school teacher was prosecuted for teaching evolution, with William Jennings Bryan and Clarence Darrow squaring off in the courtroom. H. L. Mencken, the acerbic critic and editor of the *American Mercury*, traveled to Tennessee not merely as an observer but as a participant in a media circus he dubbed "The Great Monkey Trial." Though he no doubt exaggerated his role in later recollections, Mencken claimed to have recruited and offered strategic advice to Darrow, who had reluctantly taken the case at the behest of a new and struggling legal organization called the American Civil Liberties Union. Mencken's dispatches from Dayton, syndicated in newspapers nationwide, made journalistic history and scrawled a caricature of people of faith that has been passed on to generations of journalists with only minor alterations to this very day.

Mencken denounced Christianity as a "childish theology founded upon hate" and railed against its followers, who he described as "morons," "yokels from the hills," and members of the "booboisie." He lampooned the Bible Belt as a region that resounded with "the clashing of theologians" but had nothing to drink save "a beaker of coca-cola" and nothing to read but "a pile of *Saturday Evening Posts* two feet high." Most of his reports carried little news from the trial. Instead, Mencken used the forum to undertake a vicious critique of fundamentalism, whose adherents he dismissed as "rustic ignoramuses" who knew "nothing that is not in Genesis."[1]

Mencken was a man of deep prejudice. He praised the Nazis when they came to power, heralded Hitler as a hero, and filled his correspondence with anti-Semitic jokes about "Jews in Hollywood" and "Judaized New York." This dark and bigoted side of his personality finds no audience today. But the cruel portrait Mencken painted of Christians remains.[2]

Mencken's iconoclastic bombast is still felt today, and many in the press view religion with suspicion as the refuge of losers and the domain of extremists. The *New York Times* published an editorial on its opinion page in 1993 that asserted that the religious conservative movement "confronts us with a far greater threat than the old threat of Communism." Earlier, the *Times* printed a column by Garry Wills that said of evangelicals in the Republican Party: "The crazies are in charge. The fringe has taken over." A syndicated columnist has suggested that "we tax the hell out of the churches if they open their holy yaps one more time about abortion, prayer in the schools or anything else." Some of this is mere hyperbole. It is hard to take seriously the notion that evangelicals in America are really as sinister a threat as Joseph Stalin. Still, the impression conveyed by these statements suggests that religion is irrational, intolerant, and possibly dangerous.[3]

An Associated Press report by Chicago-based reporter Sharon Cohen in May 1993 examined fundamentalists and concluded that they were prone to "riots, terrorism—and death." It compared evangelical leaders in the United States like Reverend Donald Wildmon of the American Family Association with the Ayatollah Khomeini and Sheik Omar Abdel-Rahman whose disciples allegedly planted the bomb that rocked the World Trade Center. (Wildmon is a United Methodist, not a fundamentalist. He has never been known to experiment in explosives. But no matter.) The story quoted the head of a five-year Fundamentalist Project, who predicted that persons holding to the fundamentals of their faith would wreak havoc in the years ahead. "They're going to keep ripping up governments," he shuddered. "There will be a lot of turmoil. There will be a lot of blood."[4]

Evidence of this imminent doom abounds. The *Atlanta Constitution* related a disturbing report in 1992 that drew a comparison between politically active evangelicals in the United States and rioting Hindus in India. A group of Hindus in New Delhi, the editorial intoned, had recently torn down a Muslim mosque, sparking riots in which two hundred people died. But this tragedy spoke as much to America as the near East, for ours is a "nation where a lot of highly politically active people would be quite content to have the Bible" forced upon society "as a civil law codebook." What lesson should one draw from all this? That social chaos and wholesale slaughter follow wherever "politics and religion had become dangerously commingled." These Amos-and-Andy-like caricatures of people of faith reinforce our culture's phobia of religion. This is a strange observation indeed coming from a city that was the birthplace of the civil rights movement, whose pastoral leaders transported supporters to protests in church buses.[5]

Every religion has fringe or criminal elements who commit horrible acts in the mistaken name of their God. But these persons—the rioting Hindu in India or the violent Jew on the West Bank—are aberrations rather than exemplars of their religion. The media's portrayal of religion fails to account for this ambiguity. All too often it seizes on outbreaks of violence as confirmations of the "dark" side of faith.

Part of the explanation for this bias is a cultural divide that separates journalists from middle America in matters of religion. A study by sociologists Stanley Rothman and Robert Lichter in 1981 found that 86 percent of journalists and editors attend church either infrequently or not at all. Half listed no religious affiliation whatsoever. On social issues, they are decidedly left-of-center: supporting abortion on demand (90 percent), homosexual rights (75 percent), and holding that adultery is not wrong (53 percent).[6]

However, some in the press are disturbed by the cultural chasm that separates them from churchgoing citizens. Larry Barrett of *Time* magazine recently urged that he and his colleagues "get ourselves to church, if only as observers." He points to a "profound disconnect" between the press and religious folk that has led to deepening alienation from the major media by those of devout faith.[7]

Recent surveys confirm this sense of alienation. In 1989 the Religious News Service surveyed religious reporting by daily newspapers and found that readers, representing a wide array of denominations, wanted their newspapers to give higher priority to religion than sports, entertainment, the arts, or personal advice. More than local church coverage, readers hungered for analysis of how religious values impact the great moral and ethical issues of the day.[8]

A study of how the national television networks covered religion in 1993 by the Media Research Center dramatically illustrates this problem. The study found that the networks generally provide statistically insignificant coverage of religion. Only one of the four networks (ABC) employs a religion reporter. Of 18,000 stories aired on the network evening news in 1993, only 212 dealt with religion. Islam received only five stories, while there were only three on the Jewish faith. Incredibly, there was only one story during all of 1993 by the four networks on the Southern Baptists, the largest Protestant denomination in the world.[9]

Many stories treated religion in the context of pathology and violence: sexual abuse by Catholic priests, acts of vandalism committed against abortion clinics, the bombing of the World Trade Center by Islamic terrorists, and the shooting of abortionists. One of the most tragic results of this bias is when the reputations of the innocent are harmed. After a confused and troubled young man suffering from AIDS leveled false charges of sexual abuse against Joseph Cardinal Bernardin of Chicago in November 1993, the media piled on with a vengeance. Networks led their evening news broadcasts with the sensational accusations, newspapers plastered front pages with banner headlines, and the talking heads on weekend gabfests pointed to the scandal as a further sign of the declining influence of the Roman Catholic Church. While the story may have merited a mention, murky and uncorroborated recollections eighteen years after the alleged incident by an emotionally distraught accuser should have weighed less in the balance than the denial of a respected church leader with a reputation for integrity, honor, and rectitude.

It is difficult to avoid the conclusion that what drove the Bernardin story was not mere titillation but its propensity to reinforce a stereotype of religious leaders as hypocrites. The four networks broadcast twenty-five stories on the Bernardin story, including a prime-time special on CNN. When the troubled young man who initiated the charges dropped them months later, his recanting merited only a brief mention by the same media outlets. Cardinal Bernardin had been innocent all along. But where could he go to get back his reputation?[10]

Mencken-like murmurings by editorial writers and professional provocateurs do not by themselves constitute a pattern of bigotry. But their consistently harsh view of religion chips away at our ability to respect one another and listen to each other's views without prejudice. Our culture frowns upon similar stereotypes of women, African-Americans, and those of various ethnic backgrounds, as it well should. When Bill Clinton was captured on tape in 1992 repeating rumors about the alleged mob ties of New York Governor Mario Cuomo, he swiftly apologized, not only for political reasons but because his remarks perpetrated one of the oldest stereotypes about Italian-Americans. When was the last time a political candidate or major media outlet apologized for saying something insensitive about Roman Catholics or evangelicals?

Fundamentalists are the easiest target. Cartoonist Pat Oliphant recently portrayed them as filthy rats emerging from a gutter, dragging a bloated elephant (symbolizing the Republican party) into a ghetto church with a sign emblazoned with the motto, "Fundamentalist Christian Mission House: Jesus Saves." Columnist Molly Ivins has labeled politically active evangelicals "Shiite Baptists," a bizarre formulation that suggests a correlation between evangelical Protestantism and terrorism, managing with the stroke of a pen to denigrate both Baptists and Muslims.

Roman Catholics suffer equally harsh treatment. George Weigel of the Washington-based Ethics and Public Policy Center has catalogued some examples of the rhetorical bigotry directed at Roman Catholics in recent years:

- A catalogue for an exhibit in Manhattan sponsored by the National Endowment for the Arts in 1989 called John Cardinal O'Connor "a fat cannibal" and St. Patrick's Cathedral "the house of walking swastikas on Fifth Avenue."

- In 1992 the president of a local teacher's union told a school board in Pennsylvania, "The enemy of public education . . . is the Catholic Church. If the Catholic Church were to cease to exist and disappear today, it would be better for all of us."[11]

People of faith cannot ask that they never be lampooned or ridiculed. Sadly, we have brought some of the scorn upon ourselves. The scandals that rocked religious broadcasting in the 1980s and acts of child molestation committed by a small number of Catholic priests have exposed hypocrisy and tarnished the reputation of organized religion. But we do not stigmatize all parents because a few abuse or neglect their children. Nor do we trash an entire honorable profession (in this case, the clergy) because of the crimes of a few. The personality flaws of a small number of religious leaders do not justify character assassination directed against an entire faith community.

Abraham Lincoln once said he opposed slavery as a moral evil not only because of what it did to the black person, but because of what it did to the white person. The same is true of caricatures of people of faith. It cheapens our public discourse, makes it more difficult for us to arrive at consensus, and renders us all less capable of good citizenship because we tolerate attacks on those unlike ourselves. As Catholic lay theologian Michael Novak has argued, "There is a bigotry rampant in America, against evangelicals. It is the last respectable bigotry."[12]

The cumulative effect of this prejudice has been devastating. A 1989 Gallup survey found that 30 percent of Americans would not want to have a fundamentalist live next door to them. Only 3 percent said they would mind having a Catholic neighbor, while 5 percent minded having a Jew live near them. As religion has receded from public display, those who buck the trend and speak openly about their faith find themselves subjected to disapproval and censure. Stephen Bates, a scholar who has studied religious conservatives, concludes that in our culture's zeal to enforce an ethic of tolerance we have maligned the religious views of millions of Americans.[13]

What explains the unbridled hostility directed at people of faith? The answer is complex. As Stephen Carter has observed, the abortion issue has played a major role in the marginalization of faith. Because of the evangelical idiom employed by many opponents of abortion, the politics of abortion and church-state issues have become inextricably intertwined. As the heat of the abortion issue has reached a boiling point, religion has been trapped in the crossfire. Advocates of abortion oppose pro-life Jews and Christians as a matter of politics, not of religion. They reject Catholic teaching more for its ideological content than its theological beliefs. This is ironic given the Left's reliance on religious leaders and language in the past.

Prior to the *Roe* v. *Wade* decision, most religiously based citizen activism came from the Left: the civil rights struggle, the antiwar movement, nuclear disarmament, and the push for social welfare spending. Daniel Berrigan, who was arrested in 1967 for burning draft records, was a Jesuit priest who often addressed antiwar rallies held in Catholic churches. No one suggested then that Catholicism posed a danger to the separation of church and state. But *Roe* generated political involvement by religious conservatives, whose opposition to abortion is often portrayed as violent and intolerant.[14]

Just as the civil rights movement of the 1960s distanced itself from the terrorism practiced by the Black Panthers, the pro-family movement is learning to define itself by who we are not. Martin Luther King preached nonviolence. The fact that a few (led by Huey P. Newton and Eldridge Cleaver) carried their rage to violent excess did not signal the moral bankruptcy of the crusade for a color-blind society. Similarly, the fact that a handful of pro-lifers have committed violence against abortion clinics does not mean that they speak for a majority of their coreligionists. No one blamed civil rights leaders for the riots in Watts, and mainstream religious conservatives should not be marginalized because of violence committed by a handful of extremists who happen to share their views.

One recent and tragic example was the 1993 murder of Dr. David Gunn, an itinerant abortionist, by Michael Griffin, a deeply disturbed man who had been involved in pro-life protests. The anger raging inside Griffin boiled over in a parking lot outside an abortion clinic in Pensacola, Florida, where he shot Dr. Gunn.

Responsible voices from the faith community swiftly condemned the violence committed by Griffin. Mainstream pro-life organizations recoiled in horror at the shootings in Pensacola and Wichita. "The violence of killing in the name of pro-life makes a mockery of the pro-life cause," proclaimed the U.S. Catholic Bishops Conference. The bishops were right. Murder committed in the name of life is hypocrisy, pure and simple. Yet the statement of the Catholic Church went largely ignored.

Griffin was convicted of first-degree murder after a brief trial in March 1994. He was sentenced to life in prison and will not be eligible for parole for 25 years. Justice was served.

Sadly, our culture rarely honors the silent heroes who offer humane, caring alternatives to the tragedy of abortion. There are thousands of crisis pregnancy centers in America that provide unwed mothers with love, hope, and compassion. CareNet, one of the largest such organizations, handles an estimated 200,000 inquiries from frightened and troubled women every year, and saves an estimated 50,000 babies a year that otherwise might have lost their lives. In their own silent and unheralded way, they are creating a counterculture of life within the dominant culture. But they are all but ignored by a society that only fixes its disapproving glare on the pro-life movement when there are arrests, firebombings, or shootings.[15]

Even those of us with deep faith must acknowledge that religion has been perverted by some to serve evil ends—as when the Ayatollah Khomeini sent little children to die on battlefields for the glory of Allah, or when Christian slaveholders in the South invoked Scripture to justify their mistreatment of slaves, or when the Nazis in Germany trumpeted their claim of the superiority of the Aryan race and peppered their anti-Semitic rantings with quotations from the Bible.[16] But blaming these apostles of hate on the institution of the church ignores all that is good in our various faith traditions. Michael Griffin killed not because of his religion, but in spite of it. And he acted contrary to its clear teachings.

Yet a dark thread ran through the conventional explanation for Michael Griffin's behavior: he was a devout Christian. His pathology was cast in largely religious terms. He was repeatedly identified in the media as a "fundamentalist Christian." Anthony Lewis of the *New York Times* hysterically opined that the murder in Pensacola showed that "religious fanatics" want to impose "God's word on the rest of us." One news account related that Griffin educated his children at home, a practice "largely associated with Christian fundamentalist beliefs." CBS anchorman Bob Schiefer on *Face the Nation* intoned, "We've all noticed that there has been a link between crime and religion."

Another example of American society's fascination with the pathological side of religion came during the 1993 stand-off between federal law enforcement officials and David Koresh and the Branch Davidian cult in Waco, Texas. The media devoted resources to the episode normally reserved for the Olympics. It chronicled Koresh's bizarre claims that he "hears directly from God" and spooked readers with quotations from the Book of Revelation, "a darkly allegorical work" (in the words of the *Washington Post*) that foretells the apocalypse.

When campaign season rolls around, evangelicals and their allies come under vicious attack. After Allen Quist, a farmer and former state legislator, won the Republican endorsement for Governor of Minnesota in June, 1994, the Minneapolis *Star-Tribune* ran a cartoon that showed body-snatching "Quistians" stumbling through the lobby of the convention hotel with glassy eyes and scarred faces. Columnist Mark Shields called these religious folk the "American equivalent of Shiite muslims." Democratic consultant Bob Beckel compared them to Nazis. Cued by the press, Congressman Vic Fazio of California denounced politically active evangelicals and Roman Catholics as "fire-breathing" fanatics. At a news conference in Washington, Fazio dissembled on their "subterranean tactics"—such as voter identification and phone banks. One reporter queried, "What is the difference between Christians turning out voters and what the labor unions have done for years?" Fazio weakly responded that union members acted out of "personal beliefs," something that presumably motivated people of faith as well.[17]

Religion in Popular Culture

One searches in vain for a positive portrayal of faith in popular culture. When Martin Scorcese remade the 1962 film *Cape Fear*, in 1991, he transformed the character played by Robert De Niro into a Pentecostal psychopath whose body is tattooed with Bible verses and gruesome depictions of the crucifixion. He speaks in tongues and sneers at a woman just before raping her, "Are you ready to be born again?" In Woody Allen's film *Hannah and Her Sisters*, one of the characters compares evangelical preachers to the Nazis, and states that "what is going on in Christ's name" is worse than the Holocaust. In *Alien 3*, starring Sigourney Weaver, a monster invades a penal colony in outer space populated by rapists and murderers who are identified as fundamentalist Christians, not once but twice.[18]

Television entertainment reinforces the same message. In a recent episode of the NBC program *The Mommies*, a spoof on motherhood, a Catholic priest is portrayed as a drunken boob who makes sexual advances at women. When a transvestite informs him that she used to be a male, the priest replies, "Well, I used to be a Protestant." *Dream On*, a program on Home Box Office, celebrates promiscuity and laces its plotlines with nude scenes, including one in which a Catholic priest is willingly seduced by the hero's secretary.[19]

L.A. Law (NBC) recently added some excitement to boost its sagging ratings: it brought a fundamentalist attorney into the show's conflict-ridden law firm. Steven Bochco, the successful producer and creator of *L.A. Law*, promised a fair and balanced portrait of evangelical Christianity. But what happened next was all too predictable. During cross-examination in a heated trial, the born-again attorney viciously attacked and humiliated a woman who had committed adultery and was dismissed by her employer. After the trial, the victorious employer—who also professed to be a born-again Christian—tried to seduce her. The message is clear: religion is a crutch; its adherents are judgmental hypocrites. Little wonder that a character on *Love and War* (CBS), representing a David Koresh-like fanatic, concluded, "Show me one religion that isn't at least one part brainwashing." Sometimes the caricatures are repulsive in their insensitivity. *NYPD Blue*, a sexually explicit *Dragnet* for the nineties, recently featured a Scripture-spewing rapist who used the Bible to justify his exploitation of women.[20]

Gone is our understanding of religion's vibrant role in sustaining marriages, nurturing children, and strengthening families. Gone is our appreciation for religion as the basis for individual self-initiative, social quietude, and voluntary civil obedience.

Lost Language of Shared Faith

Popular disdain for religion has debased our civic discourse until it is vulgar, vitriolic, and violent. We no longer communicate because we no longer share a common vernacular. Religionists and secularists snipe at one another across rhetorical barricades.

It was not always so. Unique among all nations in history, with the exception of Israel, America was settled by persons of faith. Our educational system was largely founded by clergy. Jonathan Edwards, one of the first presidents of Princeton University, stirred congregations with sermons that warned of "sinners in the hands of an angry God."

Benjamin Franklin was dedicated to the service of the church by his deeply religious father as the "tithe" of his ten sons. Though he later chose printing as his profession, Franklin pored over the Scriptures, memorizing entire chapters from the book of Proverbs. At the age of twenty-six, he composed a prayer that he repeated daily: "O powerful Goodness! Bountiful Father! Merciful Guide! Increase in me that wisdom which discovers my truest interest. Strengthen my resolutions to perform what that wisdom dictates." His *Poor Richard's Almanac*, first published in 1732, brimmed with biblical proverbs and sayings that highlighted the Protestant ethic. "Dost thou love life? Then do not squander time, for that's the stuff life is made of," instructed one such saying. When George Whitefield visited Philadelphia in 1739, Franklin joined open-air congregations that numbered in the thousands, marveling that "it seems as if the all the world is growing religious, so that one could not walk through the town in an evening without hearing psalms sung in different families of every street."[21]

Wide-eyed schoolchildren in early America read *McGuffey's Readers* by candlelight, memorizing Scripture verses and church hymns. *McGuffey's Readers* sold 122 million copies during the nineteenth century. Noah Webster published the first American dictionary in 1828, using Bible verses as definitions. Webster founded a college, served in government, and mastered twenty-eight languages. There was no false dichotomy between personal faith and public service in his day.

Indeed, Webster testified to the importance of faith to the survival of democracy. His *American Spelling Book* sold 24 million copies during his lifetime, exceeded only by the Bible in sales, and opened with the simple line: "No man may put off the law of God." Webster believed that religion should form the basis of the American legal system. "The moral principles and precepts contained in the Scriptures ought to form the basis of all our constitution and laws," he argued. "All the miseries and evils which men suffer . . . proceed directly from their despising or neglecting the precepts contained in the Bible."[22]

Higher education continued this emphasis on Scripture. John Witherspoon, president of Princeton and a signer of the Declaration of Independence, required his students to deliver their graduation addresses in Hebrew. College youth read the Scriptures in the original Greek and Hebrew. William Paley's *Evidences of Christianity*, a stirring defense of the Christian faith against its philosophic foes, was a standard college text at virtually every institution of higher learning in the nation. When John Adams took his college entrance exam, part of the assignment was translating the first ten chapters of the Gospel of John from Greek to Latin.[23]

This curriculum steeped America's early leaders in the Scriptures. Two historians recently completed a ten-year study of 15,000 documents from the colonial era. The most quoted source was the Bible, with 34 percent of all citations, followed by Montesquieu (8.3 percent), Blackstone (7.9 percent), and Locke (2.9 percent). The Bible informed the intellectual framework of America's founders far more than Enlightenment thinkers, Blackstone, or the Whig opposition in England.[24]

Well into the nineteenth century, two bodies of literature informed our civic discourse: the classics and the Bible. Theodore Roosevelt, who often read three books a day, claimed, "A thorough knowledge of the Bible is more important than a college education."

When Abraham Lincoln said in the 1850s that "a house divided against itself cannot stand," he was quoting the book of Matthew. His listeners needed no translator. Shared language and symbology muted disagreements and sustained national unity even when political disputes threatened to destroy it.[25]

We have lost this common language, and with it our sense of common values. As religion has been pushed to the uttermost edges of intellectual life, the media's explanation for the continued vitality of religion assumes an apocalyptic flavor.

From the gunning down of abortion doctors to the bombing of the World Trade Center by terrorists, religion in the popular mind has become virtually synonymous with fanaticism. Yes, some acts of violence are committed in the name of religion. No, they are not representative of the majority of people of faith—any faith. Preachers are drawn as Elmer Gantry-like caricatures, and their followers are portrayed as rubes and hayseeds. When religion does find its way into the national debate, it is invariably in the context of bombings, terror, murder, and cultic violence.

Civil religion was the first of American political institutions. "It was not until I went into the churches of America and heard her pulpits flame with righteousness that I understood her greatness," wrote Alexis de Tocqueville in 1835. Religion, he added, was "indispensable to the maintenance of republican institutions" in the United States. "Despotism may be able to do without faith, but liberty cannot." [26]

Tocqueville marveled at a nation of churchgoers whose political differences were tempered by shared values and a common language to express them. Until our culture begins to honor and affirm religion, civility may never return to American civic discourse. Today the victims are Roman Catholics, Jews, fundamentalists, and evangelicals. But, in truth, we are all losers. The pluralistic patchwork quilt of American democracy is less beautiful, less attractive, and less colorful because one of its boldest and brightest fabrics—its religious faith—has been torn away from public display.

CHAPTER FIVE

Faith Versus Fanaticism: How Religion Has Become Marginalized

Society is plagued by serious social problems—crime, illegitimacy, illiteracy, family breakup. Religious conservatives advocate solutions to those problems that are supported by the majority of the American people. Why, then, are they so often portrayed as zealots bent on imposing an undemocratic agenda? Part of the blame is our own. William Rusher once observed that the difference between Barry Goldwater and Ronald Reagan was that Goldwater spoke with a scowl while Reagan spoke with a smile. Sometimes how you say something is more important than what you say. Too often those of devout faith have spoken in the public square with a scowl, using language that did not embrace all their listeners.

One example was when a former president of the Southern Baptist Convention stated in 1980 that "God does not hear the prayers of Jews." Another example came in 1992, when one group of Christian leaders distributed a pamphlet that trumpeted the warning: "To vote for Bill Clinton is a sin against God." These statements presented a harsh side of religious belief that was inappropriate and counterproductive.

"Let your speech always be with grace, seasoned, as it were, with salt, so that you may know how you should respond to each person," admonished the apostle Paul (Colossians 4:6). How often have we in the Christian community spoken in anger rather than in love? In our zeal to motivate our supporters, we sometimes speak in a way that reflects poorly on our Christian faith. The fact that our opponents often attack us with religious intolerance does not relieve us of our responsibility to speak in mercy and reconciliation. "A gentle answer turns away wrath," instructs the Bible. "The tongue of the wise makes knowledge acceptable" (Proverbs 15:1–2).

I learned this lesson the hard way. Early in my service at the Christian Coalition, I occasionally used military metaphors to describe our efforts to encourage people of faith to get involved as citizens. A few appeared in print. Political adversaries lifted these phrases out of context and repeated them in an attempt to harm us. At first I was angry at them for distorting my words. But I learned an important lesson. I realized that I bore a special responsibility to speak in a way that reflected God's character and love. Those of us who bear His name have a unique obligation to choose words that represent our Lord in a way that reaches others and makes knowledge acceptable.

Despite the media's reluctance and downright refusal in many instances to cover issues important to religious conservatives, we can learn how to communicate in a way that embraces rather than condemns. Media coverage of religion tends only to report those actions and statements that reinforce a negative stereotype. But how often do we play into their hands? In May 1994 a Christian organization held a news conference in Washington to announce a fundraising campaign to defray the legal expenses of Paula Corbin Jones, who had filed suit against Bill Clinton for an alleged incident of sexual harassment. Certainly Paula Jones has the same right as every American to adequate legal representation. But this particular news conference left the impression that Christian groups were exploiting the incident for fundraising purposes.

The *Washington Post* plastered its pages with the headline: "Christian Coalition Forms Legal Expenses Fund for Clinton Accuser." The headline suggested that the Christian Coalition was involved in the fundraising effort—which it was not. I contacted the reporter of the story, who arranged for the printing of a retraction. But how many readers saw the correction? The media all too often highlights religion as pathology or hypocrisy, but this was an example when such a story was a self-inflicted wound.[1]

To the extent that religious leaders and organizations advocate an agenda consistent with the liberal views of some journalists, their moral statements are welcomed, not condemned. Martin Luther King, in his "Letter from Birmingham City Jail," proclaimed that "just law is a man-made code that squares with the moral law or the law of God." No one objected to his injecting religion into politics. Similar statements made by conservative religious leaders, on the other hand, have been greeted by hysterical warnings that they threaten the "separation of church and state."

False Charges of Censorship

In April 1994 the Texas Education Association newsletter trumpeted the warning: "Radical Right Invades Texas." The publication contained a spoof of a movie starring "stealth candidates" who were "targeting our schools with a secret agenda!" What was the proof of this dangerous plot? Pro-family candidates were seeking election as school board members, something which they presumably have every right to do in our democratic system. The teacher's union attempted to create fear in the minds of voters by accusing religious people of censorship. It cried that religious conservatives sought to ban books from school libraries "that have been enjoyed by children for generations."[2]

The idea that people of faith seek to censor ideas with which they disagree is not based in fact. Indeed, many of the attempts to remove books from school libraries have come from the Left. Liberal activists have sought to ban *The Adventures of Huckleberry Finn* because it contains negative portrayals of blacks. In 1993 a Virginia chapter of the NAACP sought to remove a novel from elementary school libraries because the main character, a slave, questioned his intelligence and referred to himself as a "nigger." There have also been attempts to remove books and films by ministries like Focus on the Family, and even cases where the Bible was taken off library shelves. Religious folk have tried to have books on witchcraft or the occult taken out of libraries, and there have been other instances where they sought the removal of books like J. D. Salinger's *The Catcher in the Rye*, or the works of Annie Dillard and Shel Silverstein.[3]

The point here is not that censorship is fine, but that it is practiced by both sides. Neither the Left nor the Right have a monopoly on such concerns. In some cases, one can sympathize with the objections of parents. African-American parents do not want their third-grader learning language that denigrates their race. Deeply religious parents do not want their children taught ideas about morality that directly contradict their religious beliefs.

Nevertheless, the system fails when either side seeks the removal of books from libraries or schools. How, then, to deal with the legitimate objections of parents to certain material? There are some things that none of us want our seven-year-olds to read. A library in Colorado recently chose not to carry the explicitly pornographic book *Sex* by Madonna for this very reason. The first answer to this dilemma is greater parental supervision at home. Second, there should be more participation in library boards by parents and citizens as to which books are age-appropriate for elementary school students. Beyond that, it is entirely proper for librarians or school boards, in consultation with parents, to have certain books placed behind the librarian's desk for check out with parental permission. In some parts of the country, few if any books would be included in this category; in other communities, there might be a handful. This is not censorship; it is simply protecting the right of parents to have a voice in what their children read. This is hardly a radical idea, and indeed it is practiced in communities all across the country.

Lost in the issue of censorship is the notion that parents have primary responsibility for the instruction of their children. One of the most distasteful aspects of the school board campaigns that are currently raging across the nation is that all too often the rhetoric of the Left—witness the Texas Education Association newsletter—treats parents as enemies. The school is there to serve the parents and their children, not the teachers or the bureaucrats. Its primary job is to reinforce the basic values taught at home, not experiment with alternative value systems. "Up until recent decades," notes Boston College professor William Kilpatrick, "schools were considered to be acting *in loco parentis*—in the place of the parent (this principle even prevailed in many colleges in the recent past). The idea that the parent is the first and foremost teacher was taken seriously: teachers acted for the parents as trustees of children's education." He adds, "The culture of the school and the culture of the home reinforce each other; both had similar goals and values."[4]

Censorship is wrong, no matter who practices it. But it is also wrong for schools to treat parents as intruders rather than partners in the impartation of knowledge and the inculcation of values to their children. In the Tennessee textbook case of 1986—dubbed Scopes II by the press—parents did not seek to ban textbooks. They merely wanted to substitute alternative texts for those they found objectionable. While their request was unusual, it was initially granted, then overruled by an intransigent school board, leading to the arrest and jailing of a mother who tried to remove her child from the school. The result was a mushrooming controversy and a bitter court trial in which no one emerged unscathed. Hopefully, such incidents can be avoided in the future. If religious conservatives can acknowledge the importance of the freedom of inquiry, and if educational leaders can respect parental rights, then perhaps we can resolve disputes about censorship when it is practiced by both the Left and the Right.[5]

Faith in the Crossfire

Part of the reason for the marginalization of religion lies in the church's abdication of its responsibility to the broader culture. After the Scopes trial of 1925, people of faith withdrew to their churches, creating a cultural ghetto of their own making. Their recent reentry into civic life after decades of neglect has been greeted with what might be called a faith phobia: an irrational fear of the integration of religious people into public life.

In seeking to redress their cultural isolation, people of faith must resist the temptation to promote political involvement as the sole answer to our social ills. The church that saves souls and restores marriages gains a platform from which it can speak to the broader society. The hand that feeds, clothes, and educates is strong enough to bang the gavel in the courthouse and state house. A caring faith community will not merely condemn the abortionist, but offer loving alternatives for women, such as homes for unwed mothers and adoption services.

A second problem is that the Left has unilaterally surrendered invocations of God and religion to conservatives. God has become a political football, used all too often by only one team on the field, usually the Republicans. I was told by one high-ranking Republican official that the Bush-Quayle campaign urged the platform committee in 1992 to "get God into the platform." There followed the appearance by President George Bush in August of that year before a Religious Roundtable meeting in Dallas, Texas, in which he said, "I am struck by the fact that the other party took thousands of words to make up its platform and left out three simple letters. G-O-D."

This oratory had an awkward and disjointed quality about it that invited criticism. Religion became a "wedge" issue that divided the electorate, and that was unfortunate. But Bush's larger point, that the Left now finds religion unfashionable, was not far from the mark. The causes of the Left—desegregation, opposition to the war in Vietnam, the war on poverty—once prominently displayed priests and rabbis as leaders and relied heavily on religious language. That is no longer true. Liberals have largely ceded religious vernacular to conservatives. Extremist groups like People for the American Way even attack those with faith who run for public office as a threat to the "separation of church and state," though they never specify why conservatives are any more of a threat than churchmen and churchwomen on the Left who have led religiously-inspired causes for decades.

The Democrats have behaved even more irresponsibly, launching personal assaults on candidates because of their religious faith. When Michael Farris, a constitutional attorney and home school advocate, ran for lieutenant governor in Virginia, the Democrats engaged in a vicious campaign of religious bigotry. The incumbent Democratic lieutenant governor broadcast television commercials that warned voters that Farris had once worked for Jerry Falwell (he had not) and was supported by Pat Robertson. Newspaper accounts included references to Farris's religion that would be considered scurrilous if directed at a Jew or a Muslim, and one reporter repeatedly asked Farris if he had heard the audible voice of God when he considered undertaking his campaign.

When a Christian businesswoman in Nebraska recently announced her candidacy for the U.S. Senate against Bob Kerrey, the state Democratic Party chairman denounced her as a "Christian Coalition type" and criticized her for attending an evangelical church. A woman elected to the state legislature in Montana in 1992 found herself attacked as a "stealth candidate" because of her religious beliefs. One newspaper accused her of attempting to create a theocracy and warned ominously: "If you're not born again and straight, you're not invited."[6]

When David Beasley, a respected state legislator and successful businessman, announced his candidacy for the Republican nomination for governor of South Carolina in 1994, a Democratic candidate quipped that his two leading qualifications were "handling snakes and being able to speak fluently in tongues." These kinds of attacks against Christians and others with devout faith have become a persistent pattern in Democratic campaigns across the nation in recent years. In the case of the South Carolina incident, neither the state party chairman nor David Wilhelm, chairman of the Democratic National Committee, disavowed the attack on the Republican candidate's religious beliefs.[7]

When Clarence Thomas was nominated to the U.S. Supreme Court in 1991, then-Governor Doug Wilder of Virginia reacted to the news by noting that Thomas "has indicated that he's a very devout Catholic" and asking, "The question is: How much allegiance is there to the Pope?" (Thomas, in fact, is not a Catholic. He attends an Episcopalian church.) These references to a prospective officeholder's religion bear a disturbing resemblance to the paranoid political style of the Know-Nothings of the 1850s. They demonstrate how intolerant some liberals can become when religion creeps beyond the stained-glass ghetto assigned to it.[8]

It is an indication of the collective amnesia that afflicts our body politic that such religious attacks are made at all. John F. Kennedy appeared to lay the religion issue to rest during his 1960 presidential campaign. In a speech to the Houston Ministerial Association on September 12, 1960, Kennedy warned, "For while this year it may be a Catholic against whom the finger of suspicion is pointed, in other years it has been, and may someday be again, a Jew—or a Quaker—or a Unitarian—or a Baptist." He predicted that America would be shamed before the entire world if "40 million Americans lost their chance of being president on the day they were baptized."[9]

Kennedy's eloquent words have proven darkly prophetic. The crooked finger of suspicion once pointed at him is indeed directed today at Baptists, fundamentalists, and pro-life Roman Catholics. Just ask

Ernest Lumpkin, the black pastor of Ebeneezer Baptist Church, who was appointed to the San Francisco human rights commission in 1991 because of his longstanding support for civil rights. When asked by a reporter whether or not he believed in the biblical passages that disapprove of homosexuality, he replied, "I believe everything the Bible says." It is difficult to imagine a Baptist minister giving any other answer. Yet the mayor's office in San Francisco was deluged with abusive phone calls of protest, and pastor Lumpkin was forced off the human rights board. One can almost imagine future candidates for the board going through a screening process that includes being asked, "Do you now or have you ever held to a literal belief in the Bible?"[10]

A Changing World

Modernity presents other challenges to the continued vitality of civil religion. Immigration has brought greater religious and ethnic diversity, making it more difficult to arrive at a cultural consensus on issues of faith. Secularization of both primary and higher education has made it difficult for young people to receive the moral teaching they hunger for and need. The welfare state has forced out church-based charity. Rising living standards and declining birth rates have reduced the importance of family in our daily lives.

The rise of mass media has also made religion less influential in the broader culture. Americans at one time poured into churches and synagogues not only to learn about the hereafter but to filter daily realities through a prism of faith. Religious bodies throughout history have spoken out on issues ranging from slavery to child labor to the prevalence of alcohol. The rise of television and other mass forms of communication has diminished the central position occupied by religion in American culture, despite the best efforts by modern religious broadcasters to keep the faith.

By the time the average child in America reaches the age of eighteen, the child has watched 22,000 hours of television, listened to 18,000 hours of radio, and spent only 3,000 hours in church. Little wonder that religion holds so little sway for most Americans: they are conditioned from their youth to pay more attention to Nintendo than to Nehemiah. Disney videos rank higher in their cosmology than their pastor or rabbi. A 1994 Times-Mirror survey asked respondents which institution they felt most decided what was important to them. An astonishing 43 percent listed the media, 22 percent listed Washington, and 10 percent listed Hollywood. Only 7 percent named religion.[11]

Religious conservatives recognize these realities. Indeed, people of faith are enthusiastically embracing the emerging technologies of computers and interactive television that will make up the information superhighway of the future. The use of satellites, fax machines, and cable television to spread the gospel message points to a Christian community that understands the need to adapt to new technology.

The growing racial and denominational diversity of the religious conservative movement also bodes well for its future. People of faith do not wish to turn back the clock to an earlier day before these demographic and cultural changes took place. Nor do they desire to establish religion by the arm of the state. Our ancestors fled Europe precisely because the scepter and the Scriptures were in the same hands. Many faced religious persecution at the hands of a government that expropriated taxes for the support of a church with which they violently disagreed. Because of this historical distrust of government, conservative evangelicals do not want to institute a theocratic form of government.

The True Meaning of the First Amendment

Some argue that those who seek to legislate values consistent with their faith tradition violate the First Amendment prohibition of an establishment of religion. The Supreme Court has explicitly rejected this notion. In several decisions in 1961, the Court upheld blue laws that outlawed conducting business on Sunday, despite the fact that some state codes referred to it as "the Lord's day." Chief Justice Earl Warren asserted that a law did not become unconstitutional solely because it coincided with the religious beliefs of its advocates. "Thus for temporal purposes, murder is illegal," observed Warren. "And the fact that this agrees with the dictates of the Judeo-Christian religions while it may disagree with others does not invalidate the regulation."[12]

Similarly, in *Harris* v. *McRae* (1980), the Court upheld the ban on taxpayer-funding of abortion, rejecting the argument that the law should be voided because it incorporated Roman Catholic teachings on the sin of abortion and human life beginning at conception. Justice Potter Stewart concluded that "the fact that funding restrictions in the Hyde amendment may coincide with the religious tenets of the Roman Catholic Church does not, without more, contravene the Establishment Clause." If a law *ipso facto* violated the separation of church and state because it was coincident with religious doctrine, we would be forced to repeal three centuries of Western jurisprudence: laws against murder, larceny, perjury, rape, and polygamy would all be stricken from the books.[13]

Much of the confusion about constitutional doctrine relating to church and state matters arises from the "wall of separation" metaphor contained in Thomas Jefferson's letter to the Danbury (Connecticut) Baptist Association in 1802. In this letter Jefferson expressed "solemn reverence" for "that act of the whole American people which declared that their legislature should make 'no law respecting an establishment of religion, or prohibiting the free exercise thereof,' thus building a wall of separation between church and state." But relying entirely on this single passage from a cursory letter paints an incomplete (and wholly inaccurate) picture of Jefferson's views. He did not, for example, feel bound by the separatist doctrine in 1824, when he instituted religious instruction on "[t]he proofs of the being of God, the creator, preserver, and supreme ruler of the universe" at the state-supported University of Virginia and required every student "to attend religious worship at the establishment of their respective sects." It did not prevent him as president from consenting to a law granting tax-exempt status to churches. Nor did it prevent him from signing a treaty with the Kaskaskia Indians in 1803—one year after his letter to the Danbury Baptists—that provided government funds for the support of the tribe's Roman Catholic Church and priest.[14]

Jefferson's Statute of Virginia for Religious Freedom of 1779, which he listed along with the Declaration of Independence and the founding of the University of Virginia as his greatest achievements, was designed to *protect* religion, not marginalize its expression. It forbade the government from causing anyone to "suffer on account of his religious opinions or belief," and protected the right of all to "profess, and by argument to maintain, their opinions in matters of religion." Jefferson's aim was limited in scope: to prevent the establishment of a state religion in Virginia.

Jefferson's purpose was not to stifle religious expression but to liberate it. "The rights of conscience we never submitted" to the government, he asserted, because "we are answerable for them to our God." Later he asked, "And can the liberties of a nation be thought secure, when we have removed their only firm basis, a conviction in the minds of the people that these liberties are the gift of God?"[15]

Jefferson acknowledged the important role of faith to the maintenance of civil society. In 1807 he wrote that America is about "the liberty to worship our creator in the way we think most agreeable to his will, a liberty deemed in other countries incompatible with good government and yet proved by our experience to be its best support."

The founders never intended for the First Amendment to restrain government, in its legitimate role of fulfilling a secular purpose, from accommodating religious faith. The price of ratification of the Constitution in Virginia had been the Federalists's acceptance of Patrick Henry's amendment that proclaimed that "no particular religious sect or society ought to be favored or established by law, in preference to others." James Madison's first draft of what later became the First Amendment addressed this concern. It pledged that "the civil rights of none shall be abridged on account of religious belief or worship, nor shall any national religion be established, nor shall the full and equal rights of conscience be in any manner, or on any pretext, infringed."

The Establishment Clause prohibited the federal government from foisting upon the populace (many of whom subscribed to dissenting faiths) a national religion. It did not contemplate hostility to religion in general. Madison thought the Bill of Rights was superfluous but politically necessary, an ironic twist given the large role it has played in guaranteeing basic liberties. "The [First] Amendment requires the state to be neutral in its relations with groups of religious believers and nonbelievers; it does not require the state to be their adversary," ruled Justice Hugo Black in 1947 in a decision upholding the use of government funds to bus students to parochial schools in New Jersey.[16]

Sadly, American legal culture has shifted from neutrality to hostility towards religion, something the founders never intended. The same House of Representatives that approved the Establishment Clause voted to open its sessions with prayer by an official chaplain—and provided government funds to pay for it. The day after the Establishment Clause passed the House, its members passed a resolution calling on President George Washington to issue a Thanksgiving Day proclamation urging the American people to join in "a day of public thanksgiving and prayer" that acknowledged "the many signal favors of Almighty God." At the same time, it reauthorized the Northwest Ordinance, originally enacted in 1787, which stated that "religion, morality and knowledge, being necessary to good government and the happiness of mankind, schools and the means of education shall forever be encouraged."[17]

In place of this tolerance of religious faith, the Supreme Court has substituted a doctrine of practiced ambivalence. In the *Lemon* v. *Kurtzman* decision in 1971, the Court struck down state aid to parochial schools as unconstitutional. The majority opinion proposed a three-pronged "lemon test" that voided any law that (1) did not have a secular purpose, (2) had the primary effect of advancing or inhibiting religion, and, (3) caused government to become "excessively entangled" in religion.

The "lemon test" is a lemon. It has transformed church-state litigation into a jurisprudential nightmare. The Supreme Court presides over an uncharted chaos, issuing edicts willy-nilly, banishing some centuries-old practices while holding identical ones to be constitutional—all without apparent rhyme or reason. As Chief Justice William Rehnquist remarked, the inconsistency of the "lemon test" has reduced it to an absurdity. The Court has allowed prayers led by chaplains in state legislatures, while voiding a brief moment of silence in public schools; permitted public bus service to church schools, but prevented the same buses from carrying parochial students to a public zoo or museum; allowed the state to buy history books for a parochial school, while forbidding it to provide the same school with a film on America's founding fathers.[18]

Whether the courts will correct their hostile treatment of religion remains to be seen. Past judicial rulings have all too often treated religion like pornography, something that consenting adults can be exposed to as long as children are kept at a distance. In 1994 the Supreme Court had a chance to reverse course in the case of Kiryas Joel village, a community of Satmar Hasidic Jews that received its own school district from the New York state legislature for the education of disabled youngsters. Hasidic children, in their uncommon garb and long side-curls, had been subjected to ridicule and abuse in other public schools. Establishing their own school allowed them to learn in an environment free from persecution. No religious teaching was introduced into the school. Its halls display no religious symbols or banners, its faculty is composed entirely of non-Hasidic teachers, and no religious classes were included in the curriculum. But in July, 1994, the Court ruled that the school's existence violated the Constitution. In ruling against Kiryas Joel, the Supreme Court squandered an historic opportunity to reverse three decades of hostile judicial rulings and allow the government to pursue secular goals that accommodate religion. No law should be held unconstitutional that does not establish a state religion, prefers no denomination over another, and has an essentially secular purpose.[19]

Russell Kirk has contended that "the corpus of English and American laws" cannot survive "unless it is animated by the spirit that moved it from the beginning: that is, by religion, and specifically, by the Christian religion." Compassion, justice, mercy, tolerance, charity, and faithfulness—these are the principles of the Judeo-Christian faith that have sustained our democratic way of life for centuries. A state church? That is more an insult to God than to the government, and it does a disservice to both. But a secular government informed by sacred principles and open to the service of persons of faith not only poses no threat to the Constitution, it is essential to its survival.[20]

I strongly support the separation of church and state in order to protect the church, not the state. I favor church-state separation because I would not entrust the sacred tablets of my faith to the same government that has given us the House Post Office scandal, the savings and loan debacle, and that delivers a first-class letter with the efficiency of a nineteenth-century stagecoach. If there must be a wall between the church and the government, let it be set at a reasonable height. Let the barbed wire be placed on the side of the state, with the razor-blades of restraint pointed towards the government rather than aimed like a dagger at the heart of religious people and institutions.

Make no mistake. The marginalization of people of faith, who number in the tens of millions, affects us all. Our institutions are in disarray. People are disillusioned. We have lost confidence in our government and our leaders. The values that once sustained us are in decline. In order to fully understand the crisis facing society, we need to see how politics as usual has marginalized not only people of faith, but the entire citizenry. We must understand how emerging technologies in telecommunications are giving this discontent with the status quo a powerful means of expressing itself. In order to do that, we must first look at the crisis affecting the most basic institution of our country—the family.

CHAPTER SIX

The Fire This Time:
Family Breakup and Social Chaos

I RECENTLY attended a play celebrating the end of the school year at the pre-school where my daughter attends kindergarten. The performance featured a series of skits and songs by young children dressed in colorful costumes. Some were dressed as spiders, others as flowers, some as birds. My five-year-old daughter came as a kite for her part in a song about the wind. But the real drama played out in the audience. Fathers clutched videocameras and crouched near the front to capture the moment for posterity. Mothers frantically waved at their children, while brothers and sisters craned their necks to see their siblings perform. The screams and coos of babies filled the air. The entire scene was one of delicious chaos.

As I looked around at the hundreds of proud parents jammed into the auditorium, it occurred to me that the entire proceeding had the flavor of a sacred ritual. To be sure, religion played little role in the play beyond the opening prayer. But like a child's baptism, first baseball game, piano recital, or their high school graduation, this was a sacred celebration. It lifted adults and children out of the world of temporal pursuits to take a moment to honor the transcendent. For days afterward, I found myself silently singing the nursery rhyme that my daughter had sung on stage. It wasn't the song that had captivated me, but my love for her. Any child can get into trouble, no matter how devoted the parents. But it struck me that few of the children in that auditorium would end up in trouble with the law as long as their parents remained so engaged in their upbringing and dedicated to loving them into adulthood.

Broken Families, Broken Homes

Sadly, the children I saw that evening are becoming a minority. Every year more than one million children are victims of divorce. There were only 393,000 divorces in 1960, and three out of every four marriages worked. By 1992, the number of divorces had risen to 1.2 million, and six of ten new marriages were failing. There are currently 15.8 million children living in single-parent homes, and there is little chance that this number will decrease during the coming decade. Indeed, according to the U.S. Census Bureau, 60 percent of all children in the United States will lose a parent to divorce before they reach the age of eighteen. As former *Time* correspondent Michael McManus warns, "Growing up in a broken home with a single parent or no parent is sadly the majority U.S. experience!"[1]

Many of these children suffer emotional and psychological trauma that lasts for years. They are more likely than children raised in homes with stable marriages to perform poorly or suffer disciplinary problems in school, to divorce as adults, and experience emotional difficulties. "There is a mountain of scientific evidence showing that when families disintegrate, children often end up with intellectual, physical, and emotional scars that persist for life," points out social scientist Karl Zinmeister. "We talk about the drug crisis, the education crisis, and the problems of teen pregnancy and juvenile crime, but all these ills trace back predominantly to one source: broken families."[2]

The scourge of illegitimacy, divorce, absentee fathers, and financially-pressed two-income households has turned children into the refuse of an aggressively individualistic culture. Young men and women once left homes of origin to form families of their own. The time separating adolescence and marriage was generally limited to the necessary interregnum needed to complete one's education and court the opposite sex. Today millions of Americans are delaying marriage and children for years—or forsaking them altogether. Nearly one-fifth of all males over the age of eighteen live alone. The result is the lowest rate of family formation in American history. Whereas in 1960 the average American spent 62 percent of their life with their spouse and children, that proportion by the late 1980s had fallen to only 43 percent—the lowest on record. Fifty-five percent of American adults are not married, also the highest figure in our history.[3]

Welfare perpetuates this cycle of family decay by subsidizing the movement of husbands and fathers out of the home. It does not help when the government systematically provides a monthly subsidy to young people if they engage (simultaneously) in three behaviors: not marrying, not working, and repeatedly bearing children out of wedlock. For those dependent on government assistance, these subsidized pathologies are nothing less than a sentence to perpetual poverty. There are three basic prerequisites for upward mobility in American society: graduate from high school, get a job and keep it, and get married.

Extensive research has demonstrated that failure to follow these prerequisites all but insures a life of privation. Single motherhood is not a "Murphy Brown" fairy tale. Half of all teenagers who bear children out of wedlock are on welfare within one year. Within five years, an astonishing 72 percent of white and 84 percent of black unwed teen mothers are on welfare. Those who graduate from high school, get married, and wait until age twenty before having a child are almost certain to climb up the social ladder. According to one study, in 1992 only 8 percent of those who did so lived in poverty. And what about those who did not finish high school, get married, and delay children? Their poverty rate was a staggering 79 percent.[4]

Not surprisingly, we have gotten more of what we have subsidized (illegitimacy and family breakup) and less of what we tax (working, intact families). According to one authority, 22.2 percent of white children and 82.9 percent of black children born in 1980 will become dependent on welfare before they are eighteen years old. The result is exploding expenditures on welfare payments. The cost of the Aid to Families with Dependent Children (AFDC) program alone has risen from $3.6 billion in 1970 to $22.4 billion this year, while we spend approximately $308 billion on all welfare programs. The bureaucratic inefficiency of this delivery system is notorious. If all the money spent on welfare at the federal, state, and local level were simply given to the poor, it would equal $24,500 for every family below the poverty level.[5]

The destructive vise of government policy tightens on those families that stay together, work, and save. The average family of four in America paid just 2 percent of their adjusted gross income in federal taxes in 1950. Today that figure is 24.5 percent. After calculating state income taxes, sales taxes, local taxes, and other fees, the average family of four actually pays 37.6 percent of their income in taxes—more than they spend on food, clothing, and housing combined. Like a twisted Robin Hood, the government takes from intact families and gives to those who bring children into the world without taking responsibility for providing for them.

Part of the explanation may be found in the increases in Social Security taxes enacted in 1983, which hit the middle-class families with children hardest while leaving the wealthy almost untouched. A second problem is the erosion in the value of the standard deduction for children, which has been ravaged by inflation. Had the standard deduction kept pace with inflation since 1948 (when it was $600), its value today would be over $8,652—enough for a second mortgage payment for many American families.[6]

The Family Schoolhouse

The frayed social fabric of America is reflected in the poor performance of our schools. Public schools cannot replace the family in inculcating character, transmitting values, and imparting knowledge to our young people. A 1988 study by the Department of Education found that 40 percent of high school seniors could not place the approximate date when the Constitution was written. Half did not recognize Patrick Henry as the individual who said, "Give me liberty or give me death." One-third did not know that the Declaration of Independence marked the separation of the American colonies from Great Britain. A recent study by the National Endowment for the Humanities found that two-thirds of high school juniors could not place the decade in which the Civil War was fought or the half-century in which Columbus discovered America. Only 25 percent of eighth-graders are proficient in mathematics, and schoolchildren in the United States trail their counterparts in other industrialized nations in standardized test scores in science, geography, and history.[7]

No amount of money thrown at education can substitute for strong families and stable homes. In 1960, we spent $2,035 per pupil on education (in constant 1990 dollars), and the average combined SAT score was 975. Despite more than doubling per-pupil spending to $5,247, SAT scores have declined precipitously since 1960. While there is no connection between government expenditures for education and student performance, there is a direct correlation between strong, close-knit families and educational achievement. Paul Barton, in a 1992 study titled *America's Smallest School: The Family*, argues that the number of two-parent households is far more predictive of scholastic achievement than either expenditures on education or teacher-pupil ratios. North Dakota, which ranks second in SAT scores, also ranks second in the nation in the percentage of students in two-parent households—but ranks near the bottom (44th out of 50 states) in expenditures for education. By contrast, the District of Columbia, which has the lowest percentage of students from two-parent households, also ranks 49th in SAT scores—despite spending more per pupil on education than all but four states in the nation. New Jersey, which spends more per pupil than any other state, has little to show for it: SAT scores for New Jersey students rank 39th out of 50 states.[8]

The connection between poor educational performance and family disintegration is undeniable. In a 1993 survey by the U.S. Department of Education on violence in the schools, half of all students with poor grades indicated that their parents had spent little or no time with them on their homework in the previous week. One-third of the students whose parents separate or divorce suffer a significant decline in their scholastic performance. And even those families that stay together suffer from a "famine" in family time—often caused by hurried parents in two-income households, multiple jobs, and long hours at the office. As Secretary of Education Richard Riley recently concluded, "The breakup of the American family and the isolation of family members from each other, even in intact families, has had a profound effect on the education of our children."[9]

Riley's observation reflects an emerging bipartisan consensus that the most critical component of a successful educational system is strong, functional families. I recall during graduate school teaching a course at Emory University in which one of my students failed to attend class for long periods of time. When she was present, she appeared bright, inquisitive, and engaged. But her attendance was sporadic, and she was on the verge of failing the course. After the final exam, she came to my office and asked if she could make up several missed assignments, explaining that she had been struggling with an alcohol problem. I gave her a temporary incomplete. She later made up the missed assignments and earned a fairly respectable grade. But like so many other young people today, her problem was not ability but personal difficulties at home. We cannot ask our schools to perform functions that only the family does well. Love, nurture, and instruction begin at the most effective Department of Health, Education, and Welfare ever conceived: the intact family.

Crime and Family Breakup

The coarseness of modern American society came crashing in on me on a sunny day in 1992, as I sat in a friend's office in the White House, watching in horror as the riots in south-central Los Angeles unfolded live on television. There we were, reclining in the ornate luxury of the building that is the symbol of power for the entire Western world, watching bloodshed and carnage spill over in the streets of one of our nation's greatest cities. When the smoke cleared, fifty-eight people were dead, more than 4,000 injured, and over $1 billion in damage had been done in a killing spree that lasted three days. The riots demonstrated yet again how very thin the veil is that separates civilization from chaos. It also underscored that violence and mayhem follows the decay of the two-parent, intact family as surely as the river flows home to the sea.

In 1965, following the Watts riots that consumed an entire section of Los Angeles, Daniel Patrick Moynihan, then a young aide to Lyndon Johnson, penned these words:

> From the wild Irish slums of the 19th century Eastern seaboard to the riot-torn suburbs of Los Angeles, there is one unmistakable lesson in American history: a community that allows a large number of young men

to grow up in broken families, dominated by women, never acquiring any stable relationship to male authority, never acquiring any set of rational expectations about the future—that community asks for and gets chaos. Crime, violence, unrest, unrestrained lashing out at the whole social structure—that is not only to be expected, it is very near inevitable.[10]

Moynihan made this observation at a time when the illegitimacy rate for African-American babies was 22 percent. The out-of-wedlock birth rate for African-American babies has risen to an astonishing 68 percent, and the rate is rising for other groups as well.[11]

These children are vulnerable to a whole range of social pathologies. They are three times as likely to drop out of high school, twice as likely to become chemically dependent on drugs or alcohol, and three times as likely to commit a violent crime as children raised in a two-parent, nuclear household. Communities with a high incidence of single-parent households are invariably plagued by violence and delinquency. As sociologists Douglas Smith and G. Roger Jarjoura have concluded, "Neighborhoods with large percentages of youth (those aged twelve to twenty) and areas with high percentages of single-parent households also have higher rates of crime."[12]

Reducing crime is at the center of a faith-based agenda for America. The crime problem can only be solved by strengthening the two-parent, nuclear family. No society can prosper in which violent predators roam the streets while law-abiding citizens cower in fear behind the bars and alarm systems of their own homes. Since 1960, population has risen only 41 percent, while violent crime has skyrocketed 560 percent. In 1960 there were 6,000 murders in the United States; in 1990 there were 21,000 murders. Every year in America, there is a murder committed every 22 minutes, a rape every 5 minutes, a robbery every 47 seconds, and a violent crime of some kind committed every 22 seconds. Five million Americans are victims of violent crime every year, while 19 million are targets of property crimes, such as larceny, burglary, or theft. The FBI estimates that 83 percent of all Americans—more than four out of every five—will be victims of crime at some point in their lifetimes.[13]

Had a foreign enemy done to us what we have done to ourselves, we would have gone to war to defend our families and homes. Indeed, as columnist Don Feder recently observed, more Americans died between 1976 and 1993 at the hands of other Americans than died on all the battlefields during World War II, the greatest military conflagration of the twentieth century. More Americans (73,000) were killed by their fellow citizens in just three years—between 1991 and 1993—than lost their lives in Vietnam between 1963 and 1973, a war that tore our society apart and convulsed our political system.[14]

We live in the most violent society in the entire Western world. We have an incarceration rate that is five times that of Germany and Great Britain, ten times that of Japan and Sweden. In 1960, we incarcerated about 110 people per 100,000 population. By 1992 we incarcerated 455 per 100,000 people. The total population of prisoners, parolees, and probationers has risen from 1.8 million in 1980 to 4.4 million in 1990, an increase of 139 percent in a single decade.[15]

The economic cost of crime is staggering. According to *Business Week* magazine, the total cost to society every year is $425 billion. The average career criminal commits about two hundred crimes per year at a cost to society of $430,000 annually. It costs approximately $25,000 a year to keep a criminal behind bars—about as much as it would cost to send the same person to Harvard. Per capita spending on prisons has increased 400 percent in the last twenty years, and the country has appropriated $30 billion in just the past decade to double its prison capacity. Yet despite the fact that more criminals are behind bars than at any time in our history, our streets are less safe and our citizens more terrorized than ever before.[16]

"Among the many objects to which a wise and free people find it necessary to direct their attention," suggested John Jay in *The Federalist Papers*, "that of providing for their safety seems to be the first."[17] Indeed, guaranteeing personal safety and domestic tranquility is the first charge of government, a task that both federal and state authorities have failed to faithfully execute. In 1990 corrections services accounted for only 2.5 percent of state and local government expenditures. Despite the best efforts of the federal government, crime will remain a primarily local responsibility.[18]

In 1994 Congress passed a crime bill (one of countless such federal crime measures passed in the past twenty years) to try to wrestle with the problem. Like all other crime bills, it is unlikely to have any discernable impact on the violence plaguing society. The act provided $9 billion to put an additional 100,000 police officers on the street in an expanded experiment in "community policing." This is an admirable program. But the truth is that we could put a police officer on every street corner in America and our communities would be no safer.

Chuck Colson, the former Watergate figure who has spent twenty years working in America's prisons, concludes that "this crisis will not be resolved by more cops and more cells." He adds, "The only real solution is the cultivation of conscience."[19] In a free society, the only guarantee of security is a citizenry animated by faith, tempered by familial obligations, and governed by an internalized code of conduct. Until there is a spiritual renewal among our people in matters of self-control and voluntary obedience, law-abiding citizens will continue to live with terror and violence as an everyday reality.

In this sense, religious conservatives would agree with many liberals that the crime problem cannot be solved without dealing with its root causes, though we would no doubt differ on what those root causes are. There is no direct correlation, for example, between poverty and crime. Rates of crime have risen in periods of economic good times as well as recessionary periods. In fact, crime actually declined during the Great Depression, after a sharp increase during the 1920s, a period of enormous financial prosperity and economic expansion.

Liberals look at areas of high unemployment and point out that they also suffer from a high crime. Fair enough. But the same areas also have a high percentage of absentee-parent households, which in many instances is the cause of poverty. The debate has degenerated into a which-came-first-the-chicken-or-the-egg argument. Liberals argue that poverty causes family break-up, while conservatives insist that family break-up causes poverty. In any case, what distinguishes the underclass from those who rise out of the ghetto is not their poverty alone but their behavior—crime, lawlessness, illegitimacy, and delinquency. As Myron Magnet argues, "Even when you look backwards to search for origins, it's hard to think that economic forces caused the underclass condition, when you consider that the underclass came into being in the mid sixties, when the U.S. economy was zooming and unemployment was low and falling."[20]

Nor is race predictive of crime. Minority children raised in two-parent homes have no greater propensity toward crime than whites. Some ethnic communities display little lawlessness in the midst of crushing poverty. In 1965 only five people of Chinese ancestry were incarcerated in the entire state of California. A similar pattern prevails today among Hispanics. Latino young men, while suffering high poverty rates, are more likely to come from two-parent households, less likely to go to prison, and far more likely to be in the labor force than African-American youth. Even here, the salient distinction is family formation, not race. A 1988 study by the Department of Health and Human Services found that at every income level up to $50,000 a year—for blacks, whites, and Latinos—children from two-parent households were far better off emotionally than counterparts from single-parent homes.[21]

Part of the explanation for rising crime rates is a lenient, liberal criminal justice system that has reduced the likelihood of punishment for those who commit crimes. Every ninety seconds a felon receives early release from prison. Of the more than thirteen million arrests by local law enforcement annually, less than 2 percent result in a prison sentence. Violent criminals incarcerated in state prisons currently serve an average of only 37 percent of their actual sentences. In some cases, the rate of incarceration is laughable. For murderers in the United States, the median prison sentence is six years; for rapists, three years; for drug dealers, one year. As we have reduced the likelihood of punishment and sanctions, the rate of violent crime has naturally increased.

According to the National Center for Policy Analysis, there are approximately 6 million burglaries in America every year, but only 72,000 burglars go to prison each year—an incarceration rate of barely one percent. In the District of Columbia between 1988 and 1990 there were 1,286 murders, but only one out of four led to convictions.[22]

The true origins of the crime problem are family disintegration in general and the large number of young men disconnected from families of origin and wives and children in particular. When young males are torn from the discipline of fathers and the socially sublime obligations of marriage and childrearing, they have no sense of obligation to the larger society. This is why, as George Gilder points out in his classic *Men and Marriage*, single men comprise only 13 percent of the population, but they make up 40 percent of the prison population and commit 90 percent of our violent crimes. An estimated 70 percent of youths in juvenile detention centers come from absentee-father households. Indeed, even as adults, single men are five times as likely as married men to commit a violent crime.[23]

Dan Quayle Was Right

What religious conservatives want is to make the restoration of the two-parent, intact family with children the central and paramount public policy priority of the nation. As Charles Krauthammer notes, this posits a role for public policy that was not so startling thirty years ago, but signals a real departure today. Liberal policy makers have thrown up their hands at the problem of family break-up, some embracing it rather than seeking to ameliorate its accompanying social pathologies. Others, such as columnist Richard Cohen, raise the white flag when confronted with illegitimacy, suggesting that all women on welfare have Norplant implanted under their skin to prevent them from bearing more children. Some have accused those concerned about intact families with wanting to turn back the clock to a Disney-like nostalgia-land of stay-at-home moms, tract houses in the suburbs, and Ward Cleavers reading the afternoon paper in overstuffed easy chairs. "The real deviants of society stand unmasked," notes Krauthammer. "Who are they? Not Bonnie and Clyde, but Ozzie and Harriet."[24]

The entire debate has often degenerated into a war of television sitcoms: *Leave It to Beaver* versus *Murphy Brown*. That is until recently, when Barbara Dafoe Whitehead grabbed headlines with her pathbreaking cover story in *The Atlantic* magazine, provocatively titled, "Dan Quayle Was Right." Marshalling mountains of studies from the social sciences, Whitehead argued that, quite apart from the politics of "family values," the disintegration of nuclear families spells trouble for children. "After decades of public dispute about so-called family diversity," she wrote, "the evidence from social science research is coming in: The dissolution of two-parent families, though it may benefit the adults involved, is harmful to many children, and dramatically undermines our society."[25]

Margaret Mead put it more succinctly in 1978 when she told a Senate committee, "As the family goes, so goes the nation." The debate about the desirability of two-parent families is over. It is time to do something constructive to promote and protect them, a task in which government should play a positive role. To this end, we should enact laws that encourage stable monogamous marriages, provide incentives for childbearing within marriage, discourage both abortion and bearing children out of wedlock, and assist parents in gaining both the resources and time necessary to meet the emotional and financial needs of their children.

Specific solutions to the problem of family break-up will be discussed in later chapters. But if Margaret Mead was right, then our politics and our culture should have declined in recent years as the family disintegrated. Before we turn to solutions, therefore, let us look at politics, media, and the culture.

CHAPTER SEVEN

Adventures in Porkland:
The End of Politics as Usual

By THE TIME you finish reading this sentence, the federal government will have gone another $40,000 in debt. Another drop of red ink has fallen into a sea of debt that is widening at a rate of $13,000 a second, $47 million an hour, $1 billion a day. The day of reckoning is drawing near. The national debt currently stands at $4.5 trillion — $17,000 for every man, woman, and child in America — and, if current trends continue, it will roar out of control to more than $13 trillion by the end of the decade.[1]

"We may consider each generation as a distinct nation, with a right by the will of its majority to bind themselves [in debt], but none to bind the succeeding generation," wrote Thomas Jefferson. What was the basis of this principle? The law of God, answered Jefferson. "The soil is the gift of God to the living, as much as it had been to the deceased generation; and the laws of nature impose no obligation on them to pay this debt." Jefferson's maxim addresses why religious conservatives are concerned about government waste and skyrocketing debt. Elsewhere, he urged, "Government should be small, taxes invisible and the public debt paid." Simply put, religious conservatives oppose deficit spending for the same reason Jefferson did. It not only makes bad economic sense, but it is immoral as well.[2]

As columnist George Will has presciently observed, deficits are part of a tax-and-spend political style. The political class taxes, borrows, spends, and elects. By delivering a dollar's worth of government for only eighty cents in taxes, it guarantees its reelection in perpetuity. Like an alcoholic who passes the tab of his drinking binge on to his children, career politicians buy victory at the ballot box by laying the true cost of their spending onto subsequent generations. Ending their profligate cycle of debt would transform our nation's political culture more than almost any other single undertaking under consideration.

The portion that federal taxes and revenues consume of our gross national product—all of the goods and services produced by Americans—has grown exponentially during the twentieth century. In 1938, at the peak of the New Deal, Franklin D. Roosevelt presided over a government with 650,000 employees and spending that accounted for only 7.7 percent of the GNP. Many condemned this level of government as "socialistic," and one critic warned, "There will be wiped out all of the liberties for which the Anglo-Saxon race has struggled for a thousand years." Today, under "New Democrat" Bill Clinton, the federal government has 2.4 million employees and accounts for 24 percent of the GNP. We spend an additional 14 percent of GNP on state and local government. If current trends continue, federal spending will account for an astonishing 42 percent of the GNP by the end of this decade.[3]

To support government, the American people spend much of the year working for Uncle Sam. The Tax Foundation illustrates the tax burden with its annual declaration of "Tax Freedom Day," the theoretical day on which the average American has earned enough money to pay his taxes. In 1993, Tax Freedom Day fell on May 7. New York taxpayers waited the longest for their freedom, May 22. Only in South Dakota were taxpayers actually freed on April 15.

Government, like a parasite sucking the life out of its victim, has now grown so large that it threatens to suffocate the economy. Since 1950, spending for state, local, and federal government (adjusted for inflation) has risen 600 percent. For the first time in the history of Western civilization, more people are now employed by government in the United States (18.7 million) than by all manufacturing enterprises combined (18.1 million). There are twelve times as many people working in government than tilling the soil on every farm in America. One in five workers in the nation is employed by federal, state, or local government.[4]

The cause of runaway debt is the loss of a "pay-as-you-go" ethic that informed fiscal policy from America's founding until the 1960s. In this sense, the deficit is not the real problem; it is a symptom of a much deeper problem plaguing our society. We no longer live according to what God provides. It no longer bothers us to pile up debt we can never repay and dump it in the laps of the next generation.[5]

What does the government do with all this money? According to studies by Citizens Against Government Waste, a watchdog group founded by Peter Grace, and by gadfly federal fussbudget Martin Gross, billions are wasted on pork and waste. They have uncovered some of the most outrageous examples:

- $119 million spent on periodicals—just for the Pentagon. This figure includes subscriptions for pornographic magazines that are made available at military installations around the world. One would think that U.S. military personnel would be able to purchase pornography with their own dime rather than taxpayer funds.

- $8 million for the Department of Defense to promote the 1994 World Cup soccer tournament and the 1996 Summer Olympics.

- $11 million for a memorial to Franklin Delano Roosevelt, which originally was supposed to be paid for with private funds. FDR said before he died that he did not want a memorial. Neither his personal wishes nor the existence of a memorial to FDR at the Little White House in Warm Springs, Georgia, dissuaded Congress from this wasteful spending.

- A $2.4 million, 200-space parking garage at a federal office in Burlington, Iowa. There are eighteen federal employees at the facility.[6]

This catalogue of pork is enough to make the average person's blood boil. In recent years the federal government has spent $107,000 to study the sex life of the Japanese quail, $19 million to investigate gas emissions from cow flatulence, $57,000 for gold-embossed playing cards on Air Force One, and $150,000 for a study of the Hatfield-McCoy feud.[7]

Ronald Reagan once quipped, "Balancing the budget is a little like protecting your virtue: You just have to learn to say no." Unfortunately, few members of Congress know how to say no, and constituents repeatedly reelect representatives who effectively "bring home the bacon." Although in 1994 Congress barely defeated President Clinton's pork-laden "economic stimulus package"—which included spending for projects ranging from swimming pools in Puerto Rico to jogging tracks in Indiana—the truth is that much of the most shocking waste never sees the light of day.[8]

Many members of Congress do not even read the budget and have no idea what it contains. In 1991, for instance, members of the House of Representatives received the thousand-page, $151 billion highway bill just one hour before they passed it 372–47. No one had even read the bill. In 1992 the House passed a $270 billion appropriation for the Pentagon after just fifteen minutes of floor debate. Little wonder that the budget reads like a catalogue from the little shop of horrors. Among the worst abuses:

- $6.4 million for an Idaho ski resort.

- $100 million annually to store enough helium to last until the 22d century. This is allegedly for national security reasons, although we already have enough helium to last for years.

- $500,000 to build a replica of the Great Pyramid in Egypt, Indiana.

- $219,000 to teach college students how to watch television.

- $1 million to preserve a New Jersey sewer as a historic monument.

- $163 million for the new National Biological Survey, an organization that would take an inventory of all the nation's plant and animal species. This ecological purpose would include the right to inspect any person's land to determine the existence of endangered species—a clear violation of property rights.[9]

Bureaucratic Nightmare

These and other expenditures are spread throughout a Byzantine bureaucracy that is remarkable for its inefficiency. The federal Department of Education has 5,500 employees and a budget of $33 billion, but it educates not a single student. Job training functions cost $17 billion, spread out over 152 programs operating out of forty-seven agencies and four cabinet departments. Thirteen agencies spend $4.7 billion on native American affairs, showering red tape and largesse on a population of only one million people still residing on Indian reservations, most of whom live in abject poverty. Much of the money is wasted on overhead and "social service" bureaucracies serving the reservations, while little ends up in the hands of the Indians themselves. The Department of Agriculture embodies the nineteenth-century mindset that afflicts the bureaucracy. It began in 1862 when 60 percent of Americans worked on farms, yet the entire department employed only nine people. Today only 3 percent of the population works on farms, but the Department of Agriculture has a $62.7 billion budget and 150,000 employees spread out over 11,000 field offices.[10]

The politicians on Capitol Hill feed on a steady diet of perks and privileges. One of their favorite pastimes is congressional junkets. In August 1992, for example, four members of Congress and twenty-five aides and spouses hopscotched across China, Thailand, and Japan. The total cost to taxpayers came to $550,000. The purpose of the trip? *Studying infrastructure.* This investigation took the congressional party on a sightseeing tour of the Great Wall of China and a day trip to a panda preserve. The meal tab alone ran to $68,000. A similar twenty-three-person expedition by members of the House Public Works Committee and their spouses in 1993 featured a ten-day itinerary with visits to Russia, Germany, and France. They flew in the comfort of an Air Force C-137 transport jet that costs $7,915 an hour to operate.[11]

Private citizens, in sharp contrast, are billy-clubbed into submission by overbearing federal regulators. Imagine combining the worst of Clint Eastwood and Barney Fife, and you have the personality profile of a growing army of government enforcers. One man in Virginia was recently sentenced to prison for scattering soil around on his lawn. His crime? He had violated a federal "wetlands" law. In 1991 Food and Drug Administration officials, accompanied by armed U.S. Marshals, seized a warehouse full of frozen orange juice. It posed no health hazard. The producer had committed the unpardonable offense of using the word "fresh" in a brand name. Meanwhile, it takes more than ten years for a new drug to clear FDA regulatory hurdles.[12]

.   .   .

The Adventures of Robin Hood

One of the programs that best demonstrates how the federal government has become a reverse Robin Hood is its lavish grants to the Public Broadcasting System. As budget-watcher Eric Felten concludes, "If ever a federal beneficiary qualified as a welfare queen, it is public broadcasting." Federal subsidies for PBS cost taxpayers more than $350 million per year, despite the fact that many of the recipients are wealthy beyond belief. The producers of *Sesame Street*, the Children's Television Workshop, reap more than $100 million *every year* in product licensing for Big Bird dolls and other merchandise. Their chief executive officer earns $647,000 a year in salary and benefits. A rate card sent out by Washington PBS affiliate WETA in 1992 noted the average net worth of contributors to the station was $627,000; one in eight was a millionaire; one in seven owned a wine cellar; and one in three had been to Europe within the past three years.

Those who operate public television stations are often as wealthy as their sponsors. In 1990 the executive producer for WNET, the PBS station in New York city, earned salary and benefits totaling $400,000. The taxpayers, meanwhile, forked over $30 million to WNET in 1989 alone. Adding insult to injury, public television and radio programming, apart from popular and profitable programs like *Sesame Street* and the *MacNeil-Lehrer News Hour*, sometimes veers off into the bizarre. During the Los Angeles riots in 1992, public radio station KPFK broadcast an anti-Semitic harangue by Steve Cokeley, a deputy to Louis Farrakhan, who once accused Jewish physicians of injecting blacks with the AIDS virus. Cokeley boasted that "many people from around the country are making a surprise visit to Los Angeles" to lead a "second round" of rioting and looting.[13]

These budget horror stories have become so much a part of modern political folklore that they hardly raise eyebrows. There is some truth to Bismarck's famous saying that there are two things one never wants to see being made: sausage and laws. Pork-barrel spending combines the worst of both. Certainly there is nothing new about the legislative practices of log-rolling, horse-trading, and back-scratching. They are as old as government itself.

What is new—and disturbing—is the tendency of government to punish those activities we value as a society while subsidizing social pathologies and destructive behavior of every kind. Planning to abandon your wife and children? Not to worry: the government will take care of them with a monthly subsidy. Getting a divorce? The federal government will pay for it. Attacking religion or distributing obscene material? Your federal grant application has been approved. Abusing drugs or alcohol? The government will send you a check every month, no questions asked. Take the values handed down through the centuries by the best traditions of Western civilization, flip them upside-down, and you have federal policy towards the family.

Representative Henry Hyde, one of the most respected members of the House of Representatives, concludes that government contributes to "the downward spiral of family life in this nation." He adds: "Let me state the obvious: The only reason there is a pro-family movement in this country is that there has long been an anti-family movement. It's never called that, but there it is." Government policies purposefully and deliberately "transfer resources from what works—the two-parent family—to what doesn't. Success must subsidize failure, not until failure succeeds, but until success fails."[14]

Welfare discourages work, savings, personal responsibility, and family formation. It subsidizes divorce, abandonment, illegitimacy, and joblessness. Beneficiaries are usually better off on welfare than if they earned an honest day's wage. Thomas G. West of the Claremont Institute has documented the economic disincentives of the existing welfare system by calculating the benefits available to a welfare mother with two children in California: a Section 8 housing voucher, AFDC, food stamps, and Medicaid coverage. The tax-free cash value of these benefits totals $1,817 per month, or $21,804 a year. (And this figure does not even account for the overhead of administration.) That is more than *twice* what the same person would earn from an entry-level job after paying federal and state taxes.[15]

One of the most egregious examples of government's bias against the two-parent family is the Legal Services Corporation, established in 1974 to look out for the legal rights of the poor. Today it bears little resemblance to its original mission. The LSC has become a $400 million-a-year army of 4,500 attorneys and 2,000 paralegals pursuing an extremist political agenda paid for with tax dollars. (President Clinton has proposed increasing the LSC budget to $500 million in his 1995 budget.) At one Legal Services Corporation-sponsored political training seminar, an instructor exclaimed that "capitalism is . . . a . . . power which bankrupts cities, which destroys jobs, which creates poverty and economic chaos." He advocated waging a full-scale "anticorporate campaign." Liberal advocacy attorneys have also engaged in lobbying and suing the government—and sent the taxpayers the bill. Registered lobbyists employed by the LSC have lobbied against cutting income taxes in California, vowed to "shove rent control down the throat" of the Arizona legislature, and distributed leaflets for local liberal candidates in Georgia.[16]

In 1990 the Legal Services Corporation spent taxpayer funds to pay for 210,000 divorces—at an estimated cost to taxpayers of $50 million. Indeed, the LSC has actively pursued litigation promoting abortion, welfare, and divorce while discouraging the maintenance of two-parent families. The average woman's income declines 73 percent within the first year of a divorce. Yet government has a policy of no-fault, taxpayer-funded divorce among those most vulnerable to its harsh economic impact. The median income for two-parent families in 1991 was $40,137. For divorced mothers, it was only $16,156. Thus does a government agency designed to ameliorate poverty end up fostering it by paying for divorce actions.[17]

Dollars for Indecency

The same federal government that claims to oppose drug and alcohol abuse is subsidizing it. In 1993 the federal government paid 250,000 drug addicts and alcoholics a total of $1.4 billion in Social Security disability benefits. Federal regulations require that these beneficiaries receive treatment as a condition of receiving an average of $434 a month in tax dollars. But according to a study by the General Accounting Office, the congressional watchdog agency, 172,000 were not in treatment or subject to any payment restrictions. Some had their disability checks sent directly to bars or liquor stores where they ran up lavish drinking tabs. The "compassionate" welfare state has bankrolled their destructive habits. According to Bob Cote, director of a Denver homeless shelter, disability payments are "helping people commit suicide on the installment plan." He adds: "Show me a government handout, and I'll show you something that encourages irresponsibility."[18]

One California alcoholic received a lump sum payment from the Social Security Administration of $49,000. That is more than the average family of four in America earns in a year. Some recipients used the cash to finance drinking binges, expensive narcotics habits, even drug dealing. Incredibly, a federal appeals court ruled in February 1994 that a heroin addict who dealt drugs on the side could not be denied benefits because of his illegal activity. The recipient, the court ruled, was still "disabled" and unable to work. Meanwhile, the Clinton administration has slashed funding for the war on drugs, reducing the size of the drug czar's office from 146 employees under George Bush to only 25. Surgeon General Joycelyn Elders went even further, claiming that "we would markedly reduce our crime rate if drugs were legalized."[19]

The government also provides funding for obscenity and attacks on religion through the National Endowment for the Arts. The NEA has been embroiled in controversy for years, primarily because of its tendency to fund programs that attack the family and ridicule the religious beliefs of Americans.

The Whitney Museum of Art in New York received $302,000 between 1990 and 1992 from the NEA. A portion of this grant supported an exhibit called "Abject Art: Repulsion and Desire," which a catalogue described as a "body of work which incorporates or suggests abject materials such as dirt, hair, excrement, dead animals, menstrual blood and rotting food."[20] In 1993 artists in San Diego used $4,500 in grant money from the NEA to pass out $10 bills to illegal aliens along the Mexican border. The exhibit's purpose? To "expand the parameters of the immigration debate," according to organizers.[21]

Critics respond that such grants represent only a fraction of the NEA's total budget. They miss the point. Even one dollar of taxpayer funds spent to attack someone's religion is unacceptable. If the NEA funded an anti-Semitic play staged by the Ku Klux Klan, the size of the subsidy would be irrelevant. Cries of censorship are equally specious. What artists do on their own time with their own dime is no business of the taxpayer. Let any artist create any image and exhibit it anywhere, any time, no matter how objectionable. But no taxpayer should be forced to subsidize attacks on his faith. As Thomas Jefferson once said, "To compel a man to furnish contributions of money for the propagation of opinions which he disbelieves and abhors is sinful and tyrannical."[22]

The federal Centers for Disease Control launched a new advertising campaign in January, 1994, allegedly designed to help prevent the spread of AIDS. The purpose of the $1 million media campaign was to heighten awareness of the disease among young people and encourage safe sex, including the use of condoms. Curiously, the CDC chose as its spokesman a certain Tony Keidis, star of the rock group Red Hot Chili Peppers. The text of one radio ad paid for with tax dollars read:

> I'm Anthony Keidis of the Red Hot Chili Peppers. I've been naked on stage. I've been naked on magazine covers. I was born naked, and of course, I'm naked when I have sex. But now I'm on the radio. So I might as well get naked again. There, I'm naked, see? And what I have here is a condom. A latex condom. I wear one whenever I have sex. Every time. Look, they're very easy to open. And best of all, they stop the spread of HIV. Now I'm naked. With a condom.[23]

The CDC apparently failed to conduct even the most routine background check on Mr. Keidis. Had they done so, they would have discovered that he was convicted of lewd and indecent exposure for attempting to force himself on a female member of the audience at a rock concert in Virginia in 1989. After a scandal erupted over Mr. Keidis's less-than-pristine past, the CDC pulled his spot, but the rest of the ad campaign continued. Washington has not demonstrated a penchant for producing role models of late. But whether or not Mr. Keidis was an appropriate role model is almost beside the point. The more disturbing question is: why does the federal government take the tax dollars of hard-working parents and use them to encourage high-risk behavior among their children?

The government indirectly subsidizes unhealthy and harmful behavior in many ways. Planned Parenthood is the nation's largest abortion provider, which it describes in classic Orwellian-speak as "comprehensive reproductive and complementary health services." In 1990 it received 36 percent of its $368 million budget from government contracts and grants. Through the Title X program, created in 1970 to provide pregnancy counseling to poor women, over $158 million is doled out to its local affiliates to provide abortion counseling and referrals. Planned Parenthood supports abortion-on-demand and federal funding of contraception, and advocates explicit sex-education. The Clinton administration, according to President Pamela Miraldo, "reflects the values of Planned Parenthood. We want to capitalize on that and seize the momentum to carve out a broader social agenda. . . ."[24]

Government Divorced from Reality

How have the governing elite managed to so completely divorce themselves from America's mainstream?

Part of the answer is Washington's permanent bureaucracy. "Washington moves like a mountain of jelly: you touch it or you carve away in one spot and it just seems to ooze back," according to William Niskanen, who served on President Reagan's Council of Economic Advisors.[25] Failed welfare and family programs have "oozed" right back to the status quo after determined efforts by conservative presidents or members of Congress who made modest changes at the margins for a few years. The media who cover the iron triangles also have an implicit interest in expanding the federal domain: Big government increases the importance of journalistic "beats." Ronald Reagan once observed, "A federal program is the closest thing we may ever have to eternal life on this earth." That truism has had enormous consequences for the two-parent family and the values that sustain it.

Washington has lost touch with the values of middle America. The career politicians who craft our laws and the bureaucrats who administer them are no longer responsive to the will of the people. The American public intuitively understands that government does not work, that its pork-laden indebtedness threatens the prosperity of the economy, and that its policies result in the withering, rather than the survival, of the family as the central institution of the social order.

We need more than new elections; we need a new politics. The old paradigms must be shattered and the old politics must go. A new politics—indeed an antipolitics—is being born, the broad outlines of which are only now coming into full relief. Its results will change the way we govern ourselves in a way more dramatic than anything since the New Deal.

The party machines have failed, giving us reelection rates for members of Congress that are higher than the old Soviet Politburo (in 1992, despite all the talk of "change," 93 percent of House members who ran for reelection won). They have also perpetuated the politics of pork and failed to check runaway spending. Not surprisingly, public support for parties has declined—suggesting the first tremors of a new politics in which the parties' role will likely be smaller.

The Decline of Political Parties

The beginning of the end of politics as usual may be seen in the relative weakness of America's two party system. This phenomenon could be seen in 1994 in microcosm during the U.S. Senate race in Virginia, the most-watched statewide race in the nation. The Republican party, its nominating process geared towards grassroots conservatives, chose Oliver North as its Senate nominee. The Democrats renominated incumbent Senator Chuck Robb. In years past, that would have been the end of it. But party loyalty carries little weight today. Former Governor Doug Wilder launched a petition drive to get on the ballot as an independent—jeopardizing Robb's hopes for reelection by taking more than half of the black vote. Republican Senator John Warner, meanwhile, publicly disavowed North, refusing to support his own party's nominee, and former state attorney general Marshall Coleman bolted the GOP to enter the campaign. At this writing, the results of the Virginia Senate race are anything but clear. But what is obvious is that party loyalty no longer carries the weight it once did for either voters or officeholders.

For most of the past half-century, institutions largely in the hands of the Left have held sway over the culture: the political party machines,

Hollywood, the universities, the labor unions, big business, the major foundations, the large publishing houses, and the media. (Those not specifically relating to politics are dealt with in the next chapter.) Until the power of these hierarchical, bureaucratic institutions is challenged, it will be impossible for conservatives to get their message out. There is growing evidence that these institutions are in long-term, precipitous decline. Shifting demographics and technological changes are weakening their grip on the culture, paving the way for a new participatory, citizen-oriented politics.

Our country's founders never envisioned a significant role for political parties. Indeed, they viewed parties as evil factions that endangered the public good and undermined what they called republican virtue: self-sacrifice, moderation, patriotism, and piety. Alexander Hamilton argued in *The Federalist Papers*: "Complaints are everywhere heard . . . that our governments are too unstable; that the public good is disregarded in the conflicts of rival parties; and that measures are too often decided, not according to the rules of justice," but based on "the superior force" of an "over-bearing majority."[26]

In his Farewell Address in 1796, George Washington warned, "It [the political party] agitates the Community with ill-founded jealousies and false alarms, kindles the animosity of one part against another, foments occasional riot and insurrection." He added that "party passion" would ultimately destroy democracy: "A fire not to be quenched; it demands a uniform vigilance to prevent its bursting into a flame, lest instead of warming it should consume." It is ironic that the institution that has most influenced the voting decisions of Americans over the two centuries is never even mentioned in the U.S. Constitution: the political party.[27]

Despite the best efforts of the founders to preserve the unity and patriotic spirit of the American Revolution, the party system had emerged by 1820. The extension of the electorate, the slavery controversy, and westward expansion all divided the body politic. Andrew Jackson, the dominant figure of the early nineteenth century, symbolized the egalitarian political style of the nascent Democratic party, which drove its loyalists to the polls with campaign songs, mass meetings, rallies, and torchlit parades. The modern functions of the party began to take shape.

The anti-Masonic party held the first presidential nominating convention in 1832, and the Democrats followed suit in 1836. By 1840 the modern two-party system as we know it had emerged: patronage, congressional caucuses, quadrennial presidential nominating conventions, local machinery, candidate recruitment, and get-out-the-vote efforts. They were, in fact, the first modern political parties in the history of the Western world, and they changed forever the way Americans chose their elected officials.[28]

The rise of the political party corresponded with a tidal wave of immigration beginning in the 1840s. Driven from the soil by a devastating potato famine and cruel absentee landowners, nearly two million Irish immigrated to the United States between 1840 and 1860. These Irish immigrants—the largest influx of Roman Catholics ever into America's mostly homogenous Protestant society—swarmed into big cities like Boston and New York, facing blatant job discrimination and religious prejudice, injustices that were softened by their involvement in political parties.[29]

Among the newcomers was a young cooper-cum-farmer named Patrick Kennedy, who died just nine years after arriving in Boston in 1849. His son Patrick Joseph became a successful saloon keeper and liquor importer, a loyal Democrat, and a dedicated precinct worker. He rose through the ranks of Boston's Democratic party machine to become a state senator and a powerful ward boss, dispensing patronage positions like candy to the hardest working troops in his army of precinct captains. His eldest son Joseph, who often accompanied his father as he made the political rounds of his ward, later became (at age twenty-five) the youngest bank president in the nation, a national player in the Democratic party, and the patriarch of the Kennedy political dynasty.[30]

After the Civil War, the Irish were joined by a flood of immigrants from southern and eastern Europe: Italians, Poles, Hungarians, Latvians, and Czechs. They flowed into the teeming tenement houses and immigrant ghettos of the eastern seaboard, providing cheap labor for the factories and cheap votes for the city machines. Most spoke little English. The big city machines not only were the vehicle of political socialization for these wide-eyed newcomers, but they performed vital social functions as well. Political bosses found jobs for the new arrivals, lined up housing, provided financial assistance when family members fell ill, steered them to a church or synagogue—and made sure they were registered to vote. In return, they required only political loyalty and service to the party.[31]

The party bosses ruled with an iron fist until well into the twentieth century. Woodrow Wilson was elected governor of New Jersey in 1910 after being anointed by James "Sugar Jim" Smith, the Democratic party boss of the state. Warren G. Harding rose to political prominence in Ohio with the backing of Cincinnati's Republican party machine, led by Joseph Benson Foraker and "Boss" George Cox. He was chosen for the Republican nomination for president in 1920 in the famed smoke-filled room of Chicago's Blackstone Hotel, where party leaders wheeled and dealed until finally settling on Harding in the wee hours of the morning. Harry S. Truman was elected county judge in 1922 and U.S. Senator in 1934 as the hand-picked candidate of the powerful and corrupt Pendergast machine in Kansas City. The Daley machine in Chicago delivered (some allege fraudulently) the heavily Democratic precincts that gave John F. Kennedy the narrowest of victories in Illinois in 1960, and thus the White House.[32]

But the days of the party bosses were numbered. The direct presidential primary took control of candidate selection out of the smoke-filled rooms and into the voting booth, crafting an expensive, arduous, and brutal primary season in which tens of millions of voters participated. Wisconsin held the first presidential primary in 1904. In 1960 sixteen states held presidential primaries that chose about one-fourth of the delegates; by 1980, the number had risen to thirty-two primaries choosing three-quarters of the delegates. Barry Goldwater was one of the first presidential candidates to bypass party leaders by surviving off a grassroots network of conservative activists and direct mail contributors. His victory over Nelson Rockefeller in the California primary in 1964 sealed his nomination and signaled the twilight of the Dewey-Scranton-Rockefeller wing in the Republican party. By 1972 George McGovern secured the Democratic nomination for president without the support of a single party boss, winning a string of primaries with a ragtag army of antiwar protesters and New Left activists. At the Democratic National Convention in Miami Beach, McGovern organizers cheered as Mayor

Richard Daley of Chicago was expelled from the convention hall. A new politics was born.

In 1976 Congress hammered another nail into the coffin of the party bosses by limiting contributions to only $1,000 per individual and greatly restricting the amount of funds party committees could contribute to candidates. Money is the mother's milk of politics. When campaign finance reform cut off the financial umbilical cord that connected candidates to political parties, it greatly reduced their influence over those seeking elected office.

Even more devastating to the party bosses than political reform has been the rise of television. It has transformed electoral politics in two important ways. First, television has made it possible for candidates to reach voters directly without resorting to the party bosses as intermediaries. Second, the high cost and increased political sophistication required by television has fueled the rise of America's new elite political class: the consultants. The tasks once performed by party leaders are now in the hands of high-priced gunslingers whose specialized skills are essential to winning campaigns in the age of television and computers: pollsters, media consultants, opposition researchers, and direct mail fundraisers. Today the political consultants are far more important than party officials and often more famous than the candidates who hire them: the late Lee Atwater, Ed Rollins, James Carville, Paul Begala, and Roger Ailes. They are the bosses of the new politics.

No one symbolizes the party machine as historic relic more than Representative Dan Rostenkowski of Chicago, the gruff and formidable chairman of the powerful House Ways and Means Committee. Rostenkowski, who was indicted on seventeen felony counts in 1994 for his involvement in the House Post Office scandal, is the last, gasping embodiment of the big-city machine. He learned politics at the feet of his father, who was a ward captain in Chicago's heavily Polish-American 32nd ward. Danny assumed his father's post as ward boss in 1956 and retained it for three decades after he came to Washington. During that period, Rostenkowski has mastered politics as practiced by the Daley machine: take care of your own, stick it to your enemies, look out for the little guy, vote early and often.

Tapped by Richard Daley for the Illinois legislature in 1952 and Congress in 1959, he became known early in his career as "Dick Daley's errand boy" on Capitol Hill. Feared as one of the most powerful men in Congress, Rostenkowski until recently seemed destined to spend the rest of his life as chairman of the Ways and Means Committee. But when the House Post Office scandal erupted, he was indicted on charges that included embezzlement and hiring phantom employees. Rostenkowski faced the prospect of the scandalous end of a forty-year political career—all for practicing the very style of politics that he and other machine politicians once took for granted.[33]

As stars like Rostenkowski set, the parties have become almost marginalized. The Perot movement signifies this reality most dramatically. Voters are so disenchanted with the two political parties that 63 percent of Americans told a Time/CNN poll in 1992 that they favored "a third political party that would run candidates for president, Congress, and state offices against the Democratic and Republican candidates." But this disenchantment predates Perot. Indeed, it has been building for decades. In 1944 only 18 percent of Americans called themselves independents. By the late 1960s, 30 percent of the electorate identified themselves as independents. An exhaustive Times-Mirror survey conducted in July 1992 showed that upwards of 40 percent of the electorate do not identify with the two major political parties. For more than four decades, the lifeblood of party loyalty has been bleeding out of an increasingly cynical and distrustful electorate.[34]

The hard-shell Perot vote is approximately 15 percent, roughly equivalent to the George Wallace vote in 1968. The committed independents (those who identify with neither Perot nor the parties) make up another 15 percent of voters. A confluence of these disaffected voters could create a "third force" in the electorate by 1996 or sooner, either in the form of a political party or as an independent citizen organization that rivals the Democrats and Republicans. This is particularly likely if Bill Clinton faces a tough primary challenge in 1996 from the Left, or if the Republicans jettison their pro-life stand, thus losing the millions of evangelical and Roman Catholic voters who have come into the Republican fold since 1980. The old adage that disaffected voters have "nowhere else to go" no longer applies. In today's volatile political environment, voters shunned by the existing institutions will flock to new vehicles.

The institutional weakness of the political parties exacerbates their tenuous position. On average, 40 percent of America's 175,000 precincts have no Republican or Democratic precinct captain. At a national level, the parties raise huge sums of money but rarely translate that financial clout into real impact. The Democratic National Committee has failed so miserably to mobilize grassroots support for President Clinton's domestic policy initiatives that its chairman, David Wilhelm, has been forced to overhaul the staff several times, firing the executive director and hiring a new finance chairman. Between 1983 and 1992, the three national Republican party committees raised and spent a total of $1 billion dollars. What did all this money buy? A loss of sixteen House seats and nine Senate seats.[35]

The 1992 election underscored the weakness of the parties. The Republican convention in Houston became a campaign issue after the media seized upon the presence of evangelical Christians, who the *Washington Post* found comprised 42 percent of the delegates. The media pilloried the Republicans for allowing people of faith to play such a large role and argued that their participation turned off large numbers of voters in November. But that is revisionist history. The Houston convention lifted George Bush from trailing Clinton by twenty-one points in the polls to within five points of victory. Most today understand that what cost Bush the election was not four days in Houston but the four years preceding the convention. The media missed the larger point: the rise of religious conservatives as a permanent fixture in American politics. Had they been reporting all along on the movement of people of faith into positions of responsibility within the GOP, they would not have been surprised when they showed up in such large numbers in Houston.[36]

On the Democratic side, Bill Clinton's campaign exemplified the new candidate-crafted, consultant-driven politics of the modern era. He called himself a "New Democrat," a calculated slap in the face at the liberal constituencies that had dominated the Democratic party since the early 1970s. He angered Jesse Jackson with his celebrated

rebuke of the rap singer "Sister Souljah" at a Rainbow Coalition meeting, a masterful execution of what Clinton aides called"counter-
scheduling," in which the candidate delivered a contrary message before
a traditionally Democratic audience. As the Governor of a right-to-work
state, his relationship with the labor unions was uneasy at best. Bill
Clinton's election was a personal victory, not a party victory. He was the
first president since John F. Kennedy to win the White House while his
party lost seats (a total of ten) in the House of Representatives.[37]

Political parties are not in danger of extinction. There are too many
cultural and historical forces insuring their survival. But the functions
they perform are vestiges of their former power. The job of mobilizing
voters and getting them to the polls is no longer performed by parties
but by ideological interest groups such as pro-life organizations, parochial and home school associations, teachers unions, black churches, or
the National Rifle Association. The rise of the modern welfare state has
obliterated the party's social function in providing charity and jobs to the
needy. Civil service has destroyed the ability of parties to reward loyalists with patronage.

Campaign finance reform has greatly restricted the ability of parties
to finance (and thus control) candidates, giving rise to a plethora of political action committees, interest groups, and "soft money" organizations that contact voters with corporate dollars. The average winning
congressional candidate in 1992 spent around $400,000. The national
party congressional committees are prohibited from giving them more
than $60,000 of that total. This financial reality, combined with grow-
ing voter sophistication and cynicism, suggests a continued decline in
the role and influence of political parties.[38]

The Politics of Pork

The organizational weakness of the two parties provides a window of opportunity for genuine reform to bubble up from the grassroots. Declines
in party loyalty reflect a general disenchantment with business as usual
and the politics of pork. Pork distracts the public from the inevitable day
of reckoning that will come when the debt bomb finally explodes.

Ladeled into districts like lard, it keeps members of Congress reelected and their constituents oblivious to the real price of profligacy. That is why one of the most coveted committee assignments on Capitol Hill is serving as one of the 63 members of the House Public Works and Transportation committee, which oversees about $50 billion in public works spending each year. Every road, bridge, building, or other federal construction project in the nation must pass through the gauntlet of this committee before it can be funded. Committee members regularly earmark huge spending projects for their home districts without hearings or debate. Representative James Traficant, D-Ohio, chairman of the Public Buildings Subcommittee, met for just seven minutes with ranking Republican John Duncan, Jr., of Tennessee before approving $763 million for a new courthouse in Traficant's Youngstown-area district and another courthouse in Scranton, Pennsylvania.[39]

These and other episodes underscore that the politics of pork are not limited to one party or the other. The entire system is biased towards spending. Consider the House appropriations committee. Its thirteen subcommittee chairmen preside over their respective domains with such unquestioned authority that they are known collectively as the "house of cardinals." No matter how many new members of different parties the voters elect, the system remains the same. Little wonder that voter anger is beginning to explode, shaking the institution of Congress and portending the end of politics as usual.

The future of American politics will likely feature a balkanized landscape in which voters remain nominally loyal to one of the two political parties but reserve their most fervent energy for a plethora of advocacy groups. Property rights, term limits, anti-tax, environmental, consumer, pro-life or pro-choice, Jewish and Christian citizen movements comprise the wave of tomorrow. Whatever separates them, they are united in their disdain for the politics of pork and the gridlock caused by partisan bickering. They want change, and they are prepared to go outside the existing political structures to achieve it.

A decade from now, the old dichotomies of Republican and Democrat, liberal and conservative will be less relevant, and a new populist politics will take their place. That populist future is not only about political change, but about cultural change as well. That fascinating story is next.

CHAPTER EIGHT

A Jurassic Jungle:
The Dinosaurs of Business, Labor,
and the Media

THE END of business as usual is about more than just political upheaval. The winds of change are howling across the American cultural landscape, uprooting old institutions that have controlled the
culture and transforming how we live. Among the most important institutions affected by this change are business, organized labor, and the
media.

For more than a century, business tycoons have personified the
American success story. From Carnegie and Rockefeller down to
modern-day figures like Lee Iacocca and Donald Trump, these risktakers
have captured the popular imagination. Even Ross Perot's appeal in 1992
was based in part on this phenomenon. But he and others represent a dying breed. One need only look at the Trump financial empire today to
see the problems that plague American business. Trump's fortune
crumbled when banks called in high-interest loans that financed his far-
flung empire. Although he avoided bankruptcy, Trump was forced to sell
off profitable assets, unload his yacht and other expensive playthings,
and cut back on his free-spending ways.

Organized labor has experienced similar trauma. Once the kingpins
of the Democratic party, the unions lost the vote over the North American Free Trade Agreement in 1993 by a wide margin. Hoping to make
examples of those who had crossed them, the unions recruited candidates in 1994 to challenge pro-NAFTA members of Congress in Democratic primaries. This strategy backfired. In May 1994 Ohio Democrat
David Mann, a freshman congressman who had voted for NAFTA, beat

back a tough challenge from a labor-backed opponent, winning by a margin of 50 to 48 percent. "Organized labor flexed its muscles but couldn't topple Mann," concluded one observer.[1]

In late 1992 I had a conversation with a reporter for *Time* magazine who was then working on a story about religious conservatives. I asked him about *Time*'s major design overhaul, which included the addition of a section titled "The Week" that summed up the previous week's news in a few pages. Why the format change? The reporter responded that reader surveys had shown that few subscribers were actually reading the magazine. The editors hoped that by summarizing the news in one or two-paragraph bites, they could hold the reader's attention. Who would have ever thought that one of the nation's leading magazines would find itself imitating television in order to survive?

Big Business

For most of America's history, the business world has been infatuated with bigness. The biggest factories, the largest annual revenues, the most employees, the biggest market share—success was bigness, period. Much of this obsession began with the rise of big business during the late-nineteenth century, when captains of industry steered ships of commerce to enormous profits. The entrepreneurs that historian Daniel Boorstin has called the Great Go-Getters—Andrew Carnegie, Henry Ford, John D. Rockefeller and J.P. Morgan—took the centuries-old production of the lone artisan, brought it under a single roof, beat down costs through mass production, and smashed competitors with large economies of scale. The financial returns reaped through bigness were astronomical. John D. Rockefeller bought into a struggling oil refinery in Cleveland for $3000 in 1863, and was refining 90 percent of all the crude oil drilled in the United States by 1880. He amassed a fortune of $200 million by 1900. Through vertical integration, monopolies, holding companies, and dramatically reduced production costs, Rockefeller and other Go-Getters became the high priests of America's secular faith of gigantism.[2]

These large corporations and the buccaneers who built them produced the economic transformation of the nation. The gross national product of the United States quintupled between 1870 and 1910, from $7.4 billion to $35.3 billion. The industrial labor force increased fivefold, from 2.5 million to 9.5 million, comprising almost one-fourth of the work force by 1910. Railroad track mileage increased from 53,000 miles in 1870 to 250,000 miles by the outbreak of the First World War. There were more railroad tracks in the U.S. than in the rest of the world *combined*. The number of banks tripled, the amount of oil drilled increased sevenfold, the amount of coal mined increased twentyfold, and iron/ steel production quadrupled. By the end of the First World War, the United States had risen from a largely agricultural society to the banking, industrial, and commercial capital of the world.[3]

This economic explosion corresponded with the rise of the corporation as a form of business organization. These enterprises were large, bureaucratic institutions that rationalized and economized production, maximizing returns for investors and lowering prices for consumers. Size became equated with success; bigness with efficiency. Monopolies and mergers were an inevitable byproduct of this cycle of industrialization, as large corporations swallowed up competitors to eliminate cutthroat price wars and vertically integrate production. Merger mania created megacorporations with enormous wealth. By 1929 the top 200 corporations in the nation controlled half of all the corporate wealth in the nation. Although Congress outlawed monopolies, the general trend towards bigness continued well into the twentieth century, as huge and monolithic corporations like General Motors and General Electric gobbled up market share, diversified product lines, and dominated entire industries.

Big business gained a stranglehold over the nation's politics. Through organizations like the Chamber of Commerce (founded in 1912) and the National Association of Manufacturers, they built formidable lobbying machines that linked cash-fat industrialists with elected officials. Before campaign finance reform in the 1970s, corporations could contribute unlimited sums of money to federal candidates. Many of these incumbents faced no opposition; the contributions provided access to key lawmakers. Because of the huge sums of money at stake and the labor force affected by legislation harmful to the large corporations, big business enjoyed unchallenged power on Capitol Hill.

Today the large corporations that once dominated American business and politics are in a state of crisis. Downsizing, restructuring, layoffs, and plant closings have wracked almost every industry. Millions of people lost jobs due to corporate restructuring in the past ten years.

The trend seems to be holding true into the 1990s. According to a 1994 study by a major business consulting firm, large companies have shed a total of two million jobs just since 1989. Every industry has been affected. General Electric has laid off over 100,000 employees, while Sears and Roebuck shed 50,000 workers. General Motors will shut down twenty-one plants and unload 75,000 workers through lay-offs and early retirements by the mid 1990s. All this has led management guru Tom Peters to conclude, "The plain truth is that every major manufacturing firm—from the Bank of America and Citicorp, to du Pont and General Motors, to IBM and Intel, to the Hospital Corporation of America—is undergoing trauma."[4]

In a recent study titled *Who's Creating Jobs*, David Birch of the Cognetics employment consulting firm divided firms into three main categories: elephants, mice, and gazelles. Elephants are the large companies whose stock is traded on the New York Stock Exchange; mice are small firms that experience little growth; and gazelles are the small, "niche" market companies that are creating 70 percent of the new jobs in the economy. According to Birch, the elephants—the engines of job growth prior to World War II—are in a state of long-term contraction. A survey by the American Management Association found that 25 percent of large companies are planning job cutbacks in the next year, and 63 percent plan to downsize again. By contrast, the gazelles created a total of 2.7 million jobs between 1990 and 1992. During the same period, firms with less than twenty employees created a staggering 4.1 million new jobs, against a loss at large companies of 501,000 jobs.[5]

There are significant political consequences to the decline of large corporations. The once-vaunted lobbying clout of big business is in danger of becoming a paper tiger. In the battle over the Clinton budget in 1993, which contained one of the largest tax increases in American history, the U.S. Chamber of Commerce sat on the sidelines, unwilling to risk offending the administration. So divisive was the issue within the Chamber's ranks that many small business members resigned, and a group of conservative Republican congressmen led by Tom DeLay of Texas—upset by the loss of a traditional ally—issued a public tongue-lashing to the group for being absent-without-leave.

By contrast, the National Federation of Independent Business generated thousands of phone calls and letters from its 600,000 members to swing members of Congress opposing the Clinton tax increase. Similarly, during the health care debate in 1994, the Chamber of Commerce was torn between large corporations seeking a government bail-out of health care costs for early retirees and the opposition of smaller firms to a job-killing payroll tax. After meeting repeatedly with Clinton administration officials to seek a possible compromise—part of the Washington game known as "eat me last"—Chamber officials finally buckled to the loud demands of its small business members and came out against the Clinton plan. In an embarrassing retreat, one Chamber lobbyist was forced to withdraw testimony already submitted to a congressional panel in support of employer-mandated health care.[6]

The relative decline in the role of big business in American economic and political life marks the end of a golden era. For large companies of over 500 employees, profit margins are thinning, job growth is stagnant, innovation rare, and market share is slipping away. Today, approximately one-fourth of all workers are employed by firms with less than ten employees, and one out of ten workers is a sole proprietor. Technology has opened up new opportunities for entrepreneurs, as small businesses operate out of home offices that are connected to customers by computer, fax, modem, and telephone. The Chrysler bailout of 1980 was perhaps the last hurrah of big business on Capitol Hill. The hand-wringing CEO swooping into Washington on a corporate jet seeking special breaks, tax windfalls, and protection from foreign competitors is a fixture of a bygone era. The future belongs to small businessmen and business-women who are creating the jobs, meeting the needs of customers, and making a payroll. In the years to come, they will be an emerging political force in opposing the burdensome federal taxes and regulations that have strangled the job-creating capacity of the U.S. economy.

There is a widespread misperception that big business is beholden to the Right. In fact, the opposite is true. Large corporations have mostly poured their financial largesse into the politically correct and pet projects of the Left. Some of the biggest beneficiaries of corporate philanthropy are liberal-left lobbies: Planned Parenthood, the Children's Defense Fund, the Urban League, the NAACP, League of Women Voters, and the Gay Men's Health Crisis. A study of patterns of corporate giving during 1991 by the Washington-based Capital Research Center found that major corporations gave $3.35 to liberal organizations for every one dollar given to conservative groups.[7]

This represents a historic shift from the heyday of American capitalism. In the late nineteenth-century, the large trusts quelled the labor unions and fought antitrust laws with uncommon ferocity. During the 1896 presidential campaign, business leaders, frightened by William Jennings Bryan's pledge to dismantle the gold standard and regulate the trusts, poured hundreds of thousands of dollars into the McKinley campaign. "Flag days" and "sound money clubs" united business and patriotism in a single sweeping impulse against the populist threat. During the New Deal, business leaders formed organizations like the Liberty League to resist what they deemed as Franklin Roosevelt's socialist schemes to seize their hard-earned profits through confiscatory tax rates.

By the end of World War II, this pitched battle between business and government ended in an uneasy truce. Large corporations began to view Washington as a source for largesse—guaranteeing government contracts, access to foreign markets, and protection from competitors. The welfare state also provided business the means to shift some of its costs to the government, especially health insurance and retirement benefits. This dynamic was evident during the recent debate over health care, in which many prominent business leaders such as Jack Smith of General Motors supported the notion of national health care as a way to reduce their own soaring health costs. As big business has lost some of its political clout, it has shifted in recent years from supporting limited government to advocating a range of liberal causes and candidates.

Organized Labor

As big business has shed jobs and slashed payrolls, organized labor has entered one of the longest periods of decline in its history. This, too, will have far-reaching political consequences. The rise of labor unions and the emergence of the Democratic party as a competitive presidential party are inextricably linked. The key figure in this marriage of labor and partisan politics was Franklin D. Roosevelt. One of the legislative land-marks of the New Deal was the Wagner Act of 1935, which guaranteed workers the right to collectively bargain, outlawed certain unfair labor practices, and established the National Labor Relations Board to mediate labor disputes. The Wagner Act institutionalized the labor unions as a powerful force in American politics.[8]

When FDR took the oath of office in March 1933, slightly less than three million workers—just 11.5 percent of the nonagricultural work force—were members of a labor union. In a dramatic about-face, the New Deal threw the power of the federal government behind the unions and their efforts to organize reluctant employers. A combination of New Deal-era labor law and rapid industrialization during World War II soon transformed the American economy—and with it American politics. By the time the United States entered World War II, 28.2 percent of all workers were unionized. By V-J Day, total union membership had sky-rocketed to 14.8 million, and 37 percent of all nonagricultural workers belonged to a labor union. The American Federation of Labor boasted 4.6 million members, the Committee for Industrial Organization had five million members, and every assembly-line worker at Ford and General Motors belonged to the United Auto Workers.[9]

Burgeoning membership made unions a major political force. In the 1936 presidential campaign they openly worked for the reelection of FDR, a development that, combined with the shift of allegiance by black voters to the Democratic party, was one of the most consequen-tial of the twentieth century. When Harry Truman stared into the jaws of defeat in 1948, he vetoed the right-to-work Taft-Hartley Act, playing to union workers in the recession-wracked industrial heartland. The unions mobilized millions of votes for Truman in states like Ohio and Illinois, and he won a stunning triumph over Dewey. In the euphoria that filled his hotel suite after Dewey conceded, Truman reportedly told his advisors, "Labor did it."[10]

Today union political clout is eroding. One reason is that union membership has plummeted on a long, downward arc since the 1960s.

Corporate restructuring has decimated the unions. The United Auto Workers' dues-paying membership, which stood at 1.5 million in 1979, is now only 862,000. Union membership fell to 27 percent of nonagricultural workers in the early 1970s, slipped to 21 percent by 1980 (when Ronald Reagan won 43 percent of the blue-collar vote), and dropped to only 16 percent in 1990. If current labor trends continue, union membership will fall to only 13 percent of the total work force by early in the next century.[11]

Union political fortunes have ebbed as membership has fallen. Ronald Reagan's successful campaign in 1981 against PATCO, the air-traffic controller's union, was the first in a series of setbacks. In 1984 the AFL-CIO leadership gambled its political fortunes by endorsing Walter Mondale for president in the Democratic primary. The result? Mondale won the nomination but carried only his home state of Minnesota—by less than four thousand votes. In 1989 the federal government assumed trusteeship of the Teamsters after numerous convictions of its leaders, many of whom were linked with organized crime. In 1994 the unions failed to pass their top legislative priority, a "striker replacement" bill that would have forced companies to rehire striking workers.

The Supreme Court dealt another blow to union political power in the 1988 decision in *Communication Workers of America* v. *Beck*, ruling that workers can only be required to pay that portion of their dues necessary for collective bargaining and may deduct the portion that goes to political advocacy. In the 1960s the unions generally supported the Vietnam War, and hard hats often clashed with hippies at protest rallies. But even as the grassroots of union members has remained fairly conservative (especially on cultural issues), the union bureaucracy has become a linchpin in the institutionalized power of the Left.

The *Beck* decision has the potential to sharply reduce this power. Workers are no longer required to watch helplessly as their mandatory union dues are diverted into "soft dollar" campaign contributions, lobbying, and ideological expenditures for the Left. In the *Beck* case, the courts ruled that 80 percent of union dues were going for political activities or other noncollective bargaining purposes; another court decision put the figure at 90 percent. It has been estimated that big labor pours as much as $350–400 million annually into voter registration drives, get-out-the-vote efforts, phone banks, and other in-kind contributions to liberal candidates. The Bush administration squandered a golden opportunity to enforce *Beck*, and Bill Clinton repealed the federal regulations enforcing it in 1993. It remains the law of the land, however, and will almost certainly be vigorously enforced by a future Republican president.[12]

Unions are not about to disappear from the American political landscape. Government unions have grown even as the smokestack industries have shriveled. The American Federation of State, County, and Municipal Employees (AFSCME) has risen from 1.2 million members in 1991 to 1.4 million today. The National Education Association boasts 2.1 million members—it has now surpassed the Teamsters as the nation's largest union—and annual revenues of $750 million. *Forbes* magazine has estimated that the NEA raised and spent approximately $22 million through federal and state political action committees in 1992. Clearly, the growth of the government sector guarantees that unions will remain a formidable political force for the forseeable future. And despite the decline in union membership as a percentage of the work force, the total number of union members today is identical to the number in 1956.[13]

Even so, organized labor faces a bleak future. The federal work force will be trimmed by 250,000 over the next five years, many states are freezing hiring, and the education labor market is beginning to shrink. Government unions may see their membership wither if these trends continue.

A bustling (nonunionized) service sector has replaced the smokestacks of industry. Service workers tend to be younger, more transient, and are more difficult to organize than factory workers. Today three out of four American workers are employed in service-related jobs, one in three is employed by a small business, and one in ten works for themselves. They no longer want or need union bosses to negotiate wages or secure generous benefits. The rapidly changing labor market has greatly reduced the economic power of unions and made their political muscle more a relic of the past than a wave of the future.

This dramatically evolving economic picture makes the obsolete political infrastructure of labor unions increasingly tenuous. Nothing demonstrated this reality more than the fight over NAFTA in 1993.

Faced with the greatest legislative battle in a generation, the unions employed strong-arm tactics on freshman congressman from blue-collar districts. When many turned their backs on organized labor and voted for the trade agreement with Mexico, they met with a furnace blast of angry threats and promises of revenge. "We won't forget what happened here," vowed Teamsters president Ron Carey after the vote. "We're gonna make sure we get even at the polls," promised Bill Bywater of the International Union of Electronic Workers.[14]

But these threats had more bark than bite. None of the freshman Democrats that the unions targeted for defeat in the primaries lost. Few members of Congress are likely to lose in 1994 because of their vote on NAFTA due to the shrinking slice of the electorate controlled by organized labor. The same holds true in the area of money. In 1994 labor contributions to candidates dropped by 11 percent, the first decline in twenty years. Teamsters giving fell the sharpest: an $800,000 drop between 1992 and 1994. For decades, organized labor has provided grassroots muscle and cash for Democratic candidates. The twilight of their dominant influence spells trouble for liberal causes and candidates in the future and suggests that a new day is dawning in American politics.[15]

The Media

The establishment media is another institution undergoing a major transition. For decades the American people have received reality through the prism of the media. The three television networks, the major newsweeklies, and the metropolitan daily newspapers have set the agenda, defined the issues, and elevated or deflated political personalities. But as new technologies emerge, these media institutions are losing their oligarchic control over the flow of information. This, too, will have enormous political consequences in the years to come.

The power of the establishment press has increased commensurate with the expansion of the government. It is impossible to understand the growth of the federal government without appreciating the symbiotic relationship between the permanent bureaucracy and a press corps protecting its beat. At the height of the New Deal in 1936, there were 2,000 congressional staff members and 430 members of the press corps who covered them. By 1968, with the onset of Lyndon Johnson's Great Society, the *Federal Register* was publishing 21,000 pages of new federal regulations a year, congressional staff had quintupled to 11,000, and the Washington press corps had increased to 1,600. In 1991 the *Federal Register* published 70,000 pages of new regulations, congressional staff numbered over 17,000, and the Washington press corps swelled to almost 5,000 reporters. There is a congressional beat, a White House beat, a State department beat, a Supreme Court beat, a health beat, an energy beat, and an education beat. There are reporters assigned to cover the Whitewater scandal, the savings-and-loan scandal, the House Post Office scandal, and the Bob Packwood scandal. Washington is a city where those who report the news are often bigger celebrities than those who make the news. For these media elites, reducing the size and scope of government is tantamount to professional suicide. "So instead of watchdogging and containing this massive explosion of government, the press has become government's biggest cheerleader," noted Warren Brookes, the late syndicated columnist for the *Detroit News.* "After all, we are its biggest beneficiaries."[16]

It was not always so. In the 1930s the newspaper empires of William Randolph Hearst and Colonel Robert McCormack, who ruled the midwest from his perch at the *Chicago Tribune,* savaged FDR and fomented opposition to the New Deal. Their unique brand of "yellow journalism," a precursor of tabloid television, sensationalized stories and entertained readers.

The rise of the city fueled the growth of the major metropolitan newspapers. After the Civil War, declining commodity prices and rural poverty drove the population from the countryside to the factories and skyscrapers that dotted the urban landscape of America's new cities. The percentage of U.S. population living in urban areas rose from 20 percent in 1860 to over 50 percent in 1920. Rural folk migrated to find higher wages and greater opportunity, scouring the classifieds for jobs and scanning the daily newspaper to make sense of their strange new surroundings. As a result, the circulation of the major dailies skyrocketed. In 1870, there were only 574 daily newspapers in the nation; by 1909, there were 2,600. The combined circulation of metropolitan dailies during the same period rose from 2.8 million to 24.2 million readers. This pattern continued for decades. In 1913, for example, the *Los Angeles Times* had a daily circulation of 242,000; by the early 1970s daily circulation exceeded *one million.* The *Washington Post* likewise saw its circulation rise from only 63,000 during the New Deal to 400,000 in the mid 1950s.[17]

Today the declining fortunes of metropolitan dailies stand in stark contrast to the heyday of print journalism. Daily newspapers are seeing their circulation level off or decline, advertising revenue dry up, and editorial budgets shrink. In the 1960s and 1970s, afternoon newspapers died by the dozens, killed off by television and the harsh economics of afternoon delivery over traffic-snarled freeways. The *Los Angeles Mirror* closed its doors in 1962, the *New York Herald Tribune* shut down in 1966, the *Chicago Daily News* in 1978, and the *Washington Star* folded in 1981. Now television, the same technological villain that strangled the afternoon papers, threatens the viability of morning newspapers as well.

Daily newspaper circulation has remained static or declined in recent years. Between 1990 and 1992, the nation's dailies lost a total of 2.1 million readers—*over 20,000 a week.* Nor does a turnaround appear likely. According to industry sources, 18 of the nation's 25 largest dailies lost circulation in 1993. Among the biggest losers: the *Chicago Tribune*, which lost 33,000 subscribers, and the *Los Angeles Times,* which lost 56,900 subscribers. If these trends continue, newspaper circulation will fall to pre-1960 (that is, before the dominance of television) levels by the year 2000, a staggering figure in light of the fact that two-thirds of the population now lives in urban areas.[18]

The demographic reality is simple. Five years ago 69 percent of the population read a daily newspaper. Today that figure is 60 percent and falling. By the early part of the next century less than half of the country will read a newspaper as part of their daily routine. Advertising revenues have fallen along with readership. Revenues for newspapers in the United States fell by 9 percent in 1991 and another 2.6 percent in 1992. The political consequences of this financial contraction are huge. Fewer print journalists setting the political agenda, downsized Washington bureaus, smaller staffs, a greater reliance on wire services, and an overall loss of prestige.[19]

Why have newspapers fallen on such hard times? Part of the answer is generational. Baby boomers raised in the era of television, computers, and videos simply do not rely on newspapers for information. One recent study found that among respondents under thirty-five years of age, only 30 percent had read any part of a newspaper the day before. Unless newspapers can replace aging subscribers with younger readers, they may be doomed financially. Another explanation is changing lifestyles in the sprawling suburbs. Loyal readers once brewed a pot of coffee and leisurely read the sports page. As the suburbs move farther and farther from the inner city, more people are in their automobiles by sunrise for a long commute, where they consume the news by listening to talk radio. Finally, there is the unspoken reality that America's newsrooms are dominated by those who consider themselves liberal, rarely attend church or synagogue, and vote almost as a bloc for liberal candidates. These elites have lost touch with their readers, and their subscribers are slowly abandoning them.[20]

Entertainment media is similarly losing its audience in middle America. The three networks once built programming schedules around wholesome situation comedies and family entertainment. From the time of Milton Berle and Lucille Ball down to the feel-good comedy of Mary Tyler Moore and Carol Burnett, parents could gather their children around the television set without worrying about what they might see. That all changed, subtly at first, with the work of Norman Lear, whose *All in the Family* debuted in 1970 and transformed television forever. Archie Bunker spoofed the television father figure of the 1950s—known to viewers through the likes of Robert Wagner and Fred MacMurray—as a hypocritical, boorish bigot. Lear's production assistants often met with liberal advocacy groups, who provided programming ideas that were in turn passed on to scriptwriters.

Themes of abortion, homosexuality, and drug use first found their way onto prime time television in Lear's programs. In 1980, after screening broadcasts by Pat Robertson and Jerry Falwell during research on a film, Lear launched People for the American Way with $200,000 in seed capital. A Lear-produced television commercial blasting religious people for exercising their right to engage in politics drew 10,000 responses to an 800 number. This became the basis of People For the American Way's membership list and its liberal agenda. Lear's politics influenced his programming and vice-versa.[21]

At first this iconoclastic, left-of-center programming enjoyed huge success. *All in the Family* and its spin-offs (*Maude*, *The Jeffersons*, and others) climbed to the top of the Nielsen charts and earned Lear a fortune. But the long-term result has been a decline in the prime time audience of network television. When pro-family advocates object to the coarse content of network programming, their opponents dismissively recommend that they simply turn off the television set. In a sense, families are following their advice. Millions of people are tuning out television—or, more commonly, changing the channel to cable, satellite TV, or talk radio—a subject to which we will return in later chapters.

News magazines have experienced a similar loss in prestige. At one time, they were the most powerful publications in the nation. *Time*, founded by Henry Luce in 1923, began as a kind of *Reader's Digest* for newspaper readers. By 1960 Luce was so powerful that Joseph P. Kennedy invited him to his hotel suite to watch his son's acceptance speech at the Democratic National Convention in Los Angeles on television. Luce, the son of Presbyterian missionaries in China and a staunch anticommunist, was wary of the senator from Massachusetts. But the elder Kennedy is reported to have assured Luce, "Don't worry about Jack. No son of mine is going to be soft on communism." Apparently mollified, and harboring his own private reservations about Richard Nixon, Luce remained conspicuously silent during the campaign, and *Life* magazine issued only a tepid endorsement of Nixon in the final days of the campaign. Many later pointed to Time-Life's equivocation as a critical factor in Nixon's defeat in the closest election of the twentieth century.

The unrivaled power of the newsweeklies could also be seen in JFK's close relationship with Hugh Sidey, *Time's* White House correspondent, and his friendship with Ben Bradlee, Washington bureau chief for *Newsweek*. Bradlee lived next to then-Senator Kennedy in Georgetown in the late 1950s and dropped by the Kennedy home frequently for buffet dinners or movies. Later, after he was elected president, Kennedy and Bradlee both exploited one another's friendship, Kennedy by feeding Bradlee juicy tidbits (or, in some cases, outright lies) about administration plans, Bradlee by gaining access to inside information from the highest source imaginable and calling in a hot story just hours before *Newsweek* went to press. Such access to presidents by magazine reporters would be far more difficult to come by as television came to dominate national politics.[22]

Lyndon Johnson so revered the newsweeklies that he would call Hugh Sidey on the phone every Thursday afternoon (just before the copy deadline) and announce, "It's *Time* magazine time." In fact, Johnson so revered *Time* that, as president, he would often have the first copy flown by Air Force jet to his ranch in Texas.

Today the newsweeklies struggle to sustain their readers in an era of television. They pump circulation numbers with discounted subscriptions and premium-driven advertising campaigns. *Newsweek*, for example, sells 93 percent of its subscriptions at a discount and 31 percent with electronic gadgets and gimmicks. But are people buying the magazine or the clock radio that comes with it? Reader surveys reveal that many do not actually read the magazine. Subscription renewal rates are dangerously low. Despite format changes at the major newsweeklies, nothing can change the fact that lifestyles are hurried and the world moves at a quicker pace.

Television, videos, and CD players have replaced magazines as a source of entertainment and news, particularly among the younger set, who feel more comfortable with emerging technologies than the stodgy print medium of their parents' generation. In this rapidly changing technological climate, the instantaneous quality of television news has made news magazines less important and timely. During the Persian Gulf War, millions of Americans sat glued to their television sets, watching exploding missiles light up the sky over Baghdad. Why subscribe to a magazine to see the same pictures one week later, when the war was over in one hundred hours? Today Americans are more likely to watch the "headlines" on CNN than to read them in a magazine. Even *Time* has come to recognize this reality. In 1991 the magazine put Ted Turner, whose Cable News Network audience skyrocketed during the Gulf War, on the cover as "Man of the Year."

Will the big newsweeklies face extinction? Highly unlikely. But in the 1930s and 1940s, *Life* magazine, *Look*, *Collier's* and the *Saturday Evening Post* were fixtures in almost every home in America. Today they are all either extinct or difficult to find. The new trend in magazines is "niche" marketing, narrow-casting to a specific demographic category such as working women twenty-five to forty-four years old, exercise and fitness enthusiasts, upscale financial investors, or hobbyists. Advertisers want to reach these targeted audiences, not scatter-shot their message across a vast, amorphous readership. This places the major newsweeklies at a long-term competitive disadvantage. Little wonder advertising pages are down across the board: off 12–25 percent at *Time*, 13.5 percent at *Newsweek*, and 10.2 percent at *U.S. News*. Although these publications will survive for years to come, their influence over the culture will be diminished and their political clout reduced.[23]

Challenging "Cultural Hegemony"

What Marxist theorist Antonio Gramsci termed the "cultural hegemony" may finally be cracking. Gramsci forwarded a Marxist critique of the all-pervasive ideology of capitalism. He suggested that the real power of the capitalist system was not its control of the economy but its complete dominance of the culture.

Gramsci might well have spoken of the cultural hegemony of the institutions controlled by elites in the United States. People of faith must build their own institutions that represent their views accurately. There is some hopeful evidence that this is occurring, witnessed by the explosion in talk radio, the growth of religious broadcasting, and increasing enrollment at church-affiliated colleges and universities. Herein lies the future, for the culture more than political involvement alone will ultimately determine the values that animate our people and inform our institutions.[24]

As people of faith build institutions that reflect their mainstream values, they often find themselves embroiled in a debate over the separation of church and state. This has been particularly true of their political activism. The notion that a disestablished church required that believers stay out of the political arena was never part of the design of this country's founders. Misconceptions about church-state separation make it more difficult to build a truly family-friendly culture. It is to those myths that we now turn.

CHAPTER NINE

Separation of Church and State: *"Christian Nation" and Other Heresies*

IN 1992 I traveled to Oregon to debate John Frohnmayer, the former head of the National Endowment for the Arts, at a college symposium on the First Amendment. Our debate was spirited but cordial. He argued that any restrictions on the funding of the arts amounted to censorship. I argued that if taxpayers foot the bill, they should be free to set reasonable, common-sense guidelines to prevent the funding of obscenity or attacks on religion.

During the question-and-answer period, one man stepped to the microphone. "If you are allowed to pass laws based on your religious beliefs, where do you draw the line?" he pointedly asked. "What about the separation of church and state?" It was a good question. But it also betrayed a common misunderstanding about the First Amendment. I explained that the Constitution prohibited the government from establishing an official state religion. But equally important, the "free exercise" clause of the First Amendment prevented the government from restricting the citizenry from worshiping God according to the dictates of their conscience or freely expressing religious ideas.

What good is religious liberty, I asked, if it can only be practiced behind stained-glass windows on Sunday? If one desires to pass a law to prohibit people of faith from engaging in political action based on their beliefs, one would need to take a knife to our history books and cut out the pages on the antislavery crusade, the temperance movement, the women's movement, the civil rights struggle, and the anti-Vietnam War protests. All these social movements flowered in their day because religious people believed that the ideas of right and wrong they found in the

Bible should be reflected in our laws. The only difference between these social movements and religious conservatives is the culture's view of what is politically correct.

Religious conservatives do not want a "Christian" nation, a "Jewish" nation, or a "Moslem" nation. They want a nation of strong families and basic goodness that respects the right of all individuals to express their faith and which does not prohibit faith to inform the laws that govern society. This is the kind of nation James Madison had in mind when he said, "We have staked the future . . . upon the capacity of each and all of us to govern ourselves, to control ourselves, to sustain ourselves according to the Ten Commandments of God."

Madison was right. Religious values are not a threat to democracy; they are essential to democracy. Indeed, the centrality of faith to the maintenance of democratic institutions was once considered axiomatic. For most of America's history, church pulpits flamed with sermons about social injustice; clergymen and women led social movements that embraced the highest ideals of faith-based reform; and the speeches, public statements, and proclamations of government officials brimmed with references to religion. No one suggested that these activities posed a threat to the separation of church and state. Americans resisted the establishment of a national religion but embraced faith as a vital ingredient in the body politic that was an essential counterbalance to government tyranny.

Only in recent times have religious conservatives, or religious people of any kind, been viewed as trying to transform this country into something that critics do not want to admit it has always been. The United States of America was founded on religious principles by religious people. Our society works best when we remember that fact and welcome into the public square those who act in its finest traditions.

Abraham Lincoln issued an order in 1862 requiring the observance of the sabbath in the Union army, noting that it corresponded "to the best sentiment of a Christian people."[1]

In the *Trinity* decision of 1892, the Supreme Court reviewed the Constitution, the Declaration of Independence, and other founding documents of America and concluded that they presupposed a Supreme Being and a religious citizenry. "Christianity," the Court stated, "general Christianity is and always has been a part of the common law. Not Christianity with an established church, but Christianity with liberty and conscience to all men."[2]

In 1931 Supreme Court Justice George Sutherland ruled that "the laws of the land . . . are not inconsistent with the will of God."[3] The North Atlantic summit in 1941 between Winston Churchill and Franklin Delano Roosevelt (who once described the United States as "the lasting concord between men and nations, founded on the principles of Christianity") featured Sunday services with a message from the Book of Joshua and the singing of hymns (selected by Winston Churchill) that climaxed with a windswept rendition of "Onward Christian Soldiers."[4] In 1947, in a letter to Pope Pius XII, President Harry Truman went further, asserting, "This is a Christian nation."

"We are a religious people whose system of government supposes a Supreme Being," concluded Justice William O. Douglas in *Zorach* v. *Clauson* in 1952. He added that there existed "no constitutional requirement which makes it necessary for government to be hostile to religion and to throw its weight against efforts to widen the effective scope of religious influence."[5]

"Our hard challenge and our sublime opportunity is to bear witness to the spirit of Christ in fashioning a truly Christian world," said Martin Luther King in 1963.[6]

These observations—many by liberal Democrats—reflected a consensus on civil religion that united Americans for the first three centuries of their history. They were not theological sermons but civil statements, some of them carrying the weight of law. They were not arguments for an established church but acknowledgements of a distinctly American piety that, until recently, permeated the entire culture, rendering the entanglement of government in religion superfluous and unnecessary.

This is the genius of America: we are a people of faith that stipulates, in order to protect the free exercise of our religion, that government stay out of the business of the church. In the 1830s, when the Second Great Awakening turned parts of western New York into a "burned over district" ablaze with the fires of revivalism, Alexis de Tocqueville observed that while religion was the first of America's civil institutions, the people nevertheless retained a healthy suspicion of government imposition of faith. "Religion in America," noted Tocqueville, "takes no direct part in the government of society, but it must be regarded the first of their political institutions; for if it does not impart a taste for freedom, it facilitates the use of it." He added that while "religion exercises but little influence upon the laws and upon the details of public opinion," it "directs the customs of the community, and by regulating domestic life, it regulates the state."[7]

Norman Sykes, in his classic *Church and State In England in the Eighteenth Century*, argued that three "pillars" sustained the social order of Great Britain during the eighteenth century: the Protestant Succession, the Established Church, and tolerated Dissent.[8] Three equally important "pillars" have sustained the social order in the United States for over two centuries: the separation of powers, the Bill of Rights, and civil religion. The separation of powers has guarded against tyranny by preventing the power of the national government from residing in a single branch.

The Bill of Rights enumerates the rights of the citizenry against which government may not encroach. These rights were extended to all Americans by the Fourteenth Amendment to the Constitution, which granted former slaves equality before the law following the Civil War.

The third pillar, civil religion, has been the glue that held American society together, bridging ethnic and racial differences by expressing the common attributes of faith while assiduously avoiding the European practice of established churches. Civil religion, like the separation of powers and the Bill of Rights, provides an insurance policy against tyranny, something that was foremost in the minds of a people that had just fought a bloody war of independence from Great Britain. By inculcating a voluntary code of behavior that included respect for one's neighbor, honesty, frugality, piety, and self-sufficiency, it kept the government small and subdued.

None of this adds up to the conclusion that America is a "Christian nation" in the sense of a theocratic state or a unicultural society. That not only ignores the enormous contribution that Jews have made to America, but it is something of an anachronism. It makes just as much sense to say that Massachusetts is a Puritan colony or that Maryland is a Catholic state. Massachusetts may have been a Puritan commonwealth in the seventeenth or even the eighteenth centuries, but it hardly qualifies today. America is not solely a Christian nation, but a pluralistic society of Protestants, Catholics, Jews, Muslims, and other people of faith whose broader culture once honored religion, but which today increasingly reflects a hostility towards faith in the public sphere. What religious conservatives want is to accommodate the historic role of faith in American civic life. In short, they seek to restore the time-honored tradition of civil religion—not to establish Christianity by law or create an official church.

When former President Richard Nixon recently died, many analysts observed that probably only Nixon, stalwart Republican and staunch anticommunist, could have gone to China. Similarly, probably only a Democrat can bring our nation back to the tradition of civil religion.[9]

There is some evidence that Bill Clinton would like to be that Democrat. While vacationing in Martha's Vineyard in the summer of 1993, Clinton read Yale Professor Stephen L. Carter's *The Culture of Disbelief* and found his theme of the marginalization of religion in American law and politics deeply compelling. Not long after returning to the White House, Clinton addressed an interfaith prayer breakfast of one hundred clergy in the State Dining Room and discussed the spiritual vacuum in America's soul. "Sometimes I think the environment in which we operate is entirely too secular," he confessed. "The fact that we have freedom of religion doesn't mean we need to try to have freedom from religion."[10]

In a sun-drenched South Lawn ceremony celebrating the passage of the Religious Freedom Restoration Act on November 16, 1993, Clinton went further. The Democrats had recently made the centerpiece of the gubernatorial campaign in Virginia an assault on the Republican ticket for being too closely aligned with religious conservatives. The result was the largest landslide for a Republican candidate for governor in the twentieth century—and the near-election of home school attorney Mike Farris as lieutenant governor. "There is a great debate now abroad in the land which finds itself injected into several political races about the extent to which people of faith can seek to do God's will as political actors," Clinton noted. "I would like to come down on the side of encouraging everybody to act on what they believe is the right thing to do." He urged his audience to "respect one another's faith, fight to the death to preserve the right of every American to practice whatever convictions he or she has, but bring our values back to the table of American discourse to heal our troubled land."[11]

This presidential rhetoric is helpful not only because it reaffirms the importance of civil religion but also because it prevents religion from becoming a wholly-owned subsidiary of the Republican party. Clinton's remarks constituted a remarkable (if oblique) slap at his own party for failing to appreciate the role of religion in public life. President Clinton should be commended for speaking out on the essential role of people of faith in renewing our society and sustaining democracy.

However, this rhetoric will be found wanting unless it is matched with actions. Clinton's call for taxpayer funding of abortion, his appointments of persons such as Joycelyn Elders with harshly anti-Catholic views, his endorsement of special rights legislation based on sexual preference (issued, oddly, on Valentine's Day), and the recent reemergence of the character issue with the Whitewater scandal and allegations of sexual misconduct make it more difficult for him to appeal to religious values. As Terry Eastland of the Ethics and Public Policy Center notes, he "has named to his administration individuals like Surgeon General Joycelyn Elders who not only dismiss religious conservatives but cast aspersions upon them." Clinton should continue to use the bully pulpit of the presidency to urge a healthy respect for religious values, but he must also take action to insure that those values are reflected in both the policies and conduct of his presidency.[12]

This does not mean that only a president who agrees with every single element in the religious conservative agenda can reinstill public confidence in religion. Jimmy Carter, despite all his other shortcomings, did speak eloquently about his faith. Americans yearn for political leaders for whom faith is important in their daily lives.

Reviving Civil Religion

Whether Bill Clinton or another politician changes the terms of the debate about religion and politics, the decline in civil religion has accelerated as elected officials have grown wary of using religious language to frame public issues. Demographic changes during the twentieth century have had a devastating effect on religion as the common bond uniting all Americans. Urbanization has depersonalized society until many of us do not even know our neighbors' names. The anonymity and alienation of modern society stands in stark contrast to America during the nineteenth century, when everyone was accountable to parents, neighbors, church or synagogue, and the community. Today we live in fear of each other, with alarm systems on our homes, bars on our windows, alarms on our automobiles, and guns in the closet. We travel to and from work in hermetically-sealed automobiles, lost in thought or the blare of the radio, rarely exchanging glances with fellow motorists except to shake fists or shout expletives.

Even the church has become uprooted from a sense of community. My wife and I attended a large church in Atlanta, Georgia, with over 10,000 members. We often went to church twice a week, but outside of a young married couples' group, knew almost no one who sat next to us in the pews. Fifty years ago, they would have been our friends, our family, and our neighbors.

Human beings are social animals. They are not designed to function properly when disconnected from the love and concern of others. Sadly, the number of such individuals represents the fastest growing demographic group in society. According to the U.S. Census Bureau, an astonishing 25 percent of all households consist of people living alone—one out of every four in the nation.[13] Among these roughly 22 million persons living alone, there are countless troubled people waiting to detonate. Estranged from dysfunctional families of origin, isolated from neighbors, unmarried, twisted by sexual or chemical addictions, and unaccountable to any faith community, some are the human consequences of an anonymous society.

Civil religion would help to soften the often brutal edges of our secular, modern society. It would not contemplate the establishment of an official church. But it would allow the healing influence of religion—all religions—to be freely expressed in the public square.

This was the original intent of our nation's founders when they framed the Constitution. Justice Joseph Story, who sat on the Supreme Court from 1811 until 1845 and taught law at Harvard University, stated unequivocally in his commentary on the Constitution: "The real object of the [First] Amendment was . . . to prevent any national ecclesiastical establishment which should give to a hierarchy the exclusive patronage of the national government." The objective was not, in Story's word, to "prostrate" Christianity by excluding it from the public square, but to prohibit the elevation of one sect or denomination above the others.[14]

Church and state jurisprudence has gradually shifted in recent decades to a point that the framers of the First Amendment would not recognize it. They saw the state as the threat; today the courts see the church as the threat. The founders viewed an established state religion as the embodiment of tyranny because it allowed the government to rule over citizens in matters of conscience. Today, we react harshly to religion itself, even when the government does not dictate its expression. The Supreme Court's opinion in *Employment Division* v. *Smith*, the so-called *peyote* case, in 1990 underscored our legal culture's hostility towards the free exercise of religion. In that case, the Court dropped the time-honored standard that government demonstrate a compelling reason for passing laws that had the effect (even when unintentional) of discriminating against religion. The ruling was later overturned by the passage of the Religious Freedom Restoration Act in 1993.[15]

This hostility contrasts sharply with the early republic, when religion was synonymous with patriotism, and Christianity became equated with republican virtue. In the famous 1811 blasphemy decision of *The People of New York* v. *Ruggles*, Federalist jurist Chancellor James Kent ruled that although the Constitution forbade an established church and New York had no specific statute banning blasphemy, for any citizen to denigrate Christianity was "to strike at the roots of moral obligation and weaken the security of social ties." Kent was not himself a committed Christian. But he agreed that religion was, in the words of Leverett Saltonstall of Massachusetts, "the great bond of civil society." This same conviction caused a New York judge in 1831 to disallow the testimony of a witness who declared himself an atheist. The judge ruled that faith in God "constituted the sanction of all testimony in a court of justice" and that no one could be "permitted to testify without such belief.[16]

No one is suggesting that we return to the days when the testimony of nonbelievers is excluded from courts of law. But if the pendulum then swayed too far in the direction of religion, can anyone deny that today it has swung too far in the opposite direction? When prosecutors are reprimanded because they quote from the Bible, when attorneys are told to remove ashes from their forehead on Ash Wednesday, and when a Rabbi's simple prayer is ruled unconstitutional, our zeal for separation of church and state has curdled into a sour distaste for religious expression. Today it is the religious person whose testimony or political activism may be called into question based solely on their belief in God.

CHAPTER TEN

We Stand at Armageddon:
Religion and the Reformist Impulse

How do we begin to restore civility, compassion, and faith to our lives? We cannot succeed unless we allow people of faith to enter the public square. Today's religious reformers are often ridiculed and misunderstood. But so were previous social dissenters who operated in a religious context. In order to benefit from the sublime principles that are contained in their faith, we must allow citizens to act out their reformist impulses.

The antislavery crusade, temperance movement, and civil rights struggle all owed their distinctive moral flavor to the messianic zeal of their adherents. Religion sparking political involvement is not an aberration of the American experience, but is perhaps its most persistent theme. This has been true of liberals and conservatives, Northerners and Southerners, capitalists and Jacobites, blacks and whites, Protestants as well as Catholics. Some might conclude that if the same religion motivated slaveholders in the South, nativists in the North, John D. Rockefeller, Cesar Chavez, Martin Luther King, and Jerry Falwell, then it must be a strange theology indeed. They might recall that Christ numbered among his first twelve disciples both a tax collector for the Roman Empire and a member of a terrorist political party devoted to its violent overthrow. Indeed, the universality of religion explains its powerful appeal—its ability to span across race, region, and ideology is its strongest and most commending attribute.

Religion inspired political activism from the earliest days of the American republic. The Great Awakening that broke out in 1739 with the open-air preaching of George Whitefield and John Wesley in the south of England soon swept the British colonies like a wildfire, converting thousands to an evangelical faith in God. Witnesses to Whitefield's preaching described huddled throngs that numbered as many as 30,000 people. They trudged across miles of deserted country roads and weathered driving rain or cold for hours, transfixed by sermons that warned of impending Judgment and offered the hope of salvation. Uproarious revivals convulsed entire towns and cities, paralyzing commerce and leading to thousands of conversions. New converts rolled around on the ground in seizures or stood immobile as if in a spiritual trance, while others thrashed about in bushes or ran to and fro shouting in joyful pleasure. The astonishing results repulsed colonial officials and those accustomed to High Church niceties. Samuel Seabury, an Anglican missionary serving in eastern Connecticut, reported on the emotional upheavals that shook his parish in 1741, including nightly services in which "ten or more [are] seized with violent agitations, many incapable of any decency crying out of their damned estate, some not speaking at all, or so much as being able to stand, fall down, as they pretend with the weight of their guilt . . . [until] they are converted and born again."[1]

The revivalism that convulsed the colonies between 1740 and 1760 carried the seeds of the American Revolution. The fiery preachers of spiritual revival became the pamphleteers and propagandists of political revolution, and their converts, steeped in the Scriptures, equated England with profligate Babylon and the colonies with Israel. John Dickinson, a prominent lawyer in Pennsylvania, argued in 1766 that the rights of the colonists were not granted by the king. "We claim them from a higher source—from the King of kings and Lord of all the earth," he trumpeted. "They are not annexed to us by parchments and seals. They are created in us by the decrees of Providence, which establish the laws of nature." Millenialism embroidered the speeches and spilled forth from the pens of revolutionaries who called their fellow colonists to arms: get ready for the return of the Lord! One even proclaimed that America, independent of corrupt and venal Great Britain, might well become "the foundation of a great and mighty empire, the largest the world ever saw founded on such principles of liberty and freedom . . . which shall be the principal seat of that glorious kingdom which Christ shall erect upon earth in the latter days."[2]

The Puritan thirst for frugality and holiness endowed the revolution with its full-throated moral fervor. As the colonists saw it, the gathering storm with Great Britain was a spiritual struggle between incorruptible righteousness and a hydra-headed evil. "The Gospel promises liberty and permits resistance," insisted Reverend Jonathan Mayhew of Boston as he organized protests against the Stamp Act. Religion and patriotism marched hand in hand. Those who resisted revivalism also tended to resent the democratic spirit that it fostered, and in many communities, the "New Lights"—converts of the Great Awakening—took up the musket, while "Old Lights" lived in fear for their safety and bravely defended the king and his established church. The itinerant ministers who preached a fire-and-brimstone, socially-leveling gospel also paved the way for the democratization of political life, and united the colonies in a single, sweeping revivalistic impulse that transcended barriers of class, gender, and geography. The Great Awakening united the American people as no other single event in the colonial period, giving them a common language, a common experience, and a common enemy: Great Britain, which Alexander Hamilton called "an old wrinkled, withered, worn-out hag."[3]

Preachers in eighteenth-century America relied heavily on Scripture to develop an apologia for the patriot cause. In the Bible they found justification for the doctrine of government deriving from the consent of the governed (Exodus 24:7) and the efficacy of representative government over autocratic rule (Exodus 18). As the colonies hurtled towards independence and bloodshed, pulpits flamed with jeremiads that condemned the evils of kings, with sermons drawn directly from the book of Samuel, where the prophet warned of the wickedness of monarchy.[4]

Thomas Paine followed their lead. When *Common Sense* appeared in 1776—selling 125,000 copies in the space of a year—the author used the Bible to make the case for revolution. "Government by kings was first introduced into the world by heathens, from whom the children of Israel copied the custom," he warned. He quoted extensively from the book of Samuel. "In short, monarchy and succession have laid (not for this or that kingdom only) but the world in blood and ashes. 'Tis a form of government which the word of God bears testimony against, and blood will attend it." Paine, though not himself a believer, knew his

pietistic audience well and spoke in the scriptural vernacular they understood, painting King George as a modern Pharaoh. Nor was he alone.
In colonial America, the Bible was the common denominator of the
culture: reading primer, history book, legal text, and literature for
the common folk. "Devotional piety or appeal to Scriptures—at the
center of education for the comparatively unschooled—was more usual
in addresses to the people than in the classical republican writings of the
newspapers," notes historian Rys Isaac. "Liberty, virtue, and pure Protestant religion were all inextricably intertwined." Little wonder that the
proclamation by a group of Philadelphia Presbyterians became the battle
cry for many as they marched off to war: "No King but King Jesus!"[5]

There was no false division between pulpit and public service as
America declared its independence. Reverend John Witherspoon taught
many of the founders as president of Princeton University, served in the
Continental Congress, and was one of the signators to the Declaration
of Independence. In 1776 in a sermon entitled "The Dominion of Providence over the Passions of Men"—delivered one month before his election to Congress—he declared that "he is the best friend to American
liberty who is most sincere and active in promoting true and undefiled
religion." The maintenance of liberty, he argued, required the coupling
of religion and politics. "God grant that in America true religion and
civil liberty may be inseparable," Witherspoon prayed, "and that the
unjust attempts to destroy the one may in the issue tend to the support
and establishment of both."[6]

During the Revolution, preacher became patriot, the parish church
was converted into a muster field, and elders and deacons donned the
tricornered cap of Minutemen. They poured out of the pews and onto
the battlefield, believing that American independence was not only a
constitutional imperative but a spiritual mission. "God presides over the
destinies of nations, and will raise up friends for us," thundered Patrick
Henry. "The battle is not to the strong alone; it is to the vigilant, the
active, the brave."

.   .   .

Preaching Liberty

Just as the Great Awakening sparked the democratic impulse of the American Revolution, so did the Second Great Awakening of the 1830s fan the flames of the antislavery movement. Charles Grandison Finney preached revivals that turned entire villages upside down and transformed cities into ghost towns as the entire population filled nightly church services. Taverns closed, gambling houses boarded up, theaters shut their doors, and churches swelled to overflowing. According to Lyman Beecher, one of Finney's ablest colaborers, this religious awakening "was the greatest work of God, and the greatest revival of religion, that the world has ever seen." An estimated 100,000 people experienced a spiritual conversion and made a religious affiliation in 1831 alone, probably the largest harvest of souls the American church had seen up to that time. The effects of these revivals were remarkable. Labor unrest, church schisms, and public vice all fell away before the demands of religion. The spark from one town's revival ignited religious enthusiasm in a neighboring village, which in turn fired other towns and hamlets, until the entire region of western New York "burned over" with the flames of revival.[7]

The Second Great Awakening also carried a political message for the moral reformation of American society. Critics of slavery, imbued with an evangelical ardor, condemned the peculiar institution as a social evil and, rejecting pragmatic or gradualist solutions, called for its immediate abolition. Their message took firm root in the soil blackened by the fires of revivalism. William Lloyd Garrison published the first issue of the *Liberator* newspaper in 1831, the same year Finney's revivals doubled church membership in New York. Whitney Cross has examined voting patterns in western New York in the 1840s and found that antislavery support in the electorate reached its highest levels in those areas with the greatest number of evangelical churches and the most uproarious revivals in the preceding decade. Temperance societies, antislavery groups, manual labor schools, and benevolence leagues sprouted forth like tendrils from the religious fervor of the 1830s.[8]

Antislavery reform waxed thickest in the years following the Second Great Awakening. Through the teachings of abolitionists like Theodore Weld (a convert of the great revivals) and the New York-based Tappan brothers, radical ideas for immediately ending slavery led to the formation of dozens of antislavery organizations. These evangelists proclaimed that slavery was not merely wrong, but a sin against God. They founded the American Anti-Slavery Society in 1831, the leading organization in the abolitionist cause, which within a decade had 1,650 local chapters with 170,000 members. Weld dispatched seventy agents into the countryside to preach the truth of abolition—a plan modeled after the New Testament recounting of Christ's commissioning of the first seventy disciples to spread the gospel. They fanned out across the North and West, making antislavery "identical with religion," urging their coreligionists "by all they esteem holy, by all the high and exciting obligations of duty to man and God, by all that can warm the heart and inflame the imagination, to join the pious work of purging the sin of slavery from the land."9

The preaching forays of Weld and the faithful seventy yielded much fruit. Church meetings, modeled explicitly after the revivalist preaching style that Finney had perfected in the religious awakening, lasted for two to five hours a night, often convening every evening for weeks. One of the most dedicated converts was a young attorney in western Ohio named Joshua Giddings, who organized a local abolitionist society and then won election to Congress in 1838 as an antislavery Whig. With Weld as his mentor, he led the abolitionist forces in the House of Representatives, later joining forces with the radical Republicans.

Another convert of the faithful seventy was Thaddeus Stevens, elected as a Whig Congressman from Pennsylvania in 1848, who argued that the immorality of slavery was the central issue in the nation. For these firebrands, public service provided a means to a moral end. Even the Union came second to the antislavery cause. "We have saved this Union so often that I am afraid we will save it to death," cried Thaddeus Stevens as the South careened towards secession.10

A direct progression from revivalism to abolitionism to Republicanism took place between the 1830s and the 1850s. The idea of the equality of all men in the eyes of God, popularized by the Great Awakening, congealed into a political doctrine that found its home in the Republican party. Congressman Edward Wade of Ohio, another Weld convert, informed Congress that he opposed slavery because it violated the strictures of Scripture, and he proclaimed that the Bible "was the supreme authority in every moral question." Republican Congressman George Julian of Indiana went further, declaring in 1853 that "the great central truth of Christianity is the great central truth of our movement as a party."

Then, as now, more moderate Republicans, many former Whigs more concerned with economic issues, resisted this moral impulse and resented those who had joined the party because of their religious convictions. Nevertheless, at the 1856 Republican National Convention in Philadelphia, the antislavery faithful dominated the platform committee, drafting a document that called the peculiar institution a "relic of barbarism" and called for its instant abolition. "I think it is ahead of all other platforms ever adopted," rejoiced Joshua Giddings, an influential member of the platform committee. "I am willing to let them [the moderates] have the offices to support our doctrines." Persons fired by faith and steeped in revivalism made a unique and lasting contribution to the ideological origins of the Republican party.[11]

The Demon of Liquor

Temperance also blossomed as a social movement directly out of the religious enthusiasm of the 1830s. Sermons and jeremiads by evangelical preachers during the period bemoaned a spreading scourge of pauperism, idleness, prostitution, and gambling, almost all of which they attributed to intemperance. As these social reformers saw it, a growing contagion of taverns, tippling joints, and liquor shops had flung open their doors to the immigrants that were arriving in ever larger numbers, enticing them to a life of alcoholism, dependency, and sorrow. Social disorder seemed endemic. Reports issued by New York and Massachusetts in 1821 and 1824 attributed more than half of all the paupers in those states to excessive alcohol consumption. One periodical proclaimed that "the unrestricted manufacture and sale of ardent spirits is almost the sole cause of all the suffering, the poverty, and the crime to be found in this country."[12]

Against this backdrop, the temperance movement began as an exercise in voluntary moral reformation. Presbyterian church services in revival-scorched regions climaxed not only with an altar call for the lost, but with the taking of "The Pledge" by the saved, a public ceremony in which the believer bound himself by a solemn oath to completely abstain from spirituous liquor. The Methodists and Baptists quickly followed suit. The transition from this act of individual contrition to reforming the larger society was an easy one. Temperance societies flourished like wildfire, boycotts against saloons proliferated, and local councils controlled by temperance forces enacted laws heavily regulating drinking establishments. Within two years of the great revival of 1831, the New York State Temperance Society had established 700 local affiliates, had signed 12 percent of the entire state population to the pledge, and had put nearly half of all the liquor distilleries in the state out of business.[13]

Later, in the 1870s and 1880s, temperance crusaders moved beyond these piecemeal efforts to campaign for state laws that allowed local governments to abolish saloons altogether. These campaigns led to the formation in 1893 of the Anti-Saloon League of America, which became one of the nation's most powerful lobbies. In one revivalist crusade led by Billy Sunday in the lumber town of Everett, Washington, the evangelist preached to crowds of 12,000 people (in a town with a total population of only 25,000), church rolls skyrocketed by 2,500, and the revival sparked an antiliquor campaign that closed every saloon in that overwhelmingly blue-collar town. By 1900 there were thirty-seven states covering three-quarters of the population that had passed local option antisaloon laws.[14]

For women the temperance movement represented their political baptism in fire. In fact, as historian Norman Clark has demonstrated, legislators supported by the temperance lobby were also those most likely to advocate women's right to vote. The minutes of early women's movement organizations are replete with references to efforts to pass laws against saloons, prostitution, abortion, and rape, as well as for the right of women to vote. Of the twelve states that allowed women to vote prior to 1919, all but two passed referendums banning saloons, most by large margins. Liquor concerns and breweries poured money into campaigns against women's suffrage, primarily because they recognized that granting women the right to vote signaled the death-knell of their industry.

Because the church provided them with a platform for their views, women found their greatest outlet for political activism from religious enthusiasm. The Women Christian Temperance Union, founded in 1874, ultimately grew to more than one million members around the world. Under the leadership of Frances Williard, the WCTU fought liquor, lobbied against the international opium trade, and promoted world peace. Its unique brand of "gospel politics" changed the way Americans viewed morality in public life. In 1896 the WCTU organized the first Mother's Day celebration. In 1915 its lobbyists delivered five million signatures in support of a prohibition amendment to the Constitution. "We believe in the coming of His Kingdom whose service is perfect freedom," proclaimed the WCTU Creed, "because His laws, written in the members as well as in nature and in grace, are perfect, converting the soul."[15]

Carrie Nation, one of the leading lights of the antisaloon movement, began her reformist career after an unhappy marriage to a violent drunk, and later married an evangelical preacher in Kansas. She took up the ax in 1899 after hearing the voice of God, and battled "visions of demons along the road" on the way to smashing her first saloon. Her mission of destruction soon gained her worldwide fame—and time in jail for her hatchet-wielding protests. Elizabeth Cady Stanton, Susan B. Anthony, and Amelia Bloomer learned the skills they later employed in the suffragist movement in their apprenticeships in the reform societies that flowered in western New York following the Second Great Awakening. Frances Willard spoke for many of her sisters when she proclaimed, "I am first a Christian, then I am a Saxon, then I am an American."[16]

The Populist Movement

The Populist revolt of the 1890s also owed its moral critique of American society to the churches. When Thomas E. Watson, who carried the

Populist banner for president twice, was nominated for Congress in Georgia in 1894, one grizzled farmer rejoiced, "I love the Bible. I love Jesus Christ. I love the People's party, and I love Tommie Watson." The Populists combined a respect for the agrarian lifestyle and a deep resentment of cities and the captains of industry with an abiding distrust of government they believed was controlled by plutocrats. Their standard-bearer, William Jennings Bryan, captured the Democratic nomination for president three times, served as Woodrow Wilson's secretary of state, and was the most consequential evangelical politician of the twentieth century. Although he is best remembered for the Scopes "Monkey Trial" of 1925, Bryan spent the preceding three decades as the "Great Commoner," giving voice to the concerns of farmers and acting as the voice and conscience of the agrarian wing of the Democratic party.[17]

Bryan described his reformist campaign as a moral crusade, one that pitted the robber barons and moneyed interests against "a larger middle class—God fearing and God worshipping; a class composed of both men and women in whom the spiritual element predominates and who . . . yearn to be of real service to mankind." He easily combined his religion with politics. He predicted that "whenever God is as faithfully served at the ballot box as He is in the church," then "the era of trusts, of imperialism, of spoliation and of corruption will be at an end." His later campaign against evolution was an extension of his belief that the triumph of Social Darwinism over belief in the Bible would lead to the oppression of workers, racial genocide, and world wars. Little wonder that William Allen White characterized his reformist politics as "an evangelical uprising." Bryan spoke in the honey-tongued style of a rural preacher, laced his speeches with quotations from the Bible, and called his coreligionists to act out their faith in the political world.

Some criticized the use of religious language by a handful of speakers at the Republican National Convention in Houston in 1992. One wonders how they might have reacted to Bryan's famous "Cross of Gold" speech at the Democratic National Convention in Chicago in 1896:

> We have petitioned, and our petitions have been scorned; we have entreated, and our entreaties have been disregarded; we have begged, and they mocked when our calamity came. We beg no longer; we entreat no

more; we petition no more. We defy them! . . . You shall not press down upon the brow of labor this crown of thorns; you shall not crucify mankind upon a cross of gold.[18]

The Bully Pulpit

The Progressives emulated their populist forebears in their appeal to religious values. They combined a zeal for reform with the social gospel popularized by Walter Rauschenbusch, a professor of theology whose socialist critique of industrial capitalism gained many followers. Many condemned the demon of alcohol for preying on the lives of the innocent poor. One of the leading progressive reformers was Jacob Riis, whose stark portrayal of poverty in the New York city slums in *How the Other Half Lives* (1890) became a classic. Riis reserved especially harsh judgment for the liquor trade and the saloons. In one of the most chilling anecdotes, he described a boy who was allowed to buy a large amount of beer for a drinking party held by some workers. After joining in the revelry until he became drunk, the boy "crept into the cellar to sleep off the effects of his own share in the rioting." His body was discovered "Monday morning, when the shop was opened . . . killed and half-eaten by rats that overran the place."[19]

Loving God implied service to the larger society, a mission the Progressives undertook through a plethora of social welfare organizations dedicated to the inculcation of Christian character and the reformation of society. Among the groups that blossomed in the early 1900s: the Boy Scouts, the Girl Scouts, Christian Endeavor, the Salvation Army, the Campfire Girls, and the Gideons, launched in 1908 to place Bibles in hotel rooms throughout the nation.

This reform impulse found powerful expression in the Reverend Charles Sheldon's best-selling novel *In His Steps* (1897), a moral fable in which several protagonists responded to the social ills plaguing society as they believed Christ would have were He still on earth. Labor organizers embraced this same ideal, recruiting directly in the churches and enlisting the pulpits of sympathetic clergy. A circular published in Chicago in 1918 by two Baptist ministers calling for the inclusion of black workers in the American Federation of Labor condemned "unscrupulous white plutocrats" and asserted that "God is the creator of all mankind and has endowed us with certain inalienable rights . . . so that peace and harmony will reign and hell on earth be subdued." They would have no doubt agreed with socialist Upton Sinclair, author of the muckraking novel *The Jungle* (1906), who declared that "the world needs a Jesus more than it needs anything else."[20]

Theodore Roosevelt, the devoted goldbug to Bryan's silverite crying in the wilderness, drew heavily on his Dutch Reformed upbringing in articulating his political philosophy. He vowed that the trusts trampled on the God-given rights of labor, that conservation was part of a broader mission to exercise stewardship over the earth, and that the Spanish-American War fulfilled Providence's plan for America's dominant role in the Western hemisphere. In Roosevelt's political theology, public service reflected one's private confession of faith. "Our being in this church," he told one congregation in 1903, "our communion here with one another, our sitting under the pastor and hearing from him the word of God, must, if we are sincere, show their effects in our lives outside." In 1912, when he bolted from the Republican party to carry the Bull Moose banner, he accepted the presidential nomination of his insurgent third party to the roars of the delegates by exclaiming, "We stand at Armageddon, and we battle for the Lord!"[21]

God and Civil Rights

Roosevelt was not alone in battling for the Lord. Three years before he uttered this call to arms, the National Association for the Advancement of Colored People (NAACP) brought together black clergy and white philanthropists repelled by the mistreatment of blacks in the South. The NAACP ultimately brought the lawsuit against the Topeka, Kansas, school board (a case argued by forty-five-year-old Thurgood Marshall) that led to the 1954 *Brown* v. *Board of Education* decision, in which the Supreme Court ruled segregation unconstitutional and struck down the "separate but equal" doctrine that had justified Jim Crow laws since 1896.

When the high expectations of *Brown* encountered the harsh reality of massive resistance, a young Baptist preacher in Montgomery, Alabama, named Martin Luther King led a successful boycott in 1957 of the city's segregated bus system. The black church was the cradle of the modern civil rights movement. Ordained clergy stood at its helm, and to carry on his struggle against segregation, King christened his new organization the Southern Christian Leadership Conference, a name he hoped would distinguish his nonviolent philosophy (culled from an amalgamation of sources that included Thoreau, Gandhi, and Jesus Christ) from the separatist teachings of Malcolm X and other Muslims. The buses that lined the Mall during the March on Washington in August 1963 bore the sign of the cross: Ebeneezer Baptist, Bethel African Methodist Episcopal, and Grace Church of God.

"Let us march on ballot boxes," proclaimed King upon completing the Selma-to-Montgomery march in 1965, "until we send to our city councils, state legislatures, and the United States Congress men who will not fear to do justice, love mercy, and walk humbly with their God." How long would segregation last? "Not long," answered King, for "mine eyes have seen the glory of the coming of the Lord, trampling out the vintage where the grapes of wrath are stored . . . Our God is marching on."[22]

The social ferment of the 1960s relied heavily on religious imagery and language. Jewish rabbis marched arm-in-arm with black Christian clergy—a unity that is all but forgotten in today's poisoned atmosphere between Jews and many African-American leaders. Opposition to the Vietnam War featured Roman Catholic priests from Father Daniel Berrigan to Theodore Hesburgh of Notre Dame University. Senator Eugene McCarthy, leader of the antiwar forces in the Senate and quixotic presidential candidate, was a devout Roman Catholic and pro-life. When Robert F. Kennedy made his fateful decision to oppose Lyndon Johnson for the Democratic nomination for president in 1968, he did so after sharing Holy Communion with United Farmworkers leader Cesar Chavez at a special Mass of Thanksgiving. Chavez was ending an extended fast of penance to pray for an end to the violence that plagued his union. Among liberal organizers in the 1960s, the union between church and politics was total.[23] Marshall Wittman, who now serves as the legislative director of the Christian Coalition, once worked as a field recruiter for Cesar Chavez. He relates that when he and other farmworker union organizers arrived in Detroit in 1975, they stayed in free housing provided by the Roman Catholic archdiocese and worked out of the diocese headquarters.

Such faith-based activism, now that so much energy has shifted from liberals to conservatives, has suddenly become suspect, to be treated as potentially subversive of our democratic institutions. In fact, it is part of a cherished American tradition of religious dissent and church-based reform that stretches back as far as the nation's founding.

Liberals have denounced those who entered politics to serve a religious end for violating the "separation of church and state." Such falsehoods might be harmless if they were merely propaganda designed to defeat candidates or legislation forwarded by people of faith. But they are more than that. They seek to redefine our national character and deny our past in a way that expresses not mere neutrality, but hostility, towards religion as a legitimate source of political ideas.

Our Religious Past

Our young people are denied the essential facts about our nation's religious heritage. *These United States,* one of the most common high school history texts in the nation, lists more than 300 important dates in American history, only three of which refer to religion. *A History of Our American People* includes only six religious events in its recounting of 642 important moments in our history—though it found room to include a discussion of the dance craze known as the Twist and to mention the introduction of ice hockey at Yale University. Mentor Books has recently issued a revised edition of Alexis de Tocqueville's classic *Democracy in America,* the most important work by a foreign observer of the United States ever published, and simply excised every reference to religion from the text. While some call for the inclusion of women, minorities, and native Americans in the discussion of our history, they present a highly inaccurate portrait of our national past by ignoring the contributions made by people of faith.[24]

America, Ronald Reagan once observed, is never a finished work; it is always being renewed. Religion, and particularly religious dissent, has been a vital part of that renewal since the early days of the republic. The fire-breathing abolitionist, the ax-wielding prohibitionist, the Bible-thumping opponent of evolution, and the beaten but unbowed civil rights protester—all these and more have made a priceless contribution to calling our nation back to its spiritual roots, even when their political crusades fell short of their holy expectations.

Those of us who follow in their footsteps would do well to emulate their zeal, which was tempered by humility. They personified Margaret Thatcher's eloquent warning, made in more recent times, that "there is little hope for democracy if the hearts of men and women in democratic societies cannot be touched by a call to something greater than themselves." She added: "Parliamentarians can legislate the rule of law," but only "the church can teach the life of faith." That faith is not a poison that ails our democracy; it is its lifeblood.[25]

The time has never been riper for a new reformist impulse of religious faith. People of faith must stand up and be counted as part of a modern renewal of the American experiment. They will face ridicule and abuse. But certainly no worse than was faced by Amelia Bloomer, William Jennings Bryan, and Martin Luther King. To insure that religious dissent takes a positive direction, people of faith must understand the mood of the country and the modern means of communication that are available to them, particularly the emerging giants of alternative television and talk radio.

CHAPTER ELEVEN

The Electronic Godzilla:
Television, Talk Radio, and Politics

O N THE MORNING of February 1, 1994, Congressman George Miller, Democrat of California, slipped into a subcommittee meeting and surreptitiously tacked an amendment onto the Elementary and Secondary Education Act (H.R. 6) that made it a violation of federal law for any teacher to teach a subject unless that teacher had been certified by state authorities. Few paid any attention to Miller's amendment at the time. The bill already contained a labyrinth of complex rules. One additional regulation hardly seemed to matter. But the Miller teacher-certification mandate was a dagger aimed at the heart of every private, parochial, and home school in the country.

On February 8 staff members for Congressman Dick Armey of Texas discovered the Miller amendment. Armey introduced a corrective amendment at a meeting of the House Education and Labor Committee that afternoon. But Armey lost and the Miller amendment survived its first challenge.

On February 14, as the bill sailed towards final passage, Armey's staff notified several pro-family groups on Capitol Hill of the dangers of the Miller amendment. One of those they contacted was Doug Phillips, the twenty-nine-year-old legislative director for the Home School Legal Defense Fund, a Virginia-based lobby group. Phillips, a graduate of George Mason University law school and a veteran of many conservative causes, alerted other pro-family organizations about the Miller amendment. Among them was the Christian Coalition, which activated its nationwide fax network, blitzing grassroots activists with action alerts and lighting up telephone trees nationwide.

By February 16, news of the Miller amendment sounded from the trumpet of conservative media outlets. Pat Robertson's *700 Club*, Marlin Maddoux's *Point of View* and Jim Dobson's radio program informed their huge audiences of the legislation and urged them to make their voices heard. The result was complete chaos on Capitol Hill. Over the next week an estimated one million phone calls jammed the Capitol switchboard as constituents demanded that Congress kill the Miller amendment. Congressional offices were buried beneath such an avalanche of calls that some took their phones off the hooks.

As the grassroots protest mounted, I received a phone call from a top aide to a member of Congress who asked, "What is this H.R. 6 and how should we vote?" I told him to vote against Miller and for the Armey amendment. "Consider it done," he said, and hung up the phone. This scene repeated itself all over Washington.

"We have decided to vote for your amendment. Please tell your people to stop calling," begged another congressman's chief of staff of a home school lobbyist. "I believe in democracy. It's just that we have had about as much democracy as we can handle for one day."

On February 18, as members of Congress headed home for a President's Day recess, activists showed up at town hall meetings to pepper them with questions about H.R. 6. Many congressmen had never even heard of the bill, much less the offending amendment. I spoke with one journalist whose daughter was interning in the House of Representatives when the firestorm erupted. She fielded more than 400 phone calls in the space of a few hours. She called her father, hoping he might know what H.R. 6 was. No one in the office knew. Another top aide in Congress told me that in ten years he had never seen such a spontaneous flood of protest.

This grassroots pressure had its desired effect. On February 23, the powerful House Rules Committee announced its plans to delete the teacher-certification requirement. At the behest of harried members who wanted to end the torrent of phone calls, the committee agreed to make the vote on the Miller amendment the first order of business on the following day.

On February 24 the Miller amendment was defeated by the staggering margin of 424-1. Dick Armey's substitute amendment that protected private, parochial, and home schools against federal regulation passed overwhelmingly.[1]

Just a few years ago, such legislative shenanigans would have gone unnoticed by the public. Not any more. A combination of legislative savvy, voter anger, and technologies like fax machines, microcomputers, and talk radio is making it possible for the average person to affect government as never before. The battle over H.R. 6 caught many members of Congress flatfooted. Even when the storm had passed, few understood that it was not merely an isolated episode but part of a remarkable new phenomenon of technopopulism. The *New York Times* called the vote a "bow to the religious right." They missed the larger point: talk radio and cable television, dominated by conservative voices like Rush Limbaugh and Pat Robertson, now rivals or eclipses the establishment press in shaping the nation's political agenda.[2]

Network Television

"American politics and television are now so completely locked together that it is impossible to tell the story of one without the other," wrote Theodore White in 1982.[3] The number of televisions in the United States rose from 7,000 black-and-white sets in 1946 to 50 million in 1960. During the peak years of the mid 1950s, Americans bought television sets at a rate of *10,000 a day*. This meteoric rise was one of the greatest technological triumphs in history, and it has impacted every facet of American life, especially politics.

John F. Kennedy was the first genuine television politician. Most historians agree that Kennedy edged past Richard Nixon when he won their first televised debate on September 26, 1960. Nixon, who had just been released from the hospital for treatment of a staph infection, appeared pale, gaunt, and haggard. Surveys taken later by the networks estimated that 120 million people watched one or all of the Kennedy-Nixon debates. Nixon lost the election by less than one vote per precinct. After the election, Kennedy is reported to have told his campaign advisors, "It was TV more than anything else that turned the tide."[4]

By 1968, when Nixon made his comeback, he had learned the hard lessons of his earlier defeat. He hired a former producer for Mike Douglas named Roger Ailes, who orchestrated a series of ten televised "town meetings," featuring friendly audiences that pitched softball questions at the candidate and wildly applauded his answers. The "new" Nixon appeared relaxed, self-assured, confident. The Ailes-created productions worked so well that the campaign bought four hours of television time on the weekend before the election for a nationwide telethon. This time, however, there were no debates. Nixon won by 500,000 votes out of 68 million cast.[5]

It was somehow appropriate that the climax of the television era would come with the election of Ronald Reagan, a former actor and host of the television's *GE Masterpiece Theater*. Michael Deaver, Reagan's resident public relations genius, understood that good pictures made for good television. Deaver and the White House advance team staged masterful settings for Reagan to deliver his lines: Reagan standing behind piles of sandbags peering through binoculars across the Korean demilitarized zone; an open-shirted Reagan speaking against the backdrop of the Statue of Liberty; a misty-eyed Reagan eulogizing Allied soldiers on a rocky cliff in Normandy overlooking the beaches where they gave their lives.

Many of these same tactics have been utilized by the Clinton White House with the assistance of David Gergen, who served as an aide to both Nixon and Reagan. After his celebrated problems with the Pentagon reached a flash point during the gays in the military controversy in 1993, Clinton visited the "no man's land" that divides North and South Korea, a shameless reenactment of the same visit by Reagan nine years earlier.[6]

These tactics were designed to reach a single medium: network television. But today network television is in a state of crisis, challenged by the emerging technologies of the information superhighway. Cable, interactive television, talk radio, computerized bulletin boards, fiber optics, and satellite transmission are democratizing the delivery of news and obliterating the power of the gatekeepers at the television networks.

"We're watching the end of the networks as we know them," predicts Fred Friendly, former president of CBS News. Cable has gobbled away at the audience share of the three big networks, ABC, CBS, and NBC. In 1980, 90 percent of television sets turned on during prime time were tuned to the networks. That penetration figure fell to 76 percent in 1985, and in 1990 slipped to around 60 percent. During the same period, cable increased its audience share to 20 percent, with the remainder going to independent stations or the upstart Fox network.

Viewership of network evening news shows has taken a similar nosedive. Since Dan Rather took over the anchor chair from Walter Cronkite in 1981, *CBS Evening News* has lost one-third of its audience. In 1980, three out of every four homes with television sets tuned in to the evening news shows of the big three. But by 1993 only slightly more than half of homes with television sets turned on watched network news. Among younger viewers, the drop-off is catastrophic: only one in thirteen viewers under age thirty-five watches one of the network news programs. Changing demographics, longer hours at the office, two-worker households, and later and longer commutes to the suburbs all suggest that this trend is likely to accelerate in the future. The evening news shows are the afternoon newspapers of the nineties, victims of rapidly changing technology and lifestyles.[7]

Not that the networks are finished. They still collectively rake in $9 billion a year in advertising revenue. Despite CBS' loss of NFL football in 1994, the cash position of the big three will enable them to outbid cable competitors for big-ticket programming such as the Olympics and the Super Bowl. They are also diversifying: NBC has launched CNBC, its own cable network with a populist mix of talk shows and call-in formats. For our purposes, the issue is not the continued financial viability of the networks, which is not in serious doubt, but the loosening of their monopolistic hold over the political culture due to declining audience share.[8]

High-Tech Populism

How are new technologies allowing citizens to replace network television and daily newspapers as the arbiters of American political life? The answer is a combination of cable, talk radio, and satellite television.

Cable subscribers now number 60 million households, and annual revenue for the cable industry has increased from around $2.5 billion in 1980 to $22 billion in 1993. The percentage of homes subscribing to basic cable service rose from 23 percent in 1980 to 63 percent today. This is changing our politics as well as our viewing habits. CNN and C-SPAN's live broadcasts of Congress are revolutionizing the way Americans view their government. In October 1991 more than 5 million Americans viewed the Clarence Thomas-Anita Hill hearings before the Senate Judiciary Committee. This is remarkable considering the fact that cameras were barred from the Senate floor until 1986.[9]

A new era in television history dawned in April of 1984, when Representative Newt Gingrich, the Republican firebrand from Georgia, strode to the well of the House of Representatives to denounce congressional Democrats for their opposition to Ronald Reagan's policies in Latin America. In the middle of Gingrich's remarks, Speaker "Tip" O'Neill interrupted him, and in the heated exchange that followed, the House parliamentarian ruled O'Neill out of order for making a personal attack on Gingrich. It was a stinging rebuke of a Speaker of the House, and two of the three networks led their evening broadcasts with the incident, which was captured live by C-SPAN.

In retaliation, O'Neill ordered House cameras to pan the empty chamber when Gingrich and other GOP backbenchers spent hours lambasting the Democratic leadership into the wee hours of the morning, all after the House had adjourned for the day, and all for the benefit of a growing C-SPAN audience. The episode not only signaled the passing of an aging generation on Capitol Hill who had come to Congress before the advent of television (Robert Byrd, "Tip" O'Neill, Jim Wright, Howard Baker) and the rise of a new, telegenic congressional leadership class, but it also put C-SPAN on the political map.

Today C-SPAN enjoys an audience of 2 million viewers (98 percent of whom vote), and its low-budget, populist programming of viewer call-in shows, congressional debates, and grassroots conferences satisfies a hunger among the American people for "just the facts, ma'am." People no longer need their daily newspaper to interpret reality for them; they watch it unfold without leaving their living room. Some viewers participate in the debates as they happen. When Congressman Pete Stark of

California recently cited an erroneous fact during hearings on health care reform, an angry C-SPAN viewer called his office and demanded a correction. The aide promised to pass the information on to Stark. "I don't want you to just take a message," the woman insisted. "I want you to get on into that hearing room and correct it." With C-SPAN, voter anger is instantaneous, and the outlet for their fury is immediate.[10]

Another historic moment in the new, participatory politics made possible by cable television came on February 20, 1992, when Ross Perot appeared on *Larry King Live*, and King prodded Perot into answering a question about a possible presidential bid. The exchange was remarkable for its spontaneity:

KING By the way, is there any scenario in which you would run for president? Can you give me a scenario in which you'd say, 'OK, I'm in'?

PEROT Number one, I don't want to . . .

KING Is there a scenario?

PEROT Now that touches me. But I don't want to fail them. That would be the only thing that would interest me . . . if you're that serious—you, the people, are that serious—you register me in 50 states, and if you're not willing to organize and do that . . .

KING Wait a minute. Are you saying—wait a minute.

PEROT . . . then this is all just talk.

KING Hold it, hold it, hold it, hold it, hold it . . .

PEROT Now stay with me, Larry . . . If you want to register me in 50 states, number one, I'll promise you this. Between now and the convention we'll get both parties' heads straight. . . . I don't want any money from anybody but you, and I don't want anything but five bucks from you because I can certainly pay for my own campaign—no ifs, ands, and buts—but I want you to have skin in the game. I want you in the ring.[11]

When Perot returned to his Washington hotel room after the program, he found an envelope stuffed under his door with the first contribution for his campaign, and an anonymous note: "Run, Ross, Run." His offices in Dallas received an estimated 100,000 phone calls in the seventy-two hours following the appearance on *Larry King Live*. He went on to garner a larger percentage of the vote than any independent or third-party candidate for president since Teddy Roosevelt. The marriage of Perot and King was more than coincidence. Each in their own way represents a new brand of politics. Perot would have been impossible before the rise of cable. He represents a challenge to the established party bosses in the same way that talk radio and cable represent a challenge to the monopoly of the broadcast networks. The launching of the Perot candidacy on CNN signaled the political power of cable in the same way that the Kennedy-Nixon debate twenty-two years earlier had signified the arrival of the networks. The torch is being passed.

Even more important to the new politics than CNN is the explosion of talk radio. Over 1,000 of the nation's 10,000 radio stations have shifted their formats to news-talk, and if current trends continue, one out of every six radio stations in America will feature some talk in their format by the end of the decade. Angry listeners, incited by fire-breathing talk jockeys, are dialing for democracy. Trapped on traffic-snarled highways during rush hour, they are fusing the new technology of cellular phones with the steam-cooker pressure of stressed commuters and hostile voters. They are deluging Capitol Hill with a volume of phone calls that has no precedent in history. Talk radio is shaking up Washington, throwing politicians off-stride and setting the political agenda for the nation. Gordon Liddy, Jerry Brown, Pat Buchanan, Larry King, and dozens more are joining this revolution in direct democracy with afternoon talk shows that have all been launched in the past two years.[12]

But the "Godzilla" of talk radio, in the words of the *Wall Street Journal,* is Rush Limbaugh. His radio audience is the largest in the nation, with 22 million listeners a week tuning in to a network of over 600 stations. His best-selling book, *The Way Things Ought to Be,* has sold over 2.5 million copies to become one of the biggest nonfiction best-sellers in history, and his "Limbaugh Letter" newsletter is read by 400,000 subscribers after less than two years in publication. His television program, now broadcast on 220 local stations, is a one-man gabfest performed before an adoring studio audience that is now the number-one syndicated late-night show on television.

In some ways Limbaugh represents a cultural throw-back to the heyday of AM radio. But more than simply a media empire, Limbaugh is a political phenomenon; he is tapping into voter anger and has found a way to channel it in a powerful (and financially lucrative) direction. His loyal and devoted audience savors his opinions, relishes his bombastic rhetoric, and laughs uproariously at his iconoclastic humor. If Rush raises an issue on Capitol Hill, his listeners charge to their phones and light up switchboards. "The same cannot be said of David Broder and William Safire, nor of Peter Jennings and Dan Rather," notes the *Washington Post*. "The more Olympian media, print and electronic, just does not have the same intimate rapport with its audiences."[13]

Limbaugh understands the importance of merging his populist message with the latest technology. Listeners bombard him with faxes, thumb-tack "listener mail" onto computerized bulletin boards, and dial in their opinions on cellular phones while rushing to their next business appointment. Indeed, there has been inadequate attention paid to the power of technology and changing demographics in driving the Limbaugh phenomenon. In today's fast-paced society, our neighbors are no longer the people who live next door, but those we talk to on the phone or listen to on radio or television. Limbaugh provides a shared experience for those who feel disconnected from society and are hungering for a sense of community, a feeling of belonging. Hundreds of "Rush Rooms" have sprouted up in restaurants across America, providing a midday haven for "dittoheads" who share Limbaugh's view of the world, and relish the fellowship of others who feel a similar alienation from elite culture. Talk radio has become a gigantic town meeting and an exercise in the best (and worst) of American democracy.

Limbaugh's Christian radio counterpart is Dr. Jim Dobson, founder of Focus on the Family, whose daily thirty-minute program is heard on 4,000 stations worldwide and has a weekly cumulative audience approaching five million listeners. The vast majority of Dobson's audience (70 percent) consists of baby boomer women, many of whom are juggling motherhood, homemaking, and responsibilities at the office. Dobson combines the bedside manner of a respected child psychologist with unswerving evangelical faith and conservative political views. His ministry's eight magazines reach 2.3 million households every month. He has authored twelve best-selling books on family issues that have sold millions of copies. But his greatest influence comes from his daily radio program, which has a loyal audience that will go to the phones or the post office to support the causes and issues he champions. Guests on the Dobson show have been known to receive as many as 15,000 letters after an appearance.

The cable TV analogue to Limbaugh and Dobson is former presidential candidate and religious broadcaster Pat Robertson, who founded the Family Channel in 1981 to provide an outlet for religious programming to the then-embryonic cable industry. Today the Family Channel is the tenth-largest cable network in the nation, with 58 million subscribers and stock valued at nearly $1 billion—about one-fourth the value of CBS and NBC. Its programming has evolved into an all-American mix of Westerns, game shows, and popular family entertainment. Robertson has purchased the rights to *The Waltons*, recently acquired Mary Tyler Moore studios with its rich library of wholesome seventies-era sitcoms, and is extensively involved in joint ventures for animated series and original programming. But the flagship program of the Family Channel remains the *700 Club*, Robertson's daily news and talk show, which has been broadcast continuously since 1961 and now has a weekly cumulative audience of 10 million viewers. Devotees of the *700 Club* combine deeply held religious beliefs with a disdain for the dominant culture and a commitment to participatory democracy.

The political sophistication of Robertson's audience has grown since his 1988 presidential campaign. In 1991, for example, during the confirmation vote on Supreme Court Justice Clarence Thomas, Robertson flashed the Capitol switchboard number on the screen. A total of 45,000 phone calls jammed the switchboard in the next five minutes, a record at the time. In February, 1993, during the height of Bill Clinton's bumbling attempt to repeal the ban on gays in the military, Robertson discussed the issue on the air and urged his viewers to call and make their voices heard. A record 450,000 phone calls descended on the U.S. Capitol. The following week, in its analysis of this new phenomenon of dial-in democracy, the *Washington Post* ascribed its power to the fundamentalist "followers" of Robertson, which it infamously described as "poor, uneducated, and easy to command." This observation signified a counter-assault by one of yesterday's powerbrokers (the metropolitan daily newspaper) against one of tomorrow's kingmakers (cable television). It is only natural that institutions threatened by new technology, and the new politics that it engenders, react to the challenge.

The latest blending of technology with populist politics is National Empowerment Television, the brainchild of Washington conservative strategist Paul Weyrich, which he describes as "C-SPAN with an attitude." NET began as an interactive satellite network that beams Weyrich's Washington strategy sessions to meetings of activists who gather in churches, colleges, or homes equipped with satellite dishes, and can join in by telephone or fax. In December 1993 NET launched a twenty-four-hour network that reaches 3.5 million satellite-dish owners and a potential audience of 5 million via cable and low-power TV. The eclectic programming includes call-in shows on Congress, the judiciary, education, personal finances, even wine-tasting. Weyrich's favorite technique is to invite members of Congress to appear on a program (egos on Capitol Hill rarely pass up a chance to appear on television), sit them in a chair under the hot lights, and then open up the phone lines, which quickly light up with calls from voters wanting to know why they voted a particular way on a bill. [14]

Like talk radio and cable, Weyrich's satellite town halls reach a targeted, narrow, and dedicated audience with enormous potential political power. Former Secretary of Education Lamar Alexander and the Republican National Committee have also launched satellite television networks that bypass the traditional press and connect grassroots activists with political leaders. Alexander's network boasts over 1,000 downlink locations that tune in to a monthly call-in show. [15]

Satellites are part of the information superhighway of the future that promises to shake up the establishment media by giving millions of Americans direct and immediate access to information they once received only from journalistic gatekeepers. Imagine a day when every single home or office computer (there are currently over 100 million personal computers) can be transformed into a fully interactive television set. Worker-viewers will be able to talk to bosses thousands of miles away, participate in visual teleconferences, communicate with colleagues on computerized bulletin boards, even order movies from a selection of thousands of titles. Computers will be attached to broadcasters via fiber optics, with greater transmission power in a single thread of glass than all the existing radio and television networks combined. Home schoolers will be able to pull down their children's algebra lessons from a menu of services, and a videotaped lesson with interactive capability will appear on the screen followed by a quick quiz that the computer grades.

Instead of the three or four channels offered by the networks, television viewers will be free to choose from 500 channels—pulled down from the galaxy by a satellite dish the size of a large grapefruit that will rest on top of a TV set, rather than sit on concrete in the backyard, like the seven-foot-diameter models currently in use. Also not far off is direct transmission satellite radio, which will allow Limbaugh-like radio entrepreneurs to bypass local stations and broadcast directly to listeners with satellite dishes the size of silver dollars that could be mounted on the trunk of an automobile.[16]

The disaggregation and splintering of our political culture that the advent of cable has already accomplished will only accelerate in the years ahead. Several projects, one headed by former Reagan media guru Mike Deaver, will combine unfiltered political news and updates with interactive communication. It is entirely possible that by the early part of the next century, activist-viewers will be able to flip channels between a feminist channel, a religious channel, a property rights channel, and a libertarian channel. What shape the information highway takes in the future will depend on technology, economics, and demographics. But one thing is certain. We are standing on the threshold of the most dramatic transformation of technology and politics since the advent of television.

This technology is near to becoming a reality. Hughes Aircraft Company recently launched a three-ton satellite as part of a $1 billion project to provide direct satellite television to millions of Americans by 1998. Receiving dishes are already available to consumers at a cost of only around $300. As prices drop and miniaturization accelerates, this technology will become ubiquitous, much as we have witnessed with home video recorders. Just a decade ago, few homes had VCRs; today there are 72 million in use, covering 80 percent of all the households in America. Satellites and fiber optics could make cable obsolete and further blur the distinctions between telecommunications and television. Even though the attempted merger between TCI, the world's largest cable company, and BellAtlantic fell through in 1994, the information superhighway remains a multi-billion dollar frontier that will transform how we live, work—and how we practice politics.[17]

John Naisbitt waxed prophetic in *Megatrends* when he argued that individualism and participatory democracy are the franchises of tomorrow, not the relics of yesterday. The bureaucratic, hierarchical institutions that have governed America and mediated power relationships for most of the twentieth century are on the wrong side of a tidal wave of technological and demographic change. These institutions will survive, but they cannot prosper. The future belongs not to them, but to a new, populist brand of politics that connects average citizens with a government they believe has lost touch with their values. They are pouring out of their homes and churches and into the precincts, and politics will never look the same again for their involvement.[18]

CHAPTER TWELVE

The Smoking Volcano:
Ross Perot and the Populist Revolt

I N 1992 Ross Perot garnered 19 percent of the vote for president, the highest total by any independent or third-party candidate in 80 years. Quixotic, straight-talking, and delightfully unpredictable, Perot is the antipolitician of the nineties. On election night, he entertained a crowd of supporters who packed shoulder to shoulder into a Dallas ballroom by dancing across the stage with his wife Margot to the tune of Patsy Cline's country hit, "Crazy." But there may have been a method to his madness. The Perot vote holds the key to the future of American politics, and whichever party gains the votes of his supporters can assemble a winning coalition as powerful and permanent as those forged by FDR and Ronald Reagan.

From the stratospheric apex of his bizarre presidential campaign, Perot plummeted to a new low during his campaign against NAFTA in 1993. Like a west Texas wildcatter who sinks everything he owns into a dry hole, he gambled all his political capital—and lost. The televised debate between a well-coached Al Gore and Perot revealed a petty and nasty dimension of his personality that left many of his supporters dismayed and voters turned off. As a result, his support in the electorate spiraled downward in a free fall. His approval rating dropped thirty-six points in a few months, when only 13 percent of the respondents said he would make a good president, compared to 33 percent at the peak of his popularity. The number of Americans who said they would consider voting for him for president fell from an incredible 45 percent in May, 1993, to only 28 percent at year's end.[1]

But in today's traumatized political environment, it is a serious mistake to discount Perot's appeal. A vote for Perot, after all, was not a vote *for* the eccentric billionaire but *against* the two political parties, a ballot marked "none of the above." This vote of no confidence in our political system reveals a depth of anger and cynicism that spells deep trouble for the future of American politics. If such a large number of citizens in any other Western democracy felt similarly alienated and betrayed, the government would fall. Elections would be called, a new ruling coalition installed, and public confidence in the government would rebound, as often takes place in parliamentary countries like Great Britain or Canada. But in the United States, our government does not fall. Instead, it staggers on like a crippled giant, stumbling from crisis to crisis with a minority president lacking any genuine mandate and a Congress held in low esteem.

Perot blossoms in this atmosphere like a violet in a greenhouse. His core supporters are unmoved by his flaws; indeed, they are the very things that attract them to him. For example, a 1992 Gallup poll found that Perot's liberal views in support of abortion and gay rights, and his opposition to the Persian Gulf War dissuaded few of his supporters. These die-hards are attracted by the hurricane force of his personality and his just-the-facts-ma'am demeanor, not his issue positions. Even his authoritarian edge becomes an asset; the battle-cry "Ross for Boss" has a double meaning. As a Detroit male Perot supporter concluded, "He reminds me a little of a dictator, but maybe we need that approach to intimidate the people in Washington."[2]

The Perot Vote

Who are the Perot supporters? They are male (52 percent), overwhelmingly white (94 percent), middle-class ($34,000 average household income), and disproportionately independents or disaffected Republicans (74 percent). Nearly one in four men supported Perot, compared to only one in six women. They also tend to be well-educated, geographically concentrated in the northeast and west, and youthful. Two-thirds of Perot's vote came from voters under forty-four years of age, a group that

Republicans carried heavily in the eighties, but lost big in 1992, garnering only 36 percent among these voters.[3]

Although they define themselves as moderates or liberals, the Perot voters are ideologically nondescript. Their movement represents a middle-class revolt against the straightjacket of traditional ideological categories. "Antiestablishment populism has been the most important force in our politics for the last twenty years," notes political commentator William Schneider. "It is neither liberal nor conservative . . . it is ideologically ambivalent." Perot voters believe that ideology is what is wrong with America, that both parties have failed, and that neither liberals nor conservatives have the solutions to our nation's social and economic ills.[4]

This ambivalence is reflected in the views of Perotistas on the social issues. A full 69 percent of Perot voters believe that abortion should be legal in all or most cases—almost as high as Clinton voters. Bush voters represent the flip-side of this equation: over 50 percent believe that abortion should be illegal in most or all cases. Perot voters are largely unchurched; only 33 percent of them attend church weekly, about the same as Clinton voters—far below the 50 percent of Bush voters who frequently attend church. The libertarian leanings of Perot voters might seem to make them unlikely coalition partners with religious conservatives. But that is misleading. For while Perot voters tend to steer left on abortion, they rarely cast their ballots based on social issues. According to network exit polls in 1992, only 5 percent of Perot voters ranked abortion as a key factor in their voting decision, compared to 12 percent of the entire electorate. Perot voters, therefore, could be attracted to a coalition with religious voters (Reagan did it in the 1980s) by emphasizing other issues of shared interest.[5]

The Politics of Discontent

Less important to the movement than Perot himself is the political wave of discontent that he rides like a Malibu surfer balancing on the crest of a tsunami. This "radical middle" combines the insurgent politics of Pat Buchanan on the Right and Jerry Brown on the Left. It seems to lack an ideological compass and a core of values. Part of the explanation for this loose-cannon effect lies in the deep pessimism that Perot supporters feel about the political system. In a March 1993 NBC News/ *Wall Street Journal* survey, 62 percent said that Bill Clinton and the Democratic Congress would make little difference in ending gridlock, and that "things will be pretty much as they were before." An astonishing 88 percent of Perot voters in 1992 said they were dissatisfied or angry with the way the federal government was working.[6]

These voters are angry because year after year almost every member of Congress who seeks reelection wins. This suggests that what ails American politics is not ideological but systemic. It is why voters are attracted by Perot's prescription to eschew ideology, roll up his sleeves and "get under the hood and fix it." Voter discontent and anger, which has simmered for years like a smoking volcano, is about to explode. Perot is only the initial tremor in the birthing of this new era. A world of politics turns upside down, and all that was solid ground becomes shifting sand. People have lost confidence in every major institution in society, including both political parties, Wall Street, the labor unions, the schools, and the major media. The rules by which these institutions have governed no longer apply. A new politics is being born—one that will affect how we live for decades to come.

In 1992 Perot was the first viable independent candidate for president in twenty-four years. But in subsequent presidential elections, we could have several splinter candidates. New parties may form, or at least pressure groups that function as para-parties outside the two-party paradigm. We can expect a growing number of independent candidates for state and federal office who will abandon party labels and run insurgent campaigns based on reformist platforms and charismatic personalities. Several have already won in recent years: Governor Lowell Weiker of Connecticut, Governor Wally Hickel of Alaska, and Congressman Bernie Sanders of Vermont, the first Socialist member of Congress in a generation. More independent candidates have emerged in Virginia and Kansas in 1994, with countless others in the wings.

.   .   .

An Unchartable Chaos

The salient and defining characteristic of this politics is chaotic and unpredictable change. A disenchanted and disaffected electorate is still in the mood to "throw the bums out," and the bums seem to be everywhere. Just a few of the recent developments in American politics demonstrate how unpredictable the landscape has become.

In July 1991 George Bush basked in the afterglow of the Persian Gulf War, buoyed by the highest approval ratings of any president since World War II. One survey showed that 90 percent of the American people approved of his job performance. Some of the most formidable candidates in the Democratic party—Mario Cuomo, Sam Nunn, Al Gore—bypassed the presidential campaign rather than face the prospect of defeat. A 1991 news report concluded that "almost every barometer indicates that Bush is on his way to a coronation next year." Eighteen months later, Bush lost in the worst landslide suffered by an incumbent president since William Howard Taft in 1912.[7]

President Bill Clinton's job approval rating in May 1993 stood at 38 percent, the lowest for any new president in sixty years. Buffeted by controversy after a failed Attorney General nomination and gays in the military, Clinton seemed destined to be another Jimmy Carter. Nine months later, he delivered his State of the Union address to standing ovations and enjoyed an approval rating of 58 percent, higher than Ronald Reagan's at the same point in his administration. Then the Whitewater and sex scandals exploded, sending his popularity plummeting to new lows. The roller-coaster ride of Bill Clinton's presidency symbolizes the vicious riptide of public opinion that is part and parcel of the new politics.[8]

After the 1992 election, political analysts staged the funeral and wrote the obituary of the Republican party. Torn apart by factional infighting and repudiated at the polls, the GOP lay in shambles. The newly formed Republican Majority Coalition announced plans to shift the party to the left by abandoning abortion and other social issues, the opening salvo in a fratricidal "holy war" between moderates and religious conservatives. "Pundits and Democrats alike are anticipating what could be the worst round of Republican bloodletting since Barry Goldwater was trounced by Lyndon Johnson in 1964," according to one press account. "Some even question whether it can survive in its present form." One year later, however, the GOP had triumphed in every statewide election in the nation, winning nine out of nine major campaigns. Among the victories: the biggest landslide for a Republican governor in Virginia in the twentieth century and the first Republican mayors of New York and Los Angeles in thirty years. The pitched battle between the religious and moderate wings of the party never materialized.[9]

No one celebrated the 1992 election outcome more than the pro-abortion lobby. Bill Clinton's first act as president was to reverse pro-life executive orders implemented by the Reagan and Bush administrations, and abortion lobbyists announced plans for the greatest expansion of abortion rights since *Roe* v. *Wade*. Six months later, their hopes were dashed. The Freedom of Choice Act, their top legislative priority, was dead on Capitol Hill. In July 1993 pro-life forces beat back their effort to repeal the Hyde amendment, which prohibited tax funding of abortion, in the House of Representatives by the stunning margin of 255–178. "Everyone thought this was a much more pro-choice Congress," said Congresswoman Pat Schroeder (D-CO). "We found out we were wrong." Efforts to include abortion in a national health care plan were jeopardized by stiff opposition. Meanwhile, the financial resources to fight these battles grew thinner. The National Abortion Rights Action League's budget fell from $12 million in 1990 to $5 million in 1993.[10]

The Coming Political Earthquake

These are all signposts along the road to one of the most turbulent periods in American political history. Today's winner is tomorrow's loser. The cycles of ups and downs are getting shorter and nastier. No one is exempt from the uncertain crosswinds that blow across the unchartable chaos that is our body politic.

In March 1992 I was sitting in the lobby just outside the Oval Office after attending several meetings at the White House. A senior aide to

President Bush passed by smiling broadly. He shared some shocking news from exit polls in the Illinois Democratic primary.

"Senator Alan Dixon has gone down in flames," he said matter-of-factly.

I could not believe my ears. Dixon was a moderate Democrat from Illinois who had been considered virtually unbeatable, had millions of dollars in his campaign war chest, and faced only token Republican opposition. But Dixon, a shoo-in for reelection, was soundly defeated by a little-known Cook County recorder of deeds named Carol Moseley-Braun. Her upset victory christened what became known as "the year of the woman."

Politicians have never engendered much sympathy from voters. But why have so many met with such brutal ends? We seem to have created a political culture in which everyone swims with the sharks and no one gets out of the tank alive. Why have our politics become so downright nasty? Some point to a loss of civility, noting the coarseness of our public discourse. Others blame "gridlock," the inability of either party to achieve a working majority in Congress that allows them to govern effectively. There is truth to these observations. But the real source of the current tremors of our system is an impending political earthquake—one that will soon shake existing institutions to their foundations and replace them with a new political order.

There are three main reasons for the current volatility of American public life. First, the end of the cold war has shattered the old liberal-conservative, hawk-dove, isolationist-interventionist dichotomies that once gave stability to domestic politics. Second, voter cynicism has generated a desire for change and an anti-incumbent backlash at the polls. Third, many Americans feel a void in their spiritual lives that has them searching for timeless values and meaning for their lives.

Cold War Consensus Has Shattered

Our domestic political consensus about the importance of confronting the Soviet threat forged political arrangements along predetermined ideological lines. Conservative hawks called for larger defense expenditures, idealistic doves resisted; cold warriors trumpeted an expansive, interventionist foreign policy to roll back communism, while liberal isolationists warned of the limits of American power. Underlying the entire debate was a consensus view that the Soviet Union posed a grave threat to the United States and required extraordinary counter-measures to protect U.S. national security interests.

Vietnam shattered this cold war consensus. But the ideological framework provided by the conflict with communism remained intact, and most political disputes took place within its parameters. With the collapse of the Soviet threat, now even the framework of our politics is gone, and with it the center of gravity that held our political system together has vanished.

The result is chaos. As analyst Alan Tonelson has observed, "ideological confusion has spilled over into domestic politics. Even ideas as basic as Left and Right are undergoing redefinition."[11] Fissures in both the Republican and Democratic coalitions over issues like NAFTA, Bosnia, Haiti, immigration and protectionism are creating confusion and conflict. The American people historically have responded to military victory by turning inward with a vengeance. This isolationist impulse was first noted by George Washington in his Farewell Address in 1796, in which he warned of "foreign entanglements" beyond the shores of the republic.

In the twentieth century, this impulse has given rise to nasty postwar politics. Part of the explanation is sheer exhaustion. The American people are generally reluctant to send their sons and daughters to foreign battlefields. When they return from war, they want to return to the status quo antebellum. Domestic politics curls into a fetal position, fending off foreign issues and involvement. Moreover, the end of war (whether cold or hot) unleashes pent-up voter frustrations, consumer demands, and social aspirations that have been bottled up during the military struggle. With the arrival of peace, these demands explode like an overheated pressure cooker.

This pattern repeats itself after every foreign conflict. After the Allied triumph in the First World War, the euphoria of Versailles soon gave way to the harsh reality of labor unrest, the rise of the Ku Klux Klan, the Palmer raids, and the Red Scare. The end of World War II brought not domestic tranquility, but massive strikes, hyperinflation, the Dixiecrats, and McCarthyism. The end of the cold war and the collapse of the Soviet Union brought a double-dip recession, military cutbacks, base closings, and lost jobs. The same racial resentments, previously muted by war, that exploded with the Ku Klux Klan in the 1920s and the Dixiecrats in the 1950s now finds expression in David Duke. At the same time, foreign conflagrations have crashed onto the American political scene in an endless barrage: the Persian Gulf War, Bosnia, Somalia, and Haiti. Instead of being flushed with victory, many Americans feel deflated, empty, and betrayed.

Voter Anger and Cynicism

"The American people are slow to wrath, but when their wrath is once kindled it burns like a consuming flame," observed Theodore Roosevelt. A second factor contributing to America's volatile political environment is unprecedented voter anger. At any moment, with almost no advance warning, it can boil over at the ballot box with white-hot intensity. Voters are fearful about a catalogue of woes: crime, high taxes, declining wages, the exploding federal debt, government corruption, urban riots, and family breakup. A growing number of middle-class voters feel alienated from society and angry at a government they believe has failed them. More than 60 percent routinely tell pollsters that America is headed in the wrong direction. Their anger has been building for years, and now has reached what political analyst Kevin Phillips calls "the boiling point."[12]

What is causing this unprecedented anger? The answer, according to pollster Daniel Yankelovich, is the "affluence effect." In the economic boom of the 1950s, those who retained memories of the Depression did not expect prosperity to last. By the late 1960s, this economic insecurity and fear gave way to an unrestrained optimism that affluence would never end. The belief that the financial lot of each generation would exceed their parents became an article of faith. But the third stage of the "affluence effect" is an equally strong conviction that economic catastrophe is just around the corner. Disorientation and pessimism choke out the optimism of consumers and voters. Based on extensive public opinion research, Yankelovich argues that the United States moved into this third stage of the affluence effect just prior to the 1992 elections. "People begin to feel cornered and disoriented," he concludes. "They grow apprehensive that opportunities for jobs, income growth, home ownership, higher education for their children, and retirement are at risk."[13]

This explains why George Bush lost despite the fact that the economy was already improving in late 1992. Voters simply did not believe that prosperity was imminent. Voter disaffection also reflects a deep cynicism about politics in general. They are so disenchanted with the two-party system that many are dropping out of the process or opting for "none of the above." In 1992 an astonishing 44 percent of voters said they were dissatisfied with the choices for president—even with Ross Perot running as an independent. Fifty-eight percent said, "The country needs a new political party to compete with the Democratic and Republican parties in offering the best candidates for public office." And 69 percent agreed that "there is no connection between what a presidential candidate promised and what he would do if elected." This fire wall of cynicism has hardened until voters distrust not only politicians, but politics itself.[14]

Against the backdrop of this voter discontent, our political discourse has degenerated into an angry and vacuous shouting match. E. J. Dionne argues in his excellent book *Why Americans Hate Politics*, "When Americans say that politics has nothing to do with what really matters, they are largely right." Both parties field candidates, but the voters do not trust them. We hold elections, but they seem to make little difference. The same problems of crime, education, and economic decline get worse year after year. Politics appears to be an obstacle rather than a vehicle for finding solutions. Dionne adds: "The result has been a democratic politics in which voters feel increasingly powerless."[15]

When this voter cynicism began to set in is not altogether clear. William Schneider and Seymour Lipset have argued in their book, *The Confidence Gap*, that the American people became increasingly skeptical of the efficacy of social institutions, especially the government, beginning in the 1960s. The shocks of Vietnam, racial discord, urban riots, and Watergate destroyed the faith of the people in the idea that elections could solve problems. With the exception of Ronald Reagan, no president has been elected to and served two full terms since Eisenhower. Voter participation has declined, party affiliation waned, and distrust of the government waxed. Until 1992, when the Perot candidacy generated additional interest, voter turnout has declined every year since 1960, from around 60 percent to barely 50 percent. Only the Swiss have voter turnout as low as the United States. [16]

This paradox of declining voter participation combined with angry and insurgent independent political movements is not confined to the United States. Protest candidates have exploded onto the scene in France, Canada, Sweden, Italy, and Japan. Election results have ranged from the dramatic to the bizarre. Following Canadian Prime Minister Brian Mulrooney's resignation in June of 1993, the Progressive Conservatives went from controlling the government to holding only two seats in Parliament. Almost simultaneously, reform-minded Morihiro Hosokawa was elected prime minister of Japan after a series of scandals rocked the government. The first prime minister in thirty-eight years not taken from the ranks of the Liberal Democratic party, Hosokawa was forced out of office himself months later by his own tarnished past.

Anti-incumbent feelings have reached a fever pitch and politicians face an electoral landscape filled with landmines. Grassroots political entrepreneurs are launching term limit initiatives, political reform proposals, "no special rights" referenda banning same-sex minority status, and "three strikes and you're out" anticrime measures. Choosing the wrong side on any one of these explosive issues can bring instant repudiation at the polls.

The first stirrings began in 1990, when a retired Florida investor and activist named Jack Gargan took out advertisements in newspapers with a screaming headline that demanded, "Throw the Hypocritical Rascals Out!" (Gargan would later play a key role in launching the presidential campaign of Ross Perot.) Term limit measures passed in three states (California, Oklahoma, and Colorado), and numerous incumbents went down to defeat. The Pennsylvania Senate race in November 1991 brought anti-incumbency exploding to the surface. Harris Wofford, a former Peace Corps operative who at one point trailed Bush's Attorney General Richard Thornburgh fifty points in the polls, won in a landslide.

Victims in 1992 and 1993 include George Bush, Senator Wyche Fowler of Georgia, Mayor David Dinkins of New York, and Governor Jim Florio of New Jersey. Still more politicians will see epitaphs carved on their political tombstones in the coming decade.[17]

The anti-incumbency backlash will remain a prominent feature of American politics for the foreseeable future. One reason is continued anxiety about the economy. A 1993 survey found that only 12 percent of the American people were positive about the state of the economy, while 87 percent felt negative. Only 37 percent viewed their own financial health positively. Declining wages, lost jobs, and middle-class anxiety all contribute to this essentially negative view of the nation's economic future. Ironically, the economy has enjoyed healthy growth since late 1992, interest rates remain low, unemployment has fallen to 6.5 percent, and many regions of the country enjoy full employment. But none of this seems to matter. Economic anxiety has voters feeling disillusioned and restless.

These rumblings of discontent have set the grassroots ablaze with protest. Citizens are lighting up switchboards, tying up fax machines, and jamming talk radio programs with their opinions on everything from taxes and health care to gay rights and abortion. The U.S. Capitol has been buried beneath an avalanche of mail and an unending torrent of phone calls. In 1974 only 17 percent of the American people had recently contacted their member of Congress; in 1993, 39 percent did so. Western Union's mailgram traffic on Capitol Hill has jumped an astonishing 66 percent since 1992. And the Capitol switchboard logged 22.8 million calls in the first seven months of 1993—more than it recorded in all of the previous year. A growing proliferation of grassroots advocacy groups with political agendas as diverse as the Christian Coalition and the Sierra Club are prodding their members to make their voices heard, and the politicians are listening.[18]

Spiritual Hunger

The public is also increasingly concerned about a loss of ethics and values in society. Every major institution that once enjoyed public confidence has been shaken by scandal in recent years—Wall Street, Washington, organized religion, the thrift industry, and sports. From Ivan Boesky to Jim and Tammy Bakker, from Pete Rose to Iran-Contra, these convulsions have left the general public exhausted and disillusioned. They are hungry for moral and spiritual renewal. Among voters under age fifty, "the breakdown in morality" is the number one concern, ahead of health care, welfare, the deficit, and crime. A recent poll by the *Washington Post* dissecting voter sentiment on the threshold of the 1994 elections found that two-thirds of the respondents listed social issues as the most important problem facing the nation today, while only 18 percent listed the economy. This is the opposite of voters' sentiment in 1992. They sense that what ails America is not merely an economic crisis, but a moral crisis.[19]

A Times-Mirror survey in 1994 confirmed this spiritual hunger, finding that morality and a breakdown in ethics ranked at the very top of voter concerns. Many Americans are finding that the materialism and hedonism that dominate our culture are ultimately unsatisfying. After a generation of experimenting with everything from sex and drugs to leveraged buyouts and junk bonds, today's baby boomer generation is turning inward in search of spiritual solace. *USA Today* calls it the "New Virtue." James Q. Wilson has called it the "moral sense," arguing that the knowledge of what is good and decent is intuitive in the human intellect. Americans are deeply troubled about a society in which homicide is the second leading cause of death among eighteen to thirty-four year olds, marriages are splintering, children are having children, and our material prosperity stands in stark contrast to the emptiness in our souls.[20]

Bill Bennett, borrowing a page from the Greeks, calls this moral drift "acedia." "What afflicts us is a corruption of the heart," he suggests, "a turning away in the soul. And only when we turn toward the right things—toward enduring, noble, spiritual things—will things get better." Even in the midst of economic abundance, the American people sense an emptiness in the soul that only spiritual values can fill. As columnist Robert Samuelson trenchantly argues, "Wealth will not bring love or civility. It will not make the dishonest honest. It will not mend broken families or stifle crime." Jim Fallows has suggested that America needs a healthy dose of "Frank Capra values": honesty, frugality, hard work, respect for neighbor. Bennett adds: "Even if we have full employment and greater economic growth—if we have cities of gold and alabaster—but our children have not learned how to walk in goodness, justice, and mercy, then the American experiment, no matter how gilded, will have failed."[21]

Populism and Perot

A new populist movement is stepping into the vacuum created by the end of the cold war, the loss of respect for our political institutions, and spiritual hunger. Ross Perot is the most visible personification of this moment. But the activists and voters that Perot has mobilized will ultimately be far more important than he is in changing our politics. These voters are more interested in finding a vehicle for their discontent at the grassroots than they are in advancing Perot's presidential ambitions. "We are not Ross Perot's people," insists John Ressler, Ohio chairman of United We Stand, America. "We are grateful for his backing, but he may not be our spokesman down the road."

The Perotistas will play a central role in creating a political climate in the 1990s that is more populist and user-friendly. In Florida, United We Stand activists have canvassed voters in shopping malls and outside post offices, collecting signatures in support of a tax limitation referendum. In Massachusetts, their leaders assisted in a petition drive to qualify a campaign finance reform initiative for the ballot. They have also worked diligently on behalf of term limit measures in states across the country. They are distributing nonpartisan "voter scorecards" to keep their members informed on where candidates stand on issues from taxes to gun control. Some disaffected activists, frustrated by slow-motion staff at Dallas headquarters, are breaking out on their own, forming new local organizations or joining forces with existing groups ranging from Common Cause to the Christian Coalition.

Other populist stirrings are sprouting at the grassroots like tender shoots of protest. The term limits movement, which has arisen almost spontaneously with little national coordination, threatens to turn career politicians into an endangered species. In 1992 term limit initiatives passed in fourteen out of fourteen states where it appeared on the ballot, garnering an average of 66 percent of the vote. Despite court challenges (led by Speaker Tom Foley), this movement will continue to pick up steam as voters look for ways to vent their rage.

Tax limitation has also reached its highest zenith since Proposition 13 brought the political establishment to its knees in 1978, presaging the election of Ronald Reagan. Voters in Montana rejected a sales tax hike in 1993 by a resounding 74 percent margin, and then, aided by the state chapter of United We Stand, began gathering petitions to suspend income tax increases. Similar tax protests have exploded in California, Colorado, and Oregon. Voters in Texas have amended their constitution to prohibit an income tax without a vote of the people, while Washington State voters passed a measure that requires that tax increases that exceed a strict limit be submitted to a referendum. No longer trusting the politicians, the voters are taking the most substantive decisions of government into their own hands.[22]

The key to understanding the Perot protest is not only the man but the movement he embodies. At its root is a middle class that feels economically violated. They believe that the current tax structure is unfair. Many are employed in the manufacturing sector, which has been ravaged by huge job losses. The Populist revolt of the 1890s erupted at the very moment that manufacturing surpassed agriculture as the leading contributor to the GNP, as an economic downturn pushed millions of credit-starved farmers into default and bankruptcy. A century later a modern "populist moment" has arrived, sparked by the loss of 2 million jobs over the past decade. This downward plunge in manufacturing employment shows no signs of abating. In 1993, while the service sector created over one million new jobs (representing 60 percent of employment growth), manufacturing payrolls declined by 180,000 jobs. Little wonder that two out of three Perot voters told exit pollsters in 1992 that they believed the country was in "serious long-term economic decline."[23]

A generation-long stagnation in family income has deepened economic despair. From the post-World War II period until the early 1970s, family income roughly doubled, ticking along at a robust annual growth rate of 2.8 percent. This income growth allowed families to purchase new homes, acquire affordable health care, and save for their children's education. Over the past two decades, that upward trend has come to a grinding halt. Between 1973 and 1992 the typical American family's income essentially stagnated, rising at only 0.1 percent per year after adjusting for inflation. During roughly the same period the percentage of the average family's income consumed by federal taxes has risen from 2 percent to 24 percent. The result is severe economic anxiety and a bitterness towards government that is driving disaffected voters into an angry politics of discontent. "I'm afraid by the year 2000 we'll be a third-rate country, and I'm afraid for our children," says one Perot supporter in Philadelphia.[24]

This middle-class anxiety manifests itself in different ways. It could be seen in the 1992 campaign of Jerry Brown, who theatrically donned a UAW jacket, denounced "economic greed and corrupt politics," and vowed to end politics-as-usual with a Zen Buddhist political platform, a $100 limit on contributions, and an 800 number. Or in the redoubtable Pat Buchanan, sludging through the snows of New Hampshire, deeply moved by the ruddy faces of proud men who had lost their manufacturing jobs, challenging "King George" to a battle for the soul of the Republican party. Ross Perot inherited their mantle in the general election (about two-thirds of Perot voters supported Brown or Buchanan), promising to restore government to its proper owners: "we the people."

Modern-day populism is also reflected in the ballot initiatives (anti-crime, antitax, school choice) that have proliferated on ballots in recent years. This trend represents a throwback to the progressive movement's emphasis on direct democracy. According to the National Conference of State Legislatures, the number of popular initiatives on state ballots has risen from fifty-four in 1982 to sixty-four in 1990, and still higher to seventy-five in 1992.[25]

Can Perot corral this tornado of voter discontent into a viable and lasting political force? Highly unlikely, though still possible. United We Stand, his lobby organization, raised an estimated $30 million in 1993 but has been plagued by internal discord and strategic blunders. Although Perot's group boasts an estimated 1.2 million members, he has failed to build a truly grassroots organization with a command structure of county leaders and precinct captains. Too often, the issue positions of United We Stand are arrived at haphazardly. There is no public opinion polling, issues research, or strategic planning. Perot's penchant for dismissing loyal staff and firing volunteers over perceived indiscretions will, over time, wreak havoc on his ability to build a local infrastructure. [26]

While the hefty percentage of the vote that Perot would command in a presidential race will make him a fixture of American politics for the foreseeable future, he may have peaked as a force for change. To reach his true potential, Perot will have to advance his unconventional message by more conventional means—something he shows no interest in doing. More likely than Perot to have a decisive impact is the pro-family movement, which embraces politics with the same enthusiasm with which Perotistas reject it. It is seasoned, battle-tested, and ready to serve. To understand the shape of the politics to come, one must first understand the religious conservative movement, what makes it tick, how it functions, and what motivates its leaders and supporters.

CHAPTER THIRTEEN

Miracle at the Grassroots: Christian Coalition and the Pro-Family Movement

P AT Hart, a member of the Lake County, Florida, school board, introduced a resolution on March 21, 1994, applauding "our republican form of government, capitalism, a free enterprise system, patriotism, strong family values, [and] freedom of religion" as principles that should be taught to students as the very best in the world. "Our students should learn about and appreciate other cultures," she said, but they should also appreciate democratic values. Quoting liberal historian Arthur M. Schlesinger, Hart argued, "Our task is to combine due appreciation of the splendid diversity of the nation with due emphasis on the great unifying Western ideas of individual freedom, political democracy, and human rights."[1]

Incredibly, the state chapter of the American Federation of Teachers sued the school district for teaching patriotism. People for the American Way and other critics denounced the resolution as "jingoistic, verging on racist and possibly illegal." A professor of multiculturalism at a nearby college saw visions of the Klan: "This policy is close to racism." The *New York Times* went further, noting that the "fundamentalists" on the school board had "never set foot outside the United States, speak no foreign languages," and had no "academic training in comparative culture, religion or government."[2]

The Lake County policy was entirely consistent with Florida law, which mandated that school districts teach patriotism, including "the content of the Declaration of Independence," "our republican form of government," and "proper flag display." Most understood that the entire affair was much ado about nothing. Even the state chapter leader of the NAACP dismissed charges of racism as a red herring, and asked, "Where does that policy downgrade blacks or Hispanics? This is a great country."[3]

In Lake County, a bedroom community fifty miles northwest of Orlando, pride in America is about as controversial as mom and apple pie. But this patriotic resolution stirred a hornet's nest. The reason? Hart led a three-member majority on the school board that consisted of members of the Christian Coalition. For years religion has been politically incorrect; now even patriotism is politically incorrect. The Lake County school board members were labeled "extremists," "bigots," and "stealth candidates." "I've had lots of media and verbal abuse because I believe in God," lamented one.

But there is a bright side to this story, one that is repeating itself in hundreds of communities all across the country. Mainstream pro-family candidates are running for local office — and winning — despite attacks on their faith. They are starting at the bottom and working their way up the ladder of our political system, gaining self-confidence and valuable apprenticeships in public service.

Does election to local office matter? You bet. The first elective office that Jimmy Carter ever held was on Sumter County school board in south Georgia in the 1950s. Later Carter won a seat in the state legislature and, after a losing campaign in 1966, won election as governor of Georgia in 1970. When he left the governorship in 1975, Carter immediately began running for the presidency. He rose from peanut farmer to the leader of the free world—all beginning with service on a school board in rural Georgia.

"All politics is local," said the late Speaker "Tip" O'Neill. The Left has put this motto into practice for decades. Now religious conservatives, who once built their entire movement around winning the White House, have learned that true service in government begins in the precincts and flows upwards. All the energy and activism that fired the Reagan campaigns and the Pat Robertson presidential bid of 1988 has been redirected to school boards, state legislatures, city councils, even local zoning boards. The result: a quiet revolution in local government in which people of faith are winning campaigns and learning to serve. By 1993 there were an estimated 4,000 religious conservatives serving on America's 15,000 school boards. In 1992, while the Republicans were losing the presidency in a landslide, an estimated 500 pro-family candidates ran for local office, and 40 percent won.

A self-conscious shift in strategy by the pro-family movement in the late 1980s is now paying huge dividends. It is the main reason why the pro-family movement is more likely than even Ross Perot to reshape the configuration of American politics in the 1990s.

The religious conservative movement has leadership that is mature, stable, and seasoned. It has benefitted from fifteen years of developing veteran talent at the grassroots. The spiritual commitment of its supporters is more conducive to a long-term political movement than the white-hot anger and discontent that feeds the Perot phenomenon. The pro-family movement has built a lucrative fundraising base of millions of small donors, far better suited to the exigencies of grassroots politics than the largesse of a single wealthy patron. Its demographic base in the electorate is large, well organized, and rooted in historic patterns of ethnocultural voting behavior. Finally, rather than expressing a distaste for politics as do many Perotistas, pro-family activists embrace it, pouring out of church pews to serve in the party machinery, volunteer on campaigns, and run for local office. The gains made by pro-family activists in the Republican party in recent years demonstrate that they are in the political arena for the duration. They have a fresh, can-do spirit that reflects real enthusiasm for civic involvement.

A Premature Obituary

In June 1989 Jerry Falwell announced at a news conference (ironically held in Las Vegas) that he was folding the Moral Majority. "The purpose of the Moral Majority was to activate the religious right," Falwell concluded. "Our mission has been accomplished." He added that "other groups have been born to take our place. We no longer need to be the quarterback." He announced his intention to return to his first loves:

Thomas Roads Baptist Church and Liberty University, both located in his hometown of Lynchburg, Virginia.[4]

Pundits greeted Falwell's announcement by gleefully writing the obituary of the so-called "religious right." They heralded the folding of Moral Majority as the swan song of the religious right, a tune they whistled like a funeral dirge over the grave of a once-feared political boss. "Rarely in modern times has a movement of such reputed magnitude and political potential self-destructed so quickly," concluded the *New Republic*. It might even be enough to cause liberals to "reconsider their skepticism about divine intervention." Political analyst Kevin Phillips proclaimed that Falwell's farewell "is just ratification of a political tide that's come and gone." Jeffrey Hadden, sociology professor at the University of Virginia, called it "totally anticlimactic," noting that though "it raised a lot of fuss, the Moral Majority never developed into much of a grassroots organization." Pat Robertson's failure to win the GOP presidential nomination, these pundits added, along with the downfall of Jim and Tammy Bakker and Jimmy Swaggart, made a mockery of the vaunted power of the Christian right.[5]

What these critics did not realize was that even as they danced on the grave of the Moral Majority, a new pro-family movement was rising, phoenix-like, from its ashes. Falwell had accomplished his objective of reawakening the slumbering giant of the churchgoing vote. He had passed the torch to a new generation of leadership who launched new organizations and redirected the pro-family impulse in a more permanent, grassroots direction. These leaders tended to be young (under forty), enjoyed extensive Washington experience, boasted impressive academic or legal credentials, and were generally political professionals rather than pastors or preachers.

The best and brightest of these new leaders included Gary Bauer, a former undersecretary of education and chief domestic policy advisor in the Reagan administration, who cofounded the Family Research Council in 1989 with family psychologist and radio host Dr. James Dobson. Bauer and Dobson strung together a nationwide network of state-based pro-family think tanks to advance the pro-family agenda at the local level. Susan Hirschmann, the savvy former executive director of the College Republican National Committee, was hired in 1989 to head the

Washington office of Phyllis Schlafly's Eagle Forum. Her predecessor, Leigh Ann Metzger, did a stint in the Bush White House and later became a top press aide at the Republican National Committee. David O'Steen, executive director of the National Right to Life Committee, was a whiz in polling and survey research who held a doctorate in mathematics. Tom Atwood, former treasurer of the Robertson presidential campaign, joined the staff of the Heritage Foundation and helped edit its influential *Policy Review* magazine.

In addition to new national leaders, the late 1980s witnessed the proliferation of local groups that lobbied for family-friendly legislation before state legislatures and local bodies. Some, like Lancaster County Action in Pennsylvania, were political action committees that contributed directly to local candidates. The Lincoln Caucus in Arizona taught evangelicals how to become involved in the Republican party and seek local office. In California a group of Christian businessmen came together to support conservative candidates for the state Assembly. In Houston, Texas, a group of pro-family activists assembled a computerized telephone tree that enabled them to reach 4,000 households in a matter of a few hours.

These low-budget, no-frills, volunteer driven, high-tech groups packed grassroots punch with blazing efficiency and little overhead. Housewives at kitchen tables, home schoolers perched before personal computers, businessmen burning fax lines, and precinct canvassers identifying voters formed a grassroots network without parallel. At first few took notice of their existence, and the absence of many headline hounds in their ranks delayed their appearance onto the national political scene. Most felt uncomfortable with the limelight. They were simply citizens, parents, and taxpayers organizing others of like mind.[6]

Pat Robertson's 1988 presidential campaign was the political crucible for many of them. Presidential politics has always been the elevator ride to legitimacy for social movements, whether for the Goldwater forces who took control of the Republican party in 1964 or for the McGovernites in 1972. Robertson became the midwife who transformed a social protest movement and direct mail-driven behemoth into a well-trained, seasoned force of savvy political operatives. Robertson defeated George Bush in the Michigan caucuses, trounced him in Iowa, and sent him reeling into New Hampshire with his political career hanging by a thread. Though Bush rebounded in New Hampshire and Robertson lost badly in the Bible-belt states on Super Tuesday, he came in a respectable third out of six candidates, garnered nearly two million votes, and built a precinct structure in thirty-two states.

After the primary season ended, the Bush campaign wisely recruited some of the best of Robertson's field organizers and adopted many of his themes. In Michigan, Robertson precinct captains assimilated easily into the state party, providing the ground forces that gave the statehouse back to the GOP in 1990 after years of Democratic rule. In South Carolina the Republicans bought peace with the Robertson forces by making an evangelical leader treasurer of the party. Just as the Jesse Jackson campaigns had catapulted operatives like Ron Brown to the top of the national Democratic party, Robertson's campaign infused the ranks of the GOP with new blood and organizational muscle.

Hardened by the battles of the 1980s and chastened by the movement's earlier shortcomings, these pro-family leaders were determined to learn from the past. Cal Thomas, syndicated columnist and a former staffer at the Moral Majority, argued that its opportunity "to transform the culture was quickly squandered when it was decided to emphasize fund raising instead of building the political machinery to exercise real power." Most local chapters "were little more than a name and a telephone number," with the result that "liberals, at first intimidated, soon emerged from hiding to confront what turned out to be a paper tiger." The new breed of pro-family operatives was grateful to Falwell and others for blazing the trail they now walked. They faced a new challenge. They combined a values-based political philosophy with bare-knuckled, brass-tacks political know-how. They were determined to build a strong grassroots infrastructure that would be a permanent fixture on the American political landscape.[7]

What Motivates Religious Voters

The demographic base of this new pro-family movement is formidable. According to surveys by the Gallup organization and the

Center for Political Studies at the University of Michigan, the born-again vote constitutes between 18 and 26 percent of the entire electorate—higher in presidential years, slightly lower in off-year elections. The frequent churchgoing vote (those who attend church or synagogue four times a month or more) is even higher, comprising about 35 percent of the electorate. The key demographic segments of this constituency are baby boomers with children, start-up families, and older couples who have completed their childrearing years. These combined segments translate into 28 million households, representing 30.3 percent of all households in the United States, with a population of 70 million people.[8]

Churchgoing voters generally tend to be middle-class, suburbanite married couples with children, usually between the ages of twenty-five and forty-nine years old. Contrary to popular stereotype, they are well educated (66 percent have attended college or earned a graduate degree), heavily female (62 percent), and are engaged in white-collar or professional occupations (59 percent). Their median household income is $40,000, well above the national average. Geographically, they are heavily concentrated in the South (50 percent) and midwest (26 percent).[9]

These voters are growing as a potent force in the electorate, and they comprise the most reliable base of the Republican party. Mainline Protestants, by contrast, are shriveling away as a political factor. According to a recent study by David C. Leege of the University of Notre Dame, the mainliners comprised 41 percent of the population in 1960, declined to 30 percent in the Reagan landslide of 1980, and fell to only 22 percent in 1992. Voter participation by mainline Protestants who regularly attend church is even lower: they comprised only 4 percent of the electorate in 1992. During the same period, evangelicals have remained a constant one-fifth to one-fourth of the population, and their participation in the electorate has skewed even higher as they have become more politically active. The political consequences of these ethnoreligious voting patterns are far-reaching. While George Bush's margin over Bill Clinton among white evangelical voters was thirty-six points, his margin of victory among mainliners slipped to only ten points. Clearly, the evangelical vote is a large and permanent reality in American politics, and it is a constituency that neither political party can afford to alienate.[10]

What motivates these voters? In a sentence, the protection, health, and welfare of their children. A large number of churchgoing voters are married (76 percent) and have children (66 percent). This is their most salient characteristic. Marriage and childrearing descends across the body politic like a gigantic fault line, dividing the electorate on party affiliation, cultural values, and voting behavior. Pollster Richard Wirthlin calls this divide the "family gap." In a survey conducted in 1992 for *Reader's Digest*, 64 percent of marrieds with children identified themselves as "conservatives," compared with only 45 percent among singles. Half of all marrieds with children regularly attend church, compared to only 28 percent for marrieds without children and 36 percent for singles. Marrieds with children favor stay-at-home parenting (74 percent), oppose legalizing drugs (83 percent), and oppose same-sex marriage (72 percent). The "family gap" explains why cultural hot-button issues resonate among voters, and points out why the pro-family movement will remain a central part of American politics for the next several decades.[11]

The Christian Coalition

As the new pro-family movement began to take shape, I was laboring in the library of Emory University, completing a doctorate in American history and looking forward to an academic career. After stints from 1982 to 1985 as director of the national College Republicans and Students for America, two groups that helped shift campus sentiment to the right during the Reagan years, I had decided to forsake politics. Convinced that the key to the future of the country lay in education, I bade farewell to politics and headed off for graduate school. The cloister of academia provided time to think, reflect, and enjoy the life of the mind. By 1989, when Jerry Falwell closed the Moral Majority, I was happily married, and my wife Jo Anne was expecting our first child. Climbing back into the political arena was the last thing on my mind.

As I described earlier in this book, I met Pat Robertson in early 1989 and an off-hand conversation turned into a chance to help build the Christian Coalition. At first the staff consisted of me, my wife, and a part-time secretary. We fielded phone calls, opened mail that eventually arrived in tubs, and began to build at the grassroots on a shoe-string budget. Rather than spend money on plush offices and high-priced consultants, we poured financial resources into grassroots training workshops, voter guides, and phone banks.

The genius of the Christian Coalition was in its emphasis on the grassroots and its avoidance of a star-studded Washington media event or rally that announced lofty goals and attracted the white glare of press attention before its time. We followed a *Field of Dreams* strategy: build it and they will come. Christian Coalition differed from earlier pro-family groups in three important ways. First, it was driven by issues, not candidates or personalities. Second, although it was a national organization, it stressed local issues and grassroots organization. Our primary goal was to build fifty state affiliates that would work on state legislation, school board races, and local ordinances. Finally, it was permanent rather than cyclical. Rather than tune the rhythm of the group to election cycles, we focused on the long-term picture, assembling a permanent organization that would represent people of faith in the same way that the Chamber of Commerce represents business or the AFL-CIO represents union workers.

Slowly, we began to hire regional field organizers who roamed across nine-state regions and recruited the first of our state leaders. Our first victory came in early 1990 when the city council of Tustin, California, attempted to ban prayer from its meetings. A newly-started Christian Coalition chapter activated telephone trees and fax networks, turning out a crowd of several hundred people who protested the decision. The city council backed down, and voluntary prayer was reinstated. The grassroots strategy was working.

By the end of 1990, the Christian Coalition had 125 local chapters, 57,000 members, and a $2.8 million budget. We launched a nationwide campaign against taxpayer-funded pornography and attacks on religion through the National Endowment for the Arts, a government agency plagued by controversy and incompetence. The Coalition placed a full-page ad in the *Washington Post* in June, 1990, that warned members of Congress that a vote for taxpayer-funded obscenity would incur the wrath of taxpayers. It created a brief stir, but after the issue came to a vote, it quickly subsided. Despite our growing presence at the grassroots, we attracted almost no media attention. The press was not interested; they had already declared our movement dead. It was one more cogent example of the media's lack of familiarity with the evangelical community reaching back and biting them. But we just kept right on organizing, led by a crackerjack field staff that crisscrossed the country establishing state and local chapters.

In 1991 the Christian Coalition catapulted on to the national political radar screen when it played a role in the confirmation of Supreme Court Justice Clarence Thomas. I vividly remember the day President Bush nominated Thomas to replace the retiring Thurgood Marshall. Because of my time in Washington in the Reagan years, I had friends who were close to Thomas, and I knew him to be a conservative with strong convictions and faith in God. Convinced that the radical left would launch a counteroffensive, we braced for a battle at least as vicious as the Bork confirmation of 1987. Throughout the summer of 1991, as Thomas appeared headed for easy confirmation, we set aside a war chest of over $500,000, assembled activist lists in the states of key senators, and launched a direct mail and advertising campaign.

This planning paid off. The Coalition aired radio and television spots in support of Thomas in seven states with undecided senators, including Pennsylvania, Georgia, Louisiana, Arizona, and Alabama. Petitions circulated by local chapters generated over 50,000 calls, letters, and telegrams to Capitol Hill in the days before the vote. State leaders lobbied members of the Senate Judiciary Committee, including Senator Arlen Specter, who would later played a critical role in the Thomas victory.

When Anita Hill's allegations of sexual harassment against Thomas became public on October 7, 1991, our staff swung into action. I received a call from a former faculty member at Oral Roberts University law school who had taught with Hill. He remembered that Hill, after the alleged sexual harassment had occurred, brought Clarence Thomas to speak on campus, spending the day with him, laughing and joking amicably in the presence of others, and driving him to and from the airport.

Based on this tip I contacted Dr. Charles Kothe, former dean of the ORU law school, for corroboration. He provided an affidavit substantiating the story. I passed the material on to Senator John Danforth's staff, who distributed the affidavit to the Judiciary Committee and members of the press. Later, Kothe was called before the committee and convincingly testified that the jovial conduct that Hill displayed towards Thomas in his presence was inconsistent with her story of harassment.

On October 15, the day of the confirmation vote, Pat Robertson flashed the U.S. Capitol switchboard number on his *700 Club* program, and an estimated 45,000 phone calls jammed the lines in a 10-minute period, a record at the time. Thomas cleared the Senate by a 52–48 vote, the closest confirmation vote for an associate Justice of the Supreme Court in American history.

In 1992 the Christian Coalition focused its attention on turning out the largest number of pro-family voters in history during the upcoming presidential election. Under the able direction of a top-notch field staff and state leaders, the coalition distributed 40 million nonpartisan voter guides in 60,000 evangelical and Roman Catholic churches. We conducted nonpartisan voter registration drives in thousands of churches. Through our leadership schools, we trained an estimated 4,000 activists in the nuts and bolts of how to effectively make their voices heard in state and local government. On election day, exit polls confirmed what we expected: the largest turnout of conservative churchgoing voters in history. A total of 24 million self-identified, born-again evangelicals cast ballots in 1992, representing one out of every four ballots cast (compared to 18 percent in 1988). These voters were the only core constituency that remained loyal to the Republican party, and their concentration in the South made it the only region that George Bush carried. Although Bush lost the White House, pro-family candidates running for state and local offices won across the country.

The Clinton Agenda

Bill Clinton's election marked a turning point for the movement, serving as a wake-up call for many churchgoing voters who had retreated from the political arena after the Reagan years. Clinton's pork-laden "stimulus package" and tax increase on the middle class evoked new stirrings of political interest for many conservative evangelicals who had stayed on the sidelines. The result was an explosion in membership. By early 1993 the Christian Coalition was adding ten thousand new members and activists to its rolls every week. Its grassroots network had grown to forty-five state affiliates (nineteen with full-time staff) and 875 chapters in all fifty states, connected by a sophisticated communications network of computers, phone banks, fax machines, and direct mail. By 1994 over one million members and activists were on the coalition's national database, and annual revenues (average gift: $19) totaled $20 million.

When the Clinton administration attempted to repeal the Hyde amendment, which prohibits the use of tax dollars to pay for abortions, the Coalition swung into action. It aired radio spots in eleven states and showered swing congressional districts with 200,000 action alerts. Of the fifty members targeted by radio ads and phone banks, forty-three voted pro-life. Despite an intense lobbying effort by the White House, ninety-eight Democrats voted pro-life and the Hyde amendment was sustained by the stunning margin of 255 to 178. The coalition also spent $1.4 million to defeat the Clinton health care plan in 1994. The campaign included full-page newspaper ads in the *Washington Post* and *USA Today*, radio spots in twenty-one states, and 30 million postcards distributed in tens of thousands of churches.

As the nation headed into the 1994 elections, the Christian Coalition was regarded as one of the most effective grassroots citizen organizations in America. But it was not resting on its laurels. It distributed fifteen million congressional "scorecards" that informed citizens on how every member of the House and Senate voted on key issues affecting the family. A nationwide media campaign featured membership television spots airing on Cable News Network, the Family Channel, and the Rush Limbaugh program. Prior to the November 1994 election day, the coalition's network of local chapters distributed leaflets to churches, shopping centers, and union halls with thirty million nonpartisan voter guides that listed candidates views on taxes, a balanced budget amendment, crime, term limits, abortion, and education. State affiliates were busily assembling a lobbying structure that by decade's end would have ten million pro-family citizens on computer tape and place precinct coordinators in each of America's 175,000 precincts.

A Two-sided Coin

In their own distinct ways, the Perot phenomenon and the pro-family movement represent two sides of the same coin. The old politics of party bosses, special interests, organized labor, and career politicians is receding from the national political stage. The hierarchical institutions that personify the old politics are in long-term decline, and their unquestioned status as powerbrokers is weakening. The pillars that people have leaned on for decades have eroded, with public confidence in many of them shattered by scandal. The people no longer believe that government works or that traditional politics can solve the nation's problems. The anchors that have provided stability are gone, and voters feel that society is drifting rudderless.

Into this vacuum a new politics is taking shape that is aggressively outsider, insurgent, stylistically populist, participatory in spirit, and technologically driven. In style if not always in substance, Perot's 800 number and satellite town hall meetings and Pat Robertson's cable television empire exemplify the same outsider-versus-insider, technopopulist political approach. Each movement is flowering outside Washington, puts forth a reformist agenda, grows like weeds at the grassroots, and operates outside the two political parties. They are giving a voice and a vehicle to citizens who heretofore have felt isolated, alienated, and marginalized from their government and the larger society. The pro-family movement is likely to have more institutional staying power than the Perot protest for the simple reason that it orbits around an issues agenda rather than a personality. But each is carving new contours into the coming shape of American politics. Together, they are the wave of the future.

Part of what drives this grassroots movement is a desire for leadership with strong moral character. I recently met with a very prominent businessman from Texas who has been involved with the fight against drugs for many years. He travels all across the country. He reported that everywhere he goes, folks say they want people in government who stand up for traditional values and live them out in their own lives.

"What you are doing," he said, "is the most important work going on in the country today. The old Reagan and Bush coalitions are gone.

The religious people are the ones with energy and enthusiasm at the grassroots."

This miracle at the grassroots is not taking place in a vacuum. When history looks back on this period in American politics, it will be remembered as the era of Bill Clinton. The reemergence of an effective pro-family movement and the ascension of Clinton to the presidency are not entirely coincidental. To fully appreciate why there will be so much hunger for moral leadership and spiritual focus in the coming years, one must first understand what makes Bill Clinton tick, and what is the long-term significance of his presidency. To be sure, Clinton has elicited a strong grassroots movement of average citizens, but why? The answer to that provocative question is next.

CHAPTER FOURTEEN

Clinton Agonistes:
Woodstock Goes to the White House

IT WAS the spring of 1994, and Bill Clinton was itching to get out of the White House. The Whitewater scandal had mushroomed into a media feeding frenzy that gnawed away at his integrity and called into question his veracity. His health care plan was pronounced dead on Capitol Hill, the victim of a barrage of attacks by Republicans and maverick Democrats. Bosnia had turned into a bloody quagmire, his policy of surgical air strikes buried beneath a hailstorm of criticism. It was time to unfurl the famed Clinton road show, escape the White House — which Clinton called "the crown jewel of the federal prison system" — and get beyond the beltway to do what he did best: press the flesh with real people.

The perfect opportunity presented itself: the University of Arkansas had reached the NCAA basketball tournament's Final Four. Clinton, a devoted Razorback fan, decided to attend the championship game in Charlotte, North Carolina.

Clinton had thrived in town hall meetings during the 1992 campaign. He answered questions with biting-of-the-lower-lip sincerity, evoked empathy with his audience ("I feel your pain"), and moved across the stage with ease. He played the role of talk show host with enough panache to make Phil Donahue blush. In Charlotte, Clinton leaned back comfortably against a stool, a live audience seated around him in an intimate makeshift studio, as dark-suited, blow-dried local news anchors prepared to pitch him softball questions in their best baritones. The program was broadcast via satellite to nine states.

The stage was set for another Clinton virtuoso performance. But in the opening minutes of the broadcast, the first question sailed at Clinton like a high fastball at the head. A young woman asked pointedly, "Many of us Americans are having a hard time with your credibility. How can you earn back our trust?"

Other members of the live audience hurled knuckle-balled questions that left Clinton flustered, distracted, and, at times, bitter. One man from Austin, Texas, after recounting Clinton's flip-flops ranging from his middle-class tax cut to his evasive statements about Whitewater, bluntly asked, "Why should we believe you?"

"I have been subject, sir, to false charges," replied a testy Clinton, his voice rising as he jabbed his finger angrily at the man's image on the television screen.[1] Like a traveling evangelist preaching to a stone-faced congregation, Clinton found himself reeling from a barrage of challenges. Audience members peppered him with questions about Bosnia, Korea, and his wife's commodity trading.

The Charlotte town hall meeting was a metaphor for the Clinton presidency. Bill Clinton, the consummate policy wonk, had come to town to talk about government. Instead, he found himself face to face with the two issues raised but never resolved during the 1992 campaign: trust and character.

The trust gap that Clinton suffers with the American people is not likely to go away and holds the key to whether his presidency succeeds. The respect and awe that Americans hold for the office of the presidency is one of the most formidable assets that an incumbent president has at his disposal. If Clinton loses it—as Johnson did during Vietnam and Nixon did during Watergate—nothing can sustain him.

Modern presidents have employed various means to capitalize on the aura associated with the presidency. Franklin Delano Roosevelt took to the airwaves during his years in the White House, delivering "fireside chats" in soothing conversational style to millions of Americans who huddled around radio sets. These were not mere political exercises but civic ceremonies that united a nation plagued by depression and war. Dwight D. Eisenhower invented the modern art of summitry when he traveled to Vienna in 1955 to meet with Soviet leader Nikita Khrushchev. During this same period came Air Force One (first commissioned in

1962), the presidential limousine, Camp David (named after Eisenhower's son), and other trappings of the office.

Kennedy's chief innovation was the televised news conference, which allowed him to display his considerable wit and command of the facts. Nixon went a step further, outfitting White House guards with plumed helmets and Victorian military garb that made them look like Buckingham Palace soldiers. Jimmy Carter mistakenly believed that the American people wanted a commoner for president. He dispensed with the playing of "Hail to the Chief," carried his own luggage, and invited Willie Nelson to croon country tunes on the South Lawn.

Clinton has contributed still further to what *Time* magazine calls the incredible shrinking presidency. At times, he carries himself in the office with dignity and grace, as in April 1994 when he delivered a eulogy to Richard Nixon at the funeral in Yorba Linda, California. But at other times, his contrived hipness and MTV-consciousness serve him poorly. During an appearance on MTV in 1994, he was asked by one girl in the audience what kind of underwear he wore. "Briefs," answered the president to coos and hearty applause. (Only the questioner was disappointed: "We all thought he was a boxers man.") Whatever one thinks of Clinton's politics, it is hard to imagine the same question being posed to Eisenhower.

The crisis of the presidency under Bill Clinton is in part generational. What happens when yesterday's rebel becomes today's leader? Bill Clinton has discovered that it is a transition fraught with difficulty. George Bush's moving speech in 1991 commemorating the fiftieth anniversary of Pearl Harbor and Bill Clinton's visit to the Vietnam veterans memorial in 1993 were studies in contrast. Bush, the youngest naval aviator in World War II, spoke with the moral authority of one who had risked his life over the Pacific; Clinton eloquently called his fellow Americans to put Vietnam behind them, yet his words elicited boos and jeers from those who gathered at the black granite wall in honor of their fallen comrades.

In the final analysis, the authority of the president flows not from the ceremonial trappings of the office but from the character of the individual. This is where Clinton leaves many voters feeling cheated. And it explains why both the Whitewater scandal and allegations of sexual misconduct have resonated so powerfully in the electorate. They confirm an impression voters have of Clinton as less than forthcoming. As *Washington Post* columnist Richard Cohen observed, voters question Clinton's candor as much as his conduct. "Whatever Whitewater and related matters might eventually be about (maybe nothing), it is now about candor," Cohen argued. "The White House seems incapable of just coming out with it—the details, the facts, the bloody truth."[2]

This unease about Clinton is deep and abiding. "Americans think he is an operator; they think his first impulse is not toward truth-telling," says Peggy Noonan, former speechwriter to Ronald Reagan and George Bush. "They have a sense that he really is Slick Willie." This was not enough to trip up Clinton in 1992, despite a primary campaign whose most memorable image was a hoarse and exhausted candidate on *60 Minutes* defending his marital infidelity as aides parroted mantralike warnings about "Republican dirty tricks" and "cash for trash." Voters wanted change, and Clinton provided it; many voters brushed aside character issues that reemerged later with a vengeance.[3]

Yet he won only 43 percent of the vote in a three-way race. In 1968, the last time that happened, Nixon turned his minority presidency into a landslide by reaching out to Wallace voters, a natural constituency. Clinton has had no such luck. Perot has opposed him on the budget, taxes, health care, and NAFTA. No single revelation—Whitewater, the Paula Jones law suit, commodities profiteering—is fatal by itself. Instead, it is death by a thousand cuts, a series of episodes that confirms the reservations of voters about Clinton's character.

The Trust Gap

"A president's words can move a nation. But talk must be backed up with action or we risk diminishing the bully pulpit to a pulpit of bull," said Bill Clinton in 1992.[4] Clinton's prophecy has been self-fulfilling. He made a middle-class tax cut one of the central and most conspicuous promises of his campaign; yet in 1993, he passed one of the largest tax increases in history. He foreswore U.S. involvement in Bosnia, then initiated air strikes that threatened to suck American forces into the conflict. During his State of the Union address in 1994, he spoke passionately about the need to restore traditional values and strengthen the family. Yet he favors paying for abortion with tax dollars and publicly advocates gay rights legislation.

The result is a president who inspires respect for his political skills but nothing else. Clinton does not evoke a healthy fear on the same raw moral level as his predecessors. Franklin Roosevelt, though despised by conservatives, wooed Republicans into his cabinet to unify the nation as he prepared for World War II. Lyndon Johnson was well known for subjecting people to "the treatment," draping his lanky arm around the shoulder of a reluctant recruit and drawling in his thick Texas accent, "How can you turn me down? Your president needs you."

Clinton possesses no such stature. He watched helplessly as Governor Mario Cuomo and Senate majority leader George Mitchell both rebuffed his offers to sit on the Supreme Court, reducing his eventual nominees to the status of also-rans. He promised to put a Republican in the cabinet, then failed to do so, begging off with the excuse that no one would come aboard. Bobby Ray Inman's bizarre withdrawal from the Secretary of Defense sweepstakes in early 1994 was only surpassed by the spectacle of Clinton standing alone, as central Europe exploded in ethnic warfare, unable to find a replacement for Les Aspin. Finally, like a high school senior frantically trying to find a date as the prom approaches, Clinton elevated Under Secretary of Defense William Perry. Not a bad choice, all other things being equal, but it was yet another episode that diminished the stature of Clinton's office.

Clinton has tried to fill this void of leadership by recruiting his own Washington "wise men": David Gergen, who served under Nixon and Reagan, and Lloyd Cutler, former counsel to Jimmy Carter. But for all their usefulness in providing adult supervision for the thirtysomething White House staff, what does one do when it is the president who needs a chaperon? This is not an altogether rhetorical question. The Clintons "have played loose with the truth," says Richard Cohen. "If they were children, they'd be grounded."[5]

Despite doubts about his truthfulness, Clinton has mastered the rhetorical function of the presidency. His speech in Memphis in November of 1993 honoring Martin Luther King and calling for an end to black-on-black violence echoed with passion and dripped with pathos. In June of 1994 he stirred listeners and won over detractors with a moving address on the windswept beaches of Normandy during the fiftieth anniversary of D-day. His considerable oratorical skills invite comparisons to Ronald Reagan. The difference, of course, is that Reagan actually believed in something. He had a set of core beliefs that animated him, defined him, and provided a compass in the howling crosswinds that is the presidency. Clinton has no such center. His north star is charm itself—ingratiating, primordial, almost suffocating. He is like the boy that a girl brings home from a date who proceeds to flirt with her sister. In this respect Clinton has no peer. Charm and charisma are his most formidable assets, and they should give caution to those who have underestimated him in the past and may be tempted to do so in the future.[6]

Charisma is a poor substitute for core beliefs. But it can make the difference between death and survival, as Clinton has demonstrated repeatedly, especially in 1992 when he was hammered by revelations about his past sexual indiscretions. Lesser charges had blasted Gary Hart's presidential hopes to pieces four years earlier. Clinton not only survived but triumphed.

I was reminded of this character trait while visiting with a prominent Republican senator in the summer of 1993. Clinton was still reeling from a snarl of snafus: Zoe Baird, Lani Guinier, gays in the military, the haircut. Byron White had recently announced that he was retiring from the Supreme Court.

"If Bill Clinton blows his pick for the Supreme Court," I offered, "this could become a battle royale. His presidency might not recover."

"Oh no," the senator replied, his face turning ashen. "This guy's good. This guy's the best. He may be in trouble now, but he will be back. Don't underestimate him. No one is as good as Clinton."

Sure enough, after a brief dalliance with Mario Cuomo, Clinton chose Ruth Bader Ginsburg, who sailed through the confirmation process with hardly a whimper of protest from Republicans, giving him a much-needed victory at a critical moment. The senator had been right: Clinton is extremely bright and a quick study. He is a formidable foe. He believes passionately in his own ability to win by the sheer force of his talents and his oratorical skill. And why shouldn't he? His resilience is remarkable, even in a business where only the resilient survive. Only the self-described "comeback kid" has taken such a beating and still leans against the ropes, almost begging for more. He is the Rocky Marciano of American politics: bloodied but unbowed, punch-drunk but refusing to go down.

Clinton combines the earnestness of a Baptist Sunday school teacher with the smooth arrogance of an Oxford graduate student. Indeed, like a secular Elmer Gantry, he represents the ultimate triumph of rhetoric over reality, style over substance, charisma over character. As he entered the White House, the press swooned over his mastery of detail and his smooth expression of ideas. In this regard, he benefitted from the Bush interregnum. Bush was never comfortable with the English language. He broke off thoughts in mid sentence, punctuated his delivery with goofy aphorisms ("don't cry for me, Louise"), and reduced expressions of empathy to the reading of cue cards ("Message: I care").

At his first news conference as president-elect in November 1992, Clinton wowed reporters by extemporaneously executing a series of lucid sentences. With Al Gore standing beside him looking strangely like a Ken doll, the president-elect took questions for thirty minutes without a note or cue card, holding forth in a seamless monologue on subjects ranging from taxes and the economy to Haiti and Korea. No remarkable feat, to be sure, but after four years of Bush's tortured syntax it tickled the ears like a high cello in a symphony of clanging cymbals. "How about this shocker," gushed the *Boston Globe*. "He can talk in complete sentences!"[7]

Asked whether he planned to follow through on his promise to repeal the ban on gays in the military, Clinton hedged with disarming eloquence. "My concern here is to do it in a way that is most appropriate for the management of the whole national security and military interests of the country," he replied. "I want to consult with a lot of people about what our options are, including people who may disagree with me about the ultimate merits." It sounded good, but what did he say?[8]

Here, indeed, was a president who could talk. For the first time since Kennedy, the country had a leader who could bring Americans together with what the *New York Times* called "the balm of rhetoric." Clinton's "masseur's touch with the English language" suggested that he had "an innate ability to explain things in terms that the average person can understand, speaking in sentences and paragraphs—in contrast with the fractured prose of George Bush, who it was virtually impossible to quote in a coherent sentence without the aide of ellipses and parentheses to patch his thoughts together." Yet there remained that gnawing doubt about Clinton's truthfulness. "Quite simply, sometimes he can seem too smooth, too eloquent for his own good," observed Thomas Friedman of the *New York Times*. "Sometimes you want to check your wallet when he's done talking just to make sure all your credit cards are still there."9

In September 1993 Clinton delivered the ultimate performance of the president as sophomore debate champion. He traveled to Capitol Hill to address a joint session of Congress and launch his campaign for health care reform. When he stood behind the podium, he discovered that someone had mistakenly entered the wrong speech in the teleprompter. Unfazed, Clinton proceeded to deliver his health care address—much of it extemporaneously—while another text rolled lifelessly across the screen before him. Halfway through the speech, his aides discovered the error and corrected it. But by then Clinton was in the middle of a stirring stemwinder, jabbing the air to make his points, gesturing to the gallery to pay homage to the First Lady, and basking in the applause that rolled over him like waves of affirmation. Yet when people began to read the 1,342-page bill, they discovered that there was little connection between Clinton's soaring rhetoric and the Byzantine nightmare contained in the bill. The Clinton plan included layers of bureaucracy, a draconian payroll tax, taxpayer-funded abortion, and medical school quotas. Support for the administration's health care plan soon plummeted on Capitol Hill and in the general public.

This is a classic pattern in Bill Clinton's personality. As William Manchester said of Douglas MacArthur, he is a great, thundering paradox of a man, an enigma, and a jumble of contradictions. As a Southern governor, he was the passionate champion of racial equality who campaigned in black churches but never passed a civil rights bill. One of the founders of the centrist Democratic Leadership Council, he has allied himself with the gay rights movement and the pro-abortion lobby. A friend of labor, he never attempted to repeal Arkansas's right-to-work law and attacked the unions during the fight over NAFTA. An advocate of women's rights and gender diversity in appointments, he dismissed feminists as "bean counters" when they demanded more posts in his administration. He denounced the 1980s as a decade of greed and avarice, but he and his wife practiced their own brand of yuppie prosperity by turning a meager investment into a handsome profit on the commodities market. He attacked George Bush for acting as an apologist for the butchers of Tiananmen Square, then reversed himself and extended most-favored-nation trading status to China. Originally an opponent of the death penalty, in 1991 he signed the death warrant of a mentally retarded murderer who had the I.Q. of a twelve-year-old.

The ease with which Clinton flip-flops, all the while projecting sincerity, is striking. Even his presidential campaign began with a broken promise. In 1990 he ran for his fifth term as governor of Arkansas, promising to serve four years if elected. When asked during a televised debate if he would bypass the presidency in 1992 and serve a full term, Clinton responded with characteristic aplomb, "You bet. I told you when I announced for governor . . . and that's what I'm gonna do." It was, of course, a lie. Horrified aides stood out of camera range in shock, apoplectic that he would make such a pledge when they were already assembling the machinery for a presidential bid. But this posed no dilemma for Clinton. He staged a secret "listening tour" in 1991, visiting dozens of small towns and hamlets across the state to find out if voters cared if he kept his promise. The locations of the meetings were not disclosed, and the sessions were heavily stacked with state employees and supporters. To no one's surprise, Clinton announced after crisscrossing the state that the voters had "released" him from his pledge. The *Arkansas Democrat* issued its own verdict: "His word is dirt."[10]

Some have concluded that Clinton's inability to tell the truth is pathological. But that view is too simplistic. Clinton, in my estimation, *knows* the truth; he simply does not believe that it serves his purposes to tell it. Clinton's propensity to shade the truth and change his story to suit his own purposes derives from his past political experiences and the lessons he took from them.

To some extent, all people are prisoners of their experiences. Clinton's are a maximum security cell. Four main experiences shaped him: the formative years working for Senator William J. Fulbright in the 1960s; his brief career as an antiwar activist during the McGovern campaign of 1972; his defeat as governor of Arkansas in 1980; and his participation in the Democratic Leadership Council, the moderate group formed in 1985 by elected officials in the South and West to move the Democrats back to the center.

Clinton is a symbol of the Woodstock generation. But his politics go back even further, rooted in a long tradition of Southern liberalism. No one personified this Southern-fried progressivism more than Senator William Fulbright of Arkansas. Fulbright was a remarkable individual. He attended Oxford University as a Rhodes scholar, went to law school, and later returned to Arkansas to teach law and seek political office. He won a seat in Congress in 1942 and was elected to the U.S. Senate two years later, where he quickly rose to prominence and later ascended to the chairmanship of the Senate Foreign Relations Committee.

Bill Clinton was an undergraduate at Georgetown University when he joined Fulbright's staff in 1967. By then the senator from Arkansas had emerged as a powerful critic of the cold war, violently opposing U.S. involvement in Vietnam and urging an accommodation with the Soviets so that money spent on defense could be diverted to social programs.

Clinton self-consciously emulated Fulbright in fashioning his own political career. He went to Oxford University as a Rhodes scholar after graduating from Georgetown University (Fulbright even wrote him a letter of recommendation). Like Fulbright, he came back to the United States to attend law school (Yale for Clinton, George Washington for Fulbright). Also like Fulbright, he briefly pursued an academic career as a professor of law before running for Congress. Fulbright had won his first campaign; Clinton lost in a heavily Republican district. Both dominated Arkansas politics for long periods of time, Fulbright as senior senator, Clinton as governor. The parallels in the two careers are remarkable.[11]

Fulbright used the Senate Foreign Relations Committee to wage a one-man crusade against U.S. involvement in Vietnam. In 1966 he staged televised hearings calling for the de-escalation of the conflict. For him, Vietnam was not simply a strategic error, but a symbol of the arrogance of American power and the excesses of the cold war.

"Of all the changes in American life wrought by the cold war," Fulbright said in 1964, "the most important by far . . . has been the massive diversion of energy and resources from the creative pursuits of civilized society to the conduct of a costly and interminable struggle for world power." The cold war, he argued, distracted Americans from charity that began at home. It "has consumed money and time and talent that could otherwise be used to build schools and homes and hospitals, to remove the blight of ugliness that is spreading over the cities and highways of America, and to overcome the poverty and hopelessness that afflict the lives of one-fifth of the people in an otherwise affluent society."[12]

In April 1966 he delivered his most famous speech at Johns Hopkins University, decrying America's fear of communism and criticizing military intervention in southeast Asia. Fulbright complained of a mechanistic view of history that saw Vietnam as "another Munich," and quoted Churchill to the effect that appeasement was "magnanimous and noble" under certain circumstances. He praised anti-Vietnam protesters as an "articulate minority" that he included "in good historical company." Abraham Lincoln, he pointed out, had opposed the Mexican War. Yet he issued a word of caution to campus protesters. "We are, for better or worse, an essentially conservative society," he said, "in such a society soft words are likely to carry more weight than harsh words and the most effective dissent is dissent expressed in an orderly — which is to say in a conservative — manner."[13]

This was classic Fulbright. Liberal in his politics but conservative in style, he expressed the ideas voiced by campus radicals in a way that sounded reasonable. Part of the explanation lay in his legal and academic background. He was no radical. He approached Vietnam with the dispassion of a professor preparing for a lecture or an attorney preparing for court. Fulbright's conservative demeanor gave reason and resonance to words that sounded like frothing-at-the-mouth extremism when spoken by Ted Kennedy or George McGovern.

The themes of Fulbright's career echo in Clinton's foreign and defense policies. The dramatic downsizing of the military, the redirection of resources to social spending, the internationalization of command of U.S. forces in Somalia and Bosnia, and subservience to the United

Nations all show the reticence about the projection of American power around the globe that Clinton first absorbed during Vietnam. Even Clinton's discomfort with foreign affairs in general reflects Fulbright's bemoaning of the tendency of military conflicts to divert resources from domestic needs.

Though often waging a lonely battle, Fulbright found an ally in the Senate in Al Gore, Sr., of Tennessee. Gore vocally opposed U.S. involvement in Vietnam and provided the framework for today's "tax fairness" debate as the leader of opposition to Richard Nixon's proposed tax cuts of 1969. He was, like Fulbright, conservative in temperament and Southern in style, struggling to reconcile his liberalism with his region, especially on matters of race. He had been a candidate for the vice-presidential nomination against John F. Kennedy at the Democratic convention in 1956—a nomination ultimately won by fellow Tennessean Estes Kefauver. Few understood the symbolism of Bill Clinton selecting Al Gore, Jr., as his running mate in 1992. A quarter-century later, it represented the reuniting of the legacies of Fulbright and Gore, two of the towering Southern Senate liberals of the 1950s and 1960s.[14]

It was three o'clock in the morning on the final day of the 1992 presidential campaign, and an indefatigable and peripatetic Bill Clinton had finally landed at an airport in Ft. Worth, Texas. He had already visited five states that day; this was one of the last stops of a long and grueling marathon that had begun two years earlier. A crowd of hundreds of supporters had weathered driving rain for hours to see the exhausted but exhilarated candidate. It was fitting that Clinton would return to the state where his political career had begun twenty years before. The smell of victory was in the air. As Clinton wrapped up his stump speech, he recognized a face in the crowd. It was one of the campaign volunteers from the McGovern campaign. Impulsively, Clinton jumped off the stage and dove into the crowd. Embracing her with a big hug, he said, "It took us twenty years, but we finally made it."

By the time Bill Clinton completed his education at Oxford and Yale, Fulbright's brand of genteel liberalism was in eclipse. Bobby Kennedy was dead; Al Gore had been defeated in 1970; Senator Wayne Morse of Oregon had been turned out of office in 1968. Presidential prospects were equally dim. Chappaquiddick still haunted Ted Kennedy and

Eugene McCarthy had given up his Senate seat in 1970. Against this backdrop, liberals and opponents of the Vietnam War like Bill Clinton had only one horse to ride in 1972: Senator George McGovern of South Dakota.

McGovern became a useful if flawed vehicle for a generation of protest. He turned his campaign over to a youthful army of grassroots guerrillas who trooped through the primaries sporting scruffy beards, long hair, tie-dye shirts, and blue jeans. Because of its youthful liberalism and campus iconoclasm, the McGovern crusade walked with a distinctive sexual swagger, personified by thirty-four-year old director Gary Hart, who Theodore White described as a "blue-eyed six footer" who wore "skin-fitting pants over slim cowboy thighs" and "drew the eyes of every maiden" in the McGovern campaign.[15]

White might have been describing Bill Clinton, who after working on the losing Senate campaign of an antiwar candidate in Connecticut, moved to Texas in the fall of 1972 to manage McGovern's campaign in the Lone Star State. One of the young women attracted to Clinton was Hillary Rodham, his Yale law school girlfriend, who followed him to Texas for the ostensible purpose of registering Hispanics to vote in San Antonio. It was during this period that their romance blossomed and their political partnership began.

McGovern had no chance of carrying Texas, but Clinton bowled over those who encountered him with his insatiable ambition and legendary stamina. He rented an apartment in Austin but was rarely there. He drove campaign volunteers with a combination of charm and fury in a state headquarters where the lights never dimmed and the doors never closed. He displayed a natural ability for the gladhanding, cajoling, and schmoozing that was critical to success in politics. "He knew how to reach people, how to play to their strengths and weaknesses," recalled Taylor Branch, Clinton's codirector and later a Pulitzer-prize winning author. "Politics is love of people and the process. Bill was naturally good at that. In that sense he was Johnsonian."[16]

The McGovern campaign provided Clinton with two important lessons. First, he learned that woolly-headed liberalism did not sell in the conservative South. McGovern won only 33 percent of the vote in Texas; he received 31 percent in Clinton's native Arkansas. The McGovern experience was a baptism in fire for Clinton, teaching him that if he hoped to succeed politically in the future he would have to downplay his antiwar sentiment and liberal leanings. Second, Clinton learned the importance of relationships to political success. He forged life-long friendships with a rising generation of Democrat operatives who had cut their teeth during the McGovern campaign. Among them: fellow Rhodes scholar and McGovern delegate hunter Richard Stearns, who later became a federal judge; Willie Brown, a young black activist from California who rose to become the speaker of the state Assembly; Gary Hart, who returned to Colorado and won election to the Senate in 1974; Patrick Cadell, a twenty-two-year old Harvard senior who was McGovern's pollster; and Betsey Wright, an activist on feminist issues who would later serve as his chief of staff in Arkansas.

The McGovern campaign was to the Democratic party what the Goldwater campaign in 1964 was to the Republican party. Despite short-term defeat, it allowed the New Left to take control of the national Democratic party, in whose hands its presidential nominating process remains today. Bill Clinton was present at that creation, and his own ascension to the presidency two decades later represented the coming-of-age of a generation of political rebels.

After McGovern's defeat, Bill Clinton returned to Arkansas to begin his long and arduous climb to power. He narrowly lost a congressional bid in the most Republican district in Arkansas in the Watergate election of 1974, but impressed Democrats as a hot political property for the future. In 1976 Clinton was elected attorney general without GOP opposition, and two years later he became the youngest governor in the nation.

This lightning-fast rise made the thirty-two-year-old political wunderkind one of the rising stars of the Democratic party. In his first term, Clinton sounded progressive themes. He railed against the timber industry and the state's utilities, raised automobile tag fees, surrounded himself with youthful and cocky aides, and generally made himself in-accessible to outside advice. As a result, Clinton's confident self-assurance curdled into short-tempered arrogance. The result was a thumping re-pudiation at the polls in 1980 during the Reagan landslide.

Then a sophomore at the University of Georgia, I recall discussing the 1980 election results with a Democrat friend who later became chief of staff to Governor Zell Miller. Reagan had not only defeated a Georgian for the presidency, but Senator Herman Talmadge had lost his seat to the first Republican senator from Georgia since Reconstruction. Yet none of this seemed to faze my friend. He was downcast about only one thing: Bill Clinton had been defeated. "I cannot believe he lost," he said, shaking his head. "Clinton was one of the future leaders of the party."

Clinton's Republican opponent had aired television commercials that blasted Clinton for housing Cuban refugees at an army base in Arkansas. That explosive issue, combined with the car tag fee increase and Clinton's bristling arrogance, sent him down in flames at the age of thirty-four. Many predicted that he was finished in politics. But they were wrong. He immediately began laying the groundwork for his next campaign.

Clinton worked aggressively to reposition himself as a centrist. In a bow to the state's traditional views of marriage, Hillary Rodham adopted her husband's last name. Bill began attending the largest Baptist church in Little Rock, even joining the choir where his beaming face could be seen on Sunday morning telecasts that reached half the state's population. It was during this period that Clinton began adopting the rhetoric of a "new" Democrat, emphasizing law-and-order, education reform, moving people off welfare, and even switching his position to support the death penalty. He made television spots in which he repented for the arrogance of the past. This conservative makeover worked like a charm: Clinton won the governor's race in 1982 with 54.7 percent of the vote. Most importantly, the lessons Clinton had learned in defeat provided the guideposts for his political future, and later inspired the themes of his presidential campaign.[17]

Thereafter, Clinton displayed a trademark penchant for equivocation on politically-loaded issues. "He wanted everyone to love him, so he would leave the impression that he was agreeing with you on every issue," said Democratic State Senator Nick Wilson. The youthful purposefulness of the old Clinton gave way to a self-serving malleability, earning him the disparaging nickname of "Slick Willie." Once fired by a desire to advance progressive causes, the new Clinton seemed preoccupied with only one thing: securing his political future. "He developed the politics of ultraconsensus, this desire to never offend a single voter," noted Paul Greenberg of the *Arkansas Democrat*. This style "accounts for the residue of distrust that haunted him during the presidential campaign a decade later. It became a continuous thread in the Clinton story."[18]

Clinton completed his image makeover in 1985 when he became one of the charter members of the Democratic Leadership Council. The brainchild of Governor Chuck Robb of Virginia, the DLC aimed to steer the Democratic party back to the center after the crushing defeat of Walter Mondale in 1984. Its leaders came mostly from the South and West: Chuck Robb, Governor Bruce Babbitt of Arizona, Senator Sam Nunn of Georgia, and Congressman Richard Gephardt of Missouri. Clinton was, at first glimpse, an unusual recruit to the organization. A former McGovern operative and antiwar liberal, he hardly fit the mold of a moderate. But he enthusiastically set about the task of shifting control of the national Democratic party away from the liberal interest groups who had controlled it for decades. The AFL-CIO, the feminists, and Jesse Jackson hardened a perception that the Democrats were a party of special interests and Great Society liberalism.[19]

Clinton became chairman of the DLC in 1990. He skillfully used this platform to make himself a national party leader, traveling to thirty-five states and setting up twenty-three state chapters, making contacts that would serve him well in his presidential campaign. In May 1991 at the annual meeting of the DLC in Cleveland, Clinton excluded Jesse Jackson from addressing the gathering, a move that signaled his own move to the center and foreshadowed later disputes between him and Jackson. The DLC gave Clinton the liberal the shiny veneer of a new Democrat. It insulated him from the charges of liberalism that had sunk Mondale in 1984 and Dukakis in 1988. As Al From, the DLC's executive director, later confessed, "Our crusade and his was always to try to modernize liberalism so it could sell again."[20]

Bill Clinton suffers from a classic case of political schizophrenia. His core beliefs are those of a William Fulbright liberal radicalized by the twin experiences of Vietnam and the McGovern campaign. But his defeat in 1980 forced him to reposition himself. Clinton personifies the crisis of a political chameleon. This, in great measure, explains his indecisiveness, his obvious frustration in exercising leadership, and the chaos that reigns in the White House under Clinton. The "war for Bill Clinton's soul," described in such devastating detail by Robert Woodward in his book *The Agenda*, rages on almost every issue confronting his presidency.[21]

This fiddle-faddle leadership style may be characteristic of junior politicians, but it is highly unusual for it to afflict someone who reaches the pinnacle of power. Ronald Reagan catapulted onto the national scene in 1964 when he gave "The Speech" for Barry Goldwater, and his basic message remained unchanged for the next twenty-five years. Harry Truman was a no-nonsense anti-Communist and New Deal Democrat who brought these values with him to the Oval Office and never wavered from his basic instincts. Not so with Bill Clinton. He is really two people trapped in the same presidency: the sixties liberal and the DLC centrist, each fighting for preeminence.

Clinton's greatest legacy will be a reawakened grassroots movement for common sense. The conservative community, largely asphyxiated during the Bush years, awoke from its slumber like Rip Van Winkle on steroids after the Clinton inaugural. Membership for pro-family organizations is up dramatically, attendance at conferences and seminars is rising, and the circulation of conservative publications is skyrocketing. Magazines like *National Review* and *American Spectator* have tripled readership. The Christian Coalition entered the Clinton era with 250,000 members and activists; that number now approaches 1.4 million. Other conservative groups display a similar pattern.

This energy must be harnessed behind a positive vision for America. If it is, history will record that Clinton did more to energize the grassroots than anyone since Ronald Reagan. This is the challenge for people of faith. They cannot simply oppose Bill Clinton. They must present their own prescriptions for the problems that plague this country. When the Clinton era draws to a close, religious conservatives must be ready to take their place at the table.

If Republicans make the gains in the U.S. Congress in 1994 that are expected by most analysts, the Clinton administration's effective term could be reduced to two years. A coalition of Republicans and conservative Democrats might well control the legislative agenda. If that happens, building a movement around opposing Clinton will achieve little.

The grassroots pro-family movement must be proactive, forwarding its own ideas about where they want to take the country. That agenda must be broader and more ambitious than what we have proposed in the past.

CHAPTER FIFTEEN

To Cast a Wider Net:
Why We Need a Broader Issues Agenda

T HE ANCIENT CITY of Corinth was the capital of venality and corruption in the Greek world. It boasted a temple to the pagan goddess Aphrodite that teemed with 1,000 temple prostitutes. Ships sailed into this port city on trading routes through the Mediterranean, disembarking sailors and traders who engaged in drunken revelry at taverns and liquor shops on the south side of the city. Everything unseemly about Greek society could be found in Corinth. So unsavory was its reputation that the Greek term "Korinthiazomai" (which meant to practice fornication) was literally translated "to act like a Corinthian."

How did the leaders of the early Christian church confront Corinthian society? The apostle Paul provides the answer. "For though I am free from all men, I have made myself a slave to all, that I might win the more," he wrote. Paul became a Jew to the Jews, a Gentile to the Gentiles, a slave to the slaves, a Greek to the Greeks. "I have become all things to all men," said Paul, "that I may by all means save some" (1 Corinthians 9:19–22).

Paul did not mean to imply that he had become all things to all persons in matters of theology. He never wavered in his bold profession of the faith. But he had learned to speak the language of his listeners so they might receive his message. The book of Acts records Paul's arrest on trumped up charges in Jerusalem, whereupon he mounted a platform and spoke to a riotous mob in a Hebrew dialect. As Paul began to speak in their native tongue, a hush fell over the crowd (Acts 21:40). Likewise, the pro-family movement should not compromise its cherished beliefs or retreat from its principled positions. But in order to receive a fair hearing, it should speak in the dialect of its listeners, using language suited to a largely secular audience.

Martin Luther King adopted this strategy during the struggle for civil rights. The difference between King and previous black leaders was that he did not preach to the choir. Although his base of support was the African-American church, his message reached beyond the black community to whites in the South who were wary of equal rights for blacks but were repelled by the violence of massive resistance. His message called for healing and reconciliation, and his language was the religious vernacular that Southerners of both races could recite with the calm self-assurance of an old gospel hymn. He purposely avoided warlike metaphors that divided African-Americans from whites, choosing instead to appeal to what united them.

"Our aim must never be to defeat or humiliate the white man but to win his friendship and understanding," proclaimed King in an address on the steps of the Alabama state capitol at the conclusion of the march from Selma to Montgomery in 1965. "We must come to see that the end we seek is a society at peace with itself, a society that can live with its conscience. That will be a day not of the white man, not of the black man. That will be the day of man as man."[1]

The civil rights movement would not have succeeded without this healing rhetoric. As Jerry G. Watts has written, "We can easily forget or underestimate the significance of the moral persuasiveness of the normative vision generated within the movement." King's essentially Christian vision contrasted sharply with extremists in the Black Power movement who advocated violence against whites, referred to the white man as "a devil," and called for the separation of the races. And, Watts adds, "because the [civil rights] movement was situated in a Christian moral discourse, the movement rhetorically reinforced the possibility of the moral/political conversion of its adversaries."[2]

The pro-family movement needs a similar language to speak to a secular culture, just as King spoke for blacks to a prevailing white culture. The American people need to know that we do not desire to exclude our political foes, only to gain our own place at the table. They cannot hear too often that our objective is not to dominate, but to participate, and that our vision of society includes protecting their right to speak and be heard as much as making our own voices heard. We are not trying to elect Billy Graham to the presidency. We are attempting to give our values—which are the values of mainstream Americans—a voice in the process.

Reaching a Larger Audience

During Adlai Stevenson's second losing campaign for the presidency in 1956, Harry Truman met with the embattled candidate to offer him some advice. Stevenson, then trailing Eisenhower badly, asked Truman what he was doing wrong. Truman led him to the window, pointed to a man walking down the street below, and said, "The thing you have to do is learn how to reach that man."[3]

This same dilemma now faces the pro-family movement. Though gifted with talented leadership, strong grassroots support, and enormous financial resources, it has not yet completely connected its agenda with average voters, 40 million of whom attend church frequently, self-identify themselves as evangelicals or orthodox Roman Catholics, and consider themselves traditionalists on cultural issues.

There are many explanations for this political disconnect. One is a basic breakdown in communication. In his incisive critique of the "family values" theme of the 1992 campaign, pollster Richard Wirthlin has pointed out that political communication proceeds on three levels: policy, personal benefit, and values. Voters support candidates and causes who enact policies from which they personally benefit: tax cuts, education vouchers, higher wages, or retirement benefits.

The pro-family movement's political rhetoric has often been policy-thin and value-laden, leaving many voters tuned out. Values are very important to voters, but they are not the highest rung on a communication ladder. Without specific policies designed to benefit families and children, appeals to family values or America's Judeo-Christian heritage will fall on deaf ears.

A related shortcoming is that pro-family activists have tended to build their movement around personalities rather than policies. The Perot movement is making a similar mistake today. Visible religious figures play a vital role in building grassroots membership and generating financial support. But their personal charisma, while an important asset, is no substitute for good policy.

Prominent personalities are always critical in building social movements. Labor unions were dominated in the 1940s and 1950s by controversial figures like John L. Lewis of the United Mine Workers or Jimmy Hoffa of the Teamsters. Today, however, labor organizers are more likely to be lower-profile political professionals. A similar transition will probably occur in the pro-family movement during the coming decade.

It is also important for pro-family citizens to adjust their tactics to changing political realities. When tactics become ends in themselves, social movements falter. Abolitionists spent decades in the early nineteenth century petitioning Congress in vain for antislavery laws before shifting their focus to the free soil movement. Cesar Chavez built the United Farmworkers Union in the 1960s with hunger strikes and boycotts. But as he continued the same tired organizational tactics, membership in his union plummeted, falling to under 20,000 by the time of his death in early 1993.

In sports, if the defensive team is preventing the ground game, the offense should pass the ball. Likewise, in politics there is nothing wrong and everything prudent in changing the game plan at halftime if necessary to win. The key is not to become wedded to the playbook but to win the game. Tactical intransigence hamstrings the effectiveness of social movements.

Sit-ins at segregated lunch counters, for example, were once the focal point of the civil rights movement. After the Civil Rights Act of 1964 mandated equality in public accommodations, the movement shifted to voter registration and get-out-the-vote efforts in the South, making tremendous gains that climaxed in Jesse Jackson's 1984 and 1988 presidential campaigns. Today there are thirty-nine members of the Congressional Black Caucus, compared to only a handful in 1965. None of those gains would have been possible had the civil rights community remained committed to the tactics of sit-ins and marches. Feminist leaders have failed to learn this lesson to their hazard. The Equal Rights Amendment died as a viable legislative strategy in 1982, when the ratification period for the federal constitutional amendment expired. Yet feminist groups continue to charge the barricades, launching ERA battles in state after state, and leading their supporters to slaughter. They have lost 25 out of 25 such efforts since 1977.

The most urgent challenge for the pro-family movement is to develop a broader issues agenda. To win at the ballot box and in the court of public opinion, it must speak to the concerns of average voters in the areas of taxes, crime, government waste, health care, and economic security.

Financial pressure on families must be addressed by the pro-family movement because it affects them as adversely as cultural decay. In June 1993 an NBC/ *Wall Street Journal* poll asked the American people what they thought was most responsible for the break-up of the family. Forty-five percent of respondents said financial pressure, while 43 percent cited a decline in moral values. Obviously, the two factors are intertwined. This suggests that the key to turning "family values" into a policy-specific message that will resonate with voters is to address the real needs of financially-pressed families.[4]

Issues such as abortion and opposition to minority rights for gays are important in building a winning coalition. The pro-family movement must never retreat from its compassionate defense of innocent human life and its support for the traditional family. Our positions on those issues should be guided by the dictates of conscience, not political expediency. But we do not compromise these cherished beliefs if we expand the cluster of pro-family issues to attract a majority of voters.

Network exit polls conducted in 1992 are instructive. Only 12 percent of voters indicated that abortion was a key issue in their voting decision. Even more startling, only 22 percent of *self-identified born-again evangelicals* (about 24 percent of the total electorate) listed abortion as an important issue. And only 16 percent of all voters listed family values as one of the most important issues in their voting behavior.

This is not to suggest that social issues are unimportant to evangelical and Roman Catholic voters. But it does suggest that the stereotype of the pro-family voter as a single-issue activist, concerned exclusively with abortion and gay rights, is largely inaccurate. Even religious leaders can play to this media-driven stereotype if they are not cautious. The purpose, therefore, of embracing a broader issues agenda is not to position ourselves differently. We are already in the mainstream. The objective is to represent the interests of our core constituency of church-going evangelicals and Roman Catholics.

There is a growing body of evidence that suggests that evangelicals and their Roman Catholics allies are concerned about the same issues as the broader electorate, but with a pro-family twist. They are not as interested in legislating against the sins of others as much as they desire to protect the health, welfare, and financial security of their own families.

In this sense, the pro-family movement and its natural constituency have passed like two ships in the night. A February 1993 survey by the Marketing Research Institute found that, aside from the economy, the chief concern of voters who attend church four times a month was not abortion, pornography, or prayer in school. It was cutting waste in government and reducing the deficit. More evangelical churchgoers were concerned about term limits than about homosexual rights.[5]

Churchgoing voters continue to view abortion and other social issues as central concerns. By a margin of better than two-to-one they support laws protecting innocent human life. Self-identified, born-again Christians support school prayer by a margin of 94 percent. Eighty percent favor school choice, and 64 percent oppose repealing the ban on gays in the military. They are also far more likely to cast their ballot based solely on these issues, and their voting patterns reveal heavy support for candidates who espouse a pro-life viewpoint.

Pocketbook Issues

The intensity of their views on these issues is remarkable. But what is equally remarkable is that they view these positions as part of a holistic view of a society that is also free from crime, drugs, deficit spending, and high taxes. Hot-button issues may have pulled religious people into politics, but survey research indicates that their interests broaden the longer they stay involved. A survey of Republican voters by Fabrizio, McLaughlin and Associates in January 1993 for example, found that the issue that most unites evangelicals and fiscal conservatives is the deficit.

The reason is simple. Taxes fall heaviest on middle-class families with children. These families must tighten their belts and balance their checkbooks every month. They wonder why government cannot do the same. The furor over federal funding of the arts is not about censorship but about eliminating government waste and abuse.

According to exit polls, 17 percent of self-identified evangelicals in 1992 cast their ballots for Ross Perot, only 2 percent less than the total electorate. Perot downplayed or avoided stating his support for taxpayer funding of abortion. The centerpiece of his campaign was deficit reduction, an issue that resonates among middle-class families.

Family tax relief is another important issue to voters. The standard deduction for children is intended to keep the tax code "family friendly" by insuring progressivity and protecting middle-class families with children from confiscatory tax rates. In 1946 the standard deduction for children was $600, an amount that protected 68 percent of the income of the average family of four from federal income taxes. Families could also itemize deductions for mortgage interest or charitable contributions, protecting most of the remainder of their income. As a result, most families paid little or no federal income taxes in the 1950s and 1960s. Today, the standard deduction for children is only $2,300, and it protects only 20 percent of the average family's income from taxation.

In 1950 the average family with children paid about 2 percent of its income in federal taxes. Today the federal government confiscates 24.5 percent of that same family's income, and when state and local taxes are included the amount jumps to 37.6 percent. This huge increase in tax burden is a major reason for women joining the work force, but it's almost a losing battle against Uncle Sam. Among married-couple families in which both husband and wife work, roughly two-thirds of the wife's earnings are taken by the federal government.[6]

Higher taxes have torn at the fabric of the American family. In many families, both parents must work just to make ends meet. According to the U.S. Census Bureau, the second income generates an average of only 27 percent of total household income. Because of confiscatory tax rates, therefore, mothers and fathers often work for the sole purpose of paying for taxes, meals, wardrobe expenses, and day care. Women should be free to pursue the career of their choice and rise as high as their talents will carry them. But they should not be forced to work simply to compensate for the huge chunk of family income that currently goes to taxes.

Children are the main victims. As employers and the government have encroached on the time and attention of their parents, children are left to pick up the crumbs from the table. The result is a famine in family time. In 1965 parents spent thirty hours each week in direct, intimate interaction with their children. By 1985 that figure had fallen to only seventeen hours per week, and shows no signs of increasing.[7]

The essential principle guiding federal tax policy should be that income dedicated to the care and nurture of children is sacrosanct and should be exempt from taxation. If the standard deduction had kept pace with inflation since World War II, its value today would be approximately $8,000. Most families would be completely exempt from paying federal income tax.

This family-oriented view of taxation is gaining ground. In 1994, for the first time in history, the Republican leadership in Congress included family tax relief in the official GOP budget alternative. Drafted by House Budget Committee firebrand John Kasich of Ohio, the budget plan included a $500 tax credit per child for every family in America. It would have transferred $103 billion from the federal bureaucracy to hard-working families, with 86 percent of the tax cut going to families earning less than $75,000 a year.

The Kasich budget could mark the beginning of a "family side" revolution within the Republican party, just as the "supply side" revolution of the 1970s paved the way for the Reagan tax cuts. Kasich gave GOP deficit hawks something they had never had before: a family-friendly face. He paid for the family tax cut by eliminating funding for the Legal Services Corporation, reducing funding for the National Endowment for the Arts, and consolidating social programs into block grants to the states. Total savings: $278 billion. Pro-family organizations generated thousands of phone calls and letters to Capitol Hill on behalf of the Kasich tax cut, demonstrating their willingness to work with other conservatives on issues of shared concern. Although the GOP budget alternative failed on a straight-party vote, the lines have been drawn in the sand: liberals believe in bureaucracy, while pro-family advocates believe families know better how to care for their children with their earnings.[8]

Health Care

Health care is another issue that directly affects the family's pocketbook. It is also an issue that is inextricably linked to the moral health of society. Good health reflects good living; poor health betrays poor living. Yet this simple fact is almost entirely missing from the current policy debate over health care on Capitol Hill.

The United States spends $800 billion a year on health care, roughly 14 percent of its entire gross domestic product. As Dr. Leroy Schwartz of Health Policy International has documented, the most expensive items in the health care budget are directly attributable to behavioral problems. Crack babies, with intensive care costs of $63,000 per infant, cost $25 billion. Drug abuse and its associated violence run up a bill of additional billions of dollars.

Cancer is the second leading cause of death in the United States. Lung cancer claimed 146,000 lives last year, 90 percent of whom were cigarette smokers. The direct cost of respiratory cancer on the economy last year was $2.6 billion, with an additional $10.1 billion of indirect costs such as lost wages. America's 18 million alcoholics suffer from cirrhosis of the liver and a host of other costly ailments. The cost of a single liver transplant costs up to $250,000.

Hospital emergency rooms overflow with the victims of gang wars, drive-by shootings, and domestic quarrels. Murder, assault, and unintentional injuries run up a bill of $100 billion a year. Sexual promiscuity has its own terrible cost. The treatment for a patient suffering from AIDS can cost up to $140,000. With 118,000 documented cases, the cost to society would be $165 billion.

Unless these widespread social pathologies are ameliorated, there can be no genuine solution to the health care crisis. Poor physiological health is often a reflection of psychological disorders such as stress, loneliness, marital discord, alcoholism, sexual promiscuity, lack of exercise, or poor eating habits. The healthiest environment for persons suffering from these disorders is not a hospital but a loving home. Even scientific evidence suggests that hugs are more therapeutic than narcotics and the sound of the laughter of loved ones is more soothing than medication.

Religious organizations have been in the forefront of the debate over health care reform. In February 1994 the Christian Coalition launched a $1.4 million campaign opposing the Clinton health care plan because it included abortion coverage and would lead to rationing of vital medical services. The campaign included radio spots, print ads, and 30 million postcards distributed in 60,000 churches nationwide. The U.S. Catholic Bishops Conference also shipped an estimated 18 million postcards to Catholic churches opposing the Clinton plan's coverage for abortion. The Family Research Council provided educational literature on pro-family health care reform to 75,000 physicians for placement in waiting rooms. Taken together, these efforts demonstrate that issues such as crime and health care are too important to be left to the special interests. People of faith must speak out and impact legislation that will affect the health and well-being of every family in America.

Crime and Safety

Crime is a major issue to voters because it is ultimately about protecting children. Parents no longer feel that their children can safely venture more than two blocks from their homes. And little wonder. The number of total crimes has increased from 4.7 million in 1965 to 14.8 million in 1990. As we have discussed elsewhere, the crime problem in America is largely a problem of single men raised in absentee-father households.

Many of their victims are children. In Washington State last year, prison officials executed convicted murderer Wesley Alan Dodd as death penalty opponents burned candles at a silent vigil outside the penitentiary. No one bothered to light a candle for Dodd's victim, six-year old Lee Iseli. Dodd was on parole after serving just four months of a ten year sentence for child molestation when he abducted Lee Iseli from a playground just a few blocks from his home. He took the boy to his apartment, strapped him to a bed, and spent all night repeatedly suffocating him, reviving him, and brutally molesting him. As the sun rose over this horrible scene, Dodd choked the child to death, hung his body in a closet, and went to work at his job as a shipping clerk.

Dodd's violence will prevail as long as the two-parent family continues its decline as the primary socializing institution in society. Liberal solutions to crime like rehabilitation and early release programs have utterly failed. Nor are traditional conservative policies like building more prisons an adequate answer. The only true solution to crime is to restore the family. Young males raised in homes with male authority will emulate their fathers in marriage and procreation. Through their families, they will have a personal stake in creating a moral climate for their own children. Moreover, the penal system needs reform to allow for redemptive sentencing for nonviolent criminals, which allows them to work, pay back their victims, and make restitution to society.

Educating Children

Education is another issue that voters view primarily through the eyes of their children. The first goal of education policy should be to make schools safe. According to the U.S. Justice Department, 100,000 children bring firearms to school every day. Stuffed in book bags or hidden in lockers, these weapons are turning schools into demilitarized zones. Violence against teachers is commonplace. In Lorraine, Ohio, a female student attempted to stab her teacher to death after a dare from classmates, who promised her their lunch money if she committed the murder. The knife-wielding student was fifteen years old.

In part because of the breakdown in discipline in public schools, churchgoing voters strongly support choice in education. A growing parental rights movement is gaining momentum at the grassroots. In Chicago a group of parents recently filed suit against the city for failing to provide their children with an adequate education. In Wisconsin in 1993, Linda Cross, a parent and school teacher, narrowly lost her campaign for state superintendent of schools after being outspent 10-to-1 by a union-backed candidate who opposed school choice.

Pro-family conservatives also believe that education should inculcate values in young people consistent with the teaching of their parents. In the

1960s and 1970s, in what educator William Kilpatrick calls a "bloodless coup," the development of morally neutered curriculum such as "values clarification" or "outcome based education" removed the transmission of values from our pedagogy. It is time to restore the schools to their function as transmitters of culture. "By withholding culture from a whole generation of youth," argues Kilpatrick, we force them to "patch together crude codes of behavior from the bits and pieces they pick up on television or in the streets." Asking a twelve-year-old to determine what is right or wrong based on what "feels good" is "wildly out of place—like a guest appearance by Madonna on *Mister Rogers' Neighborhood*."[9]

Casting a wider net means having a holistic vision of society and its problems. If the grassroots pro-family movement forwards a limited agenda that only addresses one or two issues, we will not succeed because we will not deal with the full range of voter concerns.

Some on both sides of the political aisle have misunderstood the pro-family movement's emphasis on a broader issues agenda as signaling a retreat from issues like abortion and pornography. Liberals believe moral issues are losers at the ballot box, though Bill Clinton's experience with gays in the military strongly suggests otherwise. Some conservatives fear we may be raising the white flag on vital moral issues. They need not be worried. Working on other issues—crime, taxes, education—will strengthen our voice on matters of conscience, not weaken it. During the debate over health care reform, for example, opposition to taxpayer-funded abortion interwove with concerns about physician choice and jobs like an unbroken tapestry.

The false dichotomy between our moral beliefs and the broad range of issues confronting society has been created by our foes. Religious values do not apply to only a few issues; they inform every aspect of our lives. The principles of our faith speak to financial matters, crime and punishment, education, ethics and good government, and how to raise the poor out of a cycle of dependency. If we huddle in the ideological ghetto erected for us by our opponents, we do our religious beliefs an injustice and fail society as well.

The Left does not confine itself to a narrow band of issues. Feminist groups speak out about abortion, but they also aggressively lobby for federally funded day care, equal pay for equal work, and tougher laws against sexual harassment. The NAACP and other civil rights groups pass resolutions dealing with the federal budget, urban problems, health care, and foreign policy. If the Left can speak to a broad range of issues, so too should the pro-family movement.

Meeting Real Needs

When Christ entered a village, he met the needs of the people right where they were. If they were hungry, they ate. If they were thirsty, they drank. If they were blind, they saw. If they were lame, they walked. He met their needs first and preached later, usually in easy-to-understand parables accessible to the average person. His methodology should be ours as well. Too often, those of us in the pro-family community have preached before we met real needs. We must have the same attitude that Christ had as he wept over the people of Galilee, whom He described as "sheep without a shepherd."

Do our neighborhoods resound with the rattle of gunfire? We must make them safe. Do schools fail to teach basic skills and values? We must make them work. If the roads are scarred with potholes, we must pave them. If prisons do a better job of training criminals in violence than protecting the citizenry, we must reform them. If families suffer under the crushing burden of heavy taxes, we must relieve them. If the poor are trapped in inner cities that have become war zones and a welfare system that has failed them, we must set them free. Meeting these needs of our fellow citizens, including those who do not share our faith, will soften hardened hearts and prepare minds to receive our message of spiritual renewal.

Casting a wider net also means building coalitions with others outside of our own community. Many who share our values have not joined our movement for stronger families and basic goodness simply because we have never invited them to participate. This is particularly true of minorities. Building bridges with our brothers and sisters in the minority community is one of the greatest opportunities facing the pro-family movement.

CHAPTER SIXTEEN

The Curse of Ham:
Religion and Racism in America

IN 1926 the leader of one of America's largest grassroots organizations explained why so many of its members were politically active. "Finally came the moral breakdown that has been going on for two decades. One by one all our traditional moral standards went by the boards or were so disregarded that they ceased to be binding." He decried the loss of respect for the sanctity of "our homes, of chastity, and finally even of our right to teach our children in our own schools fundamental facts and truths were torn away from us. Those who maintained the old standards did so only in the face of constant ridicule."[1]

These statements were made by Hiram Wesley Evans, the Imperial Wizard and Emperor of the Ku Klux Klan. But they bear a remarkable similarity to present-day statements by religious conservative leaders about the state of our culture. Therein lies the crucible of race for the faith community.

Evans's words are a powerful reminder of the legacy of racism that religious conservatives carry like an albatross as they seek to reenter public life after a half-century of self-imposed exile. This is not to suggest any moral equivalence between the two movements. Indeed, it is grossly unfair (and inaccurate) to suggest any historical continuity between the nativist and racist agenda of the Klan, or modern counterparts like David Duke, and the pro-family movement. As E. J. Dionne has argued, "The goal of family stability should not be abandoned simply because Duke and those like him have used the issue for racist purposes."[2]

But there is much in the language of the Ku Klux Klan, Massive Resistance, and David Duke that is disturbing for religious conservatives.

For the past complicity of the white church in the mistreatment of African-Americans and Jews is too large a blot on our history to deny. Tragically, white evangelicals did not merely look the other way as African-Americans were denied full equality and participation in American life. They were among the most fiery champions of slavery and later segregation—all the while invoking God's name and quoting the Bible to justify their misdeeds. Why are white evangelicals accorded so little respect in the public square today? Certainly part of the answer lies in our past. We are speaking the language of Charles Grandison Finney. But the larger society suspects that they hear the sneering voices of Hiram Wesley Evans and George Wallace.

Jerry Falwell poignantly records his own transformation from segregationist to supporter of civil rights. When civil rights marches convulsed the South during the sixties, Falwell used his pulpit to criticize Martin Luther King and other black ministers for entangling the church in social protest, an ironic twist given his own later public career. "Preachers are not called to be politicians," he asserted, "but to be soul winners." Shortly thereafter, a group of activists from the Congress on Racial Equality targeted his church in Lynchburg, Virginia, for nonviolent protests. They were evicted and later arrested. In his autobiography, Falwell expresses regret over these incidents and for his own insensitivity to segregation. "I must admit that in all those years it didn't cross my mind that segregation and its consequences for the human family were evil. I was blind to that reality," he confesses. "I wish even more that we who love Christ and are committed to His church had healed our own divisions before the world noticed and condemned them."[3]

Billy Graham, who grew up outside of Charlotte, North Carolina, catapulted onto the national scene when he began to preach revivals in football stadiums that filled to overflowing in the late 1940s. When the civil rights crisis ensued, Graham walked a fine line between obeying the *Brown* v. *Board of Education* decision and counseling against agitation by both blacks and whites. He insisted that his crusades be integrated wherever the law allowed (some stadiums had separate white and "colored" seating). But he generally disagreed with civil rights leaders on tactics and frowned on marches and protests, preferring less visible ways to work for desegregation. As a native Southerner and the most influential American evangelist since Billy Sunday, Graham could have greatly influenced white opinion during the civil rights struggle. That he did not remains a great regret. "Tragically, too often in the past evangelical Christians have turned a blind eye to racism," he recently wrote, "or have been willing to stand aside while others take the lead in racial reconciliation, saying it was not our responsibility. (I admit I share in the blame.)"[4]

White evangelicals, who now seek a place at the table in political life, remained on the sidelines during the greatest struggle for social justice in this century. They did so by claiming that the gospel was not a political tract and that the mission of the church was to save souls and baptize believers, not to register people to vote. Some criticized the black church for organizing dissent, accusing their ministers of "politicizing" the gospel, harboring "outside agitators," and "fomenting discord."

These words have undermined the moral authority of religious conservatives as they have sought to redress other forms of social injustice—abortion, euthanasia, religious bigotry—in recent times. Richard Land, director of the Christian Life Commission of the Southern Baptist Convention, relates the story of a biracial gathering of Baptists recently held to discuss the pain and injustice of segregation. "You just don't realize how much you hurt us," one black man told his fellow Baptists.

God and Massive Resistance

The white evangelical church marched in the vanguard of the campaign to preserve segregation in the South. George Wallace may have stood in the schoolhouse door, but evangelical clergy provided the moral framework for his actions. Reverend Tobias Egger of Charlotte, North Carolina, delivered a sermon in 1957 condemning integration and contending that segregation was a "Christian position." He used as his text the apostle Paul's letter to the Galatians: "There is neither Jew nor Greek, neither bond nor free, there is neither male or female; for ye all are one in Jesus Christ." Racial differences between blacks and whites, Egger proclaimed, paralleled distinctions between Jews and

Greeks that were sanctioned by Scripture. But his greatest concern was not biblical exegesis—it was the "breakdown of racial integrity" and "enforced physical proximity or closeness of the races" that would lead inevitably to "interbreeding." Racial equality would "create jealousy, envy, covetousness, and malice, to say nothing of sheer hypocrisy."[5]

The legal apparatus of segregation emerged haphazardly in the years after the Supreme Court's decision in *Plessy* v. *Ferguson* (1896) sanctioned the "separate but equal" doctrine as the law of the land. As C. Vann Woodward illustrates in *The Strange Career of Jim Crow*, it had little foundation in Southern jurisprudence or custom prior to the 1890s. But evangelical preachers gave Jim Crow an endorsement from the Highest Source possible.[6] Reverend G. T. Gillespie, president of Presbyterian-sponsored Belhavan College in Mississippi, argued that "an all-wise Providence" is "responsible for the distinct racial characteristics . . . which are chiefly responsible for the segregation of racial groups across the centuries and in our time." His pamphlet *A Christian View of Segregation* was published and widely circulated by the White Citizen's Councils Association, a leading organization in the massive resistance movement. Although he conceded that the Bible was silent on the separation of races, Gillespie insisted that "valid inferences may be drawn in support of the general principle of segregation as an important feature of Divine purpose and Providence through the ages."

The division of tongues at the tower of Babel, Gillespie claimed, was "an act of Divine Providence to frustrate the mistaken efforts of godless men to assure the permanent integration of the peoples of the earth." The real bogeyman in this formulation was the rampaging Negro male, who lusted after white women and threatened the purity of the Anglo-Saxon race. Gillespie thundered that "racial amalgamation, implemented by wiping out all distinctions and the fostering of the most intimate contact between the races" would "inevitably result in intermarriage."[7]

Miscegenation was one of the oldest taboos in southern society. White evangelical leaders enthusiastically exploited this fear, conjuring up the demons of black sexual stereotypes that had haunted Southern literature and folklore for generations. This rhetoric elevated the raw struggle for racial power to a chivalrous defense of white Southern womanhood. "Racial segregation is in accord with the natural law which is a product of God's creation," asserted Reverend James Dees, president of the North Carolina Defenders of States' Rights. The desegregation of schools, he warned, would lead whites down a slippery slope toward "total race mixing" and "a Negroid or mulatto culture in the South and finally throughout the country."[8]

Reverend T. Robert Ingram, rector of St. Thomas's Episcopal Church in Houston, dispensed with the fig leaf of biblical quotations. "The movement towards integration is a denial of Christ," he cried. "It is part of an effort to create one society in which there are no distinctions or differences. This is part and parcel of the Antichrist."[9] Ingram was an important intellectual leader within the Southern clergy. His booklet entitled *Essays on Segregation,* which was widely influential in white evangelical circles, argued that the only appropriate place for integration was in heaven. Another evangelical leader declared in 1956 that *Brown* v. *Board* violated the laws of God. "Segregation," he exclaimed, "predates the known history of the world. God was the original segregationist."[10]

Massive resistance borrowed heavily from religious language that had earlier been used to justify slavery. Scriptural allusions to the curse of Ham recounted in the book of Genesis embroidered sermons and brimmed over in pamphlets that defended segregation. It required a leap of faith to designate black Americans as the direct descendants of caucasian Canaanites, but preachers of massive resistance like the Reverend E. E. Colvin of Orangeburg, South Carolina, found a way. "The Old Testament Scriptures recognize the existence of things as they are," he declared. "We find that also in the New Testament, Jesus did not attempt to change or reform society in His day by the use of force. There was slavery in His day [but] never did Jesus attempt to use force or advocate force" to abolish the institution of slavery.[11]

These arguments echoed the fiery defense of the peculiar institution by James Henley Thornwell, a leading Presbyterian clergyman in South Carolina, in the years prior to the Civil War. In his famous Zion Church dedicatory sermon of 1850, Thornwell cried that the "parties in the conflict are not merely abolitionists and slaveholders; they are atheists, socialists, communists, red republicans, jacobins on the one side, and the friends of order and regulated freedom on the other." Abolitionism, he declared, "is only a single aspect—a special direction of an absorbing mania—a particular form of a general spirit of madness and fanaticism."[12]

Similarly, the defense of segregation a century later became subsumed in the larger struggle to protect primitive religion from the horrors of liberalism, unitarianism, and communism. These hydra-headed evils threatened to destroy the Southern heartland and the Christian way of life, issuing forth from the North, the Soviet Union, and the pits of hell. "[A] very considerable part of the violence agitation against segregation," warned G. T. Gillespie in 1954, "stems from sources outside the Negro race, and outside of America, and coincides with the worldwide movement for racial amalgamation which has its fountainhead in Moscow." The choice between segregation and a color-blind society, he added, "is essentially a choice between the Anglo-Saxon ideal of racial integrity" and "the Communist goal of amalgamation" that would lead ultimately to the mixing of the races, intermarriage, and a mulatto society.[13]

These jeremiads had their desired effect. The *Brown* v. *Board* decision had instructed segregated school systems to integrate "as soon as practicable." But massive resistance made a mockery of that goal. Eight years after the Supreme Court decision, public schools across the South were more segregated than ever. In Alabama in 1962, not a single black child attended public school with whites; in Georgia, 8 out of 303,000 black students were in the same schools with whites; in Mississippi, none out of 287,000; in South Carolina, none out of 265,000; and in Virginia, only 536 blacks out of a total minority student population of 217,000 attended the same public schools with whites.[14]

The intervening years of Southern "interposition" brought open defiance of the Supreme Court decision. Senator Harry Byrd of Virginia declared: "We face the greatest crisis since the War between the States."[15] Massive resistance could not have succeeded without support from white evangelical churches. Throughout the South, "white citizen's councils," often led by evangelical clergy, sprouted to fight the federal desegregation decree. The Defenders of State Sovereignty and Individual Liberty, whose chaplain was Reverend John Howard of Blackstone, Virginia, boasted 12,000 members in sixty local chapters across the state in 1956. Its membership form declared that the bearer was a "white, law-abiding citizen" who was "not a member of any organization detrimental to the peace or welfare of the U.S.A.," and believed "the segregation of the races is a right of state government." The Defenders provided grassroots support for Governor Lindsay Almond's decision to close public schools in Warren County, Norfolk, and Charlottesville in 1958 rather than allow them to be integrated.[16]

The past cannot be changed. Massive resistance is a fact of history, and the evangelical church's role as the final bulwark of segregation is a dark stain on its history. We must frankly acknowledge the errors of the past, recognize the debt we owe to those who exposed the hypocrisy of the church, and forsake racism as both an ideology and a political style. And we must do more. We must build a genuinely inclusive movement that embraces the full racial diversity of America, and makes room for our black, brown, and yellow brothers and sisters in Christ. If we flow out of lily-white churches into lily-white political organizations and support only lily-white candidates for elective office, we cannot expect the larger society to take us or our agenda seriously. "Racial reconciliation demands that we stretch ourselves beyond our comfort zones," urges Robin McDonald of the Capitol Hill Crisis Pregnancy Center in Washington, D.C. "Unless Christians stand together, our church and our nation will remain divided."[17]

Building a Multiracial Movement

As I discussed in chapter one, extensive survey data demonstrates that minorities tend to be at least as conservative (and sometimes more conservative) than whites. When asked if "government should play a role in strengthening traditional values," 70 percent of African-Americans and two-thirds of Hispanics agreed it should. Minorities favor school choice, voluntary prayer in school, tougher laws against crime, cuts in federal spending, and laws that restrict abortion. They oppose the legalization of drugs, support the death penalty, and object to the teaching of homosexuality as an acceptable alternative lifestyle in the public schools.[18]

The views of minorities mark a strong departure from the liberal positions advocated by the traditional civil rights leadership. On welfare, for example, 91 percent of blacks and 86 percent of Hispanics agreed that able-bodied welfare recipients should be required to work for their benefits. Only 38 percent of blacks and 37 percent of Hispanics support quotas, set-asides, and other special preferences for minorities to compensate for past discrimination. "According to survey data, black people have more in common with Jerry Falwell than Jesse Jackson," concludes economist Walter Williams of George Mason University. "And Jesse Jackson has more in common with white hippies than black people. But even though blacks register conservative attitudes across the board, they still say they're not Republican or conservative. There's a stigma associated with these labels in the black community."[19]

John Green, specialist in religion and American politics at the Ray Bliss Institute of the University of Akron, sees in this disconnect a potential opening for the conservative faith community. "The Democratic party has traditionally been the party of minorities. Issues like gay rights and abortion have only been recent issues," notes Green. Pollster Tony Fabrizio agrees. "Given the divergence of Hispanic and African-American opinions on several key issues from that of the civil rights establishment," he concludes, "it is possible for candidates or organizations trumpeting these conservative positions to make inroads into these two core Democratic constituencies." Yet a word of caution should precede these efforts at bridge building. For while they share the views of the pro-family movement on the issues, minorities could not be further apart in terms of party loyalty. A total of 69 percent of African-Americans and 48 percent of Hispanics are Democrats, compared to only 31 percent of whites. Green adds: "Minorities don't find Democratic issues very helpful, but they don't find the Republican party very hospitable."[20]

Therein lies the rub for the pro-family community. For more than a decade the pro-family movement has been a largely white, evangelical, Protestant phenomenon with its feet planted firmly in the Republican party. If we are truly serious about building bridges to minorities, we must move beyond the white church to make inroads into traditionally Democratic constituencies of color. The liberal and civil rights communities have lost their credibility on virtually every issue, failing to represent the traditionalist views of their constituents on crime, the death penalty, abortion, school choice, and welfare reform. The pro-family movement can compete with the civil rights establishment for minority support if it will make it a priority.

New Minority Leaders

There are signs that a multiracial Christian coalition is forming in unlikely places. The New York city school board races of 1993, cited earlier, showed what can happen when color no longer divides natural allies. Recently a group of African-American pastors in Washington, D.C. launched a campaign to deny funds to any school in the nation's capital that prevented students from engaging in voluntary prayer. This campaign, along with the recent firestorm at a largely black high school in Jackson, Mississippi, shows that the grassroots movement by people of faith is hardly a white phenomenon.

"They keep you separately divided that you might be separately fleeced," Populist firebrand Tom Watson told a biracial audience in Georgia in the 1890s. Watson might have been speaking to the pro-family movement today. It has become a cliche to observe that Sunday morning is the most segregated time in America. But that segregation—voluntary rather than legally enforced—has made it difficult for those who share the same faith and values to cooperate.

How can people of faith overcome this estrangement? Part of the answer is spiritual. Our churches should reflect the fact that God's grace is for people of all races and ethnic backgrounds. Another part of the solution is finding issues that unite whites and minorities. School choice may be the issue that finally bridges the color line. In the battle for choice in California in 1993, one survey showed that minorities favored educational scholarships by a margin of roughly two-to-one, while whites slightly opposed it. The truth is that school choice as an issue appeals not to the Republican base (affluent whites in the suburbs, whose children already attend good schools) but to the Democratic base (African-Americans, Hispanics, ethnic Roman Catholics). That is why the Christian Coalition spent $100,000 broadcasting pro-school-choice spots on urban radio stations and distributed literature in minority churches. The California school choice initiative lost in 1993, but during the campaign the pro-family movement made inroads into the minority community and built relationships with minority churches that will pay dividends for years to come.

Grassroots pro-family activists are locking arms with minorities across the nation. In 1993 they supported Charles Winburn, the African-American pastor of the Kingdom Church of Cincinnati, Ohio, in his campaign for city council. Winburn, a registered Democrat, graduated from a Christian Coalition training school, and campaigned against gay rights and for welfare reform and school choice. He received 50 percent of the black vote, 30 percent of the white Democratic vote, and a majority of the Republican vote. He unabashedly testifies to the role of faith in informing his political views, a position that is still respectable in the African-American community even as it has become taboo among white candidates. "What got me elected was the timing and positioning of God," he declares. [21]

A similar campaign unfolded in 1994 in Houston, Texas, where the National Right to Life Committee and other pro-family groups came to the aid of Beverly Clark, an African-American, pro-life woman who ran for Congress in a heavily Democratic district. The Christian Coalition distributed nonpartisan voter guides in over 100 black churches and made thousands of nonpartisan get-out-the-vote calls to African-American voters from grassroots phone banks. Clark, a former member of the Houston city council, shocked political observers by forcing former Senator Lloyd Bentsen's nephew into a run-off.

Occasionally, black and white Christians are thrown together by the exigencies of a crisis. The Bishop Knox incident, detailed earlier, exemplified the unity among white and black Christians on social issues such as prayer in school. In a statement that could have been made by Pat Robertson or Jerry Falwell, Knox argued that anything that restored moral values in our young people, including prayer, could hardly be viewed as harmful. "Most of us concede that our society is in trouble and that our children are not what we would like them to be in terms of values and morals," he said. "We need a foundation to teach them that it's wrong to steal, to kill, to lie, to disrespect our elders." The outpouring of support for his courageous stand sparked grassroots lobbying efforts, coordinated by the Christian Coalition and other groups, that bolstered legislation in Mississippi and five other states to allow student-initiated prayer in public schools. Thirty years ago, African-Americans marched on state capitols across the South for the cherished right to vote. Today blacks and whites march together for the inalienable right to free speech, including speech with a religious content.[22]

These and other breakthroughs in biracial Christian cooperation point to two themes in breaking the color barrier. First, social issues are the key to unlocking support in the minority community. Republican candidates traditionally run on taxes and cutting government spending. The result is that they have won only a small percentage of the minority vote since 1936, when blacks left the party of Lincoln for the party of FDR. Moderates in the Republican party who call for the inclusion of more minorities in the party want to beat a retreat from the social issues, a flawed strategy that would virtually lock the GOP out of the minority vote for the remainder of this century. Jesse Helms, for example, received a higher percentage of the black vote than Ronald Reagan in North Carolina in 1984 by campaigning in minority churches on issues like school prayer. Michael Farris, the home-school advocate who was the Republican nominee for lieutenant governor in Virginia, won over 20 percent of the black vote in 1993.

The second theme is the need for religious conservatives to work more actively within the Democratic party. Despite their essentially conservative views on the issues, blacks and Hispanics remain strongly Democrat in their loyalties, partly because of the legacy of civil rights. If the pro-family movement hopes to make realistic gains among these voters, it must become more aggressively bipartisan and resist the temptation to become a wholly-owned subsidiary of the Republican party. The Traditional Values Coalition has understood the importance of this strategy, working with minority pastors in a bipartisan way to oppose legislation granting minority status based on sexual preference. Religious values cross racial lines; all too often, party loyalty does not.

The watershed moment for religious conservatives and the minority community was the nomination of Clarence Thomas to the U.S. Supreme Court in 1991. While traditional civil rights organizations sat on the sidelines (the NAACP refused to endorse Thomas), pro-family groups swung into action. They built relationships with emerging voices of dissent from the liberal civil rights orthodoxy: Armstrong Williams, Phyllis Berry-Meyers, John Doggett, and others. Williams later became a popular talk radio show host in Washington, D.C.; Berry-Meyers joined the staff of the pro-family Free Congress Foundation to head a black satellite television network, and Doggett's wife Teresa ran for state treasurer in Texas in 1994 with strong backing from white evangelicals.

When the history of the nascent biracial Christian coalition is written, Clarence Thomas will be a central figure. He grew up in the segregated South and came from a disadvantaged background, yet graduated from Yale Law School and blazed a brilliant career path in government, reaching the pinnacle of the legal profession at the age of forty-three. Raised in a devoutly religious home and educated at Catholic schools in his native Georgia, Thomas eloquently testified to the importance of his faith in overcoming the barriers of racism and prejudice. And he is an authentic voice of healing and empowerment for the black community. "The issue is economics—not who likes you," Thomas said prior to his nomination to the Court. "And when you have economics, people have a way of changing their attitudes towards you. I don't see how the civil rights people today can claim Malcom X as one of their own. Where does he say black people should go begging to the Labor Department for jobs?"[23]

Other voices are joining Thomas in offering a "third way" for minorities. They are forsaking both special-interest politics and the white, country-club culture that has locked them out of the political process in the past. Kay Cole James, formerly a top aide in the Bush administration, became the Secretary of Health and Human Resources in Virginia in early 1994. For Kay, it was like coming home. She grew up in the ghetto of inner-city Richmond, surrounded by crime and economic disenfranchisement, but sustained by a strong family and her transcendent faith in God. She was one of the first black students to integrate Richmond city schools in the 1960s, suffering mistreatment and persecution. Today she spearheads efforts to reform the welfare system and empower minorities and others in poverty to rise as far as their talents can carry them.[24]

Robert Woodson with the National Center for Neighborhood Enterprise is another important figure offering fresh new leadership. He argues that minorities can never be lifted out of poverty and political dis-enfranchisement by government programs. There is a strong history of conservative traditions in the black experience. Until recently, despite the bitter legacy of slavery and racism, African-Americans had strong fami-lies, vibrant churches, and safe communities. Woodson argues that only spiritual renewal and a return to the centrality of two-parent families can reverse the social pathologies that afflict minorities.[25]

The pro-family movement must embrace and promote these and other spokespersons who are challenging us to reach beyond our racially divided churches. There is much work to do. As *Christianity Today* noted in a recent cover story on racism and the church, the segregation of people of faith has been terribly costly, not only because it has under-mined the moral message of the church, but also because of the severe consequences for the entire society.[26]

Theologian Cornel West argues in his book *Race Matters* that what has kept us divided on racial issues is a largely fruitless debate between liberals and conservatives about what ails race relations in America. "The liberal notion that more government programs can solve racial problems is simplistic—precisely because it focuses *solely* on the economic dimen-sion," he argues. Meanwhile, conservatives "highlight immoral actions [crime, illegitimacy, drugs] while ignoring public responsibility for the immoral circumstances that haunt our fellow citizens." If liberals can acknowledge that government assistance cannot substitute for strong two-parent families, and if pro-family conservatives can admit that tra-ditional values alone cannot combat institutional racism, then we can move forward together in a constructive dialogue about race in America.[27]

Judgment, the Bible teaches, begins with the church. Before we point our finger of accusation at the larger society, we must put our own house in order. That means repenting of the racist past, making amends by building a biracial future, and focusing on the real needs of minorities for better schools, safer neighborhoods, and stronger families. It also means establishing churches and civic organizations that reflect the racial diversity of America. Ironically, the curse of Ham has now fallen on us; evangelical whites are the new marginalized com-munity, those most likely to be reviled for our political activism, in part because of the religious bigotry of our foes, but also because of the sins of our fathers.

What should be our response? We must continue the initial efforts already underway in the pro-family movement to work with minority churches and leaders on issues of shared concern. Jackie Robinson succeeded in breaking the color barrier in major league baseball by letting his bat do his talking. In breaking our own color line, we must take actions that speak louder than words about our commitment to a society in which people are judged by the content of their character, not the color of our skin. This will not happen overnight. But if we accomplish it, we can heal our nation with God's help, and win unlikely allies along the road to spiritual renewal.

CHAPTER SEVENTEEN

What Is Right about America:
How You Can Make a Difference

I N 1994 the District of Columbia city council, prodded by Mayor Sharon Pratt Dixon, began to explore legalizing riverboat gambling in the nation's capital. Some argued that the tax revenues generated by the riverboat casinos would fund more police and better schools. Armstrong Williams, a former aide to Clarence Thomas and host of a talk program on a Washington radio station, read a newspaper account in which several area pastors indicated support for the measure. That afternoon Williams went on his radio program and read the names and phone numbers on the air of pastors who supported riverboat gambling.

"How can church leaders support something that would lower the moral tone of our city?" asked Williams. "I expect this kind of nonsense out of politicians, but not from people who are supposed to represent the Lord." Within minutes, calls of protest jammed the lines of the churches whose pastors had expressed support for gambling. They also barraged city council members and the mayor's office with phone calls. Within days, the gambling proposal died a quiet death.

Several months earlier, the Austin, Texas, city council had passed an ordinance granting insurance and other benefits to unmarried "domestic partners" of city employees, including unmarried heterosexual couples and same-sex couples. There was little opposition on the liberal-dominated council, and the ordinance passed by a five-to-two vote.

Austin, home to the University of Texas with its thousands of faculty and staff, has one of the most liberal voting populations in the state. Any effort to repeal the city council's action seemed futile. But one person decided to take a stand despite overwhelming odds. Reverend Charles

Bullock, pastor of the 2,000-member Christ Memorial Baptist Church, formed Concerned Texans to lead a campaign to repeal the domestic partnership ordinance.

Few gave Bullock's campaign much of a chance. But he diligently organized the churches, collected thousands of signatures on a petition favoring repeal, and placed an initiative on the ballot overturning the ordinance. A group of African-American pastors agreed to turn out a strong minority vote and testified in opposition to the policy before the city council. The Christian Coalition distributed nonpartisan voter guides in churches on the Sunday prior to the vote.

On May 7, 1994, the city of Austin repealed the domestic partnership ordinance by a whopping 62 to 38 percent margin. Political observers were shocked not only by the result, but by the overwhelming size of the victory. "There is a new conservative force in this city," said Bullock.

These two incidents reaffirm the fact that one person can make a difference. Perhaps you have asked yourself whether or not your voice matters in a political system that seems to have lost touch with the people. We are frequently told that the golden era of volunteers in politics is over, that the rise of television, political consultants, and the busy schedule of two-income households has passed control of our government out of the hands of average citizens. But Ross Perot proved those pundits wrong in 1992, and his independent candidacy pulled millions of people into the process for the first time. The Christian Coalition and other grassroots organizations are also demonstrating that the American people still want a voice in their government and are willing to gain it through hard work and sweat equity.

Does the voice of a single person make a difference? History teaches us that one vote has sometimes decided the fate of nations. President Andrew Johnson avoided conviction on impeachment charges by a single vote in the U.S. Senate in 1868. Adolf Hitler became Chancellor of Germany in 1933 by a single vote in the German parliament. In 1941 just months before the Japanese bombed Pearl Harbor, the House of Representatives extended the draft by a one vote margin. John F. Kennedy won the 1960 election over Richard Nixon by one vote per precinct. In 1986 the Republicans lost control of the U.S. Senate by a combined total of only 22,000 votes in five states. In today's era of declining voter participation and citizen apathy, a handful of votes often decides the outcome.

Perhaps you have read this book and agree with many of the issues it raises. You support efforts to strengthen our families, reform our schools, and secure our streets. You may be tired of a political and legal culture that treats faith like fanaticism and equates religion with fascism. Perhaps you have agreed with many of the stands of religious conservatives on taxes, term limits, and family values, but never considered yourself a part of what some pillory as the so-called "religious right."

If all you do is read these pages, nod in agreement, and never lift a finger to change the direction of this country, this book will not have achieved its ultimate purpose. More importantly, you will have missed a once-in-a-lifetime opportunity to help move this country back into the mainstream of respect for faith and basic goodness.

A Plan for Action

Here are some practical steps that you can take to be an effective citizen, voter, and activist to make America stronger and better. In addition, this chapter includes a discussion of suggested issues on which to work as well as some cautionary words about the limits of what political action can achieve.

The first and most important step to improving our nation is to pray. The Bible teaches, "[If] My people who are called by My name will humble themselves and pray, and seek My face and turn from their wicked ways, then I will hear from heaven, will forgive their sin, and will heal their land" (2 Chronicles 7:14). How are we to pray? We should intercede for those in positions of civil authority, asking God to grant them wisdom that we might live in peace. "I urge that entreaties and prayers, petitions and thanksgivings, be made on behalf of all men," wrote the apostle Paul, "for kings and all who are in authority, in order that we may lead a tranquil and quiet life in all godliness and dignity" (1 Timothy 2:1–2).

We should support the right of children to bow their heads in prayer in our public schools. But what ails this country is not a lack of prayer in public schools, but a lack of prayer in our private spiritual lives for those in government and for a restoration of righteousness in our nation. If we pass a constitutional amendment protecting public prayer but do not earnestly pray in private along the lines the Bible teaches, our movement for stronger families and faith in God will fail in its objectives.

Second, a person can make a difference by participating in the political process. There are various ways to fulfill this obligation. We must be responsible voters, citizens, activists, and givers of our time and finances. It is important to register to vote and go to the polls. But voting alone will not rectify the problems that plague our nation. True citizenship involves availing one's self of a full range of opportunities: becoming involved in the political party of one's choice, contributing to a candidate who shares one's values, joining the Christian Coalition or another pro-family organization, starting a ministry in your church to register Christians to vote, and perhaps running for local office.

Citizenship is not a hobby, but a way of life. In this regard, Christians can learn a great deal from the Left. It is to our own shame that many on the Left display a greater commitment to values that have failed over the last thirty years than many grassroots conservative Christians exhibit for values that work and are based on eternal principles. In order to restore America to goodness, Christians must become fully engaged in the duties of citizenship. The pulpit should not be used as a platform for candidates or political parties. But pastors and priests must not shy away from teaching the responsibilities of citizenship. Our responsibility as Christians does not end at the four walls of the church, nor can we treat politics as a "dirty business" best left to others. If those of faith are not involved in the civic process as voters, activists, and candidates, others will take their place, and the entire society will pay a heavy price for our lack of involvement.

Third, we must persuade rather than preach. The evangelical idiom with which we are comfortable in propagating the gospel is neither appropriate nor effective in a political context. Those who share our faith may find the quotation of Scripture in support of a particular policy compelling, but it is likely to fall on deaf ears in the larger society. This does not mean that we should not speak boldly for our faith. But it does mean that we have a special responsibility to articulate our views in a way that others can hear, and to add persuasiveness to our words that they might receive them. Speak "only such a word as is good for edification according to the need of the moment, that it may give grace to those who hear," says the Bible (Ephesians 4:29).

Finally, we must persist. Political change does not occur in one election, one Congress, or even one decade. Religious conservatives sometimes think that if they will roll up their sleeves and get involved for a short period of time, they can solve all the country's problems and then return to their churches and homes. Jerry Falwell once told me, "The thing about Christians is that when they lose, they quit. And when they win, they quit. They just quit."

This is not a view that will lead to true change. The National Association for the Advancement of Colored People was founded in 1909. It took forty-five years before the Supreme Court issued its *Brown* v. *Board of Education* decision, and another decade before the first comprehensive civil rights legislation passed the Congress. The ACLU was founded in 1920 and for years litigated to remove expressions of religion from the public square. Not until 1962 did the Supreme Court remove prayer from the public schools.

Run Like Lincoln

"The diligent hand shall govern," says the Bible. That means persistence and a willingness to stay in the game even when the prospects of victory appear bleak. Consider the career of Abraham Lincoln. In 1831 he failed in business and the following year lost a seat in the Illinois legislature. Afterwards, he became a partner in a general store and went bankrupt in a few months, his second failure in business. It took him seventeen years to pay off the debts. After serving several terms in the Illinois legislature, in 1843 he lost a campaign for his party's nomination to Congress. Finally winning a seat in the House of Representatives in 1846, he spoke out against U.S. involvement in the Mexican War, becoming so unpopular back home that he was not even renominated by his party to his own seat. In 1855 he ran for the U.S. Senate and lost. The next year his name was placed in nomination for the vice-presidency at the Republican National Convention, but he lost out to another contender. In 1858 he was the Republican nominee for the Senate, losing to Stephen A. Douglas. Many people faced with this string of political failures might have given up. But Lincoln persisted, winning the presidency in a five-way race in 1860. Because he never gave up, the American experiment survived and the Union was preserved.

Today our nation faces a moment of opportunity and crisis not unlike that of Lincoln's time. These times require citizens who will pray, participate, persuade, and persist. These practical steps of civic involvement can reverse the tide of antipathy towards religious faith and give Christians and others of faith a voice in government.

A Third Party?

I am often asked by grassroots activists whether or not I support a third political party. Could it be that Roman Catholics, evangelicals, Jews, Greek Orthodox, and other people of faith could come together in a coalition for change? There is no question that such a party embracing family values and smaller government would enjoy public support equal to that of the Perot movement. However, such a party would not succeed as effectively as involvement in both of the existing parties. Historically, third party movements either flounder or succeed by failing: their agendas are absorbed by one of the other parties (as happened to the Populists and Progressives), causing them to wither away and die. For this reason, the best strategy for pro-family activists and their allies is to become involved as Republicans or Democrats.

By so doing, they will make politics in general more grassroots-oriented and family-friendly. Issues like family break-up and protection of human life will no longer be swept to the periphery of the political debate. Candidates of both parties will be forced to include people of faith in their campaign strategy and address their issues.

As this process unfolds, the future of American politics will likely be characterized by continued chaos and long-term trauma. The balkanization of the electorate into factions and interest groups ranging from pro-family groups to gays, feminists, environmentalists, and term limit advocates will accelerate. Religious conservatives will continue to make inroads in local offices and the structures of both parties. Anti-incumbency and voter anger will boil over at the ballot box, causing the greatest turnover in Congress in a generation. A series of scandals breeding a loss of confidence in government will likely produce more one term or abbreviated presidencies, a rule since 1960 to which only Ronald Reagan has been the exception.

Out of this volatility and upheaval will emerge a government that will be smaller and more responsive to voters. Imagine a day when members of Congress and state legislature rotate in and out of office after only a few terms. Picture a time when technology will connect citizens and activists directly with their representatives, where television and micro-computers will allow them to know whether legislators are attending a particular committee meeting and how they are voting. Imagine a day when thousands rather than dozens pack into town hall meetings, millions of calls descend on Capitol Hill every week as a matter of course, political parties find themselves sharing power with well-organized citizen groups, and 75 percent of all registered voters go to the polls.

Our political system is totally unprepared for such an influx of voters. Its entire structure is geared towards low levels of citizen participation, abysmal voter turnout, and backroom deals between special interests and career politicians. But the old system is in the midst of a meltdown. The American people are slowly but surely taking back their government. Could it be that a citizen movement for common sense and honest change is about to transform the political landscape? Only time will tell, but the prospects are good and the time is riper than ever before for an honest-to-goodness change in the way Americans govern themselves.

Forwarding Solutions

To succeed in politics, it is more important to light a candle than curse the darkness. For years pro-family supporters have pursued a reactive, defensive agenda that only rarely put forward positive solutions of our own. As we participate in the political process, we should promote and advance the following policies and programs.

The foundation of family-friendly policy is this basic principle: income devoted to the essential needs of children and families should be exempted from taxation. The standard deduction for children should be dramatically increased to $10,000 a child, so that no family of four in America making less than $40,000 a year would pay a dime in federal and state income taxes. This personal exemption should also be permanently indexed to inflation to prevent its further erosion in value in the future. The existing tax code's marriage penalty should also be eliminated, a penalty that was exacerbated by the Clinton tax increase in 1993.

A second principle guiding public policy on the family should be, "Do no harm." Where the family meets a need better than government, let government step out of the way. This is particularly true in the area of education. Attempts at federal or state regulation of church-based, private, and home schools should be foresworn. A mountain of evidence demonstrates that the best way to improve academic performance is to involve parents in the education of their children. One of the most powerful ways to encourage this parental involvement is through education scholarships of between $1,000 and $2,500 to enable parents to send their children to the school of their choice. These scholarships or vouchers represent only about one-fourth to one-half of per-pupil expenditures on education in this country—roughly equal to what we spend on bureaucracy and overhead. These funds should be shifted from education bureaucrats to families, while leaving the funds that are actually reaching the classroom in the public schools where they belong.

The religious conservative agenda for the public schools is mainstream and effective. First, we support empowering local teachers by eliminating state and federal bureaucracy and mandates. Teachers and parents know what is best for children, and the closer we keep decisions to the home and the classroom, the better students will perform. Second, implement back-to-basics curriculum with an emphasis on basic reading and math skills, backed up by standards for promotion and regular testing.

Third, merit pay and performance standards for teachers should be adopted at the state level to encourage the best and brightest to enter the profession. Greater use of alternative certification for teachers would allow those with skills and the willingness to contribute to educate our young people without having to wade through a tangle of red tape.

Finally, abstinence-based curricula that encourages young people to resist peer pressure in the area of drugs, alcohol, and sex will greatly reduce the social pathologies that have transformed too many schools into war zones. The prophets of permissiveness have done tremendous harm to our children. One million teens get pregnant every year, sexually transmitted diseases ravage our youth, half of all American teens report being sexually active, and the average sexually-active eighteen-year-olds today have had more partners than the average forty-year-olds have had in their entire lives.[1] Abstinence programs such as Sex Respect and Teen Aid have reduced the incidence of teen pregnancy, abortion, and drug use by as much as 50 percent in some school districts. By contrast, studies indicate that exposing young people to permissive "safe sex" education and school-based clinics that dispense contraceptives actually has the opposite of the desired effect. For example, two researchers recently tracked 192 young girls in Los Angeles who received contraceptives for six months from a medical clinic. These girls averaged 13.4 acts of sexual intercourse *every month*. This contrasted with 8.8 acts for young women entering the program—a 50 percent increase in sexual activity after exposure to contraception rather than abstinence.[2]

Education reform must also address what Bill Bennett has called the "architecture of the soul." Children should be taught right from wrong. They are moral creatures, and they should be treated as such. Likewise, they should not be prohibited from exercising their right to free speech, including speech of a religious content. Values should be taught, student-initiated prayer should be protected as free speech under the First Amendment, the Bible should not be banned, and the rights of parents to mold and shape the souls of their children should be respected.

A third important principle of family-friendly reform is: cut the federal budget to find the revenue to supplement the family budget. We need a Balanced Budget Amendment to the Constitution that would limit taxation to a reasonable percentage of the gross national product (perhaps 20 percent) and require Congress to spend no more than it takes in annually. We support requiring a super-majority, similar to that required to invoke closure in the Senate, to pass tax increases in both houses of Congress. A line-item veto, already given to forty-three governors, should be granted to the president. Entitlement spending should be controlled through a combination of capping growth to inflation and population increase, means-testing, and requiring larger contributions from those most able to pay.

Strengthening the family also means ending the financial subsidies for its break-up. Welfare reform must encourage work, savings, marriage, and personal responsibility. The federal government should give serious consideration to getting out of the welfare business altogether, turning its functions over to the states, which can serve as laboratories of reform. The Wisconsin legislature has already enacted a law pulling out of the federal Aid to Families with Dependent Children (AFDC) program by the end of the decade; other states will likely follow. If a state wants a liberal, permissive welfare system, let them adopt it and pay for it themselves. But the rest of the states should be free to experiment and try new innovations in reducing illegitimacy and poverty.[3]

Charles Murray has recently sparked an invigorating debate about welfare and family decomposition by commenting on the emerging "white underclass." He points out that the illegitimacy rate of 5 percent for children born in 1960—called "a vast social calamity" by the *New York Times*—is now 30 percent. Unless current trends of out-of-wedlock births are reversed, we will have a massive underclass by early in the next century. Murray argues that we should discourage illegitimacy by effectively ending pubic subsidies for out-of-wedlock births. His proposal should be tried as an experiment in pilot states or counties with high illegitimacy rates and heavy welfare caseloads. In addition, the growth in welfare spending should be capped to prevent costs from spiraling still higher. Since 1988 the amount expended by state, local, and federal governments on welfare has risen from $217 billion to $305 billion. This explosive growth should be slowed and future increases limited by statute.[4]

We must also provide greater stability for the most important contract in civilized society: the marriage contract. We cannot ultimately solve the social problems of crime, poverty, illiteracy, and drugs without saving marriages. We should reform "no fault" divorce laws that allow men to marry and father children, then simply abandon them to a life of privation. The economic inviability of single motherhood has long been established: the average woman's income declines 70 percent during the first year following divorce. Men who shirk their responsibilities to wives and children should be slapped with stiff social and legal sanctions, including garnishment of wages if necessary to recoup the more than $10 billion in child support payments currently owed by deadbeat dads. It is also important to reform divorce laws to encourage couples to stay together, particularly when children are involved. Waiting periods before a divorce decree can be granted, accompanied by a requirement of court-approved counseling, places the law firmly on the side of marriage. Churches and synagogues must also do more to prepare young couples for the pressures of modern marriage, and offer a loving atmosphere where couples in trouble can find counseling and healing.

The crime problem can never be solved without dealing with the root causes of family break-up. For this reason, one answer to crime is alternative sentencing for youthful, first-time offenders to boot camps and halfway houses. An experiment already underway in the District of Columbia is to assign nonviolent offenders to a church and a family in the community that would report to the criminal justice system on their progress. Parole should be eliminated for violent criminals, and restitution programs should allow payment of debts directly to victims rather than to society.

Defending Life

Religious conservatives believe that government should protect innocent human life. The inalienable right to life is affirmed in the Declaration of Independence and is codified in the Fourteenth Amendment to the Constitution, which guarantees that no one will be denied life or liberty "without due process of law." The Supreme Court in 1973 discarded two centuries of American jurisprudential history, choosing instead to impose the most extreme and liberal abortion law then in existence on every state in the union. Mary Ann Glendon, professor at Harvard Law School, has reviewed abortion laws around the world and concluded U.S. law is the most radical and permissive of any Western industrialized nation in the world. Israel allows abortion only in the first trimester, only if the woman is under seventeen or over forty years of age, and even then only under strict circumstances such as fetal deformity or a threat to the mother's life. Germany requires that a woman seek a second opinion from another doctor prior to an abortion, and Sweden prohibits abortion after the eighteenth week of pregnancy.[5]

Roe v. *Wade* banned virtually all common-sense restrictions. In 1982 the Supreme Court ruled that a woman's right-to-know law (requiring that a woman be informed about the development of the child) was unconstitutional. In 1976, in *Planned Parenthood* v. *Danforth*, it struck down a law that required the consent of the spouse. These and other decisions collectively constituted the most brazen act of judicial fiat since the *Dred Scott* decision, and they have engendered no less civil discord. Religious conservatives, therefore, wish to return this issue back to the political arena where it belongs, and allow the various state legislatures to enact common-sense restrictions on abortion, such as parental consent, a woman's right to know, spousal consent, and waiting periods. Should a state seek to pass laws restricting abortion to the difficult cases of rape, incest, or the endangerment of the mother's life, they should not be prevented from doing so. While it is unlikely that a majority of states would do so, no state should be prevented from enacting laws that reflect a consensus of its citizens when innocent life is at stake. Such restrictions would lay the groundwork for protection of innocent life, as the Fourteenth Amendment requires.

In 1992 the Supreme Court permitted states to adopt some modest restrictions by upholding a Pennsylvania pro-life statute in the *Planned Parenthood* v. *Casey* decision, but a five-person majority still reaffirmed *Roe*. This decision satisfied neither side. For the feminists, it opened a Pandora's Box of future restrictions that will be enacted by other state legislatures—all of which could be upheld as long as the courts hold that they do not constitute an "undue burden" on a woman's ability to have an abortion. For the pro-life movement, which had expected a majority to overrule *Roe*, the decision was a devastating blow. It was made all the more insulting by the fact that it was rendered by a Court with three of the five members appointed by Reagan and Bush voting with the majority. After twelve years of conservative Republican judicial appointments, the pro-life cause gained only one additional vote against *Roe*, a vote that was quickly lost when Bill Clinton appointed Ruth Bader Ginsburg to replace Byron White in 1993. This brings the abortion debate full-circle. There will be no end to the civil discord and social unrest accompanying *Roe* until the issue is returned to the political arena. Ironically, persons of deep religious convictions, so often accused of undemocratic impulses and a propensity to impose their beliefs on others, are the ones seeking a level legislative playing field and a full and open debate on the issue.

Abraham Lincoln said during his first debate with Stephen A. Douglas in 1858 that "we shall not have peace until . . . the opponents of slavery will arrest the further spread of it, and place it where the public mind shall rest in the belief that its course is of ultimate extinction."[6] Lincoln envisioned the withering away of a vast social evil by cutting off its source (the slave trade) and stemming its spread (the territories). Religious conservatives have the same vision for abortion. They seek to stop taxpayer subsidies, direct and indirect, to organizations that promote or perform abortions. They seek to stop its spread by allowing states to restrict it. Coupled with compassionate alternatives to abortion, restrictions on abortion will lead to its gradual extinction. The American people agree. According to a 1993 Gallup poll, 72 percent of the American people oppose taxpayer subsidies for abortion, and a majority favor limiting abortion to the hard cases of rape, incest, and the life of the mother.

Pro-family Solution

In addition, we must encourage adoption as a matter of public policy. Our goal should not be shuttling children between foster care institutions, but providing loving homes for children born out of wedlock. There are only 370,000 children in foster care, and over one million couples seeking to adopt. Because there are so few babies, and because of the innumerable legal obstacles to adoption, a system of private adoption agencies and "surrogate mothers" has sprung up. Adoption laws should be reformed to ease the transition for adoptive parents and children—regulations that prohibit interracial adoption and force parents to meet age requirements should be relaxed.

Religious conservatives favor reforming the health care system to provide the highest quality care for American families at an affordable price. The health care plan that President Clinton proposed in 1993 to great fanfare was a bureaucratic, Byzantine, European-style syndicalist nightmare with no precursor in the American experience. Its price controls and high taxes would have led to the rationing of basic medical services, millions of lost jobs, and taxpayer-funded abortion on demand. Religious conservatives favor a free market, pro-family alternative. There are serious problems with the current health care system that can and should be fixed. Some needed reforms include portability of policies, allowing workers to take their insurance with them when they change jobs. American workers do not lose their life or automobile insurance when they change jobs; they should not lose health care coverage either. In addition, we should eliminate previous condition restrictions, enact real malpractice reform, create voluntary purchasing pools to lower premiums, enact medical savings accounts for catastrophic care, and provide tax credits to enable low-income families to purchase health insurance. These common sense reforms can be enacted without interfering with the sacrosanct doctor-patient relationship and without adversely affecting the quality of care.[7]

Beyond Politics

These policies will improve the lives of Americans who find themselves trapped in poor schools, unsafe neighborhoods, and financial poverty. But it is important to acknowledge that they will not, by themselves, solve what ails America's soul. They will not begin to ameliorate the spiritual poverty from which so many in our society suffer. For this reason, the pro-family movement must recognize the limits of what government can achieve.

Some argue that conservative Christians want to use government to legislate their religious beliefs and deny the rights of others. Let me suggest that the opposite is true. Historically, civil liberties have been most secure in the hands of people of faith—for they are convinced that those liberties are granted by the outstretched hand of God and not the fickle pen of lawmakers. If liberty is granted by a human agency, then human agencies can just as easily take them away. I can think of no one better to entrust my liberties with than one who believes they are authored by a Supreme Being, and are thus accorded His full protection.

People of faith have relied too exclusively on political solutions to address their deep sense of cultural estrangement. Retreat from politics did not cause the church's cultural isolation; it completed it. Political involvement alone will not bring about cultural renewal. The faith community that evangelizes the lost, feeds the hungry, teaches the illiterate, and provides loving care for unwed mothers gains a platform from which it can speak to the broader culture.

The plain fact is that the social regression plaguing America did not happen overnight and has festered for decades due in part to the neglect of the faith community. It will not be reversed, as if by waving a magic wand, merely by electing better lawmakers or gaining more favorable court rulings. Bill Bennett has rightly urged that "our first task is to recognize that, in general, we place too much hope in politics." People of faith should exercise the duties and privileges of citizenship (as is their right), participate in the political party of their choice, and make their voices heard from the courthouse to the White House. But we do them and our religion a disservice if we suggest that politics, even in its most noble form, is a panacea for our nation's social problems. It is a poor substitute for the work of the church in restoring marriages, healing families, educating our youth, and rebuilding the broken walls of our culture. "It is foolish, and futile," Bennett adds, "to rely *primarily* on politics to solve moral, cultural, and spiritual afflictions."[8]

This is not a new idea. Christ, whose earthly ministry was the most extraordinary the world has ever seen, resisted when some of his followers sought to make him king of Judea. That would have been a demotion. "My kingdom," he said, "is not of this world." But the faith community has swung so dramatically in recent years from completely foreswearing civic involvement to embracing it as an article of faith, that it is healthy for us to remind one another that our own lives and families have not been healed and made whole because of our political involvement but by His grace as revealed through the agency of the church. We should expect no less for the larger society.

"The central lesson of the last one hundred years is that the state can disrupt, but it cannot save families," concludes Allan Carlson.[9] It is utopian to think that we can save the family through legislative action. Our goal should be more attainable and immediate: to get government off the backs of families and out of their pocketbooks. Our first challenge is to restrict government and force its disengagement from the family, not to positively empower it to intrude further. Alexis de Tocqueville observed in the 1830s that one of the indispensable supports of American democracy was the "peaceful society" that existed in the nation's families. Tranquil homes tempered passions and moderated political extremism. "When the American retires from the turmoil of public life to the bosom of his family," observed Tocqueville, "he finds in it the image of order and peace." Restoring domestic peace and order to our families will lead naturally to the restoration of civility to the broader society. That is not ultimately a political task but a cultural and spiritual mission.[10]

Fulfilling this mission will require creating a culture of compassion. The Christian progressives of the early twentieth century, fired by the social gospel, founded social benevolence organizations like the Boy Scouts, the Salvation Army, the Campfire Girls, and Boy's Town. We need new faith-based charities to bind up the wounds of our broken society.

A new breed of charitable entrepreneurs is already lifting the scaffolding of a culture of caring. The Golden Rule Insurance Company in Indianapolis, Indiana, launched a program in 1991 to provide half-tuition educational scholarships for low-income inner city schoolchildren. In 1994 the program had 1100 students enrolled, 400 on a waiting list, and more than 10 percent of the city's school population had requested an application. Pat Rooney, president of Golden Rule, is one of only three white members of an all-black inner-city congregation, and enjoys amicable relations with the minority pastors in Indianapolis. Parents are ecstatic with the results. Barbara Lewis, whose son Alphonso once performed poorly in public school, says he is now thriving in the Catholic school he attends because it teaches values and has zero tolerance for gangs, drugs, and guns. "He's safer, he's closer to home, and his grades have gotten better," she rejoices.[11]

A similar program in San Antonio, Texas, operated by the nonprofit Children's Educational Opportunity Foundation, provides scholarships to 934 poor children. These programs have elicited howls of protest from teachers unions, not because they have failed, but because they have succeeded. Thirty years ago, scowl-faced segregationists stood in the schoolhouse door and vowed that they would not allow minority children in. Today, liberal teachers unions stand at the same door and sneer that they will not let them out—even with private money.

"Real compassion involves our whole being. It means . . . to act with passion to help end the suffering and even alleviate its cause," writes Amway Corporation founder Rich DeVos. This kind of compassion can be found in Charis Homes, a Christian ministry that builds homes for the poor in downtown Atlanta on donated lots with volunteer crews. It is seen in Detroit's Homes for Black Children, which has transcended the bureaucratic maze of foster care by placing troubled youth in loving minority homes. Or in VivaHealth Plan, an innovative health maintenance organization licensed in east Los Angeles that provides affordable health care fitted to the unique needs of inner-city Latinos.[12]

These and other silent heroes of compassion are meeting not only the physical needs but the spiritual hunger of the poor—often without a dime in federal money or the bureaucratic shackles that come with it. The prevailing cultural ethos claims that everyone is a victim, that society alone bears the blame for poverty, that there is no hope for the downtrodden apart from government handouts, and minorities are so oppressed that they cannot climb the social ladder. This view of poverty and how to ameliorate it marches to the secular drumbeat of the modern welfare state. The left, argues Myron Magnet, has "radically remade American culture, turning it inside out and upside down to accomplish a cultural revolution whose most mangled victims turned out to be the Have Nots." Only faith-based charity can replace the welfare state with a culture of caring.[13]

"Keep your behavior excellent among the Gentiles," urged the apostle Peter, "so that in the thing in which they slander you as evildoers, they may on account of your good deeds, as they observe them, glorify God in the day of visitation" (1 Peter 2:12). Good deeds speak louder than words about our commitment to building a caring society. Visiting those in prison, feeding the hungry, building housing for the homeless, teaching the illiterate to read are all acts of benevolence that silence critics who see nothing but hypocrisy and greed in the message of the church.

I recently had the opportunity to attend a graduation ceremony for Heads Up, a literacy program under the auspices of the Christian Broadcasting Network. The ceremony took place at a National Guard armory in the heart of the Mississippi Delta, perhaps the poorest region in the United States. As I walked into the armory, the hall resounded with gospel hymns sung by a church choir. Approximately one hundred men and women who just a few months earlier could barely write their own names stood on an elevated stage, dressed in gold graduation caps, their faces beaming with pride and their cheeks streaked with tears of joy. Camera flashes exploded as loved ones and family members recorded the moment for posterity. Because the Heads Up program relies on volunteers, it provides graduates with high school-equivalent reading skills for about fifty dollars a person, a fraction of the cost of government literacy programs.

Ministries like CBN's Heads Up, Chuck Colson's Prison Fellowship, and Focus on the Family's new urban outreach program that promotes fatherhood are binding up the wounds of the broken-hearted and marginalized in our society—all without government involvement or political action. This spirit of compassionate volunteerism animated by faith in God and love of our fellow man is what made America great, not government programs out of Washington. Together, we can fill the void in America's soul with one consequential act of kindness at a time.

In the nineteenth century, when rugged pioneers settled the frontier of the American west, many families sold all they owned, packed their few belongings into a covered wagon, and set off into the untamed wilderness. They settled the continent with three tools: an ax, a plow, and a Bible. Once they built their log cabins and planted their crops, these men and women erected the rudiments of the civilization from whence they came. They built churches in which they worshiped God, schools that educated their children, and courthouses that served as the seat of government and the center of the political and economic life of their communities.

When a new family arrived, their neighbors joined together to help them raise their barn. The barn-raising was a ritual that united every person in the community in a shared experience of cooperation and reciprocity. It also underscored the mutual dependence of every citizen on their neighbors for their own survival against the threats of the frontier. Today we have lost both the ethic of self-reliance and this sense of mutual dependency, and with it our feeling of community.

We Americans are a people of devout faith and boundless generosity. Confronted by the same challenges that faced our forebears, we would respond just as they did. We would build churches to serve our spiritual life, schools to teach our children, and courthouses and government buildings to provide a locus point for our civic affairs. They overcame the wilderness and tamed a continent through faith in God, fidelity to family, and cooperation with their neighbors.

By emulating their example, we can rebuild the American experiment and leave our children a better nation than we inherited. There is much work to do. Let us begin the important task that lies ahead.

NOTES

CHAPTER I
THE WINNING COALITION: PEOPLE OF FAITH UNITING TOGETHER

1   Editorial, "Church and State," *Wall Street Journal,* April 4, 1994.

2   Roger Finke and Rodney Stark, *The Churching of America 1776–1990: Winners and Losers in Our Religious Economy* (New Brunswick, N.J.: Rutgers University Press, 1992), 240–45, 248, Table 7.2.

3   Stephen L. Carter, *Culture of Disbelief* (New York: HarperCollins, 1993), 6–8.

4   Laurence I. Barrett, "The 'Religious Right' and the Pagan Press," *Columbia Journalism Review,* July/August 1993, 33–34.

5   Lynnell Hancock, "In God's Name," *New York Daily News,* March 29, 1993.

6   Editorial, "School Challenge From the Right," *New York Times,* April 6, 1993.

7   E. J. Dionne, Jr., *Why Americans Hate Politics* (New York: Simon and Schuster, 1991), 240.

8   Linda Faye Williams, "Black Leadership Shows Voter Savvy," *Insight,* March 7, 1994, 23–25.

9   Fabrizio, McLaughlin and Associates, *Findings of National Surveys of White, Hispanic, and African-American Adults,* September 8, 1993. This survey was written for the Christian Coalition by Fabrizio, McLaughlin and Associates of Alexandria, Virginia.

10   Jack Kemp, "Republican Mayors Put Empowerment to the Test," *Insight,* August 16, 1993, 30.

11   Peter Steinfels, "Conservative Christians Seeking to End Conflicts," *New York Times,* March 30, 1994.

12   Avery Dulles to Richard John Neuhaus, March 24, 1994, personal correspondence to author; David Briggs, "Catholics, Evangelicals Huddle," *USA Today,* March 30, 1994, 3.

13   David Von Drehle, "*Roe* Opinion Reshaped Nation's Public and Private Life," *Washington Post,* April 7, 1994; Kristen Luker, *Abortion and the Politics of Motherhood* (Berkeley and Los Angeles: University of California Press, 1984), 137–39, 147.

14   Frederick S. Jaffe, et al., *Abortion Politics: Private Morality and Public Policy* (New York: McGraw-Hill, 1981), 113–17.

15   Charles Belmonte and James Socias, eds., *Handbook of Prayers* (Princeton, N. J.: Scepter Publishers and Midwest Theological Forum, 1992), 109; Albert J. Nevins, *Builders of Catholic America* (Huntington, Ind.: Our Sunday Visitor Publishing House, 1985), 193–96.

16   Michael Cromartie, ed., *No Longer Exiles: The Religious New Right in American Politics* (Lanham, Md.: National Book Network, 1993), 26.

17   David Wagner, "The New Right and the New Pluralism," *National Review,* May 23, 1986, 28–31.

18   Dana Mack, "What the Sex Educators Teach," *Commentary,* August 1993, 33–38.

19   Brian Robertson, "Curriculum Warriors Brace for Round Two," *Insight*, May 17, 1993, 12–16.

20   Dick Armey, "Freedom's Choir: Social and Economic Conservatives Are Singing the Same Song," *Policy Review*, Winter 1994, 30.

21   George Weigel, "Evangelicals and Catholics: A New Ecumenism," in *Piety and Politics: Evangelicals and Fundamentalists Confront the Modern World*, ed. Richard John Neuhaus and Michael Cromartie (Washington, D.C.: Ethics and Public Policy Center, 1987), 357; Michael Novak, "The Matter of Abortion," *Crisis*, February 1994, 7.

22   Anthony Bevilacqua, "Church and State Should Not Remain Separate," in *Civil Liberties: Opposing Viewpoints*, ed. Charles P. Cozic (San Diego, Calif. : Greenhaven Press, 1994), 148.

23   Keith Fournier, *Evangelical Catholics* (Nashville: Thomas Nelson, 1991), 194–200.

24   Jay Lefkowitz, "Jewish Voters and the Democrats," *Commentary*, April 1993, 38–41.

25   Don Feder, "An Overdue Exodus," *Crisis*, July/August 1993; Don Feder, "When Jewish Liberalism's the Enemy," *Boston Herald*, April 21, 1994.

26   Robert Lakine, "Towards a Jewish-Christian Alliance: An Interview of Rabbi Joshua Haberman," *Crisis*, February 1993, 34, 38.

CHAPTER 2

WHAT THE WORLD WOULD LOOK LIKE:

A RELIGIOUS CONSERVATIVE VISION FOR AMERICA

1   John Meacham, "What the Religious Right Can Teach the New Democrats," *The Washington Monthly*, April 1993, 43–44.

2   Parts of this discussion were originally presented as a paper to the Ethics and Public Policy Center on December 10, 1993. They also appear in Michael Cromartie, ed., *Disciples and Democracy: Religious Conservatives and the Future of American Politics* (Grand Rapids: Eerdman's, 1994).

3   Richard John Neuhaus, *The Naked Public Square* (Grand Rapids: Eerdman's, 1984); Thomas C. Atwood, "Through a Glass Darkly: Is the Christian Right Overconfident It Knows God's Will?," *Policy Review*, Fall 1990, 48.

4   Bureau of the Census, U.S. Department of Commerce, *Government Finances 1989–1990* (Washington D.C.: GPO, 1991), 2; Paul McNulty, "The Crime of it All," *Rising Tide*, January/February 1994, 15.

5   Jane Gross, "Sex Educators for Young See New Virtue in Chastity," *New York Times*, January 16, 1994; DeNeen L. Brown, "Virginity Is New Counterculture Among Area Teens," *Washington Post*, November 21, 1993; Barbara Ash, "True Love Waits for Thousands of Area Students," *Tallahassee Democrat*, January 20, 1994; Roper Organization, "Abortion Study," *Roper Report*, March 1994, Table 1a.

6   Benjamin Franklin, "On the Price of Corn, and the Management of the Poor," *London Chronicle*, November 1766, in *Benjamin Franklin's Writings*, ed. J. A. Leo Lemay (New York: Library of America, 1787), 587–88, cited in Thomas G. West, "Poverty and the Welfare State," in *Moral Ideas for America*, ed. Larry P. Arnn and Douglas A. Jeffrey (Claremont, Calif. : The Claremont Institute, 1993), 57.

7 George Will, "Couple Bullied on Religious Grounds," *Seattle Post-Intelligencer*, March 13, 1994.

8 Eric Foner, *Free Soil, Free Labor, Free Men: The Ideology of the Republican Party Before the Civil War* (New York: Oxford University Press, 1970), 61–65.

1 *Roberts v. Madigan*, 921 F.2d at 1055 (10th Cir. 1990).

2 Associated Press, "Doctor Claims Prayer Use Led to Suspension," *Louisville Courier-Journal*, April 4, 1991.

3 Wes Smith, "Courting Trouble: Town Bristles as the ACLU Goes after Not Just a Sign, But a Symbol," *Chicago Tribune*, February 21, 1992; Margaret Gillerman, "Town Can Keep Sign about God: Judge Dismisses ACLU Lawsuit," *Post-Dispatch* (St. Louis), April 9, 1994; Margaret Gillerman, "'The World Needs God': Sign Stirs Debate," *Post-Dispatch* (St. Louis), April 1, 1994; Wes Smith, "ACLU May Be in for a Holy War," *The Chicago Tribune,* February 11, 1994.

4 Larry Witham, "Federal Proposal Puts Trust in Court, Not God," *Washington Times,* February 27, 1994; "HUD Denies Seeking Deletion of Religion From Ads," *Washington Times,* February 27, 1994; Gary Bauer, "Religion as Harassment?" *Washington Watch,* February 11, 1994, 4; Gary Bauer, "Religious Harassment Rules Required?" *Washington Times,* May 22, 1994. USWest, the publisher of the Yellow Page directories in question, later allowed the religious symbols to be reinstated after a bout of negative publicity.

5 George Washington, "Reply to an Address by the Synod of the Dutch Reformed Church of America, October 9, 1789," *In God We Trust: The Religious Ideas of the American Founding Fathers*, ed. Norman Cousins (New York: Harper and Brothers, 1958), 60.

6 United Press International, "School Board Implements School Prayer Law," (UPI Spotlight November 18, 1993).

7 *Religious Rights Watch*, 2, no. 11, March 1991, 1.

8 *Lee v. Weisman*, 112 S Ct 2649, 120 L Ed 2d 477 (1992).

9 *Lee v. Weisman*, 514. Scalia added, "The Court's notion that a student who simply *sits* in 'respectful silence' during the invocation and benediction (when all others are standing) has somehow joined—or would somehow be perceived as having joined—in the prayers is nothing short of ludicrous. We indeed live in a vulgar age. But surely 'our social conventions' have not coarsened to the point that anyone who does not stand on his chair and shout obscenities can reasonably be deemed to have assented to everything in his presence."

10 Wire Services, "Student Prayer Halted by Principal and Police," *Religious Rights Watch*, December 1991.

11 Dave Condren, "Book Controversy in Colden Settled," *The Buffalo News*, January 20, 1994; Kimberly J. McLarin, "Schools Trying to Observe Holiday Season Minus Religion," *New York Times*, December 16, 1993.

12 Cathy Haden, "Policy on Prayer in Schools Is Crystal Clear, Principals Say," *Clarion-*

Ledger (Jackson), November 19, 1993; Andy Kanengiser, "Prayer-Backing Students Stand Ground," *Clarion-Ledger* (Jackson), November 18, 1993; Joe Urschel, "Religion: Don't Breathe a Word About It," *USA Today*, November 30, 1993; Ronald Smothers, "School Prayer Gaining Ground in South," *New York Times*, February 22, 1994; David Snyder, "Educator Gives Voice to School Prayer Issue," *Times-Picayune* (New Orleans), December 26, 1993 2, for Lynn Buzzard quotation.

13   *Goldman v. Weinberger*, 475 U.S. 503 (1986); *Lee v. Weismann*, 112 S. Ct. 2649, 2678 (1992); Michael J. Sandel, "Freedom of Conscience or Freedom of Choice," in *Religious Liberty in the Supreme Court*, ed. Terry Eastland (Washington, D.C.: Ethics and Public Policy Center, 1993), 491–96.

14   *Commonwealth of Pennsylvania v. Karl S. Chambers*, 528 PA 584, 599 A. 2d 643 (1991); Valerie Richardson, "Bible Put on Book Blacklist by Courtrooms in Two States," *Washington Times*, December 17, 1992.

15   *Commonwealth v. Chambers*, 633–35; editorial, "Mention of God Voids a Sentence," *New York Times*, November 9, 1991.

16   Daniel Boorstin, *The Americans: The Colonial Experience* (New York: Vintage Books, 1958), 40–48; Frederick B. Tolles, *Meeting House and Counting House: The Quaker Merchants of Colonial Philadelphia, 1682–1763* (Chapel Hill, NC: University of North Carolina Press, 1948), 10–28; Benjamin Hart, *Faith and Freedom: The Christian Roots of American Liberty* (Dallas: Lewis and Stanley, 1988), 197–206.

17   Shirley E. Perlman and Phil Mintz, "Objection to Ashes: Judge Orders Attorney to Clean Symbol from Forehead," *Newsday*, February 25, 1993, 7.

18   *Constangy v. North Carolina Civil Liberties Union*, 947 F.2d at 1148 (4th Cir. 1991); Reuters News Service, "Appellate Panel Bars Prayers in Courtroom," *New York Times*, October 27, 1991; D. L. Cuddy, "Judges Have Right to Pray," *Globe-Dispatch* (St. Louis), November 20, 1990.

19   Reuters News Service, "Appellate Panel"; editorial, "Another Work," *Orlando Sentinel Tribune*, November 22, 1992; "Effort to Ban Bible from Library Defeated," *St. Petersburg Times*, November 14, 1992.

20   "Religious Material Okd in Indiana State Park Inns," *Chicago Tribune*, June 14, 1990; Ed Stattmann, "Bayh Not Backing Down on Bibles in State Park Inns," *United Press International*, June 13, 1990.

21   *Stone v. Graham*, 449 U.S. 39, 42 (1980).

22   *Allegheny County v. ACLU*, 492 U.S. 573 (1989).

23   D. James Kennedy, "Separation of Church and State," *Policy Counsel*, Fall 1992, 28–29; "No 10 Commandments on State Grounds, Court Says," *Orlando Sentinel Tribune*, June 3, 1993; "Court Rules Ten Commandments Monument Illegal," *Dallas Morning News*, June 19, 1993.

24   Kennedy, "Separation of Church and State," 28.

25   Keith A. Fournier, *Religious Cleansing in the American Republic* (Virginia Beach, Vir.: American Center for Law and Justice, 1993), 11.

26   Debbie Wilgoren and Leef Smith, "Promoting Secularity in School Paper: Louden High School Urges No Use of Christmas in Next Issue," *Washington Post*, December 11, 1993.

27   Joshua Haberman, "The Bible Belt Is America's Safety Belt," *Policy Review*, Fall 1987, 42.

28 John Corry, "In God They Trust," *The American Spectator*, July 1993, 42–43; Miriam Horn, "Timothy Healy's Sacred Trust," *U.S. News and World Report*, June 5, 1989, 52–53.

CHAPTER 4

THE NEW AMOS AND ANDY: HOW THE MEDIA PORTRAYS PEOPLE OF FAITH

1 H. L. Mencken to Raymond Pearl, July 14, 1925, in Carl Bode, ed., *The New Mencken Letters* (New York: Dial Press, 1977), 187; H. L. Mencken to Sara Haardt, July 14, 1925, in Marion Elizabeth Rogers, ed., *Mencken and Sara: A Life in Letters* (New York: McGraw-Hill, 1987), 219; H. L. Mencken, *Prejudices*, Series 6 (New York: Alfred A. Knopf, 1927), 64–75; William Manchester, *Disturber of the Peace* (New York: Harper Brothers, 1950), 174, 178, 182.

2 For a similar view on Mencken but a different interpretation of the Scopes Trial, see Garry Wills, *Under God: Religion and American Politics* (New York: Simon and Schuster, 1990), 102–3, 108–14.

3 Garry Wills, "George Bush, Prisoner of the Crazies," *New York Times*, August 16, 1992: Robert H. Meneilly, "Government is Not God's Work," *New York Times*, August 29, 1993, for "Communism" quotation; Randall Balmer, "Churches Should Tread Lightly on Tax-Exemption Issue," *The Oregonian*, February 27, 1993, for Molly Ivins quotation. For a similar argument on tax-exempt status of churches, see Elliott Beard and Elizabeth Lesly, "Pennies From Heaven: It's Time for Uncle Sam to Pass the Collection Plate," *Washington Monthly*, April 1991, 40–46.

4 Associated Press Report, *Los Angeles Times*, May 15, 1993.

5 Editorial, "Real and Rhetorical Religious Wars," *Atlanta Journal and Constitution*, December 9, 1992.

6 S. Robert Lichter and Stanley Rothman, "The Media Elite and American Values," (report printed by the Ethics and Public Policy Center, Dallas, Texas), 1982; Laurence I. Barrett, "The 'Religious Right' and the Pagan Press," *Columbia Journalism Review*, July/August 1993.

7 Ibid.

8 Marshall N. Surratt, "Can Media 'Get' Religion?" *Christianity Today*, July 19, 1993, 15.

9 Media Research Center, "Faith in A Box: Network News on Religion," (pamphlet printed by the Media Research Center in Washington, D.C.) March 3, 1994, 1–4; Larry Witham, "Negative News Dominates Sparse Religion Coverage," *Washington Times*, March 4, 1994.

10 Ibid.

11 George Weigel, "The New Anti-Catholicism," *Commentary*, June 1992, 25–31; Lois Kaplan, "Is Catholic Bashing on the Rise?" *Star Tribune* (Minneapolis), December 26, 1992.

12 Statement by Michael Novak, Empower America News Conference, January 12, 1993.

13 Stephen Bates, "Fundamentally Out of Fashion," *Washington Post*, September 7, 1993; Dan Quayle, *Standing Firm* (New York: HarperCollins, 1994), 58.

14 Stephen L. Carter, "Conservatives' Faith, Liberals' Disdain," *New York Times*, August 15, 1993.

15 Figures provided by CareNet, a network of Crisis Pregnancy Centers, May 11, 1994.

16 I am indebted to Pat Robertson's address at the Alf Landon Lecture, Kansas State University, October 12, 1993, for this analysis.

17 Dan Balz, "Democrat Fazio Assails Religious Right in GOP," *Washington Post*, June 22, 1994; Ralph Hallow, "Key House Democrat Lashes Out at Christian Conservatives," *Washington Times*, June 22, 1994.

18 Michael Medved, "Hollywood's Dirty Little Secrets," *Crisis*, March 1993, 18–23.

19 Larry Bonko, *Virginian-Pilot*, February 24, 1994.

20 "Hollywood Toys with Its Last Bias: Christians," *Los Angeles Times*, October 14, 1993; Media Research Center, "Faith in a Box," 8.

21 Benjamin Franklin, *The Autobiography of Benjamin Franklin* (New York: Macmillan, 1967), 93, 112–13; Benjamin Franklin, *Poor Richard's Almanac* (Philadelphia: n.p., 1746), 16.

22 Norman K. Risjord, *Representative Americans: The Revolutionary Generation* (Lexington, Mass.: D. C. Heath and Company, 1980), 99–107.

23 Kennedy, "Separation," 35.

24 Donald S. Lutz, *The Origins of American Constitutionalism* (Baton Rouge: Louisiana State University Press, 1988), 140–43.

25 Roy P. Basler, et al., eds., *Collected Works of Abraham Lincoln* (New Brunswick, N.J.: Rutgers University Press, 1953), 2:461; Harold Holzer, ed., *The Lincoln-Douglas Debates* (New York: HarperCollins, 1993), 64–68; Richard V. Pierard and Robert D. Linder, *Religion and the Presidency* (Grand Rapids: Zondervan, 1988), 87–113.

26 Alexis de Tocqueville, *Democracy in America,* ed. Phillips Bradley (New York: Alfred A. Knopf, 1980), 307–8.

CHAPTER 5

FAITH VERSUS FANATICISM: HOW RELIGION HAS BECOME MARGINALIZED

1 Michael Isikoff, "Christian Coalition Forms Legal Expenses Fund for Clinton Accuser," *Washington Post*, May 13, 1994.

2 Texas Education Association, "Radical Right Invades Texas," *Advocate*, April/May, 1994.

3 DeNeen L. Brown, "Virginia Parents Want Book Removed," *Washington Post*, May 18, 1993.

4 William Kilpatrick, *Why Johnny Can't Tell Right from Wrong: And What We Can Do About It* (New York: Simon and Schuster, 1992), 255–56.

5 Stephen Bates, *Battleground: One Mother's Crusade, the Religious Right, and the Struggle for Control of Our Classrooms* (New York: Poseidon Press, 1993), 83–92.

6 C. David Kotok, "Kerrey, Stoney Supporters Joust Verbally," *Omaha World-Herald*, November 24, 1993; C. David Kotok, "A Repugnant Slap at Jan Stoney's Religion," *Omaha World-Herald*, November 26, 1993; Valerie Richardson, "Christian Connections Used Against Legislator," *Washington Times*, December 12, 1993.

7 Lee Bandy, "Solicitor Rips Born-Again Beasley," *Columbia State*, April 15, 1994.

8 *Virginian-Pilot*, July 3, 1991.

9 John F. Kennedy, "Remarks on Church and State," in Theodore H. White, *The Making*

of the President, 1960: A Narrative History of American Politics in Action (New York: Macmillan, 1989), 391–93.

10 "San Francisco Aide Faces Battle for Criticizing Homosexuals," *New York Times*, August 22, 1993.

11 Times/Mirror Survey, February 3, 1994.

12 *McGowan v. Maryland*, 366 U.S. 420, 442 (1961), for Earl Warren quotation; *Braunfeld v. Brown*, 366 U.S. 599 (1966); *Gallagher v. Crown Kosher Supermarket*, 366 U.S. 458; A. James Reichley, *Religion in American Public Life* (Washington, D.C.: The Brookings Institute, 1985), 144.

13 *Harris v. McRae*, 448 U.S. 297, 320 (1980).

14 *Wallace v. Jaffree* 472 U.S. 38, (1985); Robert L. Cord, *Separation of Church and State: Historical Fact and Current Fiction* (Grand Rapids: Baker, 1988), 36–46; Robert Cord, "Church, State, and the Rehnquist Court," *National Review*, no. 46, August 17, 1992, 35; Herbert B. Adams, *Thomas Jefferson and the University of Virginia* (Washington, D.C.: GPO, 1888), 91; Benjamin Hart, *Faith and Freedom: The Christian Roots of American Liberty* (Dallas: Lewis and Stanley, 1988), 351.

15 Edward Dumbauld, *The Political Writings of Thomas Jefferson* (Indianapolis: Bobbs-Merrill, 1955), 35–36; Harvey C. Mansfield, Jr., *Thomas Jefferson: Selected Writings* (Arlington Heights, Ill.: Harlan-Davidson, 1979), 46–50; Michael Novak, "Judicial Tyranny," *Forbes*, October 28, 1992, 238; Benjamin Hart, *Faith and Freedom*, 337–53.

16 Bernard Schwartz, *The Bill of Rights: A Documentary History* (New York: McGraw-Hill, 1971), 2:1026; *Wallace v. Jaffree*, 38; *Everson v. Board of Education*, 330 U.S. 1, (1947), for Hugo Black quotation. For a differing view, see Leonard W. Levy, *The Establishment Clause: Religion and the First Amendment* (New York: Macmillan Publishing Company, 1986), 108–19; or Douglas Laycock, "'Nonpreferential' Aid to Religion: A False Claim About Original Intent," *William and Mary Law Review*, no. 27, 1986, 902–6.

17 Robert L. Cord, "Church, State, and the Rehnquist Court," 35–38; *Wallace v. Jaffree*, 38, 86; John S. Baker, Jr., "The Establishment Clause as Intended: No Preference Among Sects and Pluralism in a Large Commercial Republic," in *The Bill of Rights: Original Meaning and Current Understanding*, ed. Eugene W. Hickok, Jr. (Charlottesville, Vir.: University Press of Virginia, 1991), 41–53.

18 *Lemon v. Kurtzman*, 403 U.S. 602, 612 (1971); *Wallace v. Jaffree*, 105 S. Ct. 2479, 2508 (1971), for Rehnquist dissent; *Marsh v. Chambers*, 463 U.S. 783 (1983); *Everson v. Board of Education*, 330 U.S. 1, (1947); *Wolman v. Walter*, 433 U.S. 229, (1977); *Board of Education v. Allen*, 392 U.S. 236 (1968); *Meek v. Pittenger*, 421 U.S. 349 (1975); Bruce Fein, "Religious Season: Consideration of State Influence," *The Recorder*, December 27, 1993, 7. See Justice David Souter's own understatement: "Our precedents may not always have drawn perfectly straight lines." *Lee v. Weisman*, 120 L Ed 2d 467, 501, (1992). For a good overview of tensions on the Supreme Court, see Mary Ann Glendon, "Religion and the Court: A New Beginning?" in *Religious Liberty in the Supreme Court: The Cases That Define the Debate Over Church and State*, ed. Terry Eastland (Washington, D.C.: Ethics and Public Policy, 1993), 471–81.

19 Joseph Berger, "Public School Leadership Fight Tearing a Hasidic Sect," *New York Times*, January 3, 1992; editorial, "Another Church-State Riddle," *Chicago Tribune*, January 9, 1994; Pat Buchanan, "Court Has a Chance to Bring Back Religion,"

Arizona Republic, December 5, 1993; Russell Hittinger, "The Supreme Court v. Religion," *Crisis*, May 1993, 22–30; William B. Ball, "A Chance to Untangle the Law," *Crisis*, February 1994, 16; Joan Kiskupic, "School District for Hasidim is Target of High Court Challenge," *Washington Post*, March 28, 1994.

20   Russell Kirk, "We Cannot Separate Christian Morals and the Rule of Law," in *In the First Place: Twenty Years of the Most Consequential Ideas from Hillsdale College's Monthly Journal Imprimis* (Hillsdale, Michigan: Hillsdale College Press, 1992), 156.

CHAPTER 6

THE FIRE THIS TIME: FAMILY BREAKUP AND SOCIAL CHAOS

1   Michael J. McManus, "Churches: Wedding Factories or Marriage Savers?" *National and International Religion Report*, November 1, 1993, 1–2; Michael J. McManus, *Marriage Savers: Helping Your Friends and Family Stay Married* (Grand Rapids: Zondervan, 1993), 27.

2   Daniel Patrick Moynihan, "Defining Deviancy Down," *American Scholar*, Winter 1993, 24.

3   David Popenoe, "The Family Condition of America: Cultural Change and Public Policy," in *Values and Public Policy*, ed. Henry J. Aaron, Thomas B. Mann, and Timothy Taylor (Washington, D.C.: The Brookings Institute, 1994), 98–99.

4   William Raspberry, "Out of Wedlock, Out of Luck," *Washington Post*, February 25, 1994; Douglas J. Besharov, "Making Welfare Work," *Rising Tide*, January/February 1994, 18.

5   Moynihan, "Defining Deviancy Down," 22, for figure on welfare for children born in 1980; Robert Rector, "The Paradox of Poverty: How We Spent $3.5 Trillion Without Changing the Poverty Rate," *Heritage Lectures No. 410*, September 3, 1992.

6   Robert Rector, "Reducing the Crushing Tax Burden on America's Families," *Heritage Backgrounder*, March 7, 1994; Rod Grams and Tim Hutchinson, "Putting Families First," *Washington Times*, March 4, 1994.

7   Thomas L. Jipping, "In Defense of Accurate History Education," *Policy Insights*, no. 512, September 1993.

8   William Bennett, *The Leading Index of Cultural Indicators* (New York: Simon and Schuster, 1994), 83; Daniel Patrick Moynihan, "Educational Goals and Political Plans," *Interest*, Winter 1991, 32–48; Daniel Patrick Moynihan, "Educational Goals 2000," *Congressional Record*, February 4, 1994, S924–30.

9   Richard W. Riley, "We Must Reconnect with Children," (speech delivered at Georgetown University, February 15, 1994); Family Research Council, "Free to Be Family: Helping Mothers and Fathers Meet the Needs of the Next Generation of American Children," (press release from the Family Research Council in Washington, D.C., 1992), 17.

10   Moynihan, "Defining Deviancy Down," 26.

11   Charles Murray, "The Coming White Underclass," *Wall Street Journal*, October 29, 1993.

12   Louis Sullivan, speech to National PTA Legislative Conference, March 11, 1991, cited in Family Research Council, "Free to be Family," 29; Douglas Smith and G. Roger

Jarfoura, "Social Structure and Criminal Victimization," *Journal of Research in Crime and Delinquency*, no. 25, February 1988, 27–52; Elaine Ciulla Kamark and William A. Galston, *Putting Children First: A Progressive Family Policy for the 1990s* (Washington, D.C.: Progressive Policy Institute), 1990; Moynihan, "Defining Deviancy Down," 24.

13 Bennett, *Index*, 18–23.

14 Don Feder, "Fatherless Families Fuel Crime Explosion," *Boston Herald*, November 18, 1993.

15 *Congressional Quarterly Researcher*, February 4, 1994, 104, 115.

16 "The Economics of Crime," *Businessweek*, December 13, 1993, 72–80: Don Eberle, *Restoring the Good Society: A New Vision for Politics and Culture* (Grand Rapids: Baker, 1994), 29.

17 John Jay, Federalist No. 3, in *The Federalist Papers*, ed. Gary Wills (1787; reprint, New York: Bantam Books, 1982), 10.

18 Bureau of the Census, *Government Finances, 1989–1990,* prepared by the Department of Commerce, Bureau of the Census (Washington, D.C., 1991); Paul McNulty, "The Crime of It All," *Rising Tide,* January/February 1994, 17.

19 E. J. Dionne, "Fighting Violent Crime: Moral Sense," *Washington Post*, October 5, 1993; Chuck Colson, "Partisan Politics Handcuff Crime Efforts," *USA Today*, April 6, 1994.

20 Myron Magnet, "Emancipating the Underclass," *Commonsense*, Winter 1994, 3.

21 David Rubenstein, "Don't Blame Crime on Joblessness," *Wall Street Journal*, November 13, 1992; James Q. Wilson and Richard Herrnstein, *Crime and Human Nature* (New York: Simon and Schuster, 1986), 473; James Q. Wilson, "Culture, Incentives, and the Underclass," in *Values and Public Policy*, ed. Henry Aaron, et al. (Washington, D.C.: The Brookings Institute, 1994), 58, 62–63.

22 National Center for Policy Analysis, "1992 Update: Why Crime Pays," (report printed by the National Center for Public Policy Analysis in Dallas, Texas) December 8, 1992; McNulty, "The Crime of it All," 15; Robert Davis, "Tough Talk Has a Price: More Money," *USA Today*, October 28, 1993.

23 George Gilder, *Men and Marriage* (New York: Pelican Books, 1986), 65.

24 Richard Cohen, "Dealing with Illegitimacy," *Washington Post*, November 23, 1993; Stephanie Coontz, *The Way We Never Were: American Families and the Nostalgia Trap* (New York: Basic Books, 1993); Charles Krauthammer, "Defining Deviancy Up," *New Republic*, November 22, 1993, 21, for quotation; Brian Robertson, "In Academia, New Praise for the Nuclear Family," *Insight*, March 14, 1994, 18–20.

25 Barbara Dafoe Whitehead, "Dan Quayle Was Right," *The Atlantic*, April 1993, 47–84.

CHAPTER 7
ADVENTURES IN PORKLAND: THE END OF POLITICS AS USUAL

1 Marcia Stpanek, "Know What We Owe? Debt Boggles the Mind," *Virginian Pilot* (Norfolk), March 27, 1994; Kevin J. Price, *The Debt Crisis and You* (Houston: ELS Publications, 1992), 11–21.

2 Thomas Jefferson to John Wayles Eppes, June 24, 1813, in *Writings of Thomas*

Jefferson, ed. Merrill D. Peterson (New York: Library of America, 1984), 1280–1282.

3   Office of the President, *Proposed Budget of the United States Government* (Washington, D.C.: GPO, 1992), Historical Table 1.3; Arthur M. Schlesinger, *The Age of Roosevelt: The Politics of Unheaval* (Boston: Houghton Mifflin, 1960), 515–16, for quotation; Martin A. Gross, "Budget Chop Chart: An Open Letter to President Clinton," *Washington Times*, February 17, 1993.

4   Major Garrett, "Congress Warned of Rebellion," *Washington Times*, March 12, 1993; Meredith Bishop, "Fair Game: Government Welfare for the Well-to-Do," *Policy Review* no. 56, Spring 1991, 78–79; Stephen Moore, "How Much Government Can We Afford?" *Institute for Policy Innovation, Policy Report No. 112,* September 1991; U.S. Bureau of the Census, "Statistical Brief SB/93," report prepared by U.S. Bureau of the Census, Washington, D.C. (for employment data).

5   Robert Samuelson, "The Budget: Back to the Future," *Newsweek*, February 14, 1994, 41.

6   Robert Davis, "Tough Talk Has a Price: More Money," *USA Today*, October 28, 1993; editorial, "Much More Than Research," *Washington Post*, March 15, 1994; "Weathervane," *Dallas Morning News*, February 27, 1994.

7   J. D. Podolsky, "Mr. Fussbudget," *People Weekly*, August 9, 1993, 63.

8   Ronald Reagan, Alfred M. Landon Lecture, Kansas State University, Manhattan, Kansas, September 9, 1982.

9   The above items are from Martin L. Gross, *The Government Racket* (New York: Ballantine Books, 1992), 77–78, 178–82; Citizens Against Government Waste, "Pig Book," (press release issued in Washington D.C.,Feb. 16, 1994).

10 Lee Cullum, "Ready the Budget Hatchet," *Dallas Morning News*, April 5, 1993; Major Garrett, "Congress Warned of Rebellion," *Washington Times*, March 12, 1993.

11 Martin L. Gross, *A Call for Revolution* (New York: Ballantine Books, 1993), 190; Edward T. Pound and Douglas Pasternak, "The Pork Barrel Barons," *U.S. News and World Report*, February 21, 1994, 32–36.

12 Eric Felton, *The Ruling Class: Inside the Imperial Congress* (Washington: Regnery-Gateway, 1993), 47–48.

13 Ibid., 141–42; *Journal of the Committee for Media Integrity*, Summer 1992, 10–11; Laurence Jarvik, "Making Public Television Public," *Heritage Backgrounder*, January 18, 1992.

14 Henry Hyde, "A Mom and Pop Manifesto: What the Pro-Family Movement Wants from Congress," *Policy Review*, Spring 1994, 30.

15 Thomas G. West, "Poverty and the Welfare State," in *Moral Ideas for America*, ed. Larry P. Arnn and Douglas A. Jeffrey (Claremont, Calif.: The Claremont Institute, 1993), 51–52; Robert Rector, "Focus On: Welfare," *Intellectual Ammunition*, October 1992, 14; Kevin J. Price, *Empowerment to the People: An Economic Agenda for the 21st Century* (Washington, D.C.: Free Congress Foundation, 1993), 11–13; William J. Bennett, "The Best Welfare Reform: End It," *Washington Post*, March 30, 1994.

16 Thomas DiLorenzo, "The Anti-Business Campaign of the Legal Services Corporation," (pamphlet prepared by the Center for the Study of American Business, Washington D.C., April 1988).

17 L. Weitzman, "The Economics of Divorce: Social and Economic Consequences of Prop-

erty, Alimony and Child Support Laws," *UCLA Law Review,* no. 28, 1981: 1181, 1245; Kathleen B. deBettencourt, "Legal Services Corporation and the Impact on the Family: A Preliminary Report" (report printed by the Office of Policy Development, Legal Services Corporation, Washington D.C., 1988), 15–16; "Legal Services 1990 Summary of Case Closures—Family Law," (Legal Services Corporation Case Service Reports, 1990).

18   William L. Cohen, "We Shouldn't Be Funding the Habits of Drug and Alcohol Abusers," *Washington Times,* March 23, 1994; "Tax-Subsidized Addicts," *Wall Street Journal,* February 8, 1994.

19   Ibid.; *Congressional Quarterly Weekly Report,* Washington, D.C., February 13, 1993; U.S. Surgeon General Joycelyn Elders, speech delivered to the National Press Club, December 8, 1993. For a contrast between present government policy on alcohol and drug use and the prevailing view during the early twentieth century, see Joel Schwartz, "The Moral Environment of the Poor," *The Public Interest,* Spring 1991, 21–37.

20   Joyce Price, "Art Turns Heads, Stomachs: Repulsive Show Revives NEA Flap," *Washington Times,* July 6, 1993.

21   Joyce Price, "NEA Hit from Right: Gay-Fest Funding Riles Conservatives," *Washington Times,* August 23, 1993; Joyce Price, "Artists Hand Out $10 Bills, Give NEA Funds to Immigrants," *Washington Times,* August 7, 1993.

22   National Cultural Alliance, "The Importance of Arts and Humanities to American Society," (survey published by the National Cultural Alliance, Washington, D.C., February 1993), 13.

23   John Schwatz, "Anti-Aids Campaign Aimed At Youth," *Washington Post,* January 5, 1994.

24   Planned Parenthood information derived from Stuart Nolan and Gregory P. Conko, *Patterns of Corporate Philanthropy: Executive Hypocrisy* (Washington, D.C.: Capital Research Center, 1993), 256–57.

25   William Niskanen, "Lessons for Political Appointees," in *Steering the Elephant: How Washington Works,* ed. Robert Rector and Michael Sanera (New York: Universe Books, 1987), 60.

26   Alexander Hamilton, Federalist No. 10, *The Federalist Papers,* ed. Gary Wills (New York: Bantam Books, 1982), 42–43.

27   Barry Schwartz, *George Washington: The Making of an American Symbol* (New York: Free Press, 1987), 149–77.

28   Frank J. Sorauf, *Party Politics in America* (New York: Harper College, 1991), 18–23; Arthur M. Schlesinger, Jr. *The Age of Jackson* (Boston: Little, Brown and Company, 1953), 193.

29   Roger Daniels, *Coming to America: A History of Immigration and Ethnicity in American Life* (New York: HarperCollins, 1990).

30   Peter Collier and David Horowitz, *The Kennedys: An American Drama* (New York: Warner Books, 1984), 9–22.

31   Oscar Handlin, *The Uprooted* (New York: Little, Brown and Company, 1951, 1973), 201–26.

32   Francis Russell, *The Shadow of Blooming Grove: Warren G. Harding and His Times* (New York: McGraw-Hill, 1968), 116–19, 379–84; David McCollough, *Truman* (New York: Simon and Schuster, 1992), 158–61.

33   Edward Walsh, "A Troubled Rostenkowski Hunts Votes Far From Capitol," *Washington Post*, March 13, 1994; Hedrick Smith, *The Power Game: How Washington Works* (New York: Ballantine Books, 1988), 244–47; Irv Kupcinet, "Kup's Column," *Chicago Sun-Times*, March 16, 1994.

34   Charles M. Madigan, "Americans Lose Touch with Politics," *Chicago Tribune*, November 18, 1990; A Fabrizio-McLaughlin survey conducted on February 17–18, 1994, identified 36.8 percent Democrats, 33.8 percent Republicans, 22.3 percent independents, and 7.3 percent other/don't know. For the Times-Mirror survey, see *Chicago Tribune*, July 12, 1992.

35   Federal Election Committee, "Democrats Narrow Financial Gap in 1991–1992," *Federal Election Committee Release* (Washington, D.C.: GPO, 1994), 3.

36   Jane Ely, "Religious Right Lost More Than It Won," *Houston Chronicle*, December 9, 1992.

37   Jack Germond and Jules Witcover, *Mad as Hell: Revolt at the Ballot Box, 1992* (New York: Warner Books, 1993), 293–305.

38   Ruth K. Scott and Ronald J. Hrebenar, *Parties in Crisis: Party Politics in America*, 2d ed. (New York: Prentiss Hall, 1990), 4–10; Robert Agranoff, "The New Style of Campaigning: The Decline of Party and the Rise of Candidate-Centered Technology," in *Parties and Elections in an Anti-Party Age: American Politics and the Crisis of Confidence*, ed. Jeff Fischel (Ann Arbor, Mich.: Books on Demand, 1978), 230–40.

39   Pound and Pasternak, "Pork Barrel Barons," 32–41.

CHAPTER 8

A JURASSIC JUNGLE: THE DINOSAURS OF BUSINESS, LABOR, AND THE MEDIA

1   Tim Curran and Karen Forestal, "Hyatt Ekes a Win in Ohio," *Roll Call*, May 5, 1994.

2   Daniel Boorstin, *The Americans: The Democratic Experience* (New York: Random, 1974). For an analysis of how gigantism afflicts business today, see Tom Peters, *Thriving on Chaos: Handbook for a Management Revolution* (New York: Harper and Row, 1987), 15–17.

3   T. Harry Williams, et al., *A History of the United States* (New York: Alfred A. Knopf, 1965).

4   Peters, *Thriving on Chaos*, 5.

5   National Federation of Independent Businesses, "Shooting Gazelles: New Taxes Wound Successful Firms," (news release by the National Federation of Independent Businesses, July 1993); Coopers and Lybrand, Inc., "Fourth Annual Economic Impact of Venture Capital Study," (report printed by Coopers and Lybrand, Inc., Washington, D.C., March 1994), 12.

6   Karen Riley, "U.S. Chamber Dumps Moderate, Signals Confrontational Turn," *Washington Times*, April 6, 1994.

7   Stuart Nolan and Gregory P. Conko, *Patterns of Corporate Philanthropy: Executive Hypocrisy* (Washington, D.C.: Capital Research Center, 1993), 11.

8   Arthur M. Schlesinger, Jr., *The Age of Roosevelt: The Politics of Upheaval* (Boston:

Riverside Press, 1960), 292; Arthur M. Schlesinger, Jr., *The Coming of the New Deal* (Boston: Houghton-Mifflin, 1958), 297–315, 400–6.

9   Arthur S. Link, *American Epoch: A History of the United States Since 1900* (New York: Alfred A. Knopf, 1980), 415–20.

10 David McCullough, *Truman* (New York: Simon and Schuster, 1992), 565–66, 713 for quotation; Clark Clifford, *Counsel to the President* (New York: Random, 1991), 193.

11 Council of Economic Advisors, *Government Report*, February 14, 1994; "Unions' Recovery Linked to Change in Political Climate," (report printed by the Bureau of National Affairs, December 31, 1992).

12 Reed Larson, "Harry Beck's Earthquake," *Policy Review*, Summer 1989, 74–76; Peter Brimlow and Leslie Spencer, "The National Extortion Association," *Forbes*, June 7, 1993; "AFL-CIO Membership Reflects Growth Against Government, Service Unions," *Daily Labor Report*, November 12, 1991; Frank Swoboda, "Membership Is Shifting: Survey Shows Growing Strength Among Government, Service Union," *Washington Post*, October 31, 1991.

13 Brimelow and Spencer, "National Extortion," 74–80.

14 Michael Putzel, "Enraged Union Leaders Say They Won't Forget, Will Get Revenge At Polls," *Boston Globe*, November 19, 1993, 85.

15 Brooks Jackson, *Inside Politics*, Cable News Network, May 13, 1994.

16 Warren Brookes, "The Media and the Statist Quo," *Policy Counsel*, Fall 1992, 4–5; Daniel Oliver, "How to Think About Regulations, *The Heritage Lectures*, May 19, 1993; Ted J. Smith, III, "The Destructive Dialectic: The Decline of American Journalism and What to Do About It," *The Heritage Lectures*, September 22, 1992.

17 David Halberstam, *Powers That Be* (New York: Random House, 1979), 181, 213, 303; Richard Hofstadter, *The Age of Reform: From Bryan to FDR* (New York: Viking Press, 1955), 188.

18 Barbara Ballman, "Circulation Continues to Drop at Region's Largest Dailies," *Capital Business Review*, December 13, 1993; Barbara Ballman, "Weeklies Show Market Mix: Some Expand, While Others Can Barely Make Ends Meet," *Capital Business Review*, August 30, 1993.

19 "International Federation of Newspaper Publishers Study Shows Newspaper Sales Down in Most Countries," *Editor and Publisher*, June 12, 1993; Ann Marie Kerwin, "Advo Urges Postal Service to Test Saturday Certain: Program Could Adversely Affect Newspapers' Freestanding Insert Advertising Revenue," *Editor and Publisher*, June 12, 1993; Martha Groves, "Bad News for Newspapers," *Los Angeles Times*, December 15, 1991.

20 Pat Robertson, *The Turning Tide* (Dallas: Word, 1993), 149.

21 Kathryn C. Montgomery, *Target: Prime Time-Advocacy Groups and the Struggle Over Entertainment Television* (New York: Oxford University Press, 1989); Ronald Brownstein, *The Power and the Glitter: The Hollywood-Washington Connection* (New York: Vintage Books, 1992), 279–81, 349–57.

22 Halberstam, *The Powers That Be*, 351–61, 375–76; Richard Reeves, *President Kennedy: Profile of Power* (New York: Simon and Schuster, 1993), 287–88.

23 Johnathan Yardley, "The Magazine's Low Life Expectancy," *Washington Post*, April 23, 1990.

24　Eugene D. Genovese, *Roll, Jordan, Roll: The World the Slaves Made* (New York: Vintage Books, 1972), 25–27; Samuel T. Francis, "A Counter-Hegemonic Force," in *Winning the Culture War* (McLean, Vir.: American Cause, 1993), 3–8.

CHAPTER 9

SEPARATION OF CHURCH AND STATE:

"CHRISTIAN NATION" AND OTHER HERESIES

1　Don F. Fehrenbacher, ed., *Abraham Lincoln: Speeches and Writings, 1859–1865* (New York: Library of America, 1989), 382–83; Gary Wills, *Under God: Religion and American Politics* (New York: Simon and Schuster, 1990), 381.

2　*Church of the Holy Trinity v. U.S.*, 143 U.S. 457 (1892).

3　*U.S. v. MacIntosh*, 283 U.S. 605, 625, (1931).

4　Eric Larrabee, *Commander in Chief: Franklin Delano Roosevelt: His Lieutenants and Their War* (New York: Simon and Schuster, 1988), 239–40; Martin Gilbert, *Churchill: A Life* (New York: Holt, Henry and Company, 1992), 705; for a similar account of this incident and the preceding statements, see Larry Witham, "Christian Nation Now Fighting Words," *Washington Times*, November 23, 1992.

5　*Zorach v. Clauson*, 343 U.S. 306, (1952).

6　Martin Luther King, Jr., *Strength to Love* (Philadelphia: Fortress Press, 1963).

7　Alexis de Tocqueville, *Democracy in America*, ed. Phillips Bradley (1835; reprint, New York: Alfred A. Knopf, 1980), 304–5.

8　Norman Sykes, *Church and State in England in the Eighteenth Century* (Cambridge: Oxford University Press, 1934), 315.

9　Adam Clymer, "Tiff Over Governor's 'Christian' Remark Underscores Fault Line in G.O.P.," *New York Times*, November 22, 1992; Samuel Francis, "Pluralism Clouds Over Fordice," *Washington Times*, November 24, 1992.

10　Statement by President Bill Clinton, August 30, 1993, White House Press Office; David Lauter, "Clinton Voices Concern U.S. May Be Too Secular," *Los Angeles Times*, August 31, 1993; Bill Nichols, "New Beginning for Clinton," *USA Today*, August 31, 1993.

11　Statement by Bill Clinton, November 16, 1993, White House Press Office; Peter Steinfels, "Clinton Signs Law Protecting Religious Practices," *New York Times*, November 17, 1993.

12　Terry Eastland, "Religion, Politics, and the Clintons," *Commentary*, January 1994, 40–43. Some evangelical leaders have been enamored by Clinton's recent conversion to religion. Fred Barnes, "Rev. Bill: Clinton Courts Evangelical Leaders," *New Republic*, January 13, 1994.

13　Daniel Yankelovich, "How Changes in the Economy are Reshaping American Values," in *Values and Public Policy*, ed. Henry Aaron, et al. (Washington: Brookings Institute), 1994, 33–34.

14　John S. Baker, Jr., "The Establishment Clause as Intended: No Preference Among Sects and Pluralism in a Large Commercial Republic," in *The Bill of Rights: Original Meaning and Current Understanding*, ed. Eugene W. Hickok, Jr. (Charlottesville, Vir.: University Press of Virginia, 1991), 43.

15　*Employment Division v. Smith*, 110 S. Ct. 1595 (1990).

16 Gordon S. Wood, *The Radicalism of the American Revolution* (New York: Alfred A. Knopf, 1992), 331, for Kent and Saltonstall quotations; de Tocqueville, *Democracy*, 306.

CHAPTER 10

WE STAND AT ARMAGEDDON: RELIGION AND THE REFORMIST IMPULSE

1 Samuel Seabury to Society for the Propagation of the Gospel, *SPG Secretary,* June 5, 1741, manuscript B-9, Society for the Propagation of the Gospel archives.

2 Bernard Bailyn, *The Ideological Origins of the American Revolution* (Cambridge: Harvard University Press, 1967), 187, 141, for quotations; William G. McLoughlin, "Enthusiasm for Liberty: The Great Awakening as the Key to the American Revolution" *Proceedings of the American Antiquarian Society*, 1977, 69–95; Robert A. Gross, *The Minutemen and Their World* (New York: Hill and Wang, 1976), 10–29, 52.

3 Benjamin Hart, *Faith and Freedom: The Christian Roots of American Liberty* (Dallas: Lewis and Stanley, 1988), 247, first quotation; Bailyn, *Ideological Origins*, 137, second quotation; Alan Heimert, *Religion and the American Mind: From the Great Awakening to the Revolution* (Cambridge, Mass.: Harvard University Press, 1966), 7–15; Robert Middlekauf, *The Glorious Cause: The American Revolution, 1763–1789* (New York: Oxford University Press, 1982), 103–5; Gordon Wood, *The Radicalism of the American Revolution* (New York: Alfred A. Knopf, 1992), 144–45; Edmund Morgan, "The Puritan Ethic and the American Revolution," *William and Mary Quarterly*, January 1967, 18, 42.

4 See 1 Samuel 8:11–18; Joshua Haberman, "The Bible Belt is America's Safety Belt," *Policy Review*, Fall 1987, 42.

5 Thomas Paine, "Common Sense," in *Common Sense and Other Political Writings*, ed. Melvin Advins (New York: Bobbs Merrill, 1953), 10–13, for quotation; Eric Foner, *Tom Paine and Revolutionary America* (New York: Oxford University Press, 1976), 115; Rhys Isaac, "Preachers and Patriots: Popular Culture and the Revolution in Virginia," in *The American Revolution: Explorations in the History of American Radicalism*, ed. A. Young (Dekalb, Ill.: Northern Illinois University Press, 1976), 131, 145, for second quotation; Rhys Isaac, *The Transformation of Virginia, 1740–1790* (Chapel Hill: University of North Carolina Press, 1982), 124–31, 266–69; Peter Marshall and David Manuel, *The Light and the Glory* (Old Tappan, N.J.: Fleming Revell, 1977), 254–69.

6 John Witherspoon, "The Dominion of Providence over the Passions of Men," in *Lend Me Your Ears: Great Speeches in History*, ed. William Safire (New York: W. W. Norton, 1992), 429–30.

7 Whitney R. Cross, *The Burned-Over District: The Social and Intellectual History of Enthusiastic Religion in Western New York* (Ithaca: Cornell University Press, 1950), 151–58; Paul B. Johnson, *A Shopkeeper's Millennium: Society and Revivals in Rochester, New York, 1815–1837* (New York: Hill and Wang, 1978), 5, for Beecher quotation.

8 Cross, *Burned-Over District*, 226–28; Johnson, *Shopkeeper's Millennium*, 5–6.

9 Gilbert Hobbs Barnes, *The Antislavery Impulse, 1830–1844* (1933; reprint, New York: Harcourt, Brace, and World, 1964), 104.

10 Ibid., 79–87, 178–81; Eric Foner, *Free Soil, Free Labor, Free Men; The Ideology of the Republican Party Before the Civil War* (New York: Oxford University Press, 1970), 109, 142, for quotation.

11 Ibid., 109–10, for first and second quotations; 130, for Giddings quotation.

12 Joel Bernard, "From Fasting to Abstinence: The Origins of the American Temperance Movement," in *Drinking: Behavior and Belief in Modern History*, ed. Susanna Barrows and Robin Room (Berkeley: University of California Press, 1991), 337–51.

13 Cross, *Burned-Over District*, 211–14.

14 Norman H. Clark, *Deliver Us From Evil: An Interpretation of American Prohibition* (New York: W. W. Norton, 1976), 94–101.

15 Helen B. Tyler, *Where Prayer and Purpose Meet: The WCTU Story, 1874–1949* (Evanston, Ill.: Signal Press, 1949), 15, 137, 167.

16 Clark, *Deliver Us From Evil*, 104–5; Cross, *Burned-Over District*, 237; A. James Reichley, *The Life of the Parties* (New York: Free Press, 1992), 187, for Willard quotation; Ian Tyrell, "Women and Temperance in International Perspective: The World's WCTU, 1880s–1920s," in *Drinking: Behavior and Belief in Modern History*, ed. Susanna Barrows and Robin Room (Berkeley, Calif.: University of California Press, 1991), 217–35.

17 C. Vann Woodward, *Tom Watson: Agrarian Rebel* (1938: reprint, New York: Oxford University Press, 1969), 264; Garry Wills, *Under God: Religion and American Politics* (New York: Simon and Schuster, 1990), 97–100.

18 LeRoy Ashby, *William Jennings Bryan: Champion of Democracy* (Boston: Twayne Publishers, 1987), 97–99; Robert W. Cherney, *A Righteous Cause: The Life of William Jennings Bryan*, ed. Oscar Handlin (Boston: Little, Brown and Company, 1985), 173; William J. Bryan, "Cross of Gold," in *Lend Me Your Ears: Great Speeches in History*, ed. William Safire (New York: W. W. Norton, 1992), 769, 772.

19 Joel Schwartz, "The Moral Environment of the Poor," *The Public Interest*, no. 103, Spring 1991, 21–37, 26–27, for Riis quotation.

20 Ashby, *William Jennings Bryan*, 98–99; Carl Sandberg, *The Chicago Race Riots* (New York: Harcourt, Brace, and World, 1969), 57, for labor circular quotation; Richard Hofstadter, *The Age of Reform: From Bryan to FDR* (New York: Vintage Books, 1955), 212–14; Arthur S. Link, *American Epoch: A History of the United States Since 1900* (New York: Alfred A. Knopf, 1980), 23–25.

21 Herman Hagedorn, ed., *The Works of Theodore Roosevelt: Presidential Addresses and State Papers*, vol. 2 (New York: Scribner's Sons, 1923), 447, for first quotation; A. James Reichley, *The Life of the Parties: A History of American Political Parties* (New York: Free Press, 1992), 201, for second quotation.

22 Martin Luther King, "Our God is Marching On," in *The Eyes on the Prize Civil Rights Reader*, ed. Clayborne Carson, et al. (New York: Viking-Penguin Press, 1991), 226–27.

23 Arthur M. Schlesinger, Jr., *Robert F. Kennedy and His Times* (Boston: Houghton-Mifflin, 1978), 2:884.

24 Thomas L. Jipping, "In Defense of Accurate History Education," *Policy Insights*, no. 512, September 1993, 1–2.

25 Margaret Thatcher, "We Can't Make it Without Religious Values," *Saturday Evening Post*, July/August 1989, 60–61.

CHAPTER 11

THE ELECTRONIC GODZILLA: TELEVISION, TALK RADIO, AND POLITICS

1 "Home Schooling Movement Gives House a Lesson," *Congressional Quarterly*, February 26, 1994, 479–80.

2 Associated Press, "Home Schooling Wins Emphatic Assurance from House," *New York Times*, February 25, 1994; Carol Innerst, "Home Schoolers Sound Off: Hill Corrects Education Bill, *Washington Times*, February 25, 1994.

3 Theodore White, *America in Search of Itself: The Making of the President 1956–1980* (New York: Warner Books, 1982), 165.

4 David Halberstam, *The Powers That Be* (New York: Random House, 1979), 338–41; White, *America in Search of Itself*, 279–95.

5 Joe McGinnis, *The Selling of the President, 1968* (New York: Trident Press, 1969), 62–77.

6 Hedrick Smith, *The Power Game: How Washington Works* (New York: Ballantine Books, 1988), 398–417.

7 Harry F. Waters with Patrick Rodgers, "The Networks Come Home: After Much Tinkering, Programmers Rediscover Family Entertainment," *Time*, May 31, 1993, 71–72.

8 Elizabeth Jensen, "Major T.V. Networks Dinosaurs No More," *Wall Street Journal*, March 17, 1994.

9 Jeffery Daniels, "Media Growth Accelerates but Industry Exiting Top 5," *The Hollywood Reporter*, July 19, 1993.

10 Robin Toner, "Gold Rush Fever Grips Capital as Health Care Struggle Begins," *New York Times*, March 13, 1994.

11 *Larry King Live*, February 20, 1992, CNN Transcripts, transcript #501.

12 Howard Fineman, "The Power of Talk," *Newsweek*, February 8, 1993, 24.

13 David Remnick, "The Day of the Dittohead," *Washington Post*, February 20, 1994.

14 Howard Kurtz, "With a News Look, Partisan TV Networks Downlink Conservatism," *Washington Post*, February 10, 1994.

15 Gerald Seib, "Modem Operandi: Politics Go Digital," *Wall Street Journal*, March 16, 1994. It has been my privilege to serve on the board of directors of NET since 1991.

16 George Gilder, "Television: The Interplay of Technology and Politics," *Policy Counsel*, Fall 1993, 24–26.

17 Patrick Harverson, "Hughes Aircraft to Build 660 Million Dollar Satellite System," *The Financial Times*, December 10, 1993, 25; "Video Equipment Sales," *Video Week*, August 2, 1993.

18 John Naisbitt, *Megatrends* (New York: Warner, 1982).

CHAPTER 12

THE SMOKING VOLCANO: ROSS PEROT AND THE POPULIST REVOLT

1 Gloria Borger and Jerry Bickley, "A Giant New Sucking Sound," *U.S. News and World Report*, December 20, 1993, 18.

2 "Effect of Perot's Opinions on Vote," *Gallup Poll Monthly*, April 1992, 9; Frank Luntz, "Perovian Civilization: Who Supported Ross, and Why," *Policy Review*, Spring 1993,

19; Mike Clancy, "Ross Perot's Presidential Petition Drive Gaining Momentum," *The Reuter Library Report,* April 14, 1992.

3   "Final Presidential Heat, November 1–2, 1992," *Gallup Poll Monthly,* November 1992, 9; Luntz, "Perovian Civilization," 19; interview with Frank Luntz, February 23, 1994; Richard Blow, "The Clinton Plan to Control Perot," *Mother Jones,* January/February 1994, 22–25.

4   Kevin Phillips, *Boiling Point: Democrats, Republicans, and the Decline of Middle-Class Prosperity* (New York: HarperCollins, 1993), 58.

5   Everett Carl Ladd, "The 1992 Election's Complex Message," *American Enterprise,* January/February 1993, 50–51.

6   James Barnes, "Still on the Trail," *National Journal,* April 19, 1993, 860–64; Borger and Bickley, "Sucking Sound," 18; "Profiling Clinton, Bush, Perot Supporters," *American Enterprise,* January/February 1993, 95–96.

7   Steve Daley, "As Democrats Dribble, White House Views '92 Election as an Easy Layup," *Chicago Tribune,* July 28, 1991.

8   Editorial, "Bill Clinton's Vital Signs," *New York Times,* January 25, 1994; Charles E. Cook, "Despite a Rough Winter, Clinton's Numbers Are Good," *Roll Call,* January 24, 1994.

9   Jim Lobe, "Grand Old Party Finds Itself in Shambles," *Inter-Press Service,* November 18, 1992; Larry Sabato, "The 1993 Statewide Elections: Virginia's Twelve Year Itch Returns," (report printed by the University of Virginia Department of Government), 11–22, 27–28.

10   Richard Miniter, "Rules of the House Don't Get in the Way," *Insight,* September 27, 1993, 10–11; Karen Ball, "House Deals Blow to Abortion-Rights Forces," *Associated Press,* July 1, 1993; Devin Merida, "Abortion-Rights Backers in Congress Mull Their Mistakes," *Washington Post,* July 2, 1993.

11   Alan Tonelson, "Beyond Left and Right," *The National Interest,* Winter 1993/1994, 3–18.

12   Phillips, *Boiling Point,* 223–25, 236–42.

13   Daniel Yankelovich, "How Changes in the Economy Are Reshaping American Values," in *Values and Public Policy,* ed. Henry J. Aaron, et al. (Washington D.C.: The Brookings Institute, 1993), 16–21.

14   David Espo, "Clinton Says Bigger Deficit Forced Him to Cut Back Tax Relief Plan," *USA Today,* June 23, 1992; Janice Castro, "Is Bush Losing the Numbers Game?: As the Jobless Figure Goes Up, His Standing in the Polls Heads Down," *Time,* July 13, 1992; Matthew Cooper, "The Voters," *U.S. News and World Report,* August 31, 1992.

15   E. J. Dionne, *Why Americans Hate Politics* (New York: Simon and Schuster, 1991), 332.

16   Seymour Martin Lipset, "Why Americans Refuse to Vote," *Insight,* February 7, 1994, 24–26; William Schneider and Seymour M. Lipset, *The Confidence Gap: Business, Labor, and Government in the Public Mind* (Baltimore: Johns Hopkins University Press, 1987).

17   For a good discussion of the Pennsylvania Senate race as a precursor phenomenon of politics in the 1990s, see Jack W. Germond and Jules Witcover, *Mad as Hell: Revolt at the Ballot Box, 1992* (New York: Warner Books, 1993), 63–77.

18   Jon Meacham, "Why the Party of the People Has a Grassroots Problem," *Washington Monthly,* October 1993, 22–28.

19 Steven Pearlstein, "Consumer Confidence Index Slips: Data a New Sign of Half Recovery," *Washington Post*, May 26, 1993; Steve Mufson, "Two Reports Herald Slow Recovery: Consumer Confidence Up, Wage Inflation Modest," *Washington Post*, April 28, 1993.

20 David Zimmerman, "Looking for Virtues to Believe In, *USA Today*, April 14, 1994.

21 Steven Roberts, "High Hopes," *U.S. News and World Report*, January 25, 1993; David Hitman, "Clinton's Grand Plans," *U.S. News and World Report*, January 25, 1993; William J. Bennett, "Revolt against God: America's Spiritual Despair," *Policy Review*, Winter 1994, 19–24; Robert J. Samuelson, "It's Not the Economy, Stupid," *Washington Post*, January 7, 1994; Dionne, *Why Americans Hate Politics*, 369, for Fallows quotation; Larry Burkett, *Whatever Happened to the American Dream* (Chicago: Moody Press, 1993), 27–37.

22 Kenneth Silber, "Voters Take Control of Taxes," *Insight*, January 3, 1994, 6–9.

23 *Economic Report of the President* (Washington, D.C.: GPO, 1994), 98–102; VRS Exit Survey, in *American Enterprise*, January/February 1993, 95.

24 *Economic Report of the President*, 115; Paulette Thomas, "Widening Rich-Poor Gap Is a Threat to the 'Social Fabric,' Says White House," *Wall Street Journal*, February 15, 1994; Luntz, "Perovian Civilization," 22.

25 Phillips, *Boiling Point*, 61.

26 Guy Molyneux and William Schneider, "Ross is Boss: Ross Perot," *The Atlantic*, May 1993, 84–101, provides a good analysis of the Perot movement.

CHAPTER 13
MIRACLE AT THE GRASSROOTS:
CHRISTIAN COALITION AND THE PRO-FAMILY MOVEMENT

1 Statement by Pat Hart before Lake County School Board, March 21, 1994; Pat Hart to the Editor of the *Orlando Sentinel*, May 5, 1994; Pat Buchanan, "Lake County Scuffle in the Culture War," *Washington Times*, May 18, 1994. Hart's resolution sought to clarify the school district's compliance with a state mandate to teach multiculturalism.

2 Larry Rohter, "Battle Over Patriotism Curriculum," *New York Times*, May 15, 1994.

3 Rick Badie, "Teaching Battle Could be Needless," *Lake Sentinel*, May 12, 1994, 1; Carol Innerst, "Patriotic Emphasis Gets OK in Florida," *Washington Times*, May 15, 1994.

4 "Falwell's Farewell: Jerry Falwell Disbands Moral Majority," *National Review*, July 14, 1989, 19; "Scrapping the Moral Majority," *Time*, June 26, 1989, 26.

5 Sean Wilentz, "Strength for the Journey," *New Republic*, April 25, 1988, 30; Laura Sessions Stepp, "Falwell Says Moral Majority to Be Dissolved," *Washington Post*, June 12, 1989, for Phillips quotation; *National Review*, July 14, 1989, 19, for Hadden quotation.

6 David Shribman, "Going Mainstream: Religious Right Drops High-Profile Tactics, Works on Local Level," *Wall Street Journal*, September 26, 1989.

7 Cal Thomas, *A Layman's Briefing Book on the Issues* (Brentwood, Tenn.: Wolgemuth and Hyatt, 1990).

8 Ronald Brownstein, "Washington Outlook: Is the GOP Too Timid to Say No to the Religious Right?" *Los Angeles Times*, July 11, 1994; Burt Solomon, "His Public

Embrace of Religion Gives Clinton a Political Boost," *The National Journal*, April 6, 1994.

9   Marketing Research Institute, "National Survey of Churchgoing Voters," (report printed by the Marketing Research Institute in Pensacola, Florida, 1993); Ray C. Bliss Institute, *National Survey of American Evangelicals*, (Akron, Ohio:, University of Akron Press, 1992); Jon Meacham, "What the Religious Right Can Teach New Democrats," *Washington Monthly*, April 1993, 42–47.

10 David C. Leege, "The Decomposition of the Religious Vote: A Comparison of White, Non-Hispanic Catholics with Other Ethnoreligious Groups, 1960–1992," paper delivered to American Political Science Association, September 2–5, 1993, 15, Table 2, Table 4.

11 Reader's Digest Association, "Reader's Digest Poll Reveals Family Gap," *Wirthlin Group Survey Results* (New York: Reader's Digest Association, 1992).

CHAPTER 14

CLINTON AGONISTES: WOODSTOCK GOES TO THE WHITE HOUSE

1   Adam Nagourney, "Clinton Runs into 'Credibility' Storm," *USA Today*, April 6, 1994.

2   E. J. Dionne, Jr., "Whitewater: Who Made This Monster?" *Washington Post*, March 23, 1994; Richard Cohen, "No Longer Operative," *Washington Post*, April 13, 1994.

3   Peggy Noonan, "They Voted for Change. He Gives Them Pork," *Fortune*, April 25, 1994, 126–34.

4   Maralee Schwartz, "Clinton Proposes 6-Point Program to Aid Families: Candidate Faults GOP, Democrats on 'Family Values,'" *Washington Post*, May 22, 1992.

5   Cohen, "No Longer Operative."

6   Joe Klein, "The Politics of Promiscuity," *Newsweek*, May 9, 1994, 17–20.

7   David Nyhan, "Clinton's Talkfest Was Terrific," *Boston Globe*, December 17, 1992.

8   Michael Kelly, "Clinton, Sketching Plan for the Economy, Counsels Patience," *New York Times*, November 13, 1992.

9   Thomas Friedman, "To the Mat: Now Clinton Decides Which Promises Come First," *New York Times*, November 15, 1992.

10 David Maraniss, "Before Race Began, Clinton Resolved Pledge Not to Run," *Washington Post*, July 15, 1992.

11 William L. O'Neill, *Coming Apart: An Informal History of America in the Sixties* (New York: Random House, 1971), 321–25.

12 J. William Fulbright, "The Cold War in American Life," speech delivered at the University of North Carolina, April 7, 1964, reprinted in Haynes Johnson and Bernard M. Gwertzman, *Fulbright: The Dissenter* (Garden City, N.Y.: Doubleday, 1968), 284–85.

13 J. William Fulbright, *The Arrogance of Power* (New York: Random House, 1967), 33, 38–39.

14 Albert Gore, Sr., *Let the Glory Out* (New York: Viking Press, 1972), 222–23.

15 Theodore H. White, *The Making of the President, 1972* (New York: Atheneum Publishers, 1973), 101–40, 106, for quotation.

16 David Maraniss, "Bill Clinton: Born to Run . . . and Run, and Run," *Washington Post*, July 13, 1992.

17 David Maraniss, "Lessons of Humbling Loss Guide Clinton's Journey," *Washington Post*, July 14, 1992.

18 Ibid.

19 Paul Taylor, "Democrats' New Centrists Preen for '88," *Washington Post*, November 10, 1985; Dan Balz, "Southern and Western Democrats Launch New Leadership Council," *Washington Post*, March 1, 1985; Laurence I. Barrett, "Rising Stars of the Sunbelt: The Democratic Leadership Council Is Redefining the Party," *Time*, March 31, 1986, 30; William Schneider, "The Democrats in '88," *The Atlantic*, April 1987, 37–59.

20 Maraniss, "Before Race Began."

21 Robert Woodward, *The Agenda* (New York: Simon and Schuster, 1994).

CHAPTER 15

TO CAST A WIDER NET: WHY WE NEED A BROADER ISSUES AGENDA

1 Martin Luther King, Jr., "Our God Is Marching On!" in *The Eyes on the Prize Civil Rights Reader*, ed. Clayborne Carson et al. (New York: Viking Press, 1991), 227.

2 Jerry G. Watts, "Racial Discourse in an Age of Darwinism," *Democratic Left*, no. 18, July/August 1990, 3, cited in E. J. Dionne, Jr., *Why Americans Hate Politics* (New York: Simon and Schuster, 1991), 337–38.

3 David McCollough, *Truman* (New York: Simon and Schuster, 1992), 959. Parts of this discussion appeared previously in Ralph E. Reed, Jr., "Casting a Wider Net," *Policy Review*, Summer 1993, 31–35.

4 Gerald F. Seib, "Americans Feel Families and Values Are Eroding But They Disagree Over Causes and Solutions," *Wall Street Journal*, June 11, 1993.

5 Marketing Research Institute, "National Survey of Churchgoing Voters," (report printed by the Marketing Research Institute in Pensacola, Florida, 1993), 27.

6 Robert B. Rector, "Reducing the Crushing Tax Burden on America's Families," *Heritage Foundation Backgrounder*, no. 981, March 7, 1994, 1.

7 William R. Mattox, Jr., "The Parent Trap," *Policy Review*, Winter 1991, 6.

8 Scott A. Hodge, "Kasich Budget Means $59 Million A Year For Typical Congressional District," *Heritage Foundation Reports*, March 7, 1994.

9 William Kilpatrick, *Why Johnny Can't Tell Right From Wrong: And What We Can Do About It* (New York: Simon and Schuster, 1992), 122, 79–82.

CHAPTER 16

THE CURSE OF HAM: RELIGION AND RACISM IN AMERICA

1 Hiram Wesley Evans, "The Klan's Fight for Americanism," *North American Review*, 103, March/April/May 1926, 33–63 cited in Richard Hofstadter, *The Age of Reform* (New York: Vintage Books, 1955), 294–96.

2 E. J. Dionne, Jr., *Why Americans Hate Politics* (New York: Simon and Schuster, 1991), 367.

3 Jerry Falwell, *Strength for the Journey* (New York: Simon and Schuster, 1987), 279–99, 286, 293, for quotations. For a contemporaneous view, see T. B. Maston, *Segregation and Desegregation: A Christian Approach* (New York: Macmillan, 1959), 133–37.

4 Billy Graham, "Racism and the Evangelical Church," *Christianity Today*, October 4, 1993, 27; William Martin, *A Prophet with Honor* (New York: William Morrow, 1991), 296, 362.

5 Reverend Henry Tobias Egger, "What Meaneth This: There is No Difference," cited in Franklin Adair Tyler, *All God's Chillun: Southerners View Forced Integration* (n.p., 1958), 40–43.

6 C. Vann Woodward, *The Strange Career of Jim Crow* (1955; reprint, New York: Oxford University Press, 1974), 97–109.

7 James Graham Cook, *The Segregationists* (New York: Appleton-Century-Crofts, 1962), 211–16; Charles Everett Tilson, *Segregation and the Bible* (Nashville: Abingdon, 1958), 16, 20, for Gillespie quotations.

8 Cook, *The Segregationists*, 225.

9 Ibid., 219.

10 Tilson, *Segregation and the Bible*, 15.

11 Cook, *The Segregationists*, 210.

12 James Henley Thornwell, "Slavery and the Religious Instruction of the Coloured Population," *Southern Presbyterian Review*, no. 4, July 1850, 105–41, 114, for quotation; Charles C. Bishop, "The Pro-Slavery Argument Reconsidered: James Henley Thornwell, Millennial Abolitionist," *South Carolina Historical Magazine*, no. 73, January 1972, 18–26; H. Shelton Smith, *In His Image, But . . . : Racism in Southern Religion, 1780–1910* (Durham, N.C.: Duke University Press, 1972), 140–43.

13 Cook, *The Segregationists*, 215–16.

14 *Brown v. Board of Education of Topeka*, 347 U.S. 483, 497 (1954); Lynne Lanniello, *Milestones Along the March: Twelve Historic Civil Rights Documents* (New York: Frederick Praeger Publishers, 1965), 51–56; *Southern School News*, May 1962, for integration figures; James J. Kilpatrick, *The Southern Case for School Segregation* (Richmond: Crowell-Collier Press, 1962), 189.

15 J. Harvie Wilkinson, *Harry Byrd and the Changing Face of Virginia Politics* (Charlottesville, Vir. : University Press of Virginia, 1968), 113, 121.

16 Editorial, *Richmond Times-Dispatch*, February 25, 1956; editorial, "The Transcendent Issue," *Richmond News Leader*, November 21, 1955, reprinted in James J. Kilpatrick, ed., *Interposition: Editorials and Editorial Page Presentations. The Richmond News Leader, 1955–1956* (Richmond, Vir.: David Tennant and Bryan, 1957), 1; Robbins L. Gates, *The Making of Massive Resistance* (Chapel Hill: University of North Carolina Press, 1964), 51, 117, 161.

17 Andres Tapia, "The Myth of Racial Progress," *Christianity Today*, October 4, 1993, 23.

18 Fabrizio, McLaughlin, and Associates, "Executive Summary," (report published by Fabrizo, McLaughlin, and Associates, Inc., Alexandria, Vir., September 7, 1993), 1–5.

19 Elena Neuman, "The Right Arises in Black Politics," *Insight*, September 27, 1993, 6–15.

20 Fabrizio, McLaughlin, and Associates, "Executive Summary," 8; John Wheeler, Jr., and Paul English, "Minority Myths Exploded: Poll Shows Minorities Hold Traditional Values," *Christian American*, October 1993, 4.

21 Barbara Woerner, "African-American Christian Wins Office," *Christian American*, April 1994, 9.

22 Ronald Smothers, "School Prayer Gaining Ground in the South," *New York Times*, February 22, 1994, for Knox quotation; William Booth, "Longing for Values Drives School Prayer Crusade," *Washington Post*, April 1, 1994; David Snyder, "Educator Gives Voice to School Prayer Issue," *Time-Picayune* (New Orleans), December 26, 1993.

23 Juan Williams, "A Question of Fairness," *The Atlantic*, no. 259, February 1987, 70–80; Fred Barnes, "The Minority Minority: Black Conservatives and White Republicans," *The New Republic*, September 30, 1991, 18–21.

24 Kay Cole James, *Never Forget: The Riveting Story of One Woman's Journey From the Projects to the Corridors of Power* (Grand Rapids: Zondervan, 1993).

25 Adam Myerson, "Manna 2 Society: The Growing Conservatism of Black America," *Policy Review*, no. 68, Spring 1994, 4–6.

26 Tapia, "Myth," 16.

27 Cornel West, *Race Matters* (Boston: Beacon Press, 1993), 2.

CHAPTER 17

WHAT IS RIGHT ABOUT AMERICA: HOW YOU CAN MAKE A DIFFERENCE

1 U.S. Department of Health and Human Services, "Percent of Women 15–19 Years of Age Who Are Sexually Experienced," *National Survey of Family Growth* (Washington, D.C.: GPO, 1988); Paula K. Braverman and Victor C. Strasburger, "Adolescent Sexual Activity," *Clinical Pediatrics*, November 1993, 658–69; Donald P. Orr, et al., "Premature Sexual Activity as an Indicator of Risk, *Pediatrics*, February 1991, 141.

2 Allan C. Carlson, *Family Questions: Reflections on the American Social Crisis* (New Brunswick, N.J.: Transaction Publishers, 1991).

3 William Tucker, "The Front Lines of Welfare Reform," *Insight*, August 16, 1993, 6–12; Lauch Faircloth, "Principles of Real Reform," *Congressional Record*, November 20, 1993, S16672; John McClaughry, "Alternative Pathway to Welfare Reform," *Washington Times*, January 26, 1994.

4 Charles Murray, "The Coming White Underclass," *Wall Street Journal*, October 29, 1993; Robert Rector, "President Clinton's Commitment to Welfare Reform: The Disturbing Record," *Heritage Backgrounder*, no. 967, December 1993, 12–16; Ronald Brownstein, "GOP Welfare Proposals Becoming More Conservative," *Los Angeles Times*, March 9, 1994.

5 James Q. Wilson, "On Abortion," *Commentary*, January 1994, 22; Mary Ann Glendon, *Abortion and Divorce in Western Law* (Cambridge, Mass.: Harvard University Press, 1987).

6 Harold Holzer, ed., *The Lincoln-Douglas Debates* (New York: HarperCollins, 1993), 65.

7 Elizabeth McCaughey, "What the Clinton Plan Will Do For You," *The New Republic*, February 7, 1994, 22; Irwin Stelzer, "What Health Care Crisis?" *Commentary*, February 1993, 24; "CONSAD Research Study," (report printed by the National Bureau of Economic Research Foundation, Washington D.C.) May 1993; "An Open Letter to President Clinton," *Wall Street Journal*, January 14, 1994.

8 William J. Bennett, "Getting Used to Decadence: The Spirit of Democracy in Modern America," *The Heritage Lectures*, no. 477, December 1993, 7. For a good discussion

of this theme, see Don E. Eberly, *Restoring the Good Society: A New Vision for Politics and Culture* (Grand Rapids: Baker, 1994), 81–92.

9   Allan C. Carlson, *Family Questions: Reflections on the American Social Crisis* (New Brunswick, N.J.: Transaction Publishers, 1991), 279.

10   Alexis de Tocqueville, *Democracy in America*, ed. Phillips Bradley (1835; reprint, New York: Alfred A. Knopf, 1980), 1:304.

11   Golden Rule Insurance Company, "Educational Choice Charitable Trust: Questions and Answers," (a Golden Rule Insurance Company press release, Indianapolis, Ind.), March 30, 1994; Lynn Ford, "Parents Laud Success of Plan That Helps Inner-City Youth Attend Private Schools," *Indianapolis Star*, May 12, 1992; editorial, "Fighting the Golden Rule," *Wall Street Journal*, September 6, 1991.

12   Richard M. DeVos, *Compassionate Capitalism: Helping People Help Themselves* (New York: Penguin-Dutton Books, 1993), 125; Marvin Olasky, *Philanthropically Correct: The Story of the Council on Foundations* (Washington, D.C.: Capital Research Center, 1993), 61–71; Robert L. Woodson, ed., *On the Road to Economic Freedom: An Agenda for Black Progress* (Washington, D.C.: Regnery-Gateway, 1987), 89–92; Tim W. Fergeson, "An Ethnic-Flavored HMO vs. Clinton's Cookie-Cutter," *Wall Street Journal*, February 8, 1994.

13   Myron Magnet, *The Dream and the Nightmare: The Sixties' Legacy to the Underclass* (New York: William Morrow, 1993), 16.

INDEX

abandonment, 35; subsidizing, 99
ABC TV, 24, 56, 161
Abdel-Rahman, Sheik Omar, 54
abolition, 145, 147, 155, 224, 239
abortion, 10, 11, 14, 16, 18, 19, 23, 26, 28-32, 51,
    54, 55, 56, 58, 92, 127, 148, 172, 173, 175, 182,
    200, 225, 226, 232, 237, 241, 242, 257, 260;
    condemnation of, 71; counseling and
    referrals, 103; on-demand, 103; parental
    approval, 31; Roman Catholic teachings on,
    16-17, 76; taxpayer funding, 76; taxpayer-
    funded, 100, 102, 136, 176, 200, 207, 210,
    227, 230, 232, 262
absentee fathers, 82
absolutes, 6, 7; moral, 50
abstinence, 32, 257
abuse, 155; alcohol and drug, 99, 100;
    economic, 185
accommodationism, 27, 212
accountability, 137
acquisitiveness, 4
activism, 51, 190; faith-based, 154; Jewish, 153;
    political, 25, 27, 130, 139, 149, 247; antiwar, 212
activists, 34, 199, 252; civil rights, 236;
    conservative, 107; disaffected, 184; gay, 9;
    grassroots, 157, 167; liberal, 69; local, 3;
    New Left, 107; pro-family, 42, 45, 191, 193,
    223, 244, 254; pro-life, 17, 58; single-issue,
    225
Adams, John, 64
addictions, chemical and sexual, 137
adoption, 31, 71, 261; interracial, 262
adultery, 55, 62
advertisers, boycotting, 30
advertising revenues, newspaper, 126
advertising, radio, 200, 230
advocacy, attorneys, 44, 100; groups, 112;
    political, 122
advocates, pro-family, 228
AFL-CIO, 122, 197, 218
African-Americans, 9, 10, 12, 13, 19, 23, 41, 57,
    87, 90, 153, 190, 236, 239, 241-245, 247
age, of discovery, 5; of empire, 5; of revolution,
    5
agenda, nation's political, 159; broader issues,
    221; Clinton, 199; extremist, 100; faith-
    based, 87; liberal social, 103; mainstream, 9;
    nativist, 235; pro-family, 192; reformist, 201;

religious conservative, 11, 23, 24, 38, 39, 136;
    undemocratic, 67
agreement, Jewish-Christian, 20
Aid to Families with Dependent Children
    (AFDC), 83, 99, 258
AIDS, 32, 56, 98, 102, 229
Ailes, Roger, 108, 160
Air Force One, 204
air-traffic controllers' strike, 122
alcohol, 257; abuse, 86, 87, 99, 100, 101
alcoholism, 147, 229
Alexander, Lamar, 167
Alien 3, 61
alienation, 137; cultural, 55
Allen, Woody, 61
alliance, Catholic-evangelical, 18
Almond, Lindsay, 241
alternative sentencing for juveniles, 259
alternative value systems, 70
amalgamation, racial, 240
amendment, human life, 17
America, secular, 20
American Anti-Slavery Society, 146
American Center for Law and Justice, 49
American Civil Liberties Union (ACLU), 8, 42,
    45, 47, 53, 253
American Family Association, 54
American Federation of Labor, 121, 152
American Federation of State, County, and
    Municipal Employees (AFSCME), 123
American Federation of Teachers, 189
American Management Association, 118
American Mercury, 53
American Revolution, 105, 134, 142, 144, 145
American Spectator, 219
American Spelling Book, 63
Amos and Andy, 53
Amway Corporation, 265
Anglicans, 142
Anthony, Susan B., 149
anti-Catholicism, 17
anti-Masonic party, 106
Anti-Saloon League of America, 148
anti-Semitism, 54, 60, 101
Antichrist, 239
Aphrodite, 221
Apocalypse, 61
appeasement, 213

arbitration, 36
Archdiocese of New York, 13
Arkansas Democrat, 211, 218
Armageddon, 141, 152
Armey, Richard, 18, 157, 158
arrogance, Bill Clinton's, 215, 217
art, abject, 101; taxpayer-funded, 101, 102, 131;
    federal funding, 227
Ash Wednesday, 47, 139
Asians, 13
Aspin, Les, 207
Assemblies of God, 5
Associated Press, 54
Association of Couples for Marriage
    Enrichment, 19
associations, special-interest, 111
atheism, 138, 239
Atlanta Constitution, 54
The Atlantic, 91
attorneys, government-funded, 100
Atwater, Lee, 25, 108
Atwood, Tom, 27, 193
authority, and character, 205; honoring, 29;
    moral, 237; of father in home, 87

Babbitt, Bruce, 218
Babel, tower of, 238
baby boomers, 5, 127, 165, 183
Babylon, 142
backlash, anti-incumbency, 182
Baird, Zoe, 208
Baker, Howard, 162
Bakker, Jim and Tammy, 183, 192
balanced budget, 27, 34, 38, 95; Amendment,
    11, 34, 200, 257
Bank of America, 118
bankruptcy, 100, 115, 185; moral, 59
Baran, Jeff, 8
Barrett, Larry, 55
barriers, denominational, 15
Barton, Paul, 85
base closings, 179
basic academic skills, 33
Bates, Stephen, 58
Bauer, Gary, 192
Beasley, David, 73
Beckel, Bob, 61
Beecher, Lyman, 145
Begala, Paul, 108
behavior, 36; destructive, 99; inappropriate, 42
"behavioral poverty," 35
Belhaven Colege, 238
Bennett, William J., 5, 183, 257, 263
Bentsen, Lloyd, 244
Bernardin, Cardinal Joseph, 56, 57
Berrigan, Daniel, 59, 153
Berry-Meyers, Phyllis, 246
Bethel African Methodist Episcopal Church,
    153

Bevilacqua, Anthony, 19
bias, 9; anti-religious, 6, 56; judicial, 46
Bible, 26, 42, 46, 47, 48, 55, 62, 64, 74, 132,
    139, 143, 144, 147, 150, 151, 236, 238, 251,
    252, 253, 257, 266; Bible Belt, 53; -banning,
    48, 50; -reading, 43
Bible clubs, 35
big business, 105
bigotry, 6, 9, 51, 54, 57, 72; religious, 13, 20, 35,
    237, 248
bigots, 190
Bill of Rights, 77, 134
Birch, David, 118
birth rates, statistics, 74
Bismarck, Otto von, 98
Black Panthers, 59
Black, Justice Hugo, 78
Blackstone Hotel, 107
Blackstone, Sir William, 64
blasphemy, 138
Bloomer, Amelia, 149, 155
blue laws, 75
Boesky, Ivan, 183
Bolshevik Revolution, 27
Bonnie and Clyde, 91
book-banning, 69
books, age-appropriate, 70
Boorstin, Daniel, 116
boot camps for offenders, 28, 259
Bork, Robert, confirmation hearings, 198
Bosnia, 178, 179, 203, 204, 206, 213
Boston Globe, 209
Boston Herald, 19
Boy Scouts, 151, 264
Boy's Town, 264
boycotts, 153; of sponsors of violence on TV, 29
Bradlee, Ben, 128
Bradley, Tom, 12
Branch Davidians, 61
Branch, Taylor, 215
break-up, family, 259
Brigham Young University, 33
Bright, Bill, 14
Broder, David, 165
Brookes, Warren, 125
Brown v. Board of Education, 152, 153, 236, 239,
    240, 253
Brown, Jerry, 164, 173, 186
Brown, Ron, 194
Brown, Willie, 216
Bryan, William Jennings, 53, 120, 150, 155
Buchanan, Pat, 164, 173, 186
Buddha, 42
budget, health care, 229
Bull Moose party, 152
Bullock, Charles, 249, 250
"bullying of religion," 36
bureaucracy, 18, 37, 39, 70, 94, 96, 97, 99, 103,
    117, 210, 228, 256; inefficiency, 83; labor
    union, 122; permanent, 124

burglary, 28, 87
Burke, Edmund, 46
Bush, administration, 3, 123, 246; presidential campaign; family-values theme, 223
Bush, George, 1, 72, 101, 110, 175, 177, 182, 193, 194, 195, 198, 199, 205, 206, 209, 210, 211; "King George," 186
Bush-Quayle campaign, 72
business, 115, 116
Business Week, 88
Buzzard, Lynn, 45
Byrd, Harry, 240
Byrd, Robert, 162
Bywater, Bill, 124

C-SPAN TV, 162, 163, 167
Cable News Network (CNN), 129, 162, 164, 200
Cadell, Patrick, 216
Camp David, 205
campaign, antiliquor, 148; health care reform, 210; contributions, 25, 108; direct mail and advertising, 198; school board, 70
Campfire Girls, 151, 264
Campus Crusade for Christ, 14
candidates, 109; third-party, 171; Democratic, 124; liberal, 100; pro-family, 9, 37, 69, 190, 191; Republican, 245; school board, 8
Cape Fear, 61
Capital Research Center, 120
Capitalism, 38, 189; Marxist critique of, 130; shifting, 120
Capitol Hill Crisis Pregnancy Center, 241
care centers for needy children, 35
career politicians, 201, 255
CareNet, 60
Carey, Ron, 124
caricatures, 58, 65; Amos-and-Andy-like, 55
Carlson, Allan, 264
Carnegie, Andrew, 115, 116
Carter, Jimmy, 136, 175, 190, 205, 207
Carter, Stephen L., 6, 51, 58, 135
Carville, James, 108
Casey, Robert, 15
casinos, 249
catastrophic care, 262
Catcher in the Rye, 69
U.S. Catholic Bishops Conference, 17, 59, 230
cause(s), abolitionist, 146; liberal, 124; progressive, 217; religiously-inspired, 72
CBN TV, 3, 4
CBS TV, 60, 62, 161, 166; Evening News, 160, 161
celibacy, 18
cellular phones, 164, 165
censorship, 9, 50, 69, 70, 71, 102, 131, 227
U.S. Census Bureau, 82, 137, 227
Center for Neighborhood Enterprise, 246
Center for Political Studies, 195
Centers for Disease Control (CDC), 102

Chamber of Commerce, 9, 117, 119, 197
Chambers, Karl, 46, 47
change(s), 104, 112, 169; cultural, 75, 113; economic and social, 38; political, 113, 253; time for, 21; unpredictable, 175; voter demand for, 206
chaos, civilization and, 86; economic, 100; judicial, 78; social, 55, 87
chaplains, U.S. Senate, 48
Chappaquiddick, 214
character, 41; and authority, 205; Bill Clinton's, 204, 206; Christian, 151; inculcating, 84; judgment by content of, 248; moral, 201; redefinition of, 154
Charis Homes, 265
charisma, over character, 209
charities, 79; faith-based, 35, 39, 264, 265; church-based, 74
chastity, 235
Chavez, Cesar, 141, 153, 154, 224
Chicago Daily News, 126
Chicago Tribune, 125, 126
child abuse, 58
child labor, 74; laws, 38
child molestation, 30, 230
child neglect, 34
childrearing, 10, 91
Children's Defense Fund, 120
Children's Educational Opportunity Foundation, 265
children, concern for welfare of, 196
chilling effect, on freedom of speech, 50
Chinese-Americans, 90
Christ Memorial Baptist Church, 250
Christian Broadcasting Network (CBN), 1, 266
Christian Coalition, 3, 4, 8, 12, 13, 20, 37, 68, 72, 154, 157, 182, 184, 189, 190, 196-200, 219, 230, 243, 244, 250, 252; state and local affiliates, 200; state and local chapters, 198
Christian Endeavor, 151
Christian Life Commission, 237
Christian right, 192
Christian, born-again, 62; nation, 132-135; world, 133
Christianity, 14, 42, 53, 56, 132, 133; and republican virtue, 138; central truth of, 147; evangelical, 62; limitation of, 138; principles of, 133
Christianity Today, 247
Christians, 34; conservative, 24; fundamentalist, 53; right-wing, 8
Christmas, litigation against, 49, 50
Chrysler Corporation bailout, 119
church and state, 19, 23, 49, 58, 59, 69, 72, 76, 79, 130-132, 134, 139, 154; jurisprudence, 138
church attendance, statistics, 196
church, African-American, 222; and racism, 236; Roman Catholic, 17; white evangelical, 237
churches, 266, 267; evangelical, 5, 199;

mainline, 5, 16; racially divided, 247; Roman Catholic, 199
Churchill, Winston, 4, 37, 133
Citicorp, 118
citizen legislature, 38
citizen participation, 37
Citizens Against Government Waste, 95
citizenship, 6, 25, 58, 252, 263; duties of, 41
city councils, 28, 190
civic involvement, church-based, 12
Civil Rights Act, 224
Civil War, 39, 84, 106, 125, 134, 239, 240
civilization, 266; Western, 43, 49, 94, 99
Claremont Institute, 99
Clarence Thomas hearings, 198, 199
Clark, Beverly, 244
Clark, Norman, 148
Cleaver, Eldridge, 59
Clinton, President Bill, 16, 23, 35, 57, 67, 68, 94, 95, 109-111, 123, 135, 136, 160, 166, 174, 175, 176, 195, 203-206, 209, 212, 214, 215, 216, 218, 232; administration, 32, 101, 103, 119; 1993 budget, 118; charm and charisma, 208; era, 202; lack of core beliefs, 208; shading the truth, 211
Clinton health care plan, 15, 200, 203, 210, 230, 262
Clinton, Hillary Rodham, 210, 215, 217
Clinton presidential campaign, 214, 217
Clinton tax increase, 256
CNBC TV, 161
CNN, 56
coalition-building, 1, 233; biracial, 246; Christian, 243; ecumenical, 19; emerging, 12; Republican-Democratic, 219; winning, 225
coalitions, partners, 173; Reagan and Bush, 201; weakening of, 178
code of conduct, 89
Cognetics, 118
cohabitation, 36
Cohen, Richard, 91, 206, 207
Cohen, Sharon, 54
Cokeley, Steve, 98
cold war, 179, 212, 213
Coleman, Marshall, 104
collective bargaining, 122
College Republican National Committee, 192
College Republicans, 26, 196
Collier's magazine, 129
color line, 12
Colson, Chuck, 14, 89, 266
Columbus, Christopher, 84
Colvin, E. E., 239
Committee for Industrial Organization, 121
Committee for Jewish Education, 20
commodity trading, Hillary Rodham Clinton's, 204
common cause, 14, 17, 184
common law, 49, 133

Common Sense, 143
Communication Workers of America v. Beck, 122, 123
communications, satellite, 168, 169
communism, 54, 128, 178, 240; America's fear of, 213
communists, 239
communities, ethnic, 90; "community policing," 89
community, Christian, 67; civil rights, 224; faith, 58; marginalized, 247; pro-family, 13
computers, 75, 108, 119, 127, 159, 160, 165, 168, 193, 200, 255
Concerned Texans, 250
Concerned Women for America, 3
condoms, 32, 102
conferences, grassroots, 20
Congress, 25, 42, 45, 95, 96, 103, 106, 108, 109, 112, 115, 117, 119, 146, 147, 150, 153, 158, 159, 162, 167, 172, 177, 182, 197, 210, 212, 224, 253, 255, 258; conservative gains in, 219; Democratic, 174; reelection of, 104
Congress on Racial Equality, 236
Congressional Black Caucus, 224
congressional districts, 2
congressional junkets, 97
Connally, John, 23
conscience, cultivation of, 89; dictates of, 225; issues of, 232; rights of, 77
consensus, 58; cold war, 177; cultural, 74; on education, 85
conservatives, 141, 154, 173; pro-family, 231, 247; religious, 9, 10, 11, 23, 24, 28, 32, 33, 35, 37, 59, 67, 69, 75, 89, 93, 110, 135, 190, 191, 219, 237, 245, 251, 253, 255, 259, 262
Constancy, William, 47, 48
Constitution of Virginia, 77
Constitution, United States, 17, 34, 41, 43, 79, 84, 105, 131, 132, 137, 138, 257; basis of, 64; proposed temperance amendment, 149
consultants, 108, 250
consumerism, 112
Continental Congress, 144
contraband, Bible as, 43
contraception, 9, 103
contraceptives, 257
contributions, "soft dollar," 122; charitable, 35, 227; time and money, 252
conversion, moral/political, 222; religious, 142
convictions, religious, 147
cooperation, biracial, 245; with neighbors, 267
corporation, rise of, 117
corrections services, 29, 88
corruption, 37, 150, 179
Cote, Bob, 101
Council of Economic Advisors, 103
counterculture, 60
courthouses, 267
Cox, "Boss" George, 107
Creator, 76, 77

credibility, Bill Clinton's, 204
crime, 13, 23, 28, 33, 67, 87, 179, 180, 183, 186, 200, 225, 226, 230, 232, 242, 247, 258
Crime Bill of 1994, 89
crime, juvenile, 82; organized, 122; origins of problem, 90; and punishment, 232; rates, 87; violent, 87, 91
criminal justice system, 259
criminals, nonviolent, 231
crisis, civil liberties, 8; drug, 82; economic, 183; education, 82; health care, 229; moral, 19, 183; of political chameleon, 218; of the presidency, 205
Cronkite, Walter, 161
Cross, Linda, 231
Cross, Whitney, 145
Crow, Jim, 238
crucifixion, 61
Cuban refugees, 217
cults, 5, 65
cultural hegemony, 130
cultural isolation, 263
cultural revolution, 265
culture, American, 6; capitalist dominance of, 130; children-friendly, 30; decline of, 92; family-friendly, 130; individualistic, 82; of caring, 31, 39, 265; of compassion, 264; political, 94, 168; popular, 51, 61; secular, 9, 222; trash quotient of, 30; white country-club, 246
Cummins, Mary, 7, 8
Cuomo, Mario, 51, 57, 175, 207, 208
curriculum, abstinence-based, 257; morally neutered, 232
Cutler, Lloyd, 207

D-Day anniversary celebrations, 208
Daley political machine, 107, 108
Daley, Richard, 108, 109
"Dan Quayle Was Right," 91
Danbury Baptist Association, 76
Danforth, John, 198
Darrow, Clarence, 53
Davis, Richard Allen, 28
day care, 34, 227; federally funded, 232
De Niro, Robert, 61
deadbeat dads, 30, 35, 259
death penalty, 47, 211, 217, 242
Deaver, Michael, 160, 168
debate, abortion, 261; national, 65; Perot-Gore, 171; political, 254
debt, federal, 179; government, 18; national, 93, 94, 95
decay, cultural and moral, 39; of family, 83
Declaration of Independence, 64, 76, 84, 132, 144, 189, 259
decline, in moral values, 225; labor unions, 120; of big business, 118, 119; of liberal institutions, 105

Dees, James, 239
Defenders of State Sovereignty and Individual Liberty, 240
Deficit, 183; reduction, 226, 227; spending, 93, 226
DeLay, Tom, 119
delinquency, 87, 89
democracy, 7, 24, 37, 50, 65, 155, 158, 189; and religion, 136; and talk radio, 164; dial-in, 167; direct, 186; George Washington on, 105; participatory, 166, 169; religion as threat to, 132; survival of, 63
Democracy in America, 154
Democratic Leadership Council (DLC), 210, 212, 218
Democratic National Committee, 110
Democratic National Convention, 73; Chicago, 150; Los Angeles, 128; Miami Beach, 107
Democratic Party, 72, 105, 107, 110, 115, 121, 150, 194, 216, 218, 242, 245
democratic process, American, 51
Democrats, 12, 13, 15, 16, 19, 35, 72, 104, 124, 133, 135, 162, 200, 242, 254; liberal, 38; maverick, 203
demographics, 20, 75, 105, 126, 130, 137, 194; changing, 161, 165, 169
DeMoss, Nancy, 15, 16
Department of Agriculture, 97
Department of Defense, 95
Department of Education, 84, 85, 96
Department of Health and Human Services, 90, 246
Department of Health, Education, and Welfare, 86
Department of Housing and Urban Development (HUD), 43
Department of Justice, United States, 43
Department of Labor, 246
dependency, 35, 147, 232
depression, 204
desegregation, 72
DeSpain v. DeKalb, 49
Detroit News, 125
DeVos, Rich, 265
Dewey, Thomas E., 121
Dickinson, John, 142
Dillard, Annie, 69
Dinkins, David, 182
Dionne, E. J., 24, 180, 235
direct mail, 23, 193, 200; fundraisers, 108
disbelief, culture of, 6, 51, 135
discipline, breakdown in, 231
discourse, American, 136; civic, 19, 35, 62, 64, 65; moral, 222; public, 11, 29, 51, 58, 177; public policy, 18
discrimination, 9, 106; religious, 43
disenfranchisement, political, 247
Disney, 75, 91
disorder, social, 147; psychological, 229

disrespect for elders, 244
dissent, conservative, 213; religious, 155
dissenters, social, 141
diversity, 75, 92, 189, 247; gender, 211; racial, 241
divorce, 10, 39, 82, 83, 85, 99, 183
divorce, "no fault," 29, 100, 258; subsidies for, 258; taxpayer-funded, 100
divorce law reform, 259
Dixiecrats, 179
Dixon, Alan, 177
Dixon, Sharon Pratt, 249
Dobson, James, 158, 165, 192
Dodd, Wesley Alan, 230, 231
Doggett, John, 246
domestic partnership ordinance, 249, 250
domestic policy, 110
domestic quarrels, 229
domestic tranquility, 88, 179
"Dominion of Providence over the Passions of Men," 144
Donahue, 30
Donahue, Phil, 30, 203
Douglas, Justice William O., 133
Douglas, Mike, 160
Douglas, Stephen A., 254, 261
downsizing, corporate, 118; of the military, 213
Dragnet, 62
Dred Scott decision, 260
drive-by shootings, 229
dropouts, 10, 87
drug abuse, 229
drugs, 226, 247, 257, 258, 265; dealing, 101; fight against, 201; illegal, 29, 32, 33, 39, 44, 82, 87, 100, 127; legalization, 101, 196
Dukakis, Michael, 218
Duke, David, 179, 235
Dulles, Avery, 15
Duncan, John, Jr., 112
du Pont Corporation, 118
dynasty, Kennedy, 106

Eagle Forum, 193
early release programs, 231
earthquake, political, 176, 177
Eastland, Terry, 11, 136
Ebeneezer Baptist Church, 74, 153
economic, decline, 180; federal disincentives, 99; insecurity, 179; security, 225; "stimulus package," 95
economy, American, 121; beleaguered, 119; free market, 14
Ecumenism, 13, 16, 18, 19
education, 23, 167, 180, 200, 232, 256; reform, 251, 257; public, 9; quality of, 33; reform, 28; scholarships, 33, 256, 264, 265
educational achievement, 85
Edwards, Jonathan, 63
egalitarianism, 105

Egger, Tobias, 237
eighties, 4
Eisenhower, Dwight, 181, 204, 223
Elders, Surgeon General Joycelyn, 101, 136
electorate, attitudes toward political parties, 109; balkanization of, 254
Elementary and Secondary Education Act, 157
Emory University, 2, 86, 196
emotional problems of children, 82
Employment Division v. Smith, 138
empowerment, 13; African-American, 246; of teachers, 256
encounter weekends, 19
endangerment of mother's life, 260
enlightenment, 64; changing technology, 129
environmentalism, 112
environmentalists, 255
Equal Employment Opportunity Commission (EEOC), 42
Equal Rights Amendment, 224
equality, racial, 7, 238
equivocation, Bill Clinton's penchant for, 217
eschatology, 25
Establishment Clause, 75, 76, 77, 78, 131
estrangement, cultural, 263
eternal life, 103
ethics, 232; loss of, 182, 183
Ethics and Public Policy Center, 18, 57, 136
euthanasia, 14, 237
evangelicals, 1, 3, 15, 16, 17, 19, 21, 25-28, 51, 53, 54, 58, 65, 75, 109, 147, 198, 199, 223, 225, 237, 254; church-going, 226; estimated number, 2; politically-active, 55, 61
Evangelicals and Catholics Together, 14
evangelism, 14
Evans, Hiram Wesley, 235, 236
Evidences of Christianity, 64
evil(s), 58, 64, 143
evolution, 9, 53, 150, 155
executive orders, pro-life, 176
exit polls, statistics, 225, 227
experiment, American, 254
exploitation of women, 29
extremism, political, 264
extremists, 24, 54, 190

Fabrizio, Tony, 242
Fabrizio, McLaughlin and Associates, 226
Face the Nation, 60
fair hiring practices, 30
fair housing laws, 43
fairness, 41
faith, 8, 9, 11, 18, 24, 36, 37, 65; antipathy toward, 254; attacks on, 101, 102, 131; Christian, 27; consensus of beliefs, 14; defense of, 64; evangelical, 142, 166; in American civil life, 135; in God, 12; Judeo-Christian, 79; mainstream values of, 130; marginalization of, 6, 40, 51, 58; of

Pioneers, 267; and public service, 63; orthodox, 6; practice of, 40; public expressions of, 42, 46, 48; supremacy of, 14; tolerance of, 78
faithfulness, 79
Fallows, Jim, 183
Falwell, Jerry, 72, 127, 141, 191, 196, 236, 242, 244, 253
families, 11, 28; broken, 82, 87; dysfunctional, 137; healthy, 10; intact, 29, 39, 84, 86; tax relief for, 38; two-parent, 92, 100
family breakup, 179
Family Channel, 166, 200
"family gap," 196
family income stagnation, 186
Family Research Council, 192, 230
family, breakdown, 39; breakup, 67, 81, 83, 85, 91, 92, 225, 254; crisis of, 80; disintegration, 85, 90, 92; entertainment, 166; formation, 82, 90, 99; importance of, 74; importance ranked, 12; nuclear, 87, 91; pathology of decay, 86; religious values in, 27; two-parent, 99, 247; values, 91, 189, 225, 251, 254
famine in family time, 228
fanaticism, 6, 64, 67
fanatics, 61
Farewell Address, 105, 178
Farrakhan, Louis, 98
Farris, Michael, 25, 72, 135, 245
fascism, 6, 7, 251
fate of nations, 250
fax machines, 75, 119, 159, 165, 167, 182, 193, 197, 200
Fazio, Vic, 61
FBI statistics, 87
fear, 9, 13, 27, 87, 137, 143, 179, 207; and crime, 29; of faith, 48; racist, 238
Feder, Don, 19, 88
federal budget, 206, 233, spending, 94, 241
Federal Register, 125
federal regulations, 97
Federalist Papers, 88, 105
Fellowship of Christian Athletes, 44
Felten, Eric, 98
feminists, 211, 218, 255, 260
Fernandez, Joseph, 7
feudalism, 38
fiber optics, 160, 168, 169
fidelity, 32, 267
Finney, Charles Grandison, 145, 236
Finney, Joan, 15
"fireside chats," 204
First Amendment, 9, 30, 36, 43, 75, 77, 131, 138, 257
fiscal responsibility, 34
Florio, Jim, 182
Focus on the Family, 31, 69, 165, 266
Foley, Tom, 185
Foner, Eric, 38

Food and Drug Administration, 97
food stamps, 99
Foraker, Joseph Benson, 107
Forbes magazine, 123
Ford Motor Company, 121
Ford, Henry, 116
Fordham University, 15
foreign affairs, 214
foreign entanglements, 178
foreign policy, 21; internationalist, 38
foster care, 35, 261, 265
foundations, 105
founders, 43, 64, 78, 105, 137
Fournier, Keith, 49
Fourteenth Amendment, 134, 259
Fowler, Wyche, 182
Fox network, 161
Frame of Government for Pennsylvania, 47
Franklin, Benjamin, 35, 50, 63
Free Congress Foundation, 246
free enterprise system, 189
free exercise of religion, 76
free speech, 245
Freedom of Choice Act, 15, 176
freedom, American experiment in, 15; from religion, 135; individual, 189; of press, 43, 50; of religion, 135; of speech, 43, 50; of worship, 43; religious, 14, 15
Friedman, Thomas, 210
Friendly, Fred, 160
Frohnmayer, John, 131
From, Al, 218
Frosty the Snowman, 49
frugality, 184
Fulbright, William J., 212-214, 218
fundamentalism, 53
Fundamentalist Project, 54
fundamentalists, 24, 57, 60, 62, 65, 73, 189
fundraising, 4, 68; direct mail, 108
Furman University, 33
future, 6, 16, 18, 75, 130, 132, 167, 176; anxiety about, 3; biracial, 247; economic, 182; expectations about, 87; importance of education, 196; labor unions, 123; media trends, 161; of American politics, 172; of political movements, 201; of small business, 119; populist, 113

G.I. bill, 33
Gallup organization, 194
Gallup poll, 172; survey, 58
gambling, 147, 249
Gandhi, Mahatma, 153
gangs, 229, 265
Gantry, Elmer, 65; secular, 209
Garcia, Linda, 9
Gargan, Jack, 181
garnishment of wages, 259
Garrison, William Lloyd, 145
Gartland, Pat, 9

Gay Men's Health Crisis, 120
gays, 255; in the military, 160, 166, 175, 208, 209, 226, 232
General Accounting Office (GAO), 100
General Electric, 117, 118
General Motors, 117, 118, 120, 121
genocide, 150
geography, 84
George III, King of England, 144
George Mason University, 157, 242
George Washington University, 212
Georgetown University, 212
Gephardt, Richard, 218
Gergen, David, 160, 207
Gibbons, Cardinal James, 17
Giddings, Joshua, 146, 147
Gideons, 48, 151
Gilder, George, 91
Gillespie, G. T., 238, 240
Gingrich, Newt, 162
Ginsburg, Ruth Bader, 208, 261
Girl Scouts, 151
Glendon, Mary Ann, 259
God-shaped vacuum, 4
Godzilla, 164
gold standard, 120
Golden Rule Insurance Company, 264
Goldwater presidential campaign, 193, 216
Goldwater, Barry, 25, 67, 107, 176, 219
good and evil, clash of, 24
Gore, Al, 171, 175, 209, 214
government, assistance, 83; growth of, 123, 125; local, 190; republican, 189; responsive to voters, 255; spending, 245; state and local, 199; suspicion of, 134; waste, 225-227; workers, statistics, 94
Grace Church of God, 153
Grace, Peter, 15, 95
graduations, 64
Graham, Billy, 223, 236, 237
Gramsci, Antonio, 130
grassroots sources of energy, 202
Great Awakening, 141, 143, 145, 146; Second, 133, 145, 146, 149
Great Depression, 89, 179
"Great Monkey Trial," 53
Great Society, 125
Great Wall of China, 97
greed, economic, 186
Greek mythology, 42
Greek Orthodox, 11, 15, 16, 254
Greeks, 64, 238
Green, John, 242
Greenberg, Paul, 218
gridlock, 112, 174, 177
Griffin, Michael, 59, 60
gross national product (GNP), 94, 117, 185, 257
Gross, Martin, 95
guarantee of security, 89
guerrillas, grassroots, 215

Guinier, Lani, 208
gun control, 184
Gunn, David, 59
guns, 265

Haberman, Rabbi Joshua, 20
Hadden, Jeffrey, 192
"Hail to the Chief," 205
Haiti, 178
Ham, curse of, 239, 247
Hamilton, Alexander, 105, 143
handicaps, physical, 10
Hannah and Her Sisters, 61
Harding, Warren G., 107
Harris v. McRae, 76
Hart, Gary, 208, 215, 216
Hart, Pat, 189
Hart, Peter, 12
Harvard University, 88, 137, 216; Law School, 259
Heads Up, 266
health care, 183, 206, 225, 229, 233, 262, 265; debate, 120; employee-mandated, 119; national, 120, 176; reform, 27, 232; pro-family, 230
health insurance, 262
Health Policy International, 229
health, psychological, 229
Hearst, William Randolph, 125
Hecht, Rabbi Shea, 20
hedonism, 183
Helms, Jesse, 245
Henry, Patrick, 77, 84, 144
Heritage Foundation, 193
heritage, Judeo-Christian, 223; religious, 154
Hesburgh, Theodore, 153
Hickel, Wally, 174
higher education, 33, 64
higher wages, 223
Hill, Anita, 162, 198
Hindus, 55
Hirschmann, Susan, 192
Hispanics, 9, 12, 13, 90, 190, 215, 241-243, 245
history, 7, 16, 84; examples from, 74; lesson of, 27, 86; of religion in America, 132; religious unity in, 133; revisionist, 110; social movements in, 38; Supreme Court in, 17; view of, 5
Hitler, Adolf, 54, 250
HIV, 102
Hoffa, Jimmy, 224
holding companies, 116
holidays, religious, 45
Hollywood, 20, 51, 54, 105; evaluation of, 75
Holocaust, 61
Holy Spirit, work of, 19
Home Box Office, 62
Home School Legal Defense Fund, 157
home schooling, 33, 60

homemakers, 165
Homes for Black Children, 265
homes for unwed mothers, 35, 71
homicide, 183
homosexuality, 74, 127
"honest graft," 26
honesty, 184
Hosokawa, Morihiro, 181
Hospital Corporation of America, 118
House Appropriations Committee, 112
House Budget Committee, 228
House Education and Labor Committee, 157
"house of cardinals," 112
House of Representatives, 47, 78, 96, 99, 104,
    111, 146, 158, 162, 176, 250, 253
House Public Works and Transportation
    Committee, 112
House Public Works Committee, 97
House Rules Committee, 158
households, two-income, 250
Houston Ministerial Association, 73
How the Other Half Lives, 151
Howard, John, 240
Hughes Aircraft Company, 168
humility, 27, 155
Hyde Amendment, 15, 76, 176, 200
Hyde, Henry, 15, 99
hyperinflation, 179
hypocrisy, 56, 58, 59, 62, 68, 238, 241, 266

Iacocca, Lee, 115
IBM, 118
iconoclasm, of McGovern campaign, 215
ideological ambivalence, 173; confusion, 178
idleness, 147
ignorance, 33
illegal aliens, 101
illegitimacy, 10, 30, 39, 67, 82, 83, 87, 89, 91,
    92, 247, 258; bureaucratic bias toward, 31;
    subsidies for, 29, 258
illiteracy, 10, 39, 67, 258
immigration, 106, 178; illegal, 101; nineteenth
    century, 106
imperialism, 150
In His Steps, 151
in loco parentis, 70
incarceration, 90
incest, 31, 260, 261
inclusion, of women, minorities, and Native
    Americans, 154
"incredible shrinking presidency," 205
indecency, 100
independents, 109
Indian, religions, 42; reservations, 97
Indiana Civil Liberties Union, 48
individualism, 169
industrialization, 117
inflation, 84, 94, 186, 256, 258
influence-peddling, 37

information superhighway, 75, 160, 167, 168,
    169
infrastructure, 97, 187; grassroots, 194;
    political, 2, 123
Ingraham, T. Robert, 239
injustice, social, 237
Inman, Bobby Ray, 207
inner city, 127
integration statistics, 240
integrity, 203
Intel, 118
interest groups, ideological, 111
interest, rates, 182; mortgage, 227
intermarriage, 240; racial, 238
Internal Revenue Service (IRS), 17
International Union of Electronic
    Workers, 124
"interposition" racial resistance, 240
intolerance, 35, 50, 51, 54, 59; toward religion,
    21, 41, 49, 67
involvement, civic, 191; in Vietnam, 214;
    parental, 85; political, 25, 59, 71, 106, 141,
    252, 263
iron triangles, 103
Isaac, Rys, 144
Iseli, Lee, 30, 230
Islam, 14, 56
isolation, cultural, 71; of family members, 85
isolationism, 178
Israel, 20, 21, 63, 260; children of, 143; West
    Bank, 55
issues research, 186
Ivins, Molly, 57

Jackson, Andrew, 105
Jackson, Brooks, 25
Jackson, Jesse, 13, 111, 194, 218, 224, 242
Jacobins, 239
James, Kay Cole, 246
Jarjoura, G. Roger, 87
Jay, Justice John, 88
jealousy, 238
Jefferson, Thomas, 33, 76, 77, 93, 102
Jennings, Peter, 165
Jesus Christ, 153; lordship of, 14
Jews, 7, 9, 11, 13, 19, 51, 54, 55, 58, 65, 67, 72,
    73, 112, 134, 135, 236, 237, 254; attacks on,
    38; Hasidic, 79; orthodox, 20
job, cutbacks, 118; losses, 179, 182, 185
joblessness, 99
Johns Hopkins University, 213
Johnson, Andrew, 250
Johnson, Lyndon, 86, 125, 129, 153, 176, 204,
    207
Jones, Paula Corbin, 68, 206
Jordan, Vernon, 23
Judaism, 42, 56
judgment, 142, 247
judicial decisions, liberal, 39

judiciary, 48, 167
Julian, George, 147
The Jungle, 152
jurisprudence, 76
justice, 28, 60, 79, 105, 153, 184; racial, 14; social, 17
Justice Department, United States, 11, 231

Kaisch, John, 228
Kefauver, Estes, 214
Keidis, Tony, 102
Kennedy, D. James, 3
Kennedy, John F., 16, 73, 107, 111, 159, 205, 214, 250
Kennedy, Joseph, 106
Kennedy, Joseph P., 128
Kennedy, Patrick, 106
Kennedy, Robert F., 153, 214
Kennedy, Ted, 213, 214
Kennedy-Nixon debate, 164
Kent, Chancellor James, 138
Kerry, Bob, 72
Khomeini, Ayatollah, 54, 60
Khrushchev, Nikita, 204
kidnapping, 28
Kilpatrick, William, 70, 232
kindergarten, 81
King Jesus, 144
King of kings, 142
King, Larry, 164
King, Martin Luther, 59, 68, 133, 141, 153, 155, 207, 222, 236
Kingdom Church, 244
Kirk, Russell, 79
Kiryas Joel village, 79
Klaas, Polly, 28
Know-Nothings, 14, 73
Koppel, Ted, 24
Korea, 204
Koresh, David, 61, 62
Kothe, Charles, 198, 199
KPFK FM, 98
Krauthammer, Charles, 91
Krol, Cardinal John, 17
Ku Klux Klan, 51, 101, 178, 179, 189, 235

L.A. Law, 62
labor, 115
labor force, 117
labor trends, statistics, 122
labor unions, 19, 105, 120, 121, 210, 224; decline of, 120-123; loss of confidence, 174; reduced economic power, 123; tactics of, 124; twilight of political influence, 124
labor, unfair practices, 121
LaHaye, Beverly, 3
Lancaster County Action, 193
Land, Richard, 14, 237

Lapin, Rabbi Daniel, 20
larceny, 76, 87
Larry King Live, 163, 164
Latinos, 90, 265
law, and order, 217; enforcement, 29; civil rights, 35; dependence upon religious values, 79; of God, 69; higher, 10; moral, 69; and religion, 19; right-to-work, 211; and will of God, 133
lawlessness, 89, 90
laws, 103; abortion, 259; against crime, 241; antislavery, 224; antitrust, 120; basis of, 64; Jim Crow, 152; of nature, 142
layoffs, 118
leaders, African-American, 153; civil rights, 236; grassroots, 3; minority, 243
leadership, civil rights, 241; moral, 202
leadership schools, 199
League of Women Voters, 120
leap of faith, 239
Lear, Norman, 127, 128
Lee v. Weisman, 46
Leege, David C., 195
Lefkowitz, Jay, 19
Legal Services Corporation (LSC), 99, 100, 228
legislation, civil rights, 253; gay rights, 207
"lemon test," 78
Lemon v. Kurtzman, 78
"Letter from Birmingham Jail," 68
Lewis, Alphonso, 264
Lewis, Anthony, 60
Lewis, Barbara, 264
Lewis, John L., 224
liberalism, 214, 215, 218, 240; Great Society, 218; Southern, 212; woolly-headed, 215
liberals, 24, 89, 141, 154, 194, 215, 232; support of bureaucracy, 228
Liberator newspaper, 145
libertarians, 173
liberties, civil, 262
liberty, 43, 144, 145; civil, 50; gift of God, 77; maintenance of, 144; religious, 14, 20, 21, 131; without faith, 65
Liberty League, 120
Liberty University, 192
Lichter, S. Robert, 55
Liddy, Gordon, 164
Life magazine, 128
life of faith, 155
life of the mother, 261
lifestyle(s), agrarian, 150; alternative, 241; changing, 127, 161; gay, 7
"Limbaugh Letter," 164
Limbaugh, Rush, 159, 164, 165; radio program, 200
Lincoln Caucus, 193
Lincoln, Abraham, 58, 64, 132, 213, 253, 261
line-item veto, 34, 258
Lipset, Seymour, 180
literacy, 10, 266

litigation, church-state, 78; limits on, 36
lobbying, 122; grassroots, 244
lobbyists, registered, 100; home school, 158
local ordinances, 197
Locke, John, 64
Look magazine, 129
Los Angeles Mirror, 126
Los Angeles riots, 86
Los Angeles Times, 126
Love and War, 62
loyalty, decline in party, 112; party, 245
Luce, Henry, 128
Luker, Kristen, 17
Lumpkin, Ernest, 74
lying, 244

MacArthur, Douglas, 210
MacNeil-Lehrer News Hour, 98
Maddoux, Marlin, 158
Madison, James, 77, 132
Madonna, 70, 232
magazines, 166
Magnet, Myron, 89, 265
Malcolm X, 153, 246
malpractice reform, 262
Manchester, William, 210
mandate(s), teacher-certification, 157, 158;
    elimination of, 256
Manifest Destiny, 5
manifesto, inter-faith, 14
Mann, David, 115
marital infidelity, 206
Marketing Research Institute, 226
marriage, 91, 258; delayed, 82; importance of,
    29, 30; security of, 82
marriage counseling, 259
Marriage Encounter, 19
marriage penalty, 256
Marshall, Thurgood, 152, 198
mass production, 116
materialism, 183
Mayhew, Jonathan, 143
McCarthy, Eugene, 153, 215
McCarthyism, 179
McCartney, Bill, 31
McCormack, Col. Robert, 125
McDonald, Robin, 241
McGovern presidential campaign, 193, 212, 214,
    215, 216, 218
McGovern, George, 16, 107, 213, 215
McGuffey's Reader, 63
McKinley campaign, 120
McManus, Michael, 82
Meacham, John, 24
Mead, Margaret, 92
means-testing, 258
media, 51, 53, 74, 92, 103, 105, 110, 115, 124, 198;
    abuse, 190; beliefs of, 55; bias of, 64;
    consultants, 108; elites, 125; evaluation of,

75; expansion of, 125; feeding frenzy, 203;
    loss of confidence, 174; network monopoly,
    164; populist programming, 162, 165
Media Research Center, 56
Medicaid, 99
Medved, Michael, 20
Mencken, H. L., 53
menorahs, 36, 43
mercy, 79, 153, 184
merger, TCI-Bell Atlantic, 169
mergers, corporate, 117
merit pay for teachers, 256
Methodists, 5, 26, 54, 148
Metzger, Leigh Ann, 193
Mexican War, 213, 253
military cutbacks, 179
military intervention, 213
millenialism, 142
Miller, George, 157
Miller, Zell, 217
Minneapolis Star-Tribune, 61
minorities, 9, 10, 12, 39, 154, 247, 265;
    cooperation with, 244; religious values of,
    12
Minutemen, 144
Miraldo, Pamela, 103
miscegenation, 238
misconduct, sexual, 205, 206, 208
Mister Rogers' Neighborhood, 232
Mitchell, George, 207
mockery, 59
moderates, 24, 147
moderation, 105
modesty, 27
Mondale, Walter, 122, 218
monetary policy, 38
monopolies, corporate, 116, 117
Montesquieu, Baron de, 64
moral breakdown, 183, 235
Moral Majority, 191, 194, 196
"moral sense," 183
morality, 50; Christian, 20
Morgan, J. P., 116
Morris, Anna May, 46, 47
Morse, Wayne, 214
Moseley-Braun, Carol, 177
Mother's Day celebration, 149
motherhood, 165
movement(s), anti-incumbency, 181, 255; anti-
    tax, 112, 184, 186; antisaloon, 149;
    antislavery, 38, 134, 141, 145; antiwar, 59;
    Black Power, 222; chastity, 32; Christian
    school, 17; civil rights, 13, 39, 59, 131, 141,
    153, 222, 224, 237; fatherhood, 31; free soil,
    224; gay rights, 210; genuinely inclusive,
    241; grassroots, 219, 220; labor, 17; marriage
    enrichment, 19; massive resistance, 237,
    238, 239, 240, 241; multiracial, 241; parental
    rights, 231; Perot, 223, 254; populist, 149;
    pro-choice, 112; pro-family, 13, 17, 25, 59,

99, 187, 189, 191, 196, 201, 202, 220-223, 225, 226, 233, 242-244, 245, 247, 248; pro-life, 15-17, 112; progressive, 186; religious conservative, 38, 54, 75, 112, 187, 191; resistance, 222; social, 38, 224; suffragist, 147, 148, 149; temperance, 131, 141, 145, 147, 148; term limits, 184; women's, 39, 131, 148
movies, 32
Moynihan, Daniel Patrick, 86, 87
MTV-consciousness, Clinton's, 205
multiculturalism, 7, 189
murder, 10, 28, 30, 47, 59, 60, 65, 75, 76, 87, 90, 229, 231, 244
"Murphy Brown," 83
Murray, Charles, 258
Muslims, 55, 72, 135, 153; Shiite, 57, 61

NAACP, 69, 120, 152, 190, 233, 245, 253
Naisbitt, John, 169
narcicissism, 4
narcotics, 101
Nation, Carrie, 149
National Abortion Rights Action League, 24, 176
National Association of Evangelicals, 15
National Association of Manufacturers, 117
National Biological Survey, 96
National Center for Policy Analysis, 90
National Conference of State Legislatures, 186
national debt, statistics, 93
National Education Association (NEA), 123
National Empowerment Television (NET), 167
National Endowment for the Arts, 57, 101, 131, 197, 228
National Endowment for the Humanities, 84
National Federation of Independent Business, 119
National Labor Relations Board, 121
National Review, 219
National Rifle Association, 111
National Right to Life Committee, 15, 17, 193, 244
national security, 178, 209
Native American affairs, 96
nativism, 16, 141
nativity scenes, 36, 49
Nazis, 54, 60, 61
NBC TV, 62, 161, 166; NBC News, 174
NBC/ Wall Street Journal, 225
NCAA Final Four tournament, 203
neighborhood(s), 10, 11, 18, 28, 29, 87, 247, 262
Neill, Dr. Richard, 30
Nelson, Willie, 205
networks, grassroots, 200
Neuhaus, Richard John, 11, 14, 27
New Age, 5, 14
New Deal, 94, 104, 120, 121, 124-126
New Deal Democrat, 219

"New Democrat," 94, 110, 217, 218
New Left, 216
new political order, 177
new politics, 104, 175
New Republic, 192
"New Virtue," 183
New World, 5
New York Daily News, 8
New York Herald Tribune, 126
New York Public Library, 51
New York State Temperance Society, 148
New York Stock Exchange, 118
New York Times, 8, 51, 54, 60, 159, 189, 209, 258
news bureaus, 126
news conference, televised, 205
news coverage, emphases of, 56; of religious issues, 56
news magazines, 124, 128, 129
newspapers, 124; daily circulation statistics, 126; decline in, 127; liberal bias, 127; major, 125, 126
Newsweek, 5, 51, 128, 129, 129, 130
Newton, Huey P., 59
Nightline, 24
nineties, 62, 161, 171
Nintendo, 75
Niskanen, William, 103
Nixon, Richard, 23, 24, 128, 135, 159, 204, 206, 207, 214, 250
Noonan, Peggy, 206
Norplant contraceptive device, 91
North American Free Trade Agreement (NAFTA), 115, 123, 124, 171, 178, 206, 211
North Atlantic summit, 133
North Carolina Defenders of States' Rights, 239
North, Oliver, 104
Northwest Ordinance, 78
Novak, Michael, 58
nuclear disarmament, 59
nuclear family, 87, 91
nudity, 62
Nunn, Sam, 175, 218
NYPD Blue, 62

O'Connor, Cardinal John, 13-16, 51, 57
O'Neill, Tip, 162, 190
O'Steen, David, 193
obscenity, 101, 131; taxpayer-funded, 197
occult, 69
Oliphant, Pat, 57
Olympics, 61
"Onward Christian Soldiers," 133
operatives, pro-family, 194
opium trade, 149
opposition researchers, 108
Oral Roberts University Law School, 198
organization(s), antislavery, 146; civil rights, 245; business, 117; grassroots, 186;

grassroots political, 2, 4, 200, 235, 250; lobbying, 117; pro-family, 157, 197, 219, 228, 252, 255; pro-life, 111; religious, 21, 230; social welfare, 151; "soft money," 111; volunteer, 37; oganized labor, 201; farmworker union, 154; labor unions, 224; liberal organizers, 153
outcome based education, 232
Oxford University, 212, 214
Ozzie and Harriet, 39, 91

Paine, Thomas, 143
Paley, William, 64
Palmer raids, 178
pamphleteers and propagandists, 142
pantheism, 14
paralegals, government-funded, 100
parental, choice, 39; consent, 260; involvement, 33, 256; rights, 70, 71
parenting, stay-at-home, 196
parents, African-American, 70
Parker, Starr, 9
parochialism, 16
party bosses, 106, 107, 201
party loyalty, 104, 107
party machines, 104
Pascal, Blaise, 4
pastors, African-American, 243, 250
PATCO, 122
pathologies, social, 257
patriarchy, Jim Crow, 9
patriot, 144
patriotism, 105, 120, 189, 190; and religion, 138, 143
patronage, 106
Pax Britannica, 5
Pearl Harbor, 205, 250
Pell grants, 33
Pendergast machine, 107
Penn, William, 47
Pentagon, 95, 96, 160
People for the American Way (PAW), 12, 72, 127, 189
people of faith, marginalization of, 80
People of New York v. Ruggles, 138
perjury, 76
permissiveness, 257
Perot phenomenon, 201
Perot supporters, statistics, 172
Perot, Margot, 171
Perot, Ross, 109, 115, 163, 171, 172, 180, 181, 184, 186, 187, 191, 223, 227, 250
Perry, William, 207
persecution, 48, 75
Persian Gulf War, 129, 172, 175, 179
persistence, 253
personal finances, 167
personal responsibility, 99, 258
personal safety, 88

Peters, Tom, 118
Petition(s), 198, 250, 251
peyote case, 138
phantom employees, 109
philanthropy, 27
Phillips, Doug, 157
Phillips, Kevin, 179, 192
phobia of religion, 45, 55, 71
phone banks, 200; grassroots, 244
physician choice, 232
piety, 105; devotional, 144
Planned Parenthood, 102, 103, 120
Planned Parenthood v. Casey, 260
Planned Parenthood v. Danforth, 260
plant closings, 118
platform, political, 72; pro-life, 109; Republican, 25; Zen Buddhist, 186
Plato, 43
Pledge of Allegiance, prohibition of, 44
Plessy v. Ferguson, 238
PLO, 21
pluralism, 24, 65
Point of View, 158
police protection, 29; increased, 89
police state, 9
Policy Review, 193
policy, debate, 229; defense, 213; destructive, 84; domestic, 110; education, 231; family-friendly, 256; foreign, 21, 38, 178, 213, 233; monetary, 38; public, 10, 35, 41; to benefit families and children, 223
Politburo, 104
political action, 3; committees (PACs), 111
political correctness, 119, 132
political parties, 104, 121, 255; attitudes of electorate, 109
political reform, 108
political schizophrenia, Bill Clinton's, 218
politically incorrect, 190
politicians, career, 94
politics, 157; of discontent, 186; "gospel," 149; allure of, 26; American, 2, 7, 13, 16; as usual, 112; citizen-oriented, 105; consultant-driven, 110; corrupt, 186; decline of, 92; family-friendly, 254; fascination with, 25; future, 112; grassroots, 191; grassroots-oriented, 254; hard-ball, 25; influence on religion, 25; limits of, 25; new, 104; of pork, 104, 111, 112; of ultraconsensus, 218; of virtue, 51; old-style, 201; populist, 113, 169; postwar, 178; special-interest, 24, 246; tax-and-spend, 93; technopopulist, 201
pollsters, 108
polygamy, 76
Poor Richard's Almanac, 63
Pope Pius XII, 133
population statistics, 87; Jewish, 19, 20
populism, 173, 184; high tech, 161; modern, 186
populist revolt, 171, 185
populists, 38, 150, 151, 254

pork-barrel spending, 34, 96; statistics, 95

pornography, 14, 23, 39, 79, 95, 99, 226, 232; Bible as, 48; hard-core, 29, 30; taxpayer-funded, 197

"possession of Christian literature," 44

postcards, 200, 230

potato famine, 106

"Potomac fever," 26

poverty, 32, 35, 83, 90, 97, 100, 151, 246, 247, 258, 262, 265; pauperism, 147; and alcoholism, 148; and crime, 89; intergenerational, 39; rural, 125; spiritual, 262; war on, 72

power, political, 167; racial, 238; symbolic, 86

Prager, Dennis, 20

prayer, 16, 43; at graduations, 46; banning, 197; in schools, 11, 18, 26, 36, 41, 44, 54, 78, 226, 241, 243, 244, 245, 251, 252, 253, 257; in state legislatures, 78; intercessory, 251; prejudice toward, 42; student-led, 44; unconstitutional, 139; voluntary, 8, 197

preachers, fire-and-brimstone, 143

precinct captains, 110

precincts, 200

pregnancy, counseling, 103; termination of, 31; unwanted, 31, 32

prejudice, 57, 246; anti-religious, 58; religious, 106

Presbyterians, 5, 128, 148

presidency, diminishing stature of the office, 207

price controls, 262

primaries, Democratic, 115; political, 107

Princeton University, 63, 64, 144

principles, moral, 63; of Christianity, 133; of liberty and freedom, 142; religious, 132

Prior, Maraide, 9

Prison Fellowship, 14, 266

prison system, expanding, 28

prisons, spending on, 88

private action, 29

pro-family movement, 1

profanity, 29

Profession of Faith, Roman Catholic, 17

profiteering, commodities, 206, 211

progressives, 38, 151, 254

progresssivism, 212

prohibition, 149, 155

promiscuity, 62, 229

Promise Keepers, 31

Proposition 13, 185

prostitutes, temple, 221

prostitution, 147, 148

protectionism, 178

protest, generation of, 215; social, 236

Protestant Succession, 134

protestants, 7, 14-17, 56, 106, 135, 141; conservative, 13; mainline, 195

protests, 7, 30, 55, 59, 143, 184, 224; anti-Vietnam, 9, 122, 131, 213, 218; antiwar, 107; civil rights, 155; nonviolent, 236

Proudly Pro-Life Awards, 15

PTA, 17

public assistance, 35

Public Broadcasting System (PBS), 98

Public Buildings Subcommittee, 112

public debate, 21

public education, 34; quality, 33

public opinion, changing, 175; polling, 186

public policy, 10, 35, 41

public relations, 160

public safety, 28, 29

public service and faith, 63

"public square," 11, 36, 37, 40, 48, 51, 132, 137, 141, 236, 253

publishing houses, 105

punishment for crime, 90

Puritans, 134, 143

Quakers, 73

Quayle, Dan, 91

Quist, Allen, 61

quotas, 242; medical-school, 210

race, Anglo-Saxon, 238; barrier, 12; predictive of crime, 90

racial equality, 210

racial integrity, breakdown of, 238

racial segregation, 222

racism, 8, 35, 179, 189, 190, 237, 241, 246; and religion, 235; institutional, 247

radio, 23, 74, 165; satellite, 168

Rainbow Coalition, 111

Rainbow Curriculum, 7

rap music, 32

rape, 30, 31, 76, 87, 148, 260, 261

Rather, Dan, 161, 165

Rauschenbusch, Walter, 151

Ray Bliss Institute, 242

Reader's Digest, 128; survey, 196

Reagan administration, 26, 192

Reagan campaign, 190

Reagan, Ronald, 2, 11, 23, 67, 95, 103, 122, 155, 160, 162, 171, 173, 175, 181, 185, 206, 207, 208, 217, 219, 245, 255

recession, 179

reconciliation between races, 222; faith-based, 36, 241

Reconstruction, Southern, 217

red republicans, 239

Red Scare, 178

Reed, Jo Anne, 196

reform, antislavery, 146; campaign finance, 108, 111, 117, 184; church-based, 154; education, 217; faith-based, 132; family-friendly, 257; grassroots, 111; health care,

230; malpractice, 262; of schools, 251; political, 181
Reformation, 14
reformation, moral, 145, 148
reformers, social, 147
reforms, common sense, 262
rehabilitation of criminals, 231
Rehnquist, Justice William, 78
relationships, broken, 32
relativism, 50
religion, 6
religion, and American politics, 242; best support of good government, 77; civil, 65, 74, 133, 134, 136, 137; decline in, 136; evaluation of, 75; free exercise, 15, 43, 131, 133; freedom from, 50; freedom of, 50, 189; hostility to, 133; hostility toward, 78, 154; impact of, 5; importance of, 136; in America, 134; Judeo-Christian, 76; judicial hostility toward, 79; marginalization of, 41, 67, 71, 135; media coverage, 68; and patriotism, 143; Protestant, 144; and racism, 235; role of, 21; traditional, 183; voter evaluation, 37
"religion free zones," 44
religionists, 63
religions, Eastern, 42; Native American, 42
religious broadcasting, 130
religious dissent, 154
Religious Freedom Restoration Act, 135, 138
Religious News Service, 55
religious right, 25, 69, 191, 251; obituary of, 192
Religious Roundtable, 72
renewal, charismatic, 19; cultural, 263; marriage, 19; moral and spiritual, 183; spiritual, 89, 247, 248; spiritual and moral, 29
rent control, 100
Republican Majority Coalition, 175
Republican National Committee, 167, 193
Republican National Convention, 254; Houston, 110, 150; Philadelphia, 147
Republican party, 54, 57, 104, 107, 110, 147, 152, 175, 186, 191, 193, 195, 199, 228, 242, 245; Christian influence in, 110; Dewey-Scranton-Rockefeller wing, 107; landslide victories, 176; religious values, 136
republicanism of 1830s, 146
Republicans, 12, 15, 16, 23, 34, 35, 72, 104, 147, 162, 172, 173, 203, 208, 254; pro-life, 13; radical, 146
respect for neighbors, 184
Ressler, John, 184
restitution, 231, 259
restructuring, corporate, 118
retirement benefits, 223
revival, 5, 145; spiritual, 142
revivalism, 147
revolution, "family side," 228; "supply side," 228; political, 142

Reynolds, Quentin, 50
right and wrong, 131, 257
right to vote, 39
righteousness, 143; in the nation, 252
rights, Christian, 8; civil, 10, 12, 13, 35, 39, 59, 74, 77, 210, 222, 233, 236, 242, 245; of conscience, 77, 131; equal, 222; gay, 172, 182, 225, 242, 244; homosexual, 55, 226; human, 17, 74, 189; inalienable, 152; legal, 99; legislation, 136; parental, 8, 13, 18, 256; property, 96, 112; "separate but equal," 238; voting, 148; women's, 211; of worship, 41
Riis, Jacob, 151
Riley, Richard, 85
Riordan, Richard, 12
riots, and insurrection, 105; Los Angeles, 86, 98; urban, 179, 180; Watts, 86
Rip Van Winkle, 219
Roach, Archbishop, 21
Road to Victory Conference, 20
Robb, Chuck, 104, 218
robber barons, 150
robbery, 87
Robertson, Dede, 1
Robertson, Pat, 1, 3, 14, 19, 20, 25, 72, 127, 158, 159, 166, 190, 192, 193, 194, 196, 199, 244
Robertson presidential campaign, 1, 2, 4, 25, 193
Robinson, Jackie, 248
Rockefeller, John D., 115, 116, 141
Rockefeller, Nelson, 107
Roe v. Wade, 16, 17, 39, 59, 176, 260, 261
role models, 102
Rollins, Ed, 108
Roman Catholic Church, 56, 57, 76, 154
Roman Catholics, 1, 2, 7, 11, 13-17, 19, 21, 47, 51, 57, 58, 65, 73, 76, 106, 109, 134, 135, 141, 153, 243, 254; church-going, 226; orthodox, 223; politically-active, 61; pro-life, 73
Roman Empire, 141
Rooney, Pat, 264
Roosevelt, Franklin, 94, 95, 120, 121, 125, 133, 171, 204; relations with conservatives, 207
Roosevelt, Theodore, 64, 152, 164, 179
Roper organization, 31
Rorschach test, 19
Rose, Pete, 183
Rostenkowski, Dan, 108, 109
Rothman, Stanley, 55
rule of law, 155
Rusher, William, 67

"safe sex," 32, 102, 257
safety, 230; in schools, 231
Safire, William, 165
Salinger, J. D., 69
Saltonstall, Leverett, 138
Salvation Army, 151, 264

salvation, hope of, 142
Samuelson, Robert, 183
sanctity, of life, 7, 14; of homes, 235
Sanders, Bernie, 174
Santa Claus, 49
SAT scores, 85
satellites, 75
Saturday Evening Post, 53, 129
savings, 99, 258; medical, 262
Scalia, Justice Antonin, 44
scandal, 255; Bob Packwood, 125; House Post
    Office, 79, 108, 109, 125; Iran-Contra, 183;
    religious, 58; savings and loan, 79, 125;
    Watergate, 180, 204; Whitewater, 125, 136,
    175, 203, 204, 205
Schiefer, Bob, 60
Schlafly, Phyllis, 193
Schlesinger, Arthur M., 51, 189
Schneider, William, 173, 180
school boards, 8, 9, 33, 43, 57, 69, 189, 190, 191,
    197, 243; elections, 7, 12, 18
school choice, 8, 13, 14, 33, 38, 186, 226, 231,
    241, 242, 243, 244
school districts, 7, 50
schools, 10, 247, 262, 266, 267; Catholic, 246,
    264; Christian, 18; church, 256; guns in, 43;
    home, 157, 159, 168, 256; loss of confidence,
    174; manual labor, 145; moral purposes of,
    78; parochial, 78, 157, 159; primary and
    secondary, 33; private, 157, 159; public, 32,
    39, 44, 50, 70, 84, 231, 240, 241, 256;
    quality of, 18, 28; Roman Catholic, 246;
    successful, 32; weapons in, 32
Schroeder, Pat, 176
Schwartz, Leroy, 229
Scopes Trial, 3, 53, 150; Tennessee textbook
    case, 71
Scorcese, Martin, 61
"scorecards," 200
Scripture memorization, 63
Scripture, infallibility of, 14
Seabury, Samuel, 142
secession, 146
secularism, 14, 15
secularists, 63
secularization, 74
seed capital, 3
segregation, 236-243
self-control, 89
self-esteem, 30
self-reliance, 12
self-righteousness, political, 27
Selma civil rights march, 222
Senate Foreign Relations Committee, 212
Senate Judiciary Committee, 162, 198, 199
Senate, United States, 34, 47, 104, 153, 162, 199,
    250, 253, 254, 258; direct election of, 38
"separate sphere," 42
separation of powers, 134
Sesame Street, 98

700 Club, 158, 166, 199
seventies, 4
sex, 257
sex education, 18, 103; abstinence-based, 32
Sex Respect, 257
sexual abuse, 56
sexual assault, 28
sexual harassment, 68, 198, 199, 233
sexual revolution, 4, 36
sexually transmitted diseases (STDs), 31, 32,
    257
Shamir, Yitzak, 21
Sharpton, Rev. Al, 8
Sheldon, Charles, 151
Shields, Mark, 61
Shundler, Bret, 13
Sidey, Hugh, 128
Sierra Club, 182
Silverstein, Shel, 69
sincerity, 211; Bill Clinton's, 203
Sinclair, Upton, 152
single-parent homes, 82, 87, 90
"Sister Souljah," 111
sixties, 4, 90, 236
60 Minutes, 206
slaveholders, 239
slavery, 7, 58, 60, 74, 105, 131, 141, 145, 146, 236,
    239, 247, 261
"Slick Willie," 206, 217
small business, growth of, 118, 119
Smith, Douglas, 87
Smith, Jack, 120
Smith, James "Sugar Jim," 107
social concerns, 20
Social Darwinism, 150
social dislocation, 36
social gospel, 264
social order, 50
social programs, 212, 228
Social Security, 84, 100
social spending, 213
socialists, 239
socialization, political, 106
society, "great bond of," 138; anonymous, 137;
    caring, 266; civil, 77; coarseness, 86; color-
    blind, 59; conservative, 213; depersonalized,
    137; foundations of, 39; good, 11; holistic
    view of, 226, 232; LBJ and Great Society,
    125; liberal, democratic, 24; moral health,
    229; participatory, 38; reformation of, 26,
    151; religious foundations of, 46;
    unicultural, 134; values in, 182; violence of
    modern, 88
Somalia, 179, 213
soul, converting, 149; emptiness in, 183;
    spiritual vacuum in, 135; war for Bill
    Clinton's, 219
souls, harvest of, 145
Southern Baptist Convention, 14, 67, 237
Southern Baptists, 5, 56, 57, 73, 148

Southern Christian Leadership Conference, 153
Southern Methodist University, 33
Soviet Union, 27, 178, 179, 240
Spanish-American War, 152
special interests, 25, 37, 111, 201, 218, 230, 255
Specter, Arlen, 198
spending, entitlement, 258; pork-barrel, 98
spiritual, acedia, 183; awakening, 5; hunger, 183,
    184; hunger, 265
spousal consent, 260
St. Patrick's Cathedral, 57
St. Thomas's Episcopal Church, 239
Stalin, Joseph, 54
Stamp Act, 143
standards, 21; educational, 256; living, 74;
    moral, 235; sentencing, 28
Stanley, Charles, 3
Stanton, Elizabeth Cady, 149
Star of David, 49
Stark, Pete, 162
state church, 79
state legislatures, 28, 35, 73, 190, 197
state religions, prevention of, 77
Statue of Liberty, 160
Statute of Virginia for Religious Freedom, 76
stealing, 244
"stealth candidates," 34, 69, 73, 190
Stearns, Richard, 216
stereotypes, 9, 20, 51, 56, 68, 195, 225, 238;
    about African-Americans, 57; about
    evangelicals, 57; about Italian-Americans,
    57; about Roman Catholics, 57; about
    women, 57
Stevens, Thaddeus, 146
Stevenson, Adlai, 223
Stewart, Justice Potter, 76
"stimulus package," 199
Story, Justice Joseph, 137
strategic planning, 186
Strategy, Field of Dreams, 197
stress, 229
strikes, 179
Students for America, 196
style over substance, 209
subsidizing failure, 99
suffering and alcoholism, 148
suffrage, 149
suicide, 101; professional, 125
Summer Olympics, 95
Sunday, Billy, 148, 237
Super Tuesday, 194
Supreme Being, 132, 133, 263
Supreme Court, Pennsylvania, 46
Supreme Court, United States, 26, 44, 46, 48,
    49, 73, 75, 78, 79, 122, 125, 152, 199, 207,
    238, 240, 245, 253, 259, 260
surrogate mothers, 31, 261
surveys, minority, 12
Sutherland, Justice George, 133
Swaggart, Jimmy, 192

Sykes, Norman, 134
Symbiosis of media and government, 124

Taft, William Howard, 175
Taft-Hartley Act, 121
Talese, Gay, 51
talk radio, 127, 128, 130, 155, 157, 159, 160, 161,
    164, 182, 249
Talmadge, Herman, 217
Tappan brothers, 146
tax code, family friendly, 227
tax credits, 262
tax cut(s), 35, 214, 223; middle-class, 206;
    Reagan, 228
"tax fairness," 214
Tax Foundation, 94
Tax Freedom Day, 94
tax increase, largest in history, 206
tax limitation, 185
tax policy, federal, 228
tax rates, confiscatory, 227
tax relief, 227; for families, 228
tax, Clinton administration, 119; confiscatory
    rates, 120; credit for children, 228; largest
    increase in American history, 118; payroll,
    210; standard deduction, 227, 228, 256
taxes, 7, 10, 11, 28, 35, 75, 84, 93, 94, 99, 100,
    102, 179, 182, 184, 186, 200, 225, 226, 227,
    232, 245, 251, 262; burdensome, 119;
    confiscatory, 34; federal and state, 256;
    progressive income, 38
taxpayer(s), 197; abuse of, 227; involvement,
    34; subsidies for abortion, 261
teachers unions, 111, 265
teachers, merit pay, 8
Teamsters, 122, 123, 124, 224
technology, 75, 80, 119, 124, 159, 168; changes
    in, 105; changing, 167; miniaturization, 168;
    power of, 165
technopopulism, 159
Teen Aid, 257
teen pregnancy, 32, 82, 183, 257
telecommunications, 80, 119, 155, 160, 169
teleconferencing, 168
telephone, get-out-the-vote-calls, 244; trees,
    197
television, 12, 23, 30, 32, 56, 74, 75, 96, 108, 116,
    126, 127, 129, 155, 157, 169, 200, 250, 255;
    activist-viewers, 168; bias, 62; cable, 5, 128,
    160, 161, 164, 166, 201; changing values of,
    127, 128; decline in audience, 128;
    interactive, 160, 168; interactive satellite
    broadcasts, 167; late night, 165; limiting use
    of, 29; network, 159, 161; networks, 56, 124,
    127; Nielsen ratings, 128; participatory, 163;
    political public relations, 160; satellite, 128,
    160, 161, 246; sitcoms, 91; statistics, 159;
    tabloid, 125; viewership statistics, 161, 162
Ten Commandments, 47, 48, 132; posting, 49

Tennessee textbook case (Scopes II), 71
term limits, 11, 38, 112, 181, 184, 200, 226, 251, 255
terrorism, 64, 65, 141
Texas Education Association, 69
textbooks, banning, 71; bias against religion, 154
Thanksgiving Day, 78, 153
thanksgivings, 251
Thatcher, Margaret, 155
The Adventures of Huckleberry Finn, 69
theft, 87
theism, 25
"third force," 109
third party, 254
"third way" for minorities, 246
Thomas Road Baptist Church, 192
Thomas, Cal, 194
Thomas, Justice Clarence, 73, 162, 166, 198, 245, 246, 249
Thoreau, Henry, 43, 153
Thornburgh, Richard, 181
Thornwell, James Henley, 239
"three strikes and you're out," 181
Tiananmen Square, 211
timber industry, 216
Time magazine, 55, 116, 128, 129, 130, 205
Title X grants, 103
Tocqueville, Alexis de, 65, 133, 134, 154, 264
tolerance, 11, 35, 58, 79
Tonelson, Alan, 178
Toward Tradition, 20
town hall meetings, 160, 255; satellite, 201
trading status, China as most-favored-nation, 211
tradition, intellectual and moral, 43; Judeo-Christian, 42; of faith, 75
Traditional Values Coalition, 245
traditions, 132; American democratic, 11; religious, 20, 135
Traficant, James, 112
Treaty of Versailles, 178
Trinity decision, 132
"True Love Waits," 32
true religion and civil liberty, 144
Truman, Harry, 48, 107, 121, 133, 219, 223
Trump, Donald, 115
truth, 26; absolute, 6, 7; common defense of, 15; White House delays with, 206; with capital T, 24
truthfulness, doubts about president's, 207, 210
tuition tax credit, 35
Turner, Ted, 129
turning point, inter-faith, 14
Twerrell, Terry, 8
two-parent households, 90
two-party system, 106, 180; changing, 174
tyranny, 132, 134, 138

U.S. News and World Report, 130
Ultimate Issues, 20
underclass, 89
unemployment, 89, 90, 182
union workers, 197
Unitarianism, 73, 240
United Auto Workers, 121, 122, 186
United Farmworkers, 153, 224
United Mine Workers, 224
United Nations, subservience to, 213, 214
United We Stand, 184-186
unity, 14; national, 64; racial, 243
universities, 105; church-affiliated, 130
University of Akron, 242
University of Alabama, 9
University of Arkansas, 203
University of Colorado, 31
University of Florida, 48
University of Georgia, 26
University of Michigan, 195
University of Notre Dame, 33, 153, 195
University of Texas, 249
University of Virginia, 33, 76, 77, 192
unlawful assembly, 44
unwed mothers, 83
uprising, evangelical, 150
upward mobility, 83
Urban League, 120
urban outreach, 266
urbanization, 137
USA Today, 200

V-J Day, 121
values, 5, 13, 18, 24, 84; American, 41; American mainstream, 223; cultural, 196; democratic, 189; educating for, 257; education in, 231; family, 223, 225, 251, 254; Frank Capra, 184; in schools, 14; Judeo-Christian, 14; legislation of, 75; mainstream, 130, 226; middle-American, 103; moral, 225, 244; reinforcement of, 70; religious, 19, 132, 136, 151, 232; religiously-based, 18; shared, 11, 65; traditional, 12, 99, 201, 207, 241, 247
values clarification, 232
VCRs, 169
veracity of the president, 203
vertical integration, 116, 117
victim status, 48
victory, political, 27; turning tide of, 15
Vietnam, 10, 36, 88, 178, 214, 215
Vietnam War memorial, Bill Clinton's visit, 205
Vietnam War, effects of, 180; opposition to, 72, 153, 212; supporters, 122; trust gap of presidency, 204
Vigilante, Richard, 18
violence, 13, 33, 56, 64, 65, 87; against whites, 222; black-on-black, 39, 208; fast to end, 153; fear of, 89; in schools, 85; television, 29

violent crime, 39
virgin clubs, 32
virtue, 50, 144; protecting, 95; republican, 105
"Virtuecrats," 51
vision, 27; for America, 23, 219; Christian, 222;
    conservative, 23; cultural, 24; for schools,
    33; of society, 222; political, 11; religious, 24
VivaHealth Plan, 265
Voltaire, 43
volunteerism, compassionate, 266
volunteers, 266
vote, minority, 250
voter anger, 159, 163, 165, 172, 174, 179, 255
voter apathy, 37
voter disaffection, 180
voter discontent, 186
voter guides, nonpartisan, 8, 13, 37, 197, 199,
    244, 250
voter participation, 38, 195; declining, 181
voter registration, 224; drives, 123, 199
"voter scorecards," 184
voters, African-American, 13, 244; Christian,
    225; church-going, 195; concerns of, 232;
    evangelical, 195; minority, 13; pro-family,
    199; Republican, 226; statistics on concerns
    of, 226
voting behavior, 196
vouchers, 13; education, 223; school, 256

Wade, Edward, 147
wages, 34; declining, 179, 182; garnishment of,
    31
Wagner Act, 121
waiting periods, 260
wall of separation, 11, 76
Wall Street, 183; loss of confidence, 174
Wall Street Journal, 5, 164, 174
Wallace, George, 109, 206, 236, 237
war on crime, 29
war on drugs, 101
Warner, John, 104
Warren, Justice Earl, 75
Washington Monthly, 24
Washington Post, 9, 24, 61, 68, 110, 126, 165,
    167, 183, 197, 200, 206
Washington Star, 126
Washington, George, 43, 78, 105, 178
Watergate, 36, 89
Watson, Thomas E., 149, 150
Watson, Tom, 243
Watts riots, 59
Watts, Jerry G., 222
wave of the future, 201
Ways and Means Committee, 108, 109
Weaver, Sigourney, 61
Webster, Noah, 63
Weigel, George, 18, 57
Weiker, Lowell, 174
Weinhold, Dick, 4

Weld, Theodore, 146
welfare, 9, 19, 29, 31, 83, 91, 99, 100, 103, 241,
    258
welfare queen, 98
welfare reform, 29, 217, 242, 244, 246, 258
welfare spending, 59
welfare state, 10, 36, 39, 74, 101, 111, 120, 265
Wesley, John, 5, 141
West, Cornel, 247
West, Thomas G., 99
Westward Expansion, 105
WETA TV, 98
Weyrich, Paul, 17, 18, 167
Whigs, 64, 146, 147
White Citizen's Councils Association, 238
"white citizen's councils," 240
White House staff, thirtysomething, 207
"white underclass," 258
White, Byron, 208, 261
White, John, 15
White, Theodore, 25, 159, 215
White, William Allen, 150
Whitefield, George, 63, 141, 142
Whitehead, Barbara Dafoe, 91
Whitney Museum of Art, 101
Wilder, Douglas, 73, 104
Wildmon, Donald, 54
Wilhelm, David, 73, 110
Will, George, 36, 93
Willard, Frances, 149
Williams, Armstrong, 246, 249
Williams, Polly, 38
Williams, Walter, 242
Wills, Garry, 54
Wilson, James Q., 183
Wilson, Nick, 217
Wilson, Woodrow, 107, 150
Winburn, Charles, 244
wine-tasting, 167
wire services, 126
Wirthlin, Richard, 196, 223
witchcraft, 69
Witherspoon, John, 64, 144
Wittman, Marshall, 153
WNET TV, 98
Wofford, Harris, 181
Wolfe, Tom, 7
woman's right to know, 260
women, African-American, 9; alternatives for,
    71; choosing careers, 30; exploitation of, 62;
    in the workplace, 39, 227; stereotypes
    about, 57
Women Christian Temperance Union
    (WCTU), 149
Woo, Michael, 12, 13
Woodson, Robert, 246, 247
Woodstock, 203
Woodstock generation, 212
Woodward, C. Vann, 238
Woodward, Robert, 219

Woolsey, Monsignor John, 16
Word of God, 152
workshops, grassroots training, 197
World Cup, 95
world peace, 149
World Trade Center bombing, 54, 56, 64
world view, 15
World War I, 117, 178
World War II, 17, 46, 88, 118, 120, 121, 175, 178,
    185, 205, 207
worship, freedom of, 77
Wright, Betsey, 216
Wright, Jim, 162

Yale University, 154, 212, 214; Law School, 215,
    246
Yankelovich, Daniel, 179, 180
yarmulkes, 46
"year of the woman," 177
"yellow journalism," 125
Yeshiva University, 33

zealots, 6, 34, 67
Zinmeister, Karl, 82
zoning boards, 190
Zorach v. Clauson, 133